The Great
New York
Fire of 1776

The Great
New York
Fire *of* 1776

A Lost Story of the
American Revolution

BENJAMIN L. CARP

Yale UNIVERSITY PRESS/NEW HAVEN & LONDON

Published with assistance from the Annie Burr Lewis Fund.

Published with assistance from the income of the Frederick John Kingsbury Memorial Fund.

Yale University Press books may be purchased in quantity for educational, business, or promotional use. For information, please e-mail sales.press@yale.edu (U.S. office) or sales@yaleup.co.uk (U.K. office).

Set in Minion type by Integrated Publishing Solutions, Ltd.
Printed in the United States of America.

Library of Congress Control Number: 2022936292
ISBN 978-0-300-24695-7 (hardcover : alk. paper)

A catalogue record for this book is available from the British Library.

This paper meets the requirements of ANSI/NISO Z39.48-1992 (Permanence of Paper).

10 9 8 7 6 5 4 3 2 1

For Jedidiah

Contents

The Great
New York
Fire of 1776

Was It Just the Wind?

New York City was the most important spot on the map in 1776. The British thought it was vital to retake it, and the American rebels strained to defend it. General William Howe drove the rebels from Staten Island, Long Island, and lower Manhattan, with the help of one of the largest amphibious assault forces in history up to that time. The British hoped that a decisive victory in New York would end the rebellion. Then, six days after the British took New York City, more than a fifth of it burned to the ground on September 21. The fire crippled a city that was the focal point of the 1776 campaign just weeks after the United States declared its independence. This was New York City's first great fire.

In the summer of 1776, the rebels rapidly came to understand that they could not successfully defend New York without losing a significant portion of their fighting force. They evacuated the city, and they did not quite leave it intact. As the fire raged, almost everyone at the scene believed that the rebels had lit the spark deliberately. The incendiaries may have begun with specific targets, but the fire quickly became indiscriminate, destroying the homes of friends as well as foes. The British troops and their Loyalist supporters reacted to the fire with horror. British soldiers and sailors executed a few suspected incendiaries on the spot. Outside the city, Americans weren't sure what to think.

For months before the fire, many people had predicted that New York City was doomed, because it was too important to British success, but too difficult for the rebels to defend. The rumors sounded certain that the rebels would sooner burn New York than leave it for the British. When the redcoats arrived on September 15, they found combustible materials, which they assumed had been prepared to set fire to the city. That day, the troops extinguished a small blaze and found a trail of gunpowder leading away from it. John Baltus Dash, the fire chief, buried his valuables to keep them safe from a conflagration he knew was coming. He wasn't the only one.

Who had set the Great Fire of 1776, and why? Were they mischief-makers with no political motivation? The British soldiers or sailors themselves? Civilians who supported the rebellion? Saboteurs with orders from the Continental Army? The fire appears to have been the intentional work of perpetrators with political motivations—the more radical elements of the rebel coalition. Witnesses spoke of the fire being set by white men from across the Northeast along with women and at least one mixed-race man. They acted either of their own volition or under orders from a commanding officer. Perhaps George Washington himself gave the command.

In 1776, many Americans' allegiances were not yet fixed, and European powers had not yet committed themselves to joining a fight against the British. Both sides, therefore, were trying to convince the world that they were fighting a just war. What would people say of the American rebellion now? If the fire was deliberate, then it would be harder to call the rebellion morally righteous. Rebel politicians and newspaper publishers worked furiously, therefore, to convince the public that the fire was an accident, and not worth dwelling on. They did their best to make the story disappear, leaving the British frustrated at their failure to influence public opinion, and showing the Loyalists how little room they had to express their grievances.

Fire and mayhem were undeniable features of the Revolution that its earliest chroniclers were eager to suppress. The nation's founders dismissed the fire as an accident, cast doubt on the evidence, and exonerated Washington from suspicion.[1] Continental Army staff officers and statesmen like Benjamin Franklin tried to dispel the notion that Washington had given the order to burn New York City. The evidence is ambiguous, as it is in most arson cases: it is too late to question eyewitnesses, and we have little forensic evidence, no clear confessions, no trial record, or any other type of documentation that might lead to the absolute truth. The Anglo-American legal standard to protect an accused criminal is "beyond all reasonable doubt," but that is not the standard of proof for historians, who must use the imperfect evidence at their disposal to try their best to get at the truth of the past, given what they know about the broader historical context.

Even if the fire was an accident, as the rebels claimed, the Great Fire of 1776 reveals the mayhem and instability that accompanied the creation of the United States. It was a noteworthy disaster followed by a handful of misguided murders. The fire reveals the volatile conditions of New York City and the hundreds of people who were displaced by having their homes reduced to ash. Crowding plagued the city's British garrison for the rest of the war. New Yorkers—both renters and property owners—complained about the lasting displacement and loss they had suffered. They lived in fear of new fire scares.

This book seeks to resolve the conflicting stories about the Great Fire of New York. The Great Fire challenges and changes the story of '76 to reflect the chaos and uncertainty that people experienced on the ground. It expands the story to include ordinary soldiers and civilians from a variety of backgrounds, as well as rebels, Loyalists, and those in between. It shows the rumors and lies that people told themselves amid the carnage and wreckage that the war had wrought. The American cause looks very different if we acknowledge some of its most unsavory features. And it looks very different if we put New York City at the center of the Revolution, because New York's story was one of civil violence, fire, and military occupation. In the wake of the Revolutionary War, New York City emerged as an immortal metropolis, years before it surpassed Philadelphia's population and decades before it became one of the world's largest and most influential cities. New York had risen from the ashes, but only by forgetting the flames of war.

After the battles of Lexington and Concord, thousands of American colonists channeled their political resistance into military enthusiasm and declarations of independence; by the end of 1776, however, the war reached what some considered its darkest hour. Stories of the Revolution usually allow these months to be redeemed by later successes such as Washington's victories at Trenton and Princeton. A closer look at 1776 reveals the American Revolution as a civil war, with all its attendant violence and tragedy. Every generation of Americans has disputed the meaning of the Revolution and whether it lived up to its own stated ideals. The Great Fire urges us to remember that 1776 was a more complicated time than we generally care to remember. Instead of providing another occasion for the uncritical celebration of the American past, it offers us an opportunity to consider what ideals ought to shape the present and future.[2]

Americans and their admirers usually understand 1776 as a year of bold words. Rebellious colonists listed their grievances, declared their desire for separation, and, finally, affixed their names. They pledged to one another, took oaths before a "candid world," and trusted that God blessed their intentions. But New York City in September 1776 was a "chaos zone": people were traumatized and ready to do violence, struggling to comprehend the changes around them, unmoored from civility and propriety. The year that Americans declared their independence was transitional, chaotic, and uncertain in ways that are not easy to resolve. Although many Americans traditionally read backward from later celebrations of patriotic unity and the "common cause," the year 1776 was wracked with uncertainty and rife with disruptive violence.[3]

The Great Fire of 1776 was a nameless deed, with authors but no signatures, grievances but no declarations. Historians will probably never know whether a group of incendiaries took votes, made pledges, or received a benediction. The British had faced many uprisings in the eighteenth century: slave rebellions and indigenous resistance throughout North America and the Caribbean, the Stamp Act riots of 1765, the *Gaspée* riot of 1772, and the Boston Tea Party of 1773. After incidents like these, British authorities were desperate to find the culprits: to uncover names, to hold someone accountable. If they could make an example of individual rebels, they could restore order and allegiance. During the Revolution, Loyalists argued that "envy and malice" had led an ambitious cabal of agitators to overthrow the British government and spread turbulence among the general public, who were easily duped. Anarchy and terror, they said, were the inevitable results. These fears may have had an irrational element, but the Loyalists' observations also contained some truth.[4]

The rebels were at their most admirable when they stood tall and signed their names beneath the lofty principles of liberty, equality, and unity. They were at their worst when they skulked and deceived, burned and massacred, unleashed campaigns of terror, and denigrated people as less worthy of citizenship. In the process of achieving revolution and independence, the rebels did both. Historians have carefully studied words, ideas, and persuasion, because these provide a more solid evidentiary grounding than the realms of collective violence and destruction. Such deeds, as well as words, are crucial to understanding the history of 1776.

This was a revolution where the people did not always obey their leaders. Some men committed so fully to the cause of liberty that they overstepped boundaries and overturned hierarchies. They destroyed tea. They burned boats. They tarred and feathered. They rode people on rails. They committed war crimes. They mutinied. They even set their neighbors' homes on fire. Sometimes their leaders supported them, because the crowd's violence had a purpose that aligned with their own. Just as often, though, leaders had to disavow the actions that could not be justified before a "candid world." While many people believed in the honor of the British Empire or the notions of freedom that animated the rebellion, those ideals were always in tension with the vices of the people on the ground (and the vices of the idealists themselves).

The rebels may have burned down New York City to try to disrupt the British war effort, or they did it out of a desire for vengeance, or widespread hatred of wealthy New York Loyalists and the Church of England, or perhaps defiance of their own officers. The fire therefore disrupts the traditional story of the Revolution, because Americans were and are uncomfortable admitting to the misdeeds they might have done along the way. The British also had no reason to enshrine the story, since their own troops had committed summary executions on the night of the fire. To best understand the Great Fire, we must look to the treatment of civilian property, the characteristics and motivations of the people who made up the armies, the prevailing assumptions that governed wartime restraint, and the memory of war. We must also understand the Revolution's extralegal crowd actions, like riots, intimidation, banditry, mutiny, and the resistance of the enslaved. If civilians, spies, or disobedient soldiers burned the city, then it will be worthwhile to know more about the violent impulses that helped define the revolutionary movement.

A history that includes the Great Fire of New York forces us to rethink the kinds of people who were central to the conflict. The fire uncovers stories of politicians and generals as well as the loyal, the disaffected, and the radical, rank-and-file soldiers, women, people of color, and other people on the move. Throughout the book, I generally use "rebels" or "revolutionaries" to refer to Great Britain's adversaries, as opposed to other terms that historians have used, like "patriots," "Whigs," or "Americans." The rebels had no monopoly on patriotism, and the term "Whig" is too easily confused with other usages. The British and their Loyalist supporters had many occasions to think of the rebelling colonists as traitors, mutineers, scoundrels, and terrorists, even as they launched their own violent campaigns in turn. When discussing the period up to November 1783, I use "Americans" to refer more broadly to the people living on the continent, not only those who favored an independent United States.

I found a very different American Revolution in the stories of the disgraced, the displaced, and the prematurely deceased—amid rumors that would not die, in smoldering towns, among prisoners that slithered away from justice or insisted on their innocence, and from people who swore to believe what their eyes told them. The Great Fire brings together the thoughts and decisions of some well-known politicians and senior military officers, but also captains and privates, Loyalists, women, and people of African and indigenous descent. I have tried to treat all of them with empathy, and I have done my best to understand how they experienced the American Revolution. The marginalized people of the revolutionary era rarely got to share their stories in ways that lasted, but an anomalous story like this one offers a much better opportunity to comprehend their lives and their actions. The fire helps to show how wars matter, not just because of their contingencies and endings, but also because of the unresolved tragedies they leave behind.

A Small City Still Standing

New York is a place where I think in General the houses are better built than at Boston—they are Generally of Brick—and three stories high with the largest kind of windows—their Churches are grand their Colleges & workhouse & hospital, Most excellently situated & also exceedingly commodious, their principal streets much wider than ours,—the people—why, the people, are magnificent in their equipages which are numerous in their house furniture which is fine—In their pride & conceit which are inimitable, in their profaneness— which is intolerable, in their want of principle which is prevalent—In their Toryism which is Unsufferable & for which they must repent in dust & ashes.[1]

—Henry Knox

New York is a city that never learns its lessons. In the drive to cut deals and make money, New York City tears things down or lets them rot, paves over the ruins, and builds something new, with little remorse, reverence, or reflection. It is a city rich with history, but few reminders of its early landscape remain. Instead New York's history has been a victim of its success—and its folly.[2]

New York City's story is usually told as a story of growth. New Amsterdam began with about 270 settler-colonists in 1626. In 150 years, Manhattan grew to around twenty-five thousand people, making New York the second-largest city in the thirteen rebellious colonies, after Philadelphia. The city had about four thousand buildings, most of them concentrated at the tip of lower Manhattan, within a mile of Whitehall Slip (fig. 1.1). The rest of the island was rural.[3]

For many visitors, the remarkable thing about New York City was its diversity: the market stalls echoed with grousing dialects from the Gold Coast, the British Isles, western Europe, and the Bight of Biafra; you could ask around for an Akan healer or attend religious services in Hebrew, French, German, and Dutch. Although the city had at least eighteen houses of worship, the Great Fire of 1776 destroyed at least two, both of which had been earlier targets of vandalism and attempted arson. One was Trinity Lutheran Church, with its German and English speakers.[4]

The other was the episcopal Trinity Church, the foremost of the city's three Anglican churches. Trinity Parish derived its wealth from patrons in London and New York as well as rents from the land it owned on the west side of the city. Trinity Church itself was the most prominent building in New York, its spire 180 feet high. For members of the Church of England, the city's oldest and largest church was where they felt most connected to God and—in their minds—his most favored nation. At weekly services, which seated up to two thousand people, they prayed for the king, "that he may vanquish and overcome all his enemies," and for the royal family (fig. 1.2).[5]

New York's waterfront district faced Brooklyn. From there, New Yorkers panned for wealth from the streams of Atlantic trade; the city welcomed ships and offered access to the empire's westernmost reaches. Some cashed in on imperial connections by trading manufactured goods from Britain for farm produce or supplying the sugar plantations of the British West Indies. During the Seven Years' War, the city served as the army's headquarters and grew flush from military contracts, privateering, and soaking up soldiers' wages; military officers were toasted as part of the city's social elite. Other New Yorkers profited because the city stood

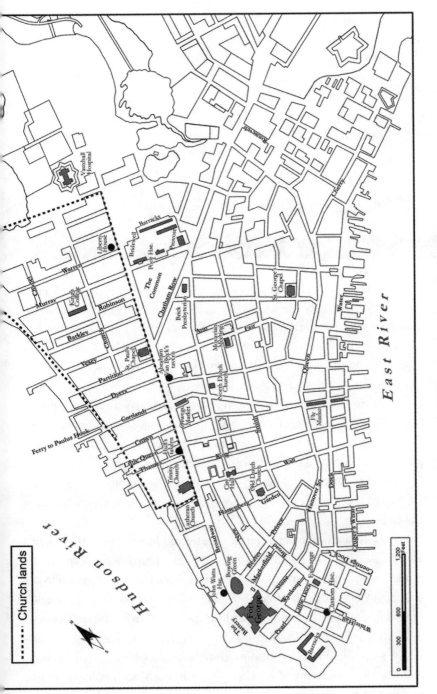

Fig. 1.1. Map of revolutionary New York City.

Fig. 1.2. In prints of colonial cities, churches symbolized status, civility, and morality. The Trinity Church steeple is especially prominent in "A View of New York from the North West," *Atlantic Neptune,* [1773?], I. N. Phelps Stokes Collection of American Historical Prints, Miriam and Ira D. Wallach Division of Art, Prints, and Photographs, New York Public Library.

on the fringes of the British Empire, where dark arts flourished: piracy (until the early eighteenth century), slave trading, smuggling from imperial enemies, and subdividing Indian lands. The imperial and local governments derived revenue from the trade in slaves and alcohol. Then, beginning in 1765, the collection of customs duties on sugar, stamps, and tea caused controversy; in 1776, New York's customs house burned during the Great Fire.[6]

The houses of lower Broadway reflected the elegance that Henry Knox observed. The merchant and councilor John Watts's house had a grand second-story room for entertaining, a garden that extended to the water, and a broad piazza that occasionally sparkled with sea spray. Such houses gleamed with japanned furniture, polished silver, and silk dresses.[7]

New York's manufacturing and retail trade, as well as its black market in stolen goods, also supported artisans, laborers, tavern keepers, and sex workers, many of whom signed ninety-nine-year leases to live on land owned by Trinity Church between Broadway and the Hudson

River. Few missed the opportunity to use the ironic nickname "Holy Ground" for the neighborhood behind St. Paul's Chapel where men visited prostitutes. This was also one of the poorest areas of the city.[8]

The colonial city suffered fires on several occasions. In the seventeenth century, imperial warfare, political factionalism, and anti-Catholic paranoia frequently threatened to engulf the town in flames. Manhattan and its vicinity had a higher concentration of enslaved people than any large city on the British-American mainland except Charleston, South Carolina. Black people's ability to overthrow this system was tightly constrained; nevertheless, white New Yorkers regularly expected that the slave revolt, when it came, would crackle with fire. In April 1712, more than two dozen enslaved Black people set fire to Pieter Van Tilburg's shed and attacked the white residents who rushed to extinguish the blaze, killing nine and wounding seven. The court carried out eighteen death sentences: three people were burned at the stake, one was broken on the wheel, and another hung in chains until his death.[9]

Perhaps New York City's slavers could have learned their lesson then. They did not. In the spring of 1741, a series of ten fires sprang up throughout the city; the first destroyed the buildings of Fort George, near the city's southern tip. The other fires did much less damage. The authorities suspected Black people and Catholics; they burned thirteen Black men at the stake, hanged seventeen more, drove one to suicide, sent eighty-four to the Caribbean, hanged four whites (two men and two women), and exiled seven other whites in what was called the "Great Negro Plot." Over the next few decades, New York newspapers occasionally reported or speculated about Black people's involvement in starting fires.[10]

Meanwhile, farther north, New Englanders were migrating into lands claimed by New York. Just as Yankees loathed New Yorkers as irreligious, vain, and selfish, with feudal ideas about land policy and taut connections to the British Empire, so New Yorkers scorned New Englanders as excessively devout, narrow-minded, sharp-elbowed, and disrespectful of social hierarchy. These tensions played out both in the city and in the hinterlands, where intercolonial conflicts over the Green Mountains or the Wyoming Valley bedeviled imperial attempts at control.[11]

After the British defeated the French in the Seven Years' War, two schools of thought developed about the future of Great Britain in North America. One school, the reformers, argued that only a standardized, centralized government with stable sources of revenue could efficiently direct the trade, defense, and statecraft of the British Empire. New York City had an important role in this newly envisioned empire: it was the seat of government for the province, it had been a military headquarters, and it was the terminus for mail packet boats from London. The other school of thought, more popular in the colonies, held that the Americans should largely govern their own affairs. The colonists wanted to carve up more Indian territory, trade and worship as they wished, and fund British garrisons at their discretion. Only with such freedoms could the Western Hemisphere attract new settlers, invest in new opportunities, and harness the willing allegiance of different peoples and the unwilling labor of the enslaved. Many New Yorkers shared this vision as well. In the long run, both camps knew what they were doing. The British had run up a debt of £42 million, and they reasoned that the American colonists owed some of that money. Parliament had fought a war largely on America's behalf and now faced further troop commitments in the American interior. By consolidating, the British metropolis developed an imperial system that eventually dominated trade and politics in many parts of the world.[12]

The rebellious colonists were right, too, and their argument led to revolution. They argued that they had forfeited none of their English liberties by putting down roots overseas. Unlike the Caribbean planters or the militarized colonies in Canada and Florida, the mainland colonists felt that a British army and navy presence was largely extraneous. As Americans foresaw an empire of their own, they resisted the idea of being taxed, governed, and garrisoned from far away, with no realistic way to be fairly represented in Parliament.[13]

The decade from 1765 to 1775 saw serious conflict over these issues. New York City was a drinking town, with a liquor license for every thirteen adult white men and a capacity for rum that sounds staggering—on average, New Yorkers drank more than seven ounces a day. The city had a reputation for drinking games, foul language, and conviviality. Abraham Van Dyck's tavern at the corner of Broadway and John Street drew crowds with public spectacles, like an eleven-foot cow and a chained leopard. Taverns were places to talk news, business, charity, books, and politics. Taverns also fomented disorder and disobedience, giving voice to the city's most radical elements. Alcohol led to broken windows, brawls with soldiers, and intimidation of imperial officials. The authorities tried to discourage some groups (particularly enslaved people and Indians) from participating in the local drinking culture and tried to curb misbehavior by bachelors, servants, seamen, sex workers, and apprentices. At the same time, new local leaders like John Lamb, Isaac Sears, and Alexander McDougall used taverns to rally their followers. Their allies toured taverns in New London, Norwich, Windham, and Boston to discuss the Stamp Act in 1765, starting the network known as the Sons of Liberty.[14]

The disputes over British imperial policies exposed the city's political fault lines and created new ones. New York had long been factious, with political divisions resembling a tribal split. The DeLancey faction roughly represented the interests of the Church of England and overseas trade, while their rivals in the Livingston faction generally stood for upstate landowners and Dissenters. Most of the DeLancey party ultimately remained loyal to the Crown. The path for the Livingston party was more complex: although they struck an alliance with the Sons of Liberty after 1769, many Livingston leaders were wary of radical resistance, and a few became Loyalists.[15]

Religion was an important source of these factional disputes. Although Anglicans hardly made up the city's majority, the Church of England was the established, state-supported church in New York County and three surrounding counties, and the only place in the Northeast with an Anglican establishment. Many of the city's most important officials and wealthiest traders owned pews at Trinity. Presbyterians and Congregationalists reacted with outrage when Anglicans moved to dictate the liturgy and presidency of King's College and then attempted to install a bishop in America. An establishment was one thing, but if the college were to become the headquarters for a church hierarchy, Dissenters worried that their religious liberty would be threatened. The resistance was led by three Yale-educated lawyers, including William Livingston, later the revolutionary governor of New Jersey; John Morin Scott, a future rebel leader of New York; and the Loyalist councilor William Smith

Jr. In 1769, Livingston called on Dissenters to oppose the Church of England, warning that if the DeLanceys prevailed in that year's elections, the Dissenters would be persecuted. Supporters of the Crown, in turn, were convinced that Presbyterians, allied with New England Congregationalists, were orchestrating the colonial resistance against the king.[16]

New York City's white working people were also politically active, proud of their status, and ready to stand up for themselves. On the one hand, more adult men could vote in New York City than in Boston or Philadelphia, and so white craftsmen had ways of making their voices heard in the realms of formal politics. On the other hand, New York City had only four assemblymen, and the province's unelected council and governor met behind closed doors. Since ballots were not secret, working New Yorkers often felt they had to vote the way their wealthy employers and patrons expected, which helped to mute class tensions. Yet on the eve of the Revolution, disparities of wealth were widening, criticisms grew louder, and the debates over the imperial crisis often showed signs of social conflict. One New York worker noted that the merchants' riches came at the expense of everyone else's misfortunes: "As a proof of it we have only to look around us," he fumed, "to see some rolling triumphantly in their Coaches on the Profits gotten by a foreign Trade," while throwing their own neighbors in prison for debt.[17]

But economic interests were never the only factor at play in the forming of alliances. Rich and poor New Yorkers might come together based on ethnicity, religion, faction, or shared resentment against the British Empire and its minions. Wealthy New Yorkers had the firmest grip on the levers of power; they sat atop a system that upheld the everyday violence of slavery and land seizure. When they objected to British policy, they could use the legislature, the courts, and petitions to enact change. Middling New Yorkers used voluntary associations to add their own voices; in a system that allowed broad political participation, they could not be ignored. The poorest and most disenfranchised New Yorkers (laborers, seamen, women, and enslaved people) had much less access to formal politics. They sang the songs of street politics: either peaceful actions like parades or outright violence against persons and property. They burned effigies, boats, and houses. They used shaming punishments like the skimmington, which was quite painful for the men whose private parts were bounced on a wooden rail. When poor peoples' interests aligned with those of a faction's wealthy leaders, then members of the upper crust might tolerate crowd action. When wealthy people felt threatened by the excesses of mass politics, however, they turned against it swiftly and attacked its legitimacy with everything they had.[18] As New Yorkers worked out their political disputes, violence was commonplace.

Fire, in particular, had a political language that everyone knew how to speak. The authorities used streetlight surveillance at night; they lit fireworks and fired ceremonial cannonades to honor the king's birthday. Rebellious crowds, in defiance, lit protest bonfires and burned the effigies of importers and Crown officials. Occasionally they threatened to destroy an offender's home. After 1765, New Yorkers joined colonists in other cities by setting things on fire during protests against Parliament and customs officials.[19]

On the night the Stamp Act was set to go into effect, New Yorkers built a gallows and dangled an effigy from it, representing the lieutenant governor, Cadwallader Colden. Then they seized Colden's carriage and burned it, along with the gallows and effigy, on Bowling Green. Meanwhile, a group of men took all the furniture out of the home of Major Thomas James (who had threatened to enforce the Stamp Act by cramming it down New Yorkers' throats) and burned it in front of his door. By the next day, New Yorkers threatened to burn Fort George—or even the whole city—unless the stamps were sent back to London. Colden tried to stash them aboard a ship for safekeeping, but the ship's captain worried that the crowd would burn down his mansion unless he surrendered the stamps. Finally, officials compromised by storing the stamps at City Hall. When the new governor arrived two weeks later and complied with the crowd's directive, they lit a bonfire in his honor.[20]

The next ten years would see more threats and fiery demonstrations. General Thomas Gage lobbied to make New York City the headquarters for the British army. With a few warships, the British could force the city to contribute supplies by threatening to "reduce it to Ashes." When Gage planted two field cannon at the entrances to the Upper Barracks in the Common (now City Hall Park), protesters responded by erecting a symbolic "Liberty Pole" nearby, leading to a series of brawls between soldiers and civilians.[21]

For all this conflict, most of New York City's actual fires had been fairly mundane; unlike Charleston in 1740, Boston in 1760, or Montreal in 1765, colonial New York never had a major fire that burned up an entire neighborhood at once. The biggest fire before the Revolution occurred in 1770, when an accidental blaze at a Masonic lodge on Ann Street destroyed sixteen buildings.[22] The city's smaller fires had many causes: bolts of lightning, unswept chimneys, dry haystacks, blacksmith's forges, sugar boilers, distillery accidents, untended candles, careless children, careless adults. Sometimes the cause was unknown. Sometimes people grumbled about lax night watchmen. Sometimes they suspected arson. Most of colonial New York's fires were apparently accidental, confined to a few houses at most. Rain, snow, firefighters, alert civilians, and sheer luck had kept the city mostly unscorched.

New York City's Common Council appointed dozens of men to serve in its eleven fire engine companies. Enginemen maintained order at fires, removed valuables from burning buildings, discouraged looters, and prevented fires from engulfing entire blocks (fig. 1.3). They protected individuals' property but also showed how much the city's residents depended on one another. Although the enginemen received no salary—they could even be fined for neglecting their duty—they were exempt from other civil and militia service. Some of the enginemen were radicals and leaders of the city's artisans, but others stood with the mayor to prevent riots and effigy burnings.[23]

While the wealthy lived in the city's fancy brick buildings, most of the city's houses used more flammable materials. In 1761, the New York Assembly passed a law that would have required city dwellers to build exclusively with brick and stone, with slate or tile roofs rather than wooden shingles, after 1766. But the law was suspended until 1768, then again until 1774, when at least a third of the city's householders petitioned to have the law suspended again. The petitioners included firefighters and future accused incendiaries, future rebels and future Loyalists. The new restrictions, they argued, would make building housing for poorer tenants too expensive, and the downturn in new construction would leave five-sixths of the city's carpenters with no employment.

Fig. 1.3. In this private fire club notice, citizens pass buckets from a pump to a fire engine, with firefighters at work. Other men carry ladders and hooks to help pull down houses. A chief engineer gives orders through a speaking trumpet, while men carry baskets and bags to safely protect movable goods. Detail of Henry Dawkins, Certificate of the Hand-in-Hand Fire Company, New York, ca. 1753, I. N. Phelps Stokes Collection of American Historical Prints, Miriam and Ira D. Wallach Division of Art, Prints, and Photographs, New York Public Library.

Given the choice of profit or safety, New York's landlords preferred to take their chances with fire. The assembly and council passed another bill "prohibiting wooden Buildings" in March 1775, but it was not slated to take effect until January 1776, out of "Condescensions to the Carpenters" and "to get Votes at the next Elections," which never took place; by then, New York had replaced its royal government with a Provincial Congress.[24]

New Yorkers may not have been enthusiastic about tinkering with their building codes, but they were ready for other changes. Some Americans agitated for republican government, as conservatives had warned.

These ideas were popular among Presbyterians and New England Congregationalists, but not exclusive to them; they arose from a long history of fights between imperial governors and colonial assemblies. The political factions who led New York needed support from the farmers and tradesmen, and the patrician desire for continued control contended with popular demands. White male workers, calling themselves "Mechanicks," supported radical leaders as they criticized the "corrupt Oligarchy." As one frightened conservative wrote in July 1775, "All authority, power, and government (though I cannot say government, as there is none), is in the hands of the lower class of people." On the fringes of this debate, even more radical agitators discussed expanding women's political participation and abolishing the slave trade.[25]

Other Americans feared the movement for independence and war. Some were members of the Church of England, who saw church and state as twin pillars of empire, monarchy, and faith, and distrusted America's many Dissenters. Other Loyalists held political appointments within the empire and saw it as their duty to uphold (or at most reform) the extant system. Many merchants—and the artisans and laborers they employed—relied on trade connections to the British Empire and had little enthusiasm for intercolonial nonimportation agreements or the rebellion. They may have shared the rebels' objections to British taxation and restrictions, but they saw their faith, prosperity, security, and traditions as being bound up in British patriotism. These friends of government—many of whom became Loyalists or "Tories"—calculated that America was better off as part of a growing empire. They saw the risks of trying to cobble together a new, untested confederation at the expense of so much blood and treasure and feared a civil war. In 1774 and 1775, moderates in Britain and America were calling for reconciliation before it was too late.[26]

Many New Yorkers feared the future, and with good reason. They feared New England and scorned the "levelling spirit" of its town halls and militias. Loyalists eagerly exploited divisions between New York's moderate leadership and the more radical revolutionaries in New England and the South. They hoped to make New York a loyal sanctuary in America. The local Anglican clergy used the city's Loyalist press to try to drive a wedge between New England and New York, attacking "the republican zealots and bigots of New-England" and warning other denominations to avoid "that *Presbyterian* yoke of bondage." The arch-Loyalists in America and hard-liners in Britain wanted Parliament to concede nothing to the agitators. They argued that Samuel Adams, Thomas Jefferson, Alexander McDougall, and other radical leaders had led Americans on a destructive path and called them "Factious and Republican Incendiaries" who had misled Americans with their "inflammatory" arguments. The Loyalists never inspired as many people as they hoped, but thousands of New Yorkers did remain loyal to the Crown.[27]

With such writers urging harsh measures against the American colonies, and with radical factions pushing toward republicanism and independence, New York's political elite tried to find a middle ground. Some became moderate rebels, and some became Loyalists. This is not as surprising as it might seem, because these groups wanted some of the same things as Britain's conciliatory faction: continued trade (but without the new taxes), compromise on divisive issues like the quartering of soldiers, better responsiveness from London, a stable social hierarchy, and peace in the streets. New York's lawyers and merchants helped send moderate delegates to the First and Second Continental Congress; they saw independence as a last resort. As open warfare began in April 1775, the possibility of compromise faded. Still, the New York delegation was the last to approve independence in the summer of 1776. Wealthy men who wanted to retain power moved either into the arms of royal government or into the fray with the rebellion. New York's moderate rebel leaders took the reins of state and national politics to keep the rebellion as orderly as they could make it, while most of their radical rivals entered the army or became refugees.[28]

The rise of the independence movement left open important questions about how much authority colonial leaders would retain in the provincial governments and the United States. Would it be the same wealthy grandees, minus the Loyalists, or would new leaders from humbler backgrounds join the state legislature and establish new rules for society? Would voting rights, taxation, legislative representation, religious toleration, landowning, slave owning, and women's property rights continue to favor a narrow elite, or would new governments allow greater rights among a greater number of people?[29]

It was a difficult coalition to keep together. New York's radical Sons of Liberty complained to their friends in New England about their neighbors' reluctance to take bold measures. Moderate leaders did dismantle New York's royal government in 1775, but their halting pace gave New York City a lasting reputation of being unresponsive to popular demands and supportive of the British government. In a series of votes between January 26 and February 23, the New York Assembly (under DeLanceyite control) rejected the First Continental Congress, failed to endorse non-importation, and refused to appoint delegates to the Second Continental Congress; instead they merely petitioned Parliament for a redress of American grievances. It fell to a new body, an extralegal convention, to select delegates. New York's leaders dragged their feet and clung to moderate tactics. As a result, both impatient radicals and hopeful Crown supporters believed that the province and city were friendly territory for the British Empire; furthermore, both sides anticipated that British occupation of the city would be crucial to suppressing the rebellion.

When news of the battles of Lexington and Concord reached New York City in April 1775, a crowd of people unloaded a sloop and threw its cargo (intended for the British army in Boston) into the water. Then another crowd broke into an armory and seized the weapons. A mass meeting in the Common called for the formation of a militia on April 23; four days later, the Sons of Liberty formed a battalion of eight hundred men, and about half marched to the customs house and commandeered the key (the customs house reopened later to enforce the regulations of a Continental Association instead of Parliament). On May 1, New Yorkers voted for a Provincial Congress, essentially replacing the old assembly.[30]

The city seethed with talk of violence. Back in March, a crowd of two hundred people beat William Cunningham, who guarded the city's barracks and stores for the British army, tore away his clothes, gold watch, and money, then threw him in jail and proceeded to plunder his house. After his release, continual threats forced him to hide in the woods until he fled to Boston. Newspapers accused arch-Loyalists of inviting "civil war, and all the calamities of towns in flames," and urged them to "fly for your lives." The New York Provincial Congress, which began meeting on

May 22, punished a few Loyalists who were actively working against the Continental Congress.[31]

British authority was slipping away. When the city's small garrison of redcoats withdrew, a group of rebel militia relieved them of a cartload of arms and ammunition, which they hid in the tennis court behind Abraham Van Dyck's tavern. Van Dyck, a former feltmaker and a marine lieutenant during the Seven Years' War, was also the captain of the New York Grenadiers, an independent company of volunteer militia. He was "a good Whig," and his tavern hosted the militia for drill exercises, recruiting, and officers' meetings.[32] When Governor William Tryon returned to New York on June 25 after a year away in England, he tried to hold the colony for the Crown by negotiating among the British warships, Loyalist sympathizers, and the Provincial Congress.[33]

The Royal Navy's warships, such as HMS *Asia*, remained in New York harbor. Naval officers warned the radicals to stay away from the cannon at Fort George. A group of Connecticut saboteurs took aggressive action on July 12 by destroying one of the *Asia*'s boats. Then, late at night on August 23, rebellious New Yorkers removed the cannon from the battery, attempted to capture Governor Tryon, and touched off a firefight with the *Asia*'s sailors. In response, Captain George Vandeput woke the whole city by firing thirty-two guns at 3 a.m., killing one person and wounding three more. Once the shock wore off, most property owners and wealthy renters left town or sent their families to the countryside. Tryon reported that a third of the city's inhabitants had left; he himself fled to a merchant ship on October 14 rather than run the risk of being kidnapped. British authorities were still confident enough in the loyalty of the city's remaining inhabitants that they never menaced New York City the way they terrorized much of the New England coast. Yet Vice Admiral Samuel Graves wrote darkly that if New York's rebels fired on the *Asia*, "I will assuredly lay their Town in Ashes the moment a Fleet can get up."[34]

The threats cowed the city's radicals for a time, giving space for moderate New Yorkers to cooperate with the Royal Navy. Captain Vandeput had little difficulty receiving supplies from New York, "nor do I expect there will be any unless some of the Rebel Troops from Connecticut, or New Jersey, should come into the Town, and prevent the Towns

People from acting as they seem at present inclined." As a result, radical New Yorkers and New Englanders grew infuriated that New York was doing too little to demonstrate solidarity with the Continental Congress. Gilbert Saltonstall, a New London militia captain, said he wished the city "was either ras'd to the Foundation" or fortified by Continentals; otherwise "I greatly fear the Virtue of the Yorkers whose Religion is Trade, & whose God is Gain." Colonel Jedediah Huntington of Norwich agreed: "That Colony has hitherto been, and I fear will forever be, a moth to us. I almost wish its capital was in ashes."[35]

New York's reluctant moderates held out the possibility of reconciliation, but they still took steps to rid the colony of its imperial political structures: they kneecapped the city government, stopped most court business, supplanted the assembly with a Provincial Congress (and a Committee of Safety that handled things during recess), raised a local militia, and sent recruits to the Continental Army. The governor was still doing his business aboard ship. Although Loyalists held most of the highest colonial offices and had significant support from the counties around Manhattan, they were relatively powerless without military support. In November, Connecticut radicals under Isaac Sears, acting without authorization, burned another boat with supposed connections to the *Asia* and then wrecked James Rivington's printing press—"the very life & Soul" of the "Tory Faction." Half the city and province of New York might be Loyalists, and the rest might be too moderate to stand up to them, but the people of Connecticut were ready to "purge the Land of such Villains," if only Congress would support them.[36]

Manhattanites experienced tremendous chaos as new leaders eclipsed the old imperial order. As revolutionaries envisioned a new, independent nation in America, New Yorkers hotly debated the imperial crisis without the luxury of deciding their own fate. The British fervently hoped to retain New York, which they imagined to be less rebellious than New England. At the same time, rebel leaders could not permit so central a colony to waver from a Continental commitment. Cities earned a reputation among many rebels as hotbeds of Loyalism and conciliatory overtures: many radicals fantasized about sacrificing these seaports for the sake of Continental unity.

Religious competition, economic hardship, party rivalries, and resistance to British policy all combined to bring down British government in 1775 and replace it with governance by New York's cautious provincial elites. A small city and often a brutal one, New York had its own rhythms, dissonance, and dynamics. For thousands of people, it was home.

And a sizable portion of it, at long last, was about to be destroyed.

Destroying Towns in a Civil War

A s British troops advanced on Bunker Hill on June 17, 1775, the rebels used Charlestown's mostly abandoned buildings as cover to fire on their enemies. The British responded by burning the houses, using incendiary shells and sailors armed with torches. The fires, easily visible from Boston, consumed about four hundred buildings—almost the entire town (fig. 2.1). Nine months later, a committee compiled more than £117,000 in damage claims. A year later, while serving in New York City, Dr. Isaac Foster ruefully reflected that "our enemies have by their wanton barbarity, from being inhabitants of Charlstown made us Citizens of the united Colonies at large."[1]

Although the rebels had stood up to the redcoats (much to the British army's surprise), they retreated from Charlestown peninsula in defeat. The day saw more than 1,400 casualties, and the rebels particularly mourned the death of local leader Dr. Joseph Warren. Meanwhile, the destruction of Charlestown caused mixed feelings. Rebel optimists refused to see it as a setback, but they lamented the loss of people's homes and property. After the battle, Abigail Adams grieved for the fallen and wrote, "The Spirits of the people are very good. The loss of Charlstown affects them no more than a Drop in the Bucket." A few days later, she changed her mind, writing that her father was deeply upset about the destruction of the place where their ancestors were buried.[2]

Fig. 2.1. Soldiers and civilians in Boston had a clear view of the burning of Charlestown. George Henry Millar (artist) and John Lodge (engraver), "View of the Attack on Bunker's Hill, with the Burning of Charles Town, June 17, 1775," in *The New, Comprehensive and Complete History of England* [. . .], by Edward Barnard (London, 1783), plate following p. 686, Library of Congress, Prints and Photographs Division.

The Continental Congress wanted to help the American people make sense of these contradictory emotions: they wanted Americans to understand the tragic loss of Charlestown as a wanton act of destruction by a perfidious ministerial army, while reassuring themselves that the united colonies could withstand the destruction of a few coastal towns so long as the countryside had brave people who would fight for liberty. John Adams, writing back to his wife, remarked, "It is a Method of conducting War long since become disreputable among civilized Nations: But every Year brings us fresh Evidence, that We have nothing to hope for from our loving Mother Country, but Cruelties more abominable than those which are practiced by the Savage Indians." (Adams, like most white Americans, had a one-sided perspective on Indian warfare.) At the same time, he offered "Consolation . . . that Cities may be rebuilt, and a People reduced to Poverty, may acquire fresh Property: But a Constitution of Government once changed from Freedom, can never be restored. Liberty once lost is lost forever." Rebel leaders believed it was important to blame British tyranny for the destruction of towns; otherwise people would blame the anarchic situation that the revolutionaries themselves had produced.[3]

The British also wrestled with the kind of war they wanted to wage. Their political and military leaders juggled several problems as they tried to suppress a civil war. They had to estimate the numbers of loyal (or potentially loyal) people in America, on the basis of reports from their most ardent supporters. They believed that a few agitators, mostly in New England, had misled their neighbors into rebellion. Moderates (or conciliators) hoped that a few concessions would solve the American disagreement and restore the Americans to their fidelity. The hard-liners argued that only force could persuade the colonists to accept parliamentary sovereignty; an even smaller faction suggested bringing devastation to any colonies whose leaders refused to bend the knee. Although the British leaders of the Revolution ultimately decided against a "fire and sword" approach, they still favored coercion: American subjects would only resume their allegiance if they dreaded the ships and armies of King George III.[4]

This was hardly a simple disagreement: before the war began, a British official conceded that Great Britain could easily "harass, lay Waste, & Depopulate America, to destroy the Towns, settlements & provisions & consequently to Reduce their Boasted numbers in a few Months by Famine & Misery. But all considerations of humanity out of the question that would prove a very unprofitable as well as ineffectuall method of conducting the War." The British ministry's attempts to placate both the moderate and aggressive factions of Parliament in 1775 and 1776 led to a middle path that pleased neither. Throughout the war, Great Britain acted just aggressively enough to further alienate Americans, and just conciliatorily enough to cede the initiative in its military campaigns.[5]

Destroying a densely populated settlement was especially outrageous because the effects were indiscriminate. When warships fired hot shot or explosive carcasses (incendiary shells) into American towns, then Loyalists, too, would suffer. In spite of the rebellion, American families were sympathetic figures—after all, most shared a heritage with Great Britain, and even some of the rebels had probably fallen under the sway of irresponsible demagogues. Their allegiance could still be redeemed and restored. Devastation, however, would discourage potential allies. Yet reconciliation was also an unpopular choice: the radicals, particularly the New Englanders, had taken things too far. To accede to all the rebels' demands would invite further disobedience, and that was no way to run an empire.[6]

To be thought of as an enlightened world power, Great Britain had to adopt European norms, treat prisoners and civilians humanely, and avoid the kinds of atrocities that horrified newspaper readers. They had developed codes of honor and humanity, combined with pragmatism, to foster a culture of wartime restraint. Inevitably, exceptions arose: the English (like most Europeans) had fewer qualms about unleashing indiscriminate violence against the indigenous people of Africa, the Americas, Asia, and the Pacific, and they had exacted pitiless retribution against rebels in Ireland and Scotland. When the English could paint their enemies as barbaric or rebellious, they could justify much harsher tactics.[7]

Such tactics included devastating the countryside to goad the enemy into submission. Devastation carried risks in a civil war scenario like the American Revolution, because the rebels worked the levers of public opinion to publicize smoldering fields and towns. Leaders therefore expressed a desire to protect white civilians' private property (although not the property of Native Americans) from plunder and devastation, as long as civilians stayed out of the way. The rules were never hard-and-fast. Destroying bridges, naval ships, or fortifications raised few eyebrows. Destroying hay and provisions was generally perceived as regrettable but sometimes necessary. A house was inviolate, but not if it harbored a sniper or a merchant who was supplying the enemy, and not if it was part of a town that put up a defense for too long. Devastation might burn a path to victory, but it would be foolish to offend local civilians whom you held in some esteem. Military leaders had to make case-by-case decisions that sometimes proved incorrect—or were deemed immoral—in hindsight. People understood the need for restraint as well as the desire for victory—even through fiery means.[8]

During the Seven Years' War, officers threatened to punish soldiers who pillaged, marauded, or burned civilian structures on their own initiative, reminding the men that such actions dishonored their country. The gentlemen who led British armies believed that certain types of tactics— guerrilla raids, devastation, assassination of officers, and violence against noncombatants—were essentially criminal. In an ideal army, officers might legitimately order the destruction of houses and churches, and they could justify doing so to create a smoke screen, to destroy obstructions to the army's line of fire, to eliminate cover for enemy snipers, or even to sow fear and encourage obedience. Rank-and-file soldiers, however, were discouraged from taking such activities upon themselves. Officers who instilled proper discipline could lead a more effective infantry, maintain social hierarchy, and curb the chaos that spiraled beyond the battlefield. Commanders tried to discipline their soldiers, but they never had complete control. They understood that rage, hatred, frustration, and revenge sometimes got the better of the soldiers, and they often protected marauding soldiers from punishment.[9]

Still, plenty of British officers condoned devastation. On September 1, General Thomas Gage gave Vice Admiral Samuel Graves his blessing "to lay Waste such Sea Port Towns" in New England that the king would not need for supplies. In October, Captain William Glanville Evelyn said he hoped that "Boston, New York, Philadelphia, and all the capital towns on the Continent" would be, in a year, "but stacks of chimneys like Charlestown here." Everyone understood that the British navy had the power to enact this vision, but they also knew the Americans could strike back by targeting Loyalists, sending out privateers, or committing acts of sabotage. Devastation invited revenge, not peace.[10]

Benjamin Franklin warned his correspondents in England that their destruction of towns was counterproductive. "She has begun to burn our seaport towns," he wrote to Joseph Priestly on July 7; "secure, I suppose that we shall never be able to return the outrage in kind. She may doubtless destroy them all; but if she wishes to recover our commerce, are these the probable means?" Franklin argued that the British Ministry was cutting off its nose to spite its face; burning towns and firing on cities filled with women and children "are by no means Acts of a legitimate Government," he wrote in September. "They are of barbarous Tyranny and dissolve all Allegiance." Great Britain had revealed itself as shortsighted and illegitimate; Franklin warned that the Americans would someday yearn to retaliate.[11]

Americans (and some Britons, too) were infuriated when the British navy conducted a premeditated burning of Falmouth in what is now Maine, a town of two thousand people, causing an estimated loss of almost £55,000. The British threatened to do the same to other towns along the northern New England coast. From Norwich, Connecticut, a sermon wailed, "Cast thine eye upon thy seaports, from *Falmouth* to *Carolina*, and see the ocean full of engines of death, destined for the destruction of *America*." General George Washington called the destruction of Falmouth an "Outrage exceeding in Barbarity & Cruelty every hostile Act practised among civilized Nations." John Adams joined a committee to collect a precise account of British damages and seizures. Congress would trumpet British atrocities across the globe and for "all Posterity." He added, "It may pave the Way to obtain Retribution and Compensation, but this had better not be talked of at present." Even as he contemplated sending privateers to raid Nova Scotia a few weeks later, Adams wrote, "The late conduct, in burning towns, so disgraceful to the English name and character, would justify anything, but similar barbarity. Let us preserve our temper, our wisdom, our humanity and civility, though our enemies are every day renouncing theirs. But let us omit nothing necessary for the security of our cause." Panic spread down the coast, and rebel generals convinced themselves that Loyalist inhabitants would eagerly help the British burn American cities.[12]

A pattern had emerged. Radical Americans were outraged at British acts of destruction, raised it repeatedly as a grievance driving Americans to independence, but also loudly proclaimed that they would sooner see their own cities burn than submit to Parliament's unjust acts. After all, as William Pitt, the earl of Chatham, had said to the House of Lords back in January, "You might destroy their towns, and cut them off from the superfluities, perhaps the conveniencies of life," but Americans "would not lament their loss, whilst they had . . . their woods and liberty."[13]

As men of sentiment, Continental leaders wept at the tragedy of burning towns and vowed they would never stoop so low—unless provoked by necessity. Yet they were also awed by the vision of a great city "destroyed by a conflagration." A thrilling sight like that was beautiful, baleful, sublime, and provocative. Edmund Burke had written, "Terror is a passion which always produces delight when it does not press too close." Fire and terror had their political uses, but for many Americans, the fires were pressing much too close. Like Abigail Adams's father, Americans experienced destruction as a horrid loss of hearth and shelter, tangible goods, and intangible memories. Such people could not afford to be as philosophical as Burke, John Adams, and Benjamin Franklin.[14]

The destruction of Charlestown and Falmouth also stirred Americans' traditional antipathy toward seaport cities, often viewed as hotbeds of violent radicalism and ardent Loyalism. They were the marketplaces where a merchant paid too little for crops, the countinghouses where rich men charged interest on a debt, and the courthouses where lawyers seized a defendant's property. Town houses, playhouses, and alehouses were places of opulence, live performance, drunkenness, and other temptations. As Franklin had written, cities "generally import only Luxuries and Superfluities," so the British were doing Americans a favor by disrupting this wasteful trade. While the virtuous countryside was worth defending, the cities had festered with slave trading, luxury, and wickedness. When the British attacked these vulnerable coastal points, some Americans believed that the cities were getting what they deserved.[15]

A seaport city's function made it potentially complicit in the British war effort. So long as a port city was vulnerable to naval ordnance, it could never be truly independent. Loyalists counted on the Royal Navy for protection as they withheld their oaths and aid from the rebels, provided intelligence to royal officials, recruited men, and sheltered refugees. Even people sympathetic to the rebellion might aid the British by supplying naval vessels or otherwise defying Congress's restrictions on trade. A town within range of the British navy was a town in thrall. These cities, already distrusted by rural folk, now seemed even more corruptible, because they could integrate so readily and intimately with the needs of the British army and navy.[16]

As Congress focused its energies on the invasion of Canada and the siege of Boston, it let local authorities manage Newport and New York. In those towns, moderate rebels clung to a strategy of delay and passivity: they continued supplying British naval vessels, while refraining from provocative action, to prevent the warships from firing on them.

Meanwhile, the Continental Army considered storming Boston to drive the British out. As early as July 1775, Thomas Jefferson reported from Congress that the New Englanders "are now intent on burning Boston as a hive which gives cover to regulars; and none are more bent on it than the very people who come out of it and whose whole prosperity lies there." Jefferson argued for delaying such an action until winter, when it would cause the British "irremediable distress."[17]

Congress had sent Washington to take charge of the siege. An enterprising Virginia slave owner and aristocrat who had served in the Seven Years' War, he strained to unite and retain an army mostly made up of New Englanders, and he struggled to maintain discipline with so little material support. He had been a delegate to Congress and acknowledged at the outset that he did his duty "in their service & for the Support of the glorious Cause." For practical reasons, including the slow pace of communication, Washington had some leeway to decide when and how to attack Boston. He thought it was rash to attack the British there, but he felt the pressure to take decisive action.[18]

Washington's war council considered the practicalities of a strike and decided on September 11 to postpone an attack, fearful of sending young, inexperienced troops on such a dangerous errand and reluctant to destroy Boston while so many rebel sympathizers were still trapped there. The subject came up again at a dinner Franklin attended at the Continental camp at Cambridge on October 21. Three of those present, a Connecticut judge and two southern congressional delegates, said they "wished to see Boston in flames." General Charles Lee, a British army veteran who had joined the Continentals, argued that "it was impossible to burn it, unless they sent men in with bundles of straw at their backs to do it." Firing carcasses and hot shot would fail to do the trick.[19]

A few days later, Washington held another conference with delegates and local leaders, proposing to take advantage of the winter weather and frozen harbor to bombard the town. The group referred the question to Congress, but by November it seemed safer to wait, since disease, desertion, and privation would eventually force the British out of Boston.[20]

In Philadelphia, Congress debated the question on December 21 and 22. The lawyer John Dickinson, holding out hope for reconciliation, spoke eloquently against storming Boston. "Liberty & Life may be obtain'd at too dear a Price," he argued: casualties would include women and children, as well as allies of the rebels, and injure the rebels' reputation. On the other hand, John Hancock, president of the assembled delegates, spoke in favor. Since Hancock was one of Boston's richest residents, his word carried weight. Congress authorized Washington to attack Boston, though he had neither enough troops nor enough artillery to do the job.[21]

Meanwhile, the sixth-largest city in the thirteen colonies was about to meet its fate. Norfolk, Virginia, was the largest city in its province, heavily populated by Loyalists who provided aid to the royal governor, John Murray, the earl of Dunmore. (Dunmore had been Tryon's predecessor as governor of New York.) As Thomas Jefferson called for Norfolk to be treated like ancient Carthage, his friend, the Gloucester County leader John Page, wrote: "Rather than the Town should be garrisoned by our Enemies and a Trade opened for all the Scoundrels in the Country, we must be prepared to destroy it." Echoing Franklin and Hancock, he went on, "We care not for our Towns, and the Destruction of our Houses would not cost us a Sigh. I have long since given up mine as lost." Colonels Robert Howe and William Woodford, commanding Virginia and North Carolina militiamen around Norfolk in 1775, noted the Loyalist presence in Norfolk, its value to the British as barracks, and the impossibility of retaining it for America, and recommended its destruction. Lord Dunmore and his officers wanted to preserve the seaport, but they stood ready to bombard Norfolk if the rebels showed up in force.[22]

On New Year's Day of 1776, the British bombarded Norfolk, Virginia, burning about nineteen buildings. They had intended to burn only a few houses that were concealing the rebel positions, but the rebel commanders then ordered their soldiers to destroy the rest of the houses. Over the next few days, Virginia and North Carolina militiamen went on a rampage, burning more than eight hundred buildings. The following month, the Virginia Convention ordered its militia to burn the rest. By the time they finished, 1,331 structures lay in ruins, valued at over £175,000. Of these, 70.2 percent had been torched by the rebel troops.[23]

Yet the rebels denied any responsibility. The British lieutenant John Dalrymple predicted correctly that rebel writers would take "the Inhumanity of the Action off their Shoulders" and place it "upon our own." Virginia's rebellious whites already hated Lord Dunmore for his recruitment of runaway slaves as troops, his theft of the Norfolk printing press, and other supposed depredations. They were all too happy to blame him for Norfolk's destruction. Pinkney's *Virginia Gazette* emphasized the British "design" and lauded the rebel colonels' efforts to prevent the fire's spread. Hancock compared Dunmore's "barbarity against the defenceless town of Norfolk" to the burning of Falmouth.[24]

Rebels expected that white southerners would now rally to the cause of American independence; the destruction of Norfolk, coupled with Dunmore arming slaves, had helped expand the Revolution beyond New England. Washington hoped that the "barbarous" burning of Norfolk would "unite the whole Country in one indissoluble Band" against Britain. He believed that actions like the torching of Falmouth and Norfolk, along with Thomas Paine's *Common Sense,* would lead more people to advocate for separation from Britain. To Washington, the political value of British destruction of towns was equal to that of the century's most influential pamphlet.[25]

Delegates to the Continental Congress echoed Washington's prediction, as British depredations convinced many Americans that reconciliation was impossible. Robert Morris predicted that Great Britain's "destructive War" would backfire: "The burning of Towns, seizing our Ships, with numerous acts of wanton barbarity & Cruelty perpetrated by the British Forces has prepared Men's minds for an Independency, that were shock'd at the idea a few weeks ago." Franklin reported to a British colleague, "Every Day's Plundering of our Property and Burning our Habitations, serves but to exasperate and unite us the more. . . . Our Primers begin to be printed with Cuts of the Burnings of Charlestown, of Falmouth, of James Town [Rhode Island], of Norfolk, with the Flight of Women & Children from these defenceless Places, some Falling by Shot in their Flight." Though these scenes were exaggerated, the rantings

of the delegates helped to mobilize their colleagues in favor of independence.[26]

Had the British stopped at Falmouth, Charlestown, and a few other
New England towns, they might have been able to divide the colonies
by singling out the New England militants. Samuel Adams, sensitive to
the idea that many people on both sides of the Atlantic perceived recent
events as a New England rebellion, was gleeful when the tide began to
turn: "The burning of Norfolk & the Hostilities committed in North
Carolina have kindled the Resentment of our Southern Brethren who
once thought their Eastern Friends hot headed & rash." Some moderates
still clung to the idea of reconciliation, and Dickinson warned against
"Destroying a House before We have got another." The Middle Colonies'
delegates were slower to embrace the cause of independence. Perhaps
more ruined towns would change their minds.[27]

The burning of Norfolk set the stage for 1776, one of the most
physically destructive years in American history. During the siege of
Quebec, rebels burned dozens of homes in the vicinity, tried to set fire
to Montreal, and started several more fires as they retreated. In spring,
Georgians threatened to burn Savannah and Loyalists' plantations; Colonel Archibald Bullock led Creeks along with white men "painted and
dressed like Indians" to Tybee Island, where they burned the homes of a
Maroon community; in late summer, Georgia militiamen also attempted
their first destructive raid on East Florida. Meanwhile thousands of militiamen from Virginia and the Carolinas marched through Cherokee
lands, destroying dozens of towns and displacing thousands of people.
The fall saw the burning of White Plains and other depredations in Westchester County, New York. After a summer of white panic in Jamaica,
the whites on St. Kitts suspected that enslaved incendiaries set a fire on
September 4 that did £200,000 of damage to Basseterre. In England, an
itinerant named John the Painter, with support from the rebel diplomat
Silas Deane, burned the rope house at Portsmouth dockyard in December and began reconnoitering Bristol.[28]

As 1776 dawned and Norfolk smoldered, Continental forces and
British warships still surrounded Boston. Washington wanted to attack
before the British reinforced their garrison. He waited for the harbor to
freeze and asked Congress for more men and gunpowder: "No man upon

Earth wishes more ardently to destroy the Nest in Boston, than I do." Colonel Joseph Ward acknowledged that storming his hometown, "that nest of Tories Pirates Robbers and Murders," would lay it waste, but he shrugged, "We must build it again when Peace returns." By mid-February, Washington's council of war overruled the idea of attacking Boston— they were willing to attempt a bombardment, but not until the artillery was better supplied.[29]

General William Howe had, by now, replaced Gage as the senior British commander in Boston. Concluding that the town was no longer defensible, Howe opted to evacuate. He assured the town's selectmen, who were "very Anxious" for Boston's preservation, that he had "no intention of destroying the Town Unless the Troops under his Command are molest[ed] during their Embarkation, or at their departure," by the Continental Army. The selectmen warned Washington on March 8, "If such an Opposition should take place we have the greatest reason to expe[ct] the Town will be exposed to Intire destruction." They begged him for "Assurances that so dreadfull a Calamity may not be brought on by measures without." The selectmen sent messengers with Howe's request that the rebels keep their troops out of Boston until after the British had departed. Through intermediaries, Howe made it known that Washington would have no one to blame but himself if Boston were destroyed.[30]

After reading this message and hearing other reports, Washington grew confident that Howe was going to leave Boston; yet he still could not bring himself to trust Howe's intentions. The selectmen's message was not addressed to Washington. Howe was not bound by it. Washington and his officers determined that he "shou'd give it no Answer" except to acknowledge receipt. The rebel general was not prepared to give his word, but he still wanted to let Howe know that he had listened to the proposal for a truce. Washington refused to take responsibility for Boston's fate and still hoped to pin it on his opponent.[31]

A soldier on either side who disobeyed orders might have caused a conflagration, with thousands of civilians trapped on the peninsula. Howe warned his troops, as he ordered the evacuation to begin, that "the utmost Care be taken that the Town be not set on fire, by Accident or Design. Any person Detected in Setting fire to the Town without Authority will Suffer immediate Death." He did not want to provoke Washington to attack, but he also probably feared that his own troops—after two years of resentment and deprivation ending in retreat—were contemplating undisciplined acts. He limited the soldiers' access to alcohol, confined them to quarters at night, and threatened to hang anyone "caught Plundering." He wanted no "Irregularities."[32]

Washington told his artillerymen that they "must not fire upon the Town of Boston tonight unless the Enemy first begin a Cannonade," and then should fire on the British shipping, not the town. He feared that Howe would make a surprise attack. Three days later, on March 13, Washington wrote, "Whether the Town will be destroyed is a matter of much uncertainty." The British were hacking up furniture, carts, and wagons, which he took as a good sign—after all, if they intended to burn the whole city, why bother?[33]

The British troops departed on the morning of St. Patrick's Day, March 17. They were wary of a rebel bombardment. Captain John Bowater wrote that Washington's men "chose to save the Town as the principal seat of their Rebellion, and we wou'd not destroy it as the principal part of it belongs to the Friends of Government." The rebels did not move until the British ships departed, which was a good thing: "If they had the Town Certainly wou'd have been Burnt," wrote Lieutenant William Feilding, "as every thing was laid for that purpose." An old officer said he had never seen an army so silent and obedient as the British soldiers on that morning. Feilding concluded, "I shou'd have been sorry to have seen the Town destroyd, tho I think its the only one on the Continent that ought not to be saved, as it was there the seeds of Sedition was first Sown, Nursed and Cherish'd." Hard-line soldiers thought Boston should have paid the ultimate price for its stubborn resistance to the Crown.[34]

Neither Washington nor Howe had been sure of a peaceful evacuation, but by some miracle, the two generals (and their men) abided by their wary, unconfirmed agreement, and Howe departed for Halifax, Nova Scotia. The beleaguered selectmen of Boston did not stint on their gratitude to Washington: "You have not only saved a large, elegant, & once populous City, from total Destruction, but relieved the few wretched Inhabitants from all the Horrors of a besieged Town." Still, Bostonians seethed at the damage the British troops had done, especially to their Congregational churches, which were pulled down for firewood, used as barns and riding schools, and filled with soldiers. "What Marks of Devastation and Rapine do we behold!" thundered the Reverend Samuel Cooper, "a Disgrace to any civilized Nation: but of a Piece with their Barbarity in burning so many Towns."[35]

Howe and Washington were ready to destroy Boston, yet for political reasons, they each hoped to hold the moral high ground. If Boston had burned, with "the Eyes of the whole Continent" on him, Washington would have had to find a way to blame the enemy or a subordinate. In Boston, both sides' leaders had issued a warning, for those who cared to hear it. The British army and navy might destroy an American town to discourage its inhabitants from supporting an armed insurrection. Some members of Congress had, conversely, endorsed the destruction of Boston, New York, Norfolk, and other towns for their purported loyalty to the king. A major city might have to serve as sacrifice to support the common cause.[36]

The year of America's birth was far more fiery than is generally appreciated. The mobilization of an American rebellion did not necessarily mean that people immediately began obeying the authority of the Continental Congress or the new provincial governments; instead armed parties began crossing colonial borders to commit radically destructive acts. Up and down the coast of North America, most of the governors of the thirteen colonies had fled. The rebels had forced loyal officeholders into exile or prison or cowed them into silence. The British army was largely absent from the rebellious colonies for four months (mid-March to July), and state governments were newly coming into being. It was a year of cutting ties, and authority would never again be quite so loose. History shows that this is when things start to burn.

The Armies Approach New York

Continental leaders believed it was vital to keep New York City out of British hands. John Adams wrote to George Washington of "the vast Importance of that City, Province, and the North [Hudson] River . . . in the Progress of this War, as it is the Nexus of the Northern and Southern Colonies, as a Kind of Key to the whole Continent, as it is a Passage to Canada to the Great Lakes and to all the Indians Nations." Adams worried about the Loyalists in and around the city and concluded, "No Effort to secure it ought to be omitted." As the war's focus shifted away from Boston, New York City descended into chaos and violence. The city was a tinderbox.[1]

George Washington sent the colorful General Charles Lee to oversee the city's defense (fig. 3.1). Lee was a former member of the British army who urged Americans toward confrontation with the king and encouraged the rebels to pursue irregular (or guerrilla) tactics. Disgusted with the moderate pusillanimity of New Yorkers, Lee dared the British warships that were still in the harbor to fire on the city. According to William Smith Jr., a conciliatory member of the governor's council, Lee inflamed his troops with the rumor that New York's leaders planned to supply the British garrison at Boston. Governor William Tryon believed that Lee had ordered the Connecticut and New Jersey men to provoke a bombardment and then plunder the town. Smith believed their mission

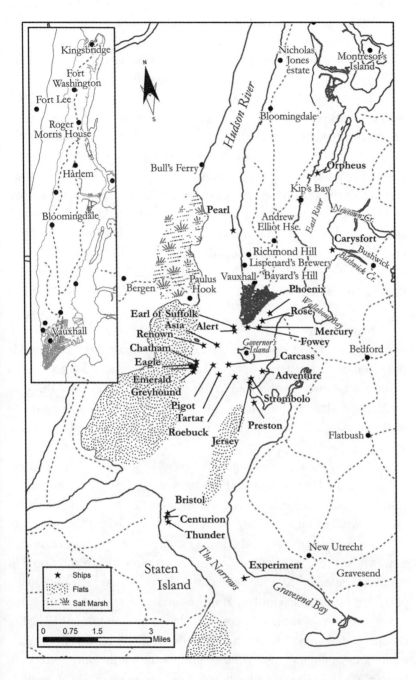

Fig. 3.1. Map of New York harbor region. This map shows the area around Manhattan as well as the approximate locations of British ships, particularly those named in the text, on September 21, 1776, when the Great Fire began. In addition to the ships shown, hundreds of British transports and other vessels were in the harbor at the time. Inset: Manhattan Island.

was to burn New York outright. Had Lee not been temporarily sidelined with gout, he might have reduced the city to ruins.[2]

Lee thought New York should be "strongly garrisoned, and fortified, or destroyed." He told Washington that he was losing sleep over the prospect of a British occupation. General Nathanael Greene urged the preparation of New York for defense, stressing its importance for control of the Hudson River and communication with Quebec and Montreal. Once the British were in, it would be difficult to get them back out, and Greene was afraid that a British occupation would drain the whole state of rebel support. The rebels faced a choice: either fortify the city or burn it. If Washington could not adequately defend New York City, then he should destroy it to keep it from the British. Washington agreed. If the British got into New York City, it would be a "Capitol blow," perhaps "irremediable."[3]

Many residents had already fled town, lest the rebels harass or imprison them. Others worried that a hotheaded commander on one side or the other would start a fight with devastating consequences. British naval captains were authorized to fire on any American town that was fortifying itself. Were Lee to provoke them, Smith wrote, it "might end in the burning of the City." New York City hardly seemed like a safe place.[4]

Wanting to keep the peace, the New York Committee of Safety (which handled the province's affairs between sessions of the Provincial Congress) asked General Lee not to bring men into New York. The committee reassured him that they would "cheerfully devote this city to sacrifice for advancing that great and important cause," yet they reminded him that "the judgment of the Continent" was still "deeply interested in the preservation of this metropolis." Lee answered that he would do his part, "but I declare solemnly that if they make a pretext of my presence to fire on the town, the first house set in flames by their guns, shall be the funeral pile of some of their best friends." Lee was certain the British were bluffing, anyway, since "the seaport towns are the only holds they have in America; they are considered as pledges of servitude." A visiting committee from the Continental Congress, reluctant to provoke a fight in New York, arrived to smooth things over. They urged inhabitants to squirrel away their valuables.[5]

The Congressional delegates' truce did not last. Major General Henry Clinton, third in command of the British army, arrived off Sandy Hook on February 4, 1776, the same day Lee finally reached the city. Clinton was only passing through, but New Yorkers worried that an attack was imminent. Lee pushed new provocations. He removed the cannon from the fort and battery. Tryon asked Clinton and Captain Hyde Parker of HMS *Phoenix* to retaliate by firing on the city, but Clinton declined: "I could not reconcile the idea of burning the only town in which we had friends in America." He considered burning an isolated part of the city as a demonstration but would "not wantonly fire shot into the town without effect, a plan I had ever disapproved."[6]

Tryon and Parker might threaten the town, but Lee thought it was all bluster. He was not the only one: John Adams also thought the British would not fire on the city, because "it has too much Tory Property to be destroyed by Tories." In the middle of the day on February 11, Lee's men spirited the cannon away, "and no cannonade ensued." The wind and ice prevented Parker from aiming his artillery at the fort and battery; his only option was to fire on the city. At that moment, Tryon changed his mind and stood down: bombarding the city would have done nothing to save the stores and artillery, since the rebel troops from New Jersey and Connecticut would have plundered them (and other property) as soon as the king's ships started firing.[7]

Lee mocked Captain Parker's hesitation. Parker said he refused to indulge the New Englanders' desire to damage a Loyalist town, but Lee retorted, "The People here laugh at his nonsense." Lee adopted the most aggressive possible stance and damned the British no matter what they did: he laughed in the face of a bombardment yet also condemned it "as a wanton piece of cruelty which cannot be of the least service to the cause of Tyranny in which you are engaged." Furthermore, he repeated his threat to make a "funeral pile" of the Loyalists as justifiable retaliation. Lee soon departed to help defend the southern seaports, leaving careful instructions for fortifying New York. (He even suggested not just disarming the Loyalists but taking their children hostage.) For the next few months, the army put extensive resources and manpower into batteries, forts, and redoubts to defend the city. The British themselves would later marvel at the rebels' efforts.[8]

Both sides had a chance to show how much they valued New York. The British navy had bombarded several towns in 1775 to show how serious it was, but at New York in February 1776, the warships balked. The radicals placed less value on preserving New York City: the New Englanders, in particular, believed that the city was a "Tory Town" worthy of destruction. They apparently believed that it would be better to goad the British into destroying the city: not only would they be rid of a troublesome place, but they would once again be able to accuse the British of burning colonial towns.[9]

In late January, a broadside from "THE SENTINEL" warned that New York's Loyalists were providing intelligence to Governor Tryon at his floating headquarters aboard the *Duchess of Gordon*. "This City becomes more and more the scoff and wonder of America!" the writer began, calling New Yorkers "dastards and poltroons" for "suffering a parcel of fellows belonging to this city, to be constantly employed to effect your destruction." These Loyalists, Washington warned, were only waiting for the right moment to "declare themselves openly" for the British. Washington arrived in New York City on April 13, determined to defend the city. After he personally took command, he asked the New York Committee of Safety to stop all communication between the city and the British warships. The British naval vessels had little choice but to move farther from the harbor and await the reinforcements that they knew were coming.[10]

Now the city had swapped one problem for another. After the Provincial Congress had spent months trying to keep the New England and New Jersey troops from occupying the city, the Continental Army was now in garrison, preparing defenses against the imminent British assault. Stopping in New York on his way to Canada, Benjamin Franklin crowed about the voluntary "Spirit" that animated "Merchants and Gentlemen working with Spades and Wheelbarrows among Porters and Negroes." Van Dyck's Grenadiers, for instance, volunteered to build a circular battery on the Hudson River. Meanwhile four hundred rebels rowed to Bedlow's Island (now Liberty Island), "an asylum for the Tory refugees," where they burned all the buildings except for a single cottage, which would shelter the women and children. A couple of weeks later,

Tryon ordered the burning of the pilot's house at Sandy Hook, New Jersey, so that rebel troops could not use it.[11]

Loyalists guessed at the rebel troops' intentions and nervously eyed the half-empty city. A disgraced Anglican clergyman named John Milner believed that Philadelphians were using "every art to inflame the Provincials to destroy this City her dreaded & hated rival," as he wrote in January. A week after Washington's arrival, a Loyalist merchant, John Wetherhead, concluded, "Nothing but a miracle can save a City the Philadelphians & Yankeys have devoted to Destruction." Two-thirds of the population had fled. The Loyalist storekeeper Frederick Rhinelander wrote, "To see the vast number of houses shut up, one would think the city almost evacuated. Women and children are scarcely to be seen in the streets."[12]

The rebel soldiers became an unavoidable presence. "Troops are daily coming in," Rhinelander complained; "they break open and quarter themselves in any houses they find shut up. Necessity knows no law. Private interest must give way to the publick good." Another Loyalist described houses stuffed with troops, "Occupied by the dirtiest people on the continent!" The Reverend Bernard Michael Houseal, translator for Governor Tryon, complained that a company of rebel soldiers used up his food, fuel, and alcohol and damaged his furniture, calling him a "d_mned Tory" who had "gone to counsel with the Enemy." People cursed the Reverend Charles Inglis in the streets, calling him a "traitor"; one Sunday a fully armed company of a hundred rebel soldiers, playing their fifes and drums, interrupted his services and lingered in the aisles for fifteen minutes, because Anglicans continued to pray for the king. Women fainted, and people were afraid the soldiers would fire at Inglis or massacre the congregation. William Tudor, a judge advocate general from Massachusetts, guessed that it was unpleasant for the city's inhabitants to live in a garrison town, but he had no pity to spare. New Yorkers deserved it, Tudor wrote, because they were responsible for America's woes: "Thousands would join . . . the Enemies of America & without Hesitation butcher their best Friends." He complained about the inhabitants' unfriendliness toward the army, and he remarked on the greed and "Dutch Subtlety" that led them to charge outrageously high prices for food.[13]

The pious New Englanders were particularly scandalized by the debaucheries of the city, which a captain from New Hampshire called "one of the wickedest Places this side of Hell." The "Holy Ground" struck them as a sinister arrangement of prostitutes paying rent to the Church of England, and many suspected the prostitutes of being part of Loyalist plots. During the week of April 22, the officers heard rumors that prostitutes from the Holy Ground beheaded two men, one of whom they also castrated. The soldiers responded by pulling down the bawdy houses, leading General Washington to threaten punishment. Notably, the Great Fire destroyed much of the "Holy Ground" on September 21, 1776; the rebels may have targeted the area deliberately.[14]

Whatever the sex workers' political sentiments, the city still had civilians of all political stripes. Ever since April 1775, New York rebels had made sporadic moves against Loyalists throughout the province: forcing them to swear oaths to the new government; ostracizing, fining, or disarming people who refused; and occasionally throwing people in prison. Many had to hide in the woods and swamps, fleeing the rebels' "savage Fury." For the first five months of 1776, rebel leaders had focused on the Loyalists who were mobilizing in Queens and Staten Island. In late May, General Washington asked the newly elected New York Provincial Congress to delegate a secret committee, led by John Morin Scott and Gouverneur Morris, to deal with local Crown supporters. The city's Loyalists lived in fear of the rebels' wrath.[15]

On June 5, the Congress made a list of enemies from New York and the surrounding counties: among others, it named John Baltus Dash, a tinman and firefighter; Theophilus Hardenbrook, a lumber merchant, architect, and firefighter; Christopher Benson, a mariner, wine seller, and militia captain; Henry Law, a mariner and customs official; the retailer Frederick Rhinelander; and the Reverend John Milner. While these men were not the colony's most prominent Loyalists—most of whom had already fled or been imprisoned—they were still thought to be aiding the Crown. On June 9, rebel authorities arrested an enslaved Black man and a free Black boatman who were carrying provisions and intelligence to Governor Tryon aboard the *Duchess of Gordon;* a rebel remarked that recruiting Black allies was evidence of the Loyalists' disgraceful methods and tactics. Local rebels decided that suppressing the Loyalists' activities was an urgent matter.[16]

New York's civilians and militiamen moved to intimidate Crown supporters further. Mobs of local rebels demanded oaths of allegiance. On the night of June 10, at least two hundred people approached Benson's house "in a riotous & tumultuous manner . . . declaring they would kill him for a damned Tory." Benson drew his sword and blocked the door, while the crowd "began pelting him with Stones" and hit him in the forehead. Moving on, the crowd carted some other Loyalists around the city and abused them. The next night, Benson heard the crowd forming again on Cortlandt Street and escaped over his back fence. Two days later, at noon, New York's rebels began looking for their most hated enemies. They did not find Benson, who had heard that "the Grenadiers" (almost certainly Abraham Van Dyck's militia company) would soon arrive to murder him, and found a place to hide overnight. Nor did they find alderman William Waddell, who slipped away and hid for the next three months, but they still did £694 worth of damage and plunder to his furniture, linens, wine, and liquor, "Ill treated his Family," and beat an enslaved woman of his household so badly that she died soon afterward. The crowd had also missed the Dublin-born leather dresser Cornelius Ryan; a Loyalist spy named Lorenda Holmes had warned him just in time, telling him where to find shelter. Ryan left Holmes with his wife Isabella, who was lying in. Then "a Mobb . . . surrounded the House," while "the City Committee [entered] with Drawn Swords and Dragged M.rs Ryan from her Bed." A committee man seized Holmes and ordered her "to stripp off her Cloaths to examine if any Letters was concealed," then dragged her to the window, "exposing her to many Thousands of People Naked."[17]

They found Theophilus Hardenbrook, a fire engine company foreman and the city's chief builder; they stripped him, his sister's husband, and two other men naked and hoisted them in the air with a rail between their legs, pelting and beating them along the way. A town crier read aloud their offenses at major intersections, and onlookers gave three cheers—the Loyalist justice Thomas Jones later wrote that the Provincial Congress and Washington himself gave sanction to the crowd. The "mangled" Hardenbrook, experiencing extreme pain and blood loss, fled to the woods around Bloomingdale. For the next two months, he hid in barns, friends' houses, and the forests "in the greatest Terror and distress" while the rebels confiscated £4,000 worth of his lumber. The crowd had been large enough to discourage the Continental Army's picket guards from interfering. Generals Israel Putnam and Thomas Mifflin (but not Washington) complained to the Provincial Congress about the violence and disorder. The legislature expressed its disapproval but also resolved that the city's inhabitants "have proceeded from a real regard to liberty" and a "detestation" of those particular Loyalists.[18]

On June 13, the day after these "Grand Toory Rides," Benson complained to Washington and "begged him to protect him," noting that citizens, soldiers, and even two officers had been in the crowd. Washington denied that the officers were under his command and told Benson "that he did not want to hear any of [his] Complaints," nor would Washington "trouble himself with any Thing of the kind." Word went around that if "Provincials," the Grenadiers, or the inhabitants wanted to assault—or even execute—a few of the city's Crown supporters, they would not have to answer to the Continental Army, because Washington was willing to look the other way. By the sixteenth, Benson had fled: he attested to his six-day ordeal before Governor Tryon aboard the *Duchess of Gordon*. The following month, Van Dyck's Grenadier company was folded into Colonel John Lasher's regiment of New York levies, a move that Van Dyck had resisted back in January.[19]

The climate was ripe for a retaliatory war to begin, and the imminent destruction of the city still loomed large in the imagination. On June 20, the rebel colonel Edward Hand of Pennsylvania was riding the ferry to New Jersey when another passenger mouthed off that "the *British* troops would . . . destroy the city by bombardment." Two days later, Colonel Loammi Baldwin reported the discovery of "a Hellish plot laid by the Tories to Assassinate his Excellency Gen[l] Washington," to aid the enemy's attack, and "blow up our Magazines." Captain Ebenezer Huntington of Norwich, Connecticut, believed that Governor Tryon was at the bottom of the plot; James Townsend of the Provincial Congress wrote that the Loyalists had planned to "set fire to the Town in nine places"; Lorenda Holmes and her aunt were accused of trying to poison the general's peas. Although the conspirators did little more than pass counterfeit money and encourage a few men to defect, Americans on the eve of independence were ready to believe that a "Diabolical Plott" had been hatched to burn New York. The regiments of Connecticut seemed particularly outraged.[20]

The rebels imprisoned the city's Loyalist mayor and hanged Thomas Hickey, one of Washington's personal guards, in the Common on June 28. Shortly afterward, Colonel Baldwin reported that Loyalists had fired shots from cover at the Continental Army's sentries for two straight nights, wounding one. Baldwin imagined that the city, with all its vices and Loyalism, was doomed to destruction.[21]

By that time, the military picture had changed considerably. On June 29, General William Howe, commander in chief of His Majesty's land forces in America, arrived aboard the *Greyhound* with transports carrying thousands of soldiers and more than 130 other warships. The next day, the Provincial Congress voted to decamp to White Plains; the last remnants of civil government in New York City were falling away. On July 2, the British took Staten Island unopposed, the same day that the Continental Congress passed its resolution for independence. Five hundred Staten Islanders swore allegiance to the king and began organizing regiments, Loyalists started arresting known rebels and pillaging their homes, and others housed and fed the British and German troops. In Manhattan, "The Inhabitants of the City are moving out with their effects as fast as possable," Colonel Baldwin wrote; the Provincial Congress appointed a committee to shelter and support the city's impoverished refugees. The soldiers in Manhattan heard a reading of the Declaration of Independence on July 9, then celebrated by defiantly tearing down a golden statue of King George III in Bowling Green (fig. 3.2). On July 12, General Howe welcomed the arrival of his older brother, Vice Admiral Richard, Lord Viscount Howe, aboard his flagship, HMS *Eagle*. Admiral Howe assumed command of the North American fleet and shared with his brother their joint commission to work toward peace. On the same day, the *Phoenix* and the *Rose* sailed up the Hudson, sending cannonballs hurtling into the city and exposing the rebels' impotence.[22]

The Howe brothers were tall, dark, and quiet; both had sterling military reputations, and each had performed deeds of almost legendary

Fig. 3.2. New Yorkers enacting symbolic action against the Crown on July 9, 1776. This fanciful European rendering of the destruction of the statue of King George III in Bowling Green mistakes both the city's buildings and the statue itself; no evidence indicates that Black people did most of the work. Franz Xaver Habermann, *La destruction de la statue royale a Nouvelle Yorck* (Paris, [1778?]), Library of Congress, Prints and Photographs Division.

courage. William and his older brother, Brigadier General George Augustus Howe, fought alongside the colonists during the Seven Years' War; after George was killed in 1758, Massachusetts had funded a monument for him at Westminster Abbey. As members of Parliament, the surviving Howe brothers had taken conciliatory stances (unlike the ministry), but both agreed to do their duty and suppress the rebellion. In July 1776, the brothers arrived in New York harbor with two mandates: as peace commissioners, empowered to offer pardons to the American rebels and negotiate with them (but only after they had submitted to British authority); and as commanders in chief of the largest overseas force the British ever sent to the Western Hemisphere. By mid-August, William Howe had between 23,000 and 24,000 soldiers under his command, which was almost as much as the entire prewar population of New York City; his brother had thirty warships, almost four hundred transports, and their crews. Washington doubted that peace was truly on their agenda.[23]

The Howes were, however, more conciliatory than their predecessors, Gage and Graves, or Captain Evelyn, and did not share the fantasy of pounding American cities into smithereens. General Howe tried to "afford protection to the inhabitants" to show the superiority of royal government, as he later claimed in Parliament when defending his failures. He wanted to take "every means to prevent the destruction of the country," in contrast to the seacoast raids of 1775. Without explicit authorization from the ministry, he would not "turn the plan of the war into an indiscriminate devastation," and he implied that he would have either disobeyed such an order or else resigned.[24]

New York City provided strategic access to New England, the mid-Atlantic, the Hudson River, and the northern backcountry; from there, the British could set up a naval base, draw in Loyalists through military recruitment and the resumption of trade, and pursue a twinned strategy of intimidation through military force and persuasion through pardons (and, with luck, other diplomatic overtures). It was not a well-coordinated plan. Lord George Germain, the cabinet secretary in charge of American affairs, favored more aggressive tactics than the Howes, but all three wanted to conserve British forces and overestimated the amount of Loyalist support the British would receive. So long as Washington's army could retreat to the countryside, Howe would have trouble winning the kind of victory that would entice Americans to flock to his colors. Still, by July, Howe felt more confident that thousands of Loyalists would join him as soon as the army had a foothold on Manhattan. The strategy relied on New York City's preservation, as the British well knew. "The hearty Wish of our People is to save it," wrote Ambrose Serle, the admiral's secretary, "if it be consistent with any Degree of Safety, upon the Attack." Serle and Henry Strachey, the secretary for the peace commission, were with Admiral Howe aboard the *Eagle*. Strachey wrote, "It would be indeed a lamentable thing to see so fine a City destroyed."[25]

The rebels under Washington could not win the battle of New York. They found themselves trying to defend an archipelago at the mouth of the Hudson River against four hundred vessels of the Royal Navy, knowing they were outgunned. Washington came to understand that he primarily had to keep his army from handing General Howe a decisive victory and maybe inflict some casualties before his inevitable retreat. The rebels mainly needed to sustain commitment, suppress dissent, and open supply lines to Europe; they could afford to slink away from their defensive works and make a stand somewhere else.[26]

Still, Washington knew that Congress, the rebels, and potential allies also needed to see him make a respectable stand at New York. He tried to rally his army of about twenty-eight thousand men. When the British first landed on Staten Island, Washington said, "The time is now near at hand which must probably determine, whether Americans are to be, Freemen, or Slaves; . . . whether their Houses, and Farms, are to be pillaged and destroyed." Regarding the local Loyalists, he made his wishes clear: "I would shew them all possible Humanity & Kindness consistent with our own Safety," but the time for niceties had passed. The Declaration of Independence had "submitted to a candid world" that King George III had "burnt our towns," a reference to Falmouth, Charlestown, Norfolk, and other bombardments. This grievance helped conclude the list of indictments against the king: he and his agents had hired German mercenaries, seized merchant seamen, and offered to arm Native American allies and Black men who were enslaved by rebel owners. Thus the fear of foreign troops, coastal raiding, and destruction matched the rebels' terrified allegations that the British had incited indigenous and enslaved Black people to commit violence. After a reading of these grievances, the soldiers and sailors at New York tore down the king's statue. In the coming days, more than 150 New Yorkers petitioned for further Loyalist purges. The crowds and soldiers had helped declare an independent America, in a city where conspiring Loyalists seemed to lurk around every corner, in a broader American climate of destruction that threatened to devolve into violent retaliation.[27]

Both sides waited for the rest of Howe's army to arrive. On August 18, after two months in hiding, Theophilus Hardenbrook decided he had cowered in the woods long enough. He packed up his papers, including sketches he had drawn of the rebel fortifications. Along with a younger Loyalist, Hardenbrook rowed a canoe out to the *Rose* as it came down the Hudson River with the *Phoenix* and two other vessels to rejoin the rest of the British fleet. The rebels unleashed their shore batteries, and the warships returned fire. As cannon roared and hardwood shattered, as the rain lashed and the wind blew, the *Rose* barreled into the canoe and capsized it; the younger man scrambled aboard the *Rose*, but Hardenbrook drowned. The British lamented the loss of an important local Loyalist, while the rebel general, William Heath, called it "the reward of Such Unrighteousness." Hardenbrook's body washed up at Burdett's Ferry three days later, and the rebels buried him. Two days after that, the British began their landing on Long Island.[28]

Had Hardenbrook waited a month, New York City would have been a British garrison. He had fought fires for more than a decade, but he was not with his fellow firefighters when the Great Fire began on September 21. A widower, he left behind three orphaned children. The British army and navy later used his property without paying rent. His nephew reflected sixty years later that the stories about his uncle's fate, "often repeated by my dear mother, have sunk deep into my heart, and their influences can never be done away."[29]

The Rankled Rank and File

Enoch Hawksworth, a Crown supporter, heard about a shocking plan. Deserters from the rebels, and Loyalist refugees from New York, told a rumor to people in the British armed forces. The rumor reached his ears right before he left New York harbor on August 12. He carried it to Ireland and sent a letter to William Knox, Parliament's undersecretary for American affairs. The informants from New York, Hawksworth wrote, "unanimously report the Rebels are determined to put N. York in Flames if attacked & found untenable, for which purpose have deposited combustible matter in various parts of the town for facilitating an instantaneous & total conflagration." The rumors read like prophecy. Hawksworth's news was weeks old, but combustion was days away.[1]

By September 1776, reports like Hawksworth's had been coming into London newspaper offices for months, and they propagated through the British press. Talk of plans to burn New York wafted through the streets and camps, and people in high places wrote about it. Of course, as Ambrose Serle, secretary to Admiral Howe, wrote, "The English Newspapers teem with Falshoods respecting American Affairs." By themselves, then, the rumors about the imminent immolation of New York City offer uncertain evidence about the intentions of the rebel troops—but they offer more concrete evidence about the perceptions of Crown supporters who sifted and spread the rumors, and they show what the British were willing to believe about the enemy. Weeks—even months— before the British took Manhattan, they concluded that the rebels were ready to burn New York City. Perhaps they were deluded, conjuring a fake story from their own preconceptions.[2]

Or perhaps they were right. Even as rebel soldiers had committed themselves to the common cause, they developed a reputation for infighting and indiscipline. Could the men's rowdy enthusiasm have led some of them to burn New York City? What motivated these men, and what were their experiences in the summer of 1776?

Rebel soldiers were politically conscious, and the ideology of the Revolution fired many of them with patriotic feeling for the enormous confederation that declared its independence on July 4. Yet these soldiers also retained a loyalty to the towns and provinces where they were born. A soldier weighed his ingrained regional allegiance and identity against the demands of brand-new national institutions, like Congress and the army. The soldiers of '76 were also prickly about their liberty. Because they thought of their service in contractual terms, they believed that the authority figures who commanded them owed them obligations in return. The soldiers were concerned not just with the British Empire and its minions but also with their own leaders' capacity for tyranny.[3]

Today Americans celebrate the ragtag army that so fiercely defended liberty—both the nation's and their own individual independence. At the time, however, the soldiers earned a mixed reception (fig. 4.1). Alexander Graydon, a Pennsylvania captain, scoffed at this "motley army." When he arrived at the Continental Army camp in late June, he wrote: "The irregularity, want of discipline, bad arms, and defective equipment . . . gave no favorable impression of its prowess." He found the soldiery "contemptible in the extreme." From the British side of the line, Ambrose Serle formed a similar impression: "Their army is the strangest that ever was collected: Old men of 60, Boys of 14, and Blacks of all ages, and ragged for the most part, compose this motley Crew." Serle was exaggerating, and both men made apparent their condescending prejudice; nevertheless the Continental Army was full of men too young to have acquired property, with a high proportion of poor, recently immigrated, and otherwise rootless men. Officers—particularly

Fig. 4.1. This satirical image and verse, by a Crown supporter, depict "Yankie"
soldiers as ragged, cold, ill, drunken, cowardly, lawless, and fanatical, led
by laborers and hypocritical parsons. Rebel officers sometimes levied the
same criticisms. "The Yankie Doodles Intrenchments Near Boston 1776,"
[London, 1776], courtesy of the John Carter Brown Library.

those from the southern and middle colonies—took a dim view of these
troops.[4]

The army depended on the men's spirit of voluntary self-sacrifice
and their willingness to obey commands. Washington repeatedly told
Congress that he needed proper authority to keep these men in line. On
New Year's Day, he proclaimed, "An Army without Order, Regularity &
Discipline, is no better than a Commission'd Mob." Good officers had
to instill "Subordination & Discipline (the Life and Soul of an Army),"
which would "make us formidable to our enemies, honorable in ourselves, and respected in the world." Washington also called for longer
enlistments, since a regular army would outclass one filled with home-

sick, short-term militiamen and volunteers. Too many of the soldiers of 1776 were "Raw, and undisciplined Recruits" who were unlikely to stay in the army. Washington was having trouble motivating them to stand against the British.[5]

Most historians agree that Washington eventually succeeded at transforming the Continental Army into a better-disciplined, professional fighting force, especially after the Valley Forge winter of 1777–78. This transformation had not yet happened in the summer of 1776; instead the early army was a mixture of men with mixed feelings about army discipline. The rigors of the 1776 campaign were discouraging: disease was rampant, and problems of supply and pay led to hunger and discomfort. Many of the field officers were untrained and incompetent, and the men did not automatically respect them. Worst of all, the cause seemed doomed to defeat at the hands of a superior army and navy. As a result, many soldiers developed grievances of their own in solidarity with their brothers-in-arms.[6]

New England soldiers made up at least half of Washington's army in 1776, and New Englanders had distinct radical traditions with deep roots. Almost all grew up learning to read in the tradition of the Congregational, or "Independent," churches where they worshipped. Disparities of wealth and status were not quite as stark in New England as they were in the other colonies, so New Englanders nurtured a fiercely communitarian ethos. The younger generation of Yankee men had also developed a "defensive independence"; they had grown up expecting that they might die at sea or at war, and they prided themselves on their political equality and their service to God's mission. They generally deferred to their elders or their social betters, but they reacted quickly when outsiders threatened their liberty. The soldiers of New England developed a reputation for obstreperous complaint, and even violence, when they felt that the authorities were impinging on their contractual rights.[7]

Governor Jonathan Trumbull of Connecticut warned Washington, therefore, "The pulse of a New England man beats high for liberty—His engagement in the service he thinks purely voluntary." Americans wondered what it meant to be a liberty-loving soldier who was also expected to obey. William Tudor, a Harvard-educated lawyer who advised Congress on its military law codes, argued that a soldier "must be content to submit to a temporary Relinquishment of some of his civil Rights." Two days after the burning of New York City, Tudor went even further: "An absolute Tyranny is essential in the Government of an Army, and . . . every Man who carries Arms, from the General Officer to the private Centinel, must be content to be a temporary Slave." Soldiers tolerated such treatment, but only because it was contractual, conditional, and temporary.[8]

In return for obedience, officers had to provide for the soldiers' health and sustenance and pursue tactics that would not waste lives. The army had to honor the soldiers' terms of enlistment regarding payment and duration of service, and the officers had to earn the men's respect. Were a commander to forfeit his obligations—by treating the men too harshly, making poor tactical decisions, or failing to provide—then soldiers became less willing to obey. As morale declined, they tended to commit crimes, to desert (sometimes en masse), and in extreme cases to mutiny.[9]

John Adams observed that officers from outside New England wanted to widen the pay disparities between officers and privates. Washington insisted that officers remain aloof from their men, while his adjutant general, Colonel Joseph Reed, scorned the "levelling spirit" that sought to equalize all ranks and pull down the upper classes. "These Gentlemen are accustomed, habituated to higher Notions of themselves and the Distinction between them and the common People, than We [New Englanders] are," Adams wrote. Over the long term, he worried about these differences in character between New England and the other regions.[10]

Graydon also disliked the New England officers because they did too little to distinguish themselves from the rank and file. As a result, "Any thing above the condition of a clown . . . was truly a rarity." New Englanders also had a tendency to include Black and Indian soldiers; Captain Persifor Frazer of Pennsylvania thought they made "a most shocking spectacle," and to Graydon they "had a disagreeable, degrading effect." More than other parts of the army, the New England regiments blurred the expected differences between officers and soldiers, and among soldiers of different races. These "testy" New England men, who made up the plurality of the Continental Army, had distinct expectations about how their officers should treat them, and they were not afraid to express their discontent.[11]

When rebel soldiers' confidence in their leaders declined, Washington had to find other means to compel them. He had few tools at his disposal—shame, the lash, and the hangman's rope. On February 9, he argued that "fear of punishment," more than "Natural bravery" or "hope of reward," transformed a man into a true soldier.[12]

Physical punishment was common in the eighteenth century: husbands abused their wives, parents beat their children, people brawled with each other, and masters thrashed their apprentices, servants, and slaves. Criminals, merchant seamen, sailors, and soldiers could expect physical correction for their mistakes. The British army allowed at least one thousand stripes for some offenses—a difficult ordeal to bear. The slave systems of the South and the Caribbean ruled through torture and tolerated ghastly mortality rates. Washington, as a young Virginia colonel during the Seven Years' War, had used the lash and the noose to enforce discipline. As harsh as everyday discipline could be, there were limits. Gentlemen almost never received corporal punishment. Heads of household were expected to treat wives, servants, and children justly. The New England authorities placed strict upper limits on masters' and magistrates' ability to inflict pain, and the Continental Army of 1775–76 followed this practice by imposing an upper limit of thirty-nine lashes for most sentences (as stipulated in 2 Corinthians 11:24) and restricting capital punishment. Congress and the states were, at first, reluctant to use extreme punishments in a volunteer army.

Americans from the South and the mid-Atlantic grew up with wider differences of rank, though they did not always accept them. Washington and most of his staff officers were gentlemen of the Chesapeake and mid-Atlantic, men of substantial property. They believed that the greatest honor accrued to the gentry, who expected deference and obedience from those below them. While social hierarchy could not ensure obedience, it at least reinforced the officers' expectations. Over time, most soldiers, even the New Englanders, yielded to the ways that social difference bolstered military rank, separating men into gentlemen officers and common soldiers. Still, the men had their limits. Rank-and-file soldiers could be quite indignant about enduring corporal punishments that they associated with slaves. When Continental Army officers looked down on the rank and file, criticized their behavior, and asked Congress to impose more painful punishments, the men refused to accept their scorn impassively.[13]

Tudor, who supervised the army's courts-martial as judge advocate general, soon grew frustrated with the congressional articles of war that outlined disciplinary codes. New York City was "debauch'd enough to corrupt the best Forces in the World," and he was constantly prosecuting the garrison's misbehaving soldiers. With Washington's blessing, on July 7, 1776, Tudor begged Congress to revise the articles and instill "a Severity of Discipline," for instance by raising the limit on lashes to one or two hundred instead of thirty-nine. (In practice, this applied only to regular Continental Army troops, not the militia.) Colonel Reed added his voice to Tudor's: to the disorderly men of the Continental Army, "thirty-nine lashes is so contemptible a punishment" that they would trade even more lashes for "a pint of rum."[14]

Washington needed better men and better field officers. Tudor (now a lieutenant colonel) had grown disgusted with constant desertions, "Shameless Ravages," and "mutinous Behaviour" among the Continental Army and the militia. Without a better system of discipline, the army was "breeding Highwaymen and Robbers," not soldiers. The men had "lost that Virtue which first engaged them to fight." If they would not be bound "by a Sense of Honour or of Duty, pray make them governable by a Fear of Punishment." The men had become so ungovernable that Tudor was desperate for a more rigorous system of corporal and capital punishment.[15]

In late summer of 1776, Congress responded by adopting new articles of war based on the British model, with its more vigorous corporal punishments. Although army discipline was "a very difficult and unpopular Subject," John Adams wrote, the new articles "laid the foundation of a discipline" that would enable the army to face the British. Washington and his officers could now threaten to inflict much more pain. Yet they still led an army of liberty-minded men who refused to lay aside their prickly principles. With the British launching their massive assault on New York, the rebel soldiers grew restless.[16]

Fig. 4.2. This British satire depicts America attacking Britannia and criticizes the Opposition members of Parliament who supported the colonists. Snake-headed Discord (*left*) carries flaming torches; readers associated rebellion with fire and chaos. "The Parricide. A Sketch of Modern Patriotism," *Westminster Magazine* 4 (May 1776): 216, Library of Congress, Prints and Photographs Division.

Rumors like Hawksworth's were reaching England as early as March 1776: "The inhabitants of New York intend to fire the town and shipping, in case any of the King's troops should land there." Londoners read in May that the rebels had burned several houses already (see also fig. 4.2). By late August, three newspapers printed the charge that "Congress have given orders to the Provincial troops . . . to set fire to that city," as soon as the British victory looked like a sure thing.[17]

After talking with soldiers, rebel deserters, and local Loyalists, Ambrose Serle learned of the social resentment and regional rivalries that simmered among the troops and inhabitants in New York City. The Connecticut soldiers were angling to destroy the town because first, "a

The PHŒNIX *and the* ROSE *Engaged by the* ENEMY'S FIRE SHIPS *and* GALLEYS *on the 16 Aug.ᵗ* 1776.
Engrav'd from the Original Picture by D. Serres from a Sketch of Sir James Wallace's.

Fig. 4.3. In August 1776, rebel forces used fire to disrupt the Royal Navy. Sir James Wallace (artist) and Dominic Serres (engraver), "The Phoenix and the Rose engaged by the enemy's fire ships and galleys on the 16 Augst. 1776," *Atlantic Neptune,* Apr. 2, 1778, I. N. Phelps Stokes Collection of American Historical Prints, Miriam and Ira D. Wallach Division of Art, Prints, and Photographs, New York Public Library.

Rival would be demolished, which they have ever hated," and second, "the King's Troops would be deprived of a convenient Station." As a result, "The mad multitude who have no Interest or Property in the Town, which appears a very fine one, are alone intent upon its Destruction." The people threatening arson were either visitors, like the New England soldiers and their camp followers, or local tenants who were too poor to own a town house. Serle's snobbery was showing, but the rumors arose from real tensions. After HMS *Phoenix* and HMS *Rose* brazenly sailed past the rebels' defenses on July 12, Serle heard that the New England soldiers were agitating to replace the New Yorkers at their posts (fig. 4.3). These "Eastern Rebels" so distrusted New Yorkers and their loyalism, Serle wrote, "that they declare openly that they may consider themselves as in an Enemy's Country." Two weeks later, he added, "the Connecticut

People would have set it [New York City] on Fire before this Time," if not for the New York troops and local householders who wanted to protect the town's property. A bit gleefully, Serle saw this as evidence of regional factionalism among the rebels; such rifts would ensure the dissolution of the rebellion.[18]

The rivalries over who should guard Manhattan had apparently broken into open disputes. The Connecticut troops had insisted so intently on undertaking the duty that they almost came to the point of brawling with the New Yorkers. Once these New Englanders occupied the city, Serle predicted that the city was as good as destroyed. By the end of July, Serle was sure that disaffected New Englanders (and maybe lower-class New Yorkers) would burn the city to keep it out of British hands. He concluded that the rebels were contemptible, disorderly, and uncivilized, and he did not put it past them to burn the city: "In all respects, these People make War like Savages."[19]

Although the Continental Congress tried to unify Pennsylvanians, Marylanders, and Yankees in a common cause, regional rivalries and resentments bedeviled Continental Army commanders in the first years of the war. With new recruits constantly arriving, the army camps forced strangers from distant towns to confront one another. Washington worried that the men—officers as well as soldiers—had begun to "irritate each other," which would "injure the noble cause in which we are engaged." In early August, Washington had to address complaints by the first battalion of Brigadier General John Morin Scott's New York brigade (which included Captain Abraham Van Dyck). These local soldiers distrusted "strangers" like the multiracial Connecticut troops; they wanted to defend New York themselves, and the Provincial Congress (now a "Convention") had assured them that they would continue to serve close to home. Washington consented by moving Scott's brigade to the city, but he warned them to "observe their engagement to the public," even if—he may have implied—the public good might require the town's abandonment and destruction.[20]

All the soldiers, wherever they came from, had a lot to gripe about besides their prejudices. "They desert in large bodies, are sickly, filthy, divided, and unruly," wrote one Loyalist, noting deaths from "putrid disorders, the small-pox in particular." Serle, too, heard about contagion and poor sanitation in the rebel camps and the city: the troops were "covered only with Rags & Vermin." Rebel deserters gave accurate reports about the thousands of men who were too ill to fight. Militia desertions were another contagion, and the rebel general Hugh Mercer reported, "Some Battalions are in very ill humour and very abusive to their Officers." A correspondent to a London newspaper wondered whether the suffering soldiers were "tired of the Dispute." Rebel-occupied New York smelled thickly of petulance and pestilence, and the British believed that the rebels were ready to purify it with fire.[21]

By the middle of August, with their landing on Long Island imminent, British officers and Loyalists were speaking with one voice: Major Francis Hutcheson wrote, "Its Generaly thought, the Rebell Army at New York will destroy it, as soon as we make our approches." The rebels believed that "the preservation of it, is an object to us for Winter Quarters," and "they are determined to burn all the towns they cannot keep." A week later, Captain John Bowater affirmed, "We hear they intend burning the Town." Other officers wrote to British newspapers: "We have a fine view of New York from this place, which we expect soon to see in flames." The rebels had removed the city's fire engines and water buckets and "filled many Houses with Combustibles," and Washington had filled "every fourth house" with pitch and tar, ready to ignite the whole city in half an hour. Correspondents were surprised that the city was not already in ashes. Another newspaper conjured an imaginary exchange: General William Howe asked Washington "not to burn New York," and Washington replied, "when he could defend it no longer, he should certainly burn it and retire, so as to cut off all supplies." One outlying correspondent swore that "Lord Howe is determined to have possession, or burn it to the ground," but almost everyone else believed the rebels were preparing to destroy New York.[22]

Even as the British grew more confident about the campaign, they began to doubt whether they would conquer anything but ruins. The New York Provincial Convention had unanimously appointed four of its members (including Connecticut-born John Sloss Hobart) to investigate whether Brooklyn residents were about to abet the British landing; if disarming the populace and removing its grain proved insufficient, the committee was empowered "*to lay the whole county waste*" with the Continental Army's help. British newspapers were therefore not too far off when they reported that "a committee was appointed to burn the city" upon retreat. On August 13, the Reverend Benjamin Trumbull (a chaplain who lived with several of Connecticut's high-ranking officers) said he was confident that the rebels could "burn and destroy the Town should the Enemy get into it." He told his wife not to worry: "We have many Ways to destress the Enemy." With some justice, the British believed that a scorched-earth campaign was imminent.[23]

Washington, meanwhile, warned Manhattan's inhabitants that the Royal Navy was about to destroy the city. On August 17, broadsides went up announcing that the general expected "a Bombardment and Attack . . . by our cruel, and inveterate Enemy" any minute. He advised all "Women, Children, and infirm Persons" to leave town as quickly as possible if they valued "their own Safety and Preservation." The general asked for help assisting the poor with their removal. In advance of the British attack, he wanted civilians out of the way. According to the Moravian pastor Ewald Gustav Shewkirk, Washington's proclamation "caused a new fright."[24]

In Paris, Silas Deane—the Continental Congress's secret envoy to France—reported to Charles Dumas (his counterpart at the Hague) on American news, dated August 20: the British were preparing to attack New York, the rebels were entrenched in a ring around New York City, and the city's houses were "filled with combustibles ready to be set on fire." Deane, of Groton, Connecticut, may have had no better source for this information than British newspapers, but his letter is significant for two reasons. First, it shows that a rebel statesman was also sharing the belief that Continental soldiers were prepared to incinerate New York City. Second, Deane himself was weeks away from slipping some money to a wandering criminal named James Aitken, or "John the Painter," who tried to burn down Portsmouth and Bristol, England, in late 1776 and 1777, and claimed to have done so on the rebels' behalf.[25]

The British began landing soldiers on Long Island on August 22. Colonel William Douglas of the 6th Connecticut Regiment was optimistic about the army's chances as he watched them parade: "Almost one half of this Grand Army now Consists of Connecticut Troops." He called the militia "a fine Set of Men," and believed the British would pay a high price when they attacked the city; "They may Burn it, but they Cant Take it, and it is of no Service to them to Destroy it."[26]

Over the course of the next few days on Long Island, the Continental Army fulfilled its enemies' expectations; Colonel Edward Hand's Pennsylvania riflemen burned grain, hay, houses, and barns, with special attention to the property of Loyalists. Philip Vickers Fithian, a Presbyterian chaplain for a New Jersey militia regiment, said his "Heart fluttered . . . To see the Ravages of War presented visibly in view—Valuable Property, indeed the Staff and Comfort of human Subsistence consuming in prodigeous Fires as Far as we could see." Serle looked at Brooklyn, "covered with Smoke," and exclaimed, "Ignoble Warfare becoming only such ignoble Minds!" Weeks later, a Hessian lieutenant would reflect sadly on the sketch of Flatbush he had made shortly before: "It was a beautiful village before these *Mordbrenner* [murderous incendiaries] burned most of it down."[27]

Things had gotten out of hand: Washington complained about his men's "disorderly & unsoldierlike" behavior and ordered them to comport themselves like a "well regulated army" by avoiding "the licentious & disorderly behaviour" of "a mob." He asked his officers "to prevent every kind of abuse to private property." Soldiers ought to act "in defense of the rights of mankind," not "invaders" of people's worldly estates. He specifically cautioned against "the burning of houses, where the apparent good of the service is not promoted by it," adding, "by duty & every rule of humanity they ought to aid, & not oppress, the distress'd in their habitations." Washington wanted an orderly and disciplined army, and he expressed humanitarian concern for civilians' homes. Still, he implied that property destruction might serve the Continental cause, and even the appearance of justification might exonerate the men from a charge of disorder or brutality. Washington reserved the right to punish the guilty while acknowledging that soldiers might need to burn houses on America's behalf.[28]

By the evening of August 27, the Howes had outwitted Washington in the battle for Long Island; the British took 900 rebels prisoner and killed or wounded 200 more. By dawn on the thirtieth, Washington successfully evacuated his army from western Long Island to Manhattan. Still, morale was sinking. "It seemed a general damp had spread" among the soldiers, Pastor Shewkirk wrote. "Many looked sickly, emaciated, cast down," and more than a few deserted their posts and went home. The New England soldiers' poor performance became notorious.[29]

General Scott concluded that the rebels could no longer hold the city. The soldiers were downcast about Long Island and the inevitable loss of Manhattan. They complained about the lack of pay and provisions, and many had already deserted. Some battalions had not been paid in more than two months. The soldiers' low spirits, combined with dismal camp conditions, made them unruly and prone to disobedience.[30]

That day, Alexander Bridges remembered, a group of people threw apples through the windowpanes of the house where he lodged. When the landlord, Mr. Cummins, asked them why they had done it, they replied, "It did not signify anything as they meant to burn the City." Bridges later testified about this before a British commission that was investigating the fire in October 1783.[31]

Joseph Plumb Martin, a fifteen-year-old private in the 5th Connecticut Regiment, offered the perspective of the rank-and-file soldier. Usually it was need, not malice, that drove the men to plunder, but sometimes, "to keep the blood from stagnating," his craving for amusement would "get the upper hand of me . . . and sometimes it would run riot with me." Like many of his fellow soldiers, Martin was young, occasionally hungry, and bored. The men were also thinking ahead: they knew the British would commandeer civilian property as stores, so "they imagined that it was no injury to supply themselves when they thought they could do so with impunity." At one point, "levity, necessity, or roguery" led Martin and some of his companions to liberate some wine from a cellar on Stone Street. The enemy would take the city one way or another. There was more than one way to deprive them of the spoils.[32]

The British were in a much better mood, but they fretted about the city: "Matters go on swimmingly," wrote one British officer, "and I don't doubt the next news we send you is, that New York is ours, though in ashes; for the Rebels Troops have vow'd to put it in flames if the Tory Troops get over." The rumors resumed. A Dublin newspaper reported that General Howe had asked "the Magistrates of New York . . . to surrender the town, or evacuate it." The magistrates replied that "they had orders from the Congress to defend it . . . and if Lord Howe should be able to force the intrenchments, they would fire the town." General Howe and his council of war supposedly retorted that "in case the town of New York should be burnt, the British soldiers should have order to give no quarter, but put the Americans to military execution." Again, no evidence indicates that this exchange took place, but the newspaper item spoke to a fear that a war of retaliation might break out at any moment.[33]

Serle gave further reports of illness in the Continental Army camp: "The Hand of GOD seems every way upon them; rent with Distractions, about 3000 sick of a contagious Disorder, distressed in their Circumstances, and all in a Panic, they have little to hope & every thing to fear." From a sodden tent on Long Island, Lieutenant Colonel Richard Grenville of the Coldstream Guards wrote, "We hear great dissatisfaction appears amongst them, the New Yorkers & New Englanders cannot agree together."[34]

The bickering between New Englanders and other troops had erupted into blows. From Newtown, Long Island, Captain James Murray of the 57th Regiment wrote, "It is just now reported that they [the rebels] have quarrelled amongst themselves; there was certainly a great deal of firing heard in town." Although Murray distrusted the rumors, he concluded: "The New Englanders it seems insisted upon burning the town at their departure, which the inhabitants as strenuously opposed." Colonel Charles Stuart also heard gunfire, and deserters later informed the British that "the inhabitants had rose in arms to protect their town from being burnt by the rebels, on which a fray issued between them and the people of Connecticut." The rumor was an exaggeration, however: Stuart also reported that five hundred men were killed before two of the mutinous regiments laid down their arms. Even so, such stories reached several British newspapers, telling of battles between New Englanders and mid-Atlantic troops over the fate of the city. One correspondent revived Serle's story from July, reporting that Washington had tried to place the city's defense in the hands of Connecticut troops, but the New York battalions refused, "assured that the Connecticutians would burn and destroy all the houses." The paper expressed its hopes that "this ever loyal city wil not be sacrificed to the inexorable fury of fanatical and congressional proscription."[35]

Although these stories seem far-fetched, no one could deny that morale was low and the men were becoming disorderly. Dr. Barnabas Binney of Boston wrote, "I am very sorry to see so little Harmony between ye Southern & Northern Forces," and he blamed the southerners: "They are puffed up at Nothing." The officers and soldiers were "dispirited," Washington wrote. Their defeat at the Battle of Brooklyn had "filled their minds with apprehension and despair." The militia were "dismayed, Intractable, and Impatient to return." Thousands had already left.[36]

Washington had been warning for months about his dangerously undisciplined army. Now, after the defeat at Brooklyn, the militia's "want of discipline & refusal of almost every kind of restraint & Government" had led to "an entire disregard of that order and subordination necessary to the well doing of an Army," all of which had "Infected" the Continental regiments. Thus, he concluded, "I am obliged to confess my want of confidence in the Generality of the Troops." Without men willing to hold the line in the face of musket fire, the campaign was lost; Washington was ordering officers at Kingsbridge to forcibly stop deserting militiamen from leaving Manhattan. While he stoically promised, "Every power I possess shall be exerted to serve the Cause," even his considerable powers might not be enough. He reminded his troops, "Now is the time for every man to exert himself and make our country glorious or become contemptible." The outcome seemed in doubt.[37]

Desertion, plunder, and other crimes arise not just from bad morals but also from bad morale. Bad morals come from an individual lack of virtue: cowardice, selfishness, and so on. Bad morale is collective. Discontented soldiers had real grievances and might direct their ire at one another, at their own commanders, or at the citizenry. Bad morale could lead, in other words, to radical political action.[38]

Civilian and military leaders among the rebels were already anxious about their troops' poor discipline and worse morale. Such reports lend credibility to the metastasizing rumor that the men were contemplating arson. Rebel soldiers were evidently threatening to burn the city, and this loose talk may well have indicated some very real plans. A close look at the Continental Army in its first year and a half reveals a climate of discontent, disobedience, and disorder that certainly might have turned men's thoughts to fiery words and fiery deeds.

As the British drew closer, Washington grew even angrier with his men. He mentioned "some instances of infamous Cowardice, and some of scandalous Plunder, and Riot" in his orders of September 3; he called such actions "utterly destructive of all Honesty or good Order," and he would call for hangings unless his officers put a stop to such behavior. Three days later, he declared that any officer who failed to report plundering would be court-martialed as an accomplice; "For let it ever be remembered, that no plundering Army was ever a successful one."[39]

Washington also wrote about militiamen feigning illness, with more deserting every day. Soon there would be few left. On eastern Long Island, the militia melted away; many of its members would end up serving under General Howe. Major Lewis Morris Jr. wrote that an entire Connecticut brigade "have got the cannon fever and very prudently skulked home"; Morris thought them a "nuisance" that the army was well rid of. Edward Hand's Pennsylvania regiment "plunder everybody in Westchester County indiscriminately," while other rebel troops pillaged on Long Island and Manhattan and committed "unwarrantable destruction" on Montresor's Island (now Randall's Island). As terrified militia deserted by the hundreds, Colonel Daniel Hitchcock complained that they were "not worth a farthing." Their defeatist attitude as they cried, "All is gone and the Regulars must overcome Us," was bringing down morale throughout the army. John Adams replied, "This despondency of Spirit, was the natural Effect, of the Retreats you have made, one after another."[40]

After hearing from five men who had fled New York on September 3, Serle concluded, "The Rebels are in a State of Animosity, Feud, and Distrust, among themselves." Major Hutcheson also reported hearing from deserters that the rebels "are in the greatest Confusion," disheartened and mutinous. He added that "the New England party have met with great opposition in their wishes to burn it, which the[y] will not be able to Effect." Henry Strachey wrote hopefully that "a Fight amongst themselves" over the destruction of the city "or any other Point, would save us a great deal of trouble." He believed that the four thousand sick men in town would be so difficult to move that it might stop the rebels from starting a fire.[41]

In the rebel camp, Colonel Douglas, once so sanguine about his men, now complained about the militia in his brigade, who gave him "much Fateague and Trouble"; he blamed his irresponsible junior officers. A number of the men were deserting; Douglas noted acidly that "many of them would sell amarica to git home." Astonishingly, some civilians were even coming into the camp to bring their friends home. The remaining men would not submit to discipline, and Douglas feared the ruin of the army was at hand. He was so exhausted from dealing with his men that his cough was getting worse—Douglas died from his illness, at the age of thirty-five, the following spring.[42]

In the city, civilians were getting nervous. Ivy Mucklewrath, coachman to William Smith Jr., removed some of his employer's most valuable possessions on August 29, because he heard the soldiers declare that "the Town should be destroyed before they withdrew from it whether General Washington forbid it or not." Several New Yorkers later recalled frequent threats of incendiarism during the rebels' occupation. John Baltus Dash, a Loyalist tinman and fireman, remembered that "those who intended to remain in the City were in general apprehensive" that the rebels would burn it. Andrew Kerr remembered that "the N. Eng.'d people" applied to Washington "to have N York burnt," but he threatened to "severely punish" anyone who tried. John Le Chevalier Roome, an imprisoned Loyalist, remembered his rebel jailers threatening to "lock up the Goal [jail] & set fire to the City & go off" when the British arrived, but they transferred him to Norwich, Connecticut, instead. Sometime around September 5, Samuel Bayard Sr.'s old friend Joseph Smith told him frankly that he would sooner burn Bayard's own house than let British troops occupy the city.[43]

Again, these rumors may mean little; many of them may have been variations on the same report prevailing among the British forces. The rumors fueled the wishful expectations of Crown supporters that the American rebellion was too internally divided to succeed. They also reflected the prejudice of many Crown supporters, which held that New Englanders and their most radical New York allies were so fanatical that they would burn New York out of spite. Much of the intelligence that Serle gathered was true: there really were tensions between troops from different regions. Illness and desertion really were significant problems in the rebel army of 1776. The threats to burn the city were almost certainly real as well. The British hoped that New Yorkers wanted to protect their own property and the safety of the army's ailing and recuperating men. They hoped that these considerations would act as the city's security. They must have been discomfited when Washington gave the order on September 8 to move the hospital across the Hudson River to Orangetown. The evacuation was proceeding. The British and their allies feared that the redcoats' boots would land on nothing but scorched earth.[44]

As the British conquest of Manhattan drew nearer, these rumors reached New York's provincial legislature and motivated its delegates to confront General Washington about them. The state's leaders took these rumors seriously, without dismissing them as British slander and paranoia. They faced the very real possibility that rebel soldiers would burn the city.

We have no proof that Washington had secret permission to burn New York. Still, in thinking about whether rebel leaders would have authorized the destruction of the city, it is worth considering how much authority these distant legislatures and imperious commanders actually held over common soldiers and civilians. Evidence strongly suggests that rebel leaders faced a rising tide of radical insubordination. The fire rumors gave them no small degree of alarm. They may sincerely have wanted to stop the burning of New York City for humane reasons and to protect the residents' property. At the same time, rebel leaders began to worry about an impending fire because it would prove that they had finally lost control.

General Washington's Bad Options

With his men plagued by illness and indiscipline, facing a British army well positioned to attack Manhattan, Washington could either defend the city or retreat. On the one hand, holding New York City was vital to maintaining rebels' morale and allegiance, and its loss would signal disaster. Washington also had to consider the future threats that would emanate from British-occupied New York. On the other hand, Washington could not afford the casualties his army would suffer in a British assault. Forced to choose between losing the city and losing his army, he chose to save his army. Once he decided to retreat, would he burn the city behind him?

Washington understood the strategic value of destroying New York and discussed it with his staff. Adjutant General Joseph Reed had written on August 4, "I should be for destroying the city and retiring when we cannot defend it longer. It is a mere point of honour which keeps us here now." Besides, the city was filled with Loyalists: "I do not see the propriety of risking the fate of America . . . to defend a city, the greater part of whose inhabitants are plotting our destruction." Two weeks after the Great Fire, Washington would write to his cousin Lund about his mind-set beforehand. He had agreed that destroying New York City was necessary: "Had I been left to the dictates of my own judgment,

New York should have been laid in Ashes before I quitted it." He argued
that the rebels' failure to order the city's destruction "may be set down
am[on]g one of the capitol errors of Congress." The British would enjoy
"warm & comfortable Barracks" for the winter, and it would be "next to
impossible" for the rebels to retake the city.[1]

Everyone seemed to share Washington's strategic assessment and
predict, therefore, that the rebels planned to burn New York City behind
them as they retreated. New York's legislature hoped it would not come
to this. The Provincial Convention had resolved on July 15 that they
would "cheerfully cooperate" if Washington needed "to abandon the city
of New-York" when he "should think it expedient for the preservation
of this State, and the general interest of America." They hoped he would
defend New York for as long as possible. Washington's relationship with
the provincial legislature was tense during these months. Although he
made it a policy to defer to legislative authorities, he had to look out for
his army; still, his correspondence with the legislature was a useful reminder that civilians were paying attention to his decisions.[2]

Now, as British and Hessian troops began landing on Long Island,
the Provincial Convention called on Washington to answer for the dis-
turbing rumors coming out of the city. On August 22, Abraham Yates Jr.,
the convention's president pro tempore, asked about "a Report Prevailing
amongst the Army, 'that if the fortune of War should oblige our Troops
to abandon that City, it should be immediately burnt by the retreating
Soldiery, and that any Man is authorized to set it on fire.'" To the legislators' horror, permission to burn New York was so diffuse that anyone—
even a common soldier—could kindle the spark.[3]

Yates reiterated that he and his colleagues "will chearfully submit
to the fatal Necessity of destroying that Valuable City whenever Your
Excellency shall deem it essential to the Safety of this State or the general
Interest of America." If Washington took responsibility, the legislators
would support his decision. Yet they noted that their "Duty . . . to their
Constituents obliges them to take every possible Precaution that Twenty
thousand Inhabitants may not be reduced to Misery by the wanton Act
of an Individual." They bristled at the idea of some lowly Connecticut
private taking matters into his own hands, and they asked Washington
"to take such Measures in preventing the evil Tendency of such a Report

as You shall deem most expedient." Washington could burn the city if necessary, but he needed to suppress this army rumor and ensure his men's obedience.[4]

Washington could not afford to alienate New York's leaders, who controlled the flow of militiamen and provisions. He hastened to "assure you Gentlemen, this Report is not founded on the least Authority from me." Then he spelled out his thoughts: "I am so sensible of the Value of such a City and the Consequences of its Destruction to many worthy Citizens & their Families that nothing but the last Necessity and that such as should justify me to the whole World, would induce me to give Orders for that purpose." Washington rationalized the rumor: although he and the New York Convention were both urging families to evacuate the city, many people were stubbornly staying put. To discourage them from staying, some gossips had spread the rumor that the soldiers were authorized to burn the city. The rumormongers' motives were "honest and innocent," Washington wrote; they hoped to keep people safe from the coming battle by terrorizing them into leaving. Realizing that this sounded like wild speculation, he disclaimed any certain knowledge: "I cannot pretend to say by whom or for what purpose it has been done." The rest of his letter asked the convention for help evacuating women, children, and the indigent from the city. He wanted to protect civilians from whatever might happen next.[5]

Washington consistently expressed his abhorrence of undisciplined soldiers, and so it is doubtful that he ever considered giving them blanket authorization to burn New York City during his retreat. Still, he knew that his own officers had also discussed the value of destroying the city, so he was being a bit disingenuous about the rumors' origins. It is strange that Washington defended the rumormongers' good intentions—perhaps he was supporting a concrete plan. Certainly, he wanted to preserve his own virtuous image: if he overtly put New York City to the torch, he needed "the whole World" to affirm that his actions were beyond reproach.[6]

Washington must have considered allowing this rumor to keep spreading; that way, the city might burn even as he kept his own hands clean. Much as King Henry II supposedly wondered aloud whether his courtiers would rid him of Thomas Becket, that "turbulent priest," Washington must have been tempted to let a trustworthy fellow destroy this troublesome city. At the same time, he must have worried that "the whole World" would scorn him if he ordered the city's destruction himself. So maybe he made known his tacit approval—maybe that was enough.[7]

It is tempting to imagine that rebel soldiers would not dare set fire to the city without the explicit sanction of their superiors, but Washington was under no such illusions. His letters show rising dismay about the misbehavior of his soldiers and the laxity of his field officers. Many already ignored the drumbeat of orders to behave with better discipline. They stepped outside the ranks, misbehaved, and violated civilian property. Some quite zealously hated the British. Some may have decided to serve the common cause with accelerants and torches.

The rebels' strategic position had become dire. The men—disgusted and frightened—were slipping away. On August 30, the chaplain Philip Fithian described the army as "filled with Anxiety—the prevailing Opinion is we cannot keep this Capital more than two or three Days." Britain's larger warships "beat up a little nearer every Tide, & we hourly expect them before the Town." That same day, General Nathanael Greene mentioned Washington's plan to retreat and make his stand at Kingsbridge, and put the odds at "two to one New York is laid in ashes."[8]

Washington was not quite ready to call for a withdrawal, but most people knew New York City was untenable. While the army shifted troops to Kingsbridge, civilians were leaving with everything they could carry; on August 31, Fithian wrote, "They consider the Ruin of the Town to be near." The next day, Captain Jonathan Birge of Bolton, Connecticut, wrote, "It is generaly supposed that the town will soon be abandon[ed] or burnt." Ludwigh Russell said the same: "It is the general opinion of all Ranks, that our People will Set it on fire themselves." William Shippen predicted on September 2, "I think it likely that [that] City will be deserted or burnt or both"; and Fithian reported, "Whispers are among the men that this Town is to be evacuated & burned," though he added, "We do not believe it." This was the same day as the supposed fight (according to British sources) between New Englanders and other rebel troops about burning the city. Two days after that, the militia captain Benjamin Bogardus reported the prevailing belief that one side or the other would destroy the city, and "it Does not Look Likely that the Enemy wants to Destroy the Town." Rumor had it that General William Howe had sent a flag of truce warning Washington that "he would then Burn Every Seaport town on the Continent" if Washington destroyed the city; "however," Bogardus wrote, "it Cant be Expected that our people will Leave the City as it is for them to harbor in."[9]

The region's Loyalists and enslaved people were also undermining the rebels' defense of New York. Washington wrote desperately to the Provincial Convention on September 1, asking for the Hudson Valley militia to help reinforce him at Kingsbridge. The state legislature replied that the large number of Loyalists and enslaved people in those counties required them to keep the militia at home, lest "our enemies . . . stir up our slaves to bear arms against us." Over the course of the war, tens of thousands of enslaved Black people took advantage of chaotic disruptions like this to emancipate themselves or take up arms for the British. Black men felt encouraged by the recruitment efforts of British officials like Lord Dunmore and Major General Henry Clinton: the Black Pioneers were now in New York harbor, enlisting more men, and the British were forming other African American units on Staten Island.[10]

Fithian wrote that "Freedom is likely to suffer her sorest Persecution" in New York City. Washington, knowing he was about to lose the city to the British, told Congress that he hoped to "serve the Cause" and save his army, but "Our situation is truly distressing." The British army outnumbered his "dispirited" forces. They now occupied western Long Island and Governor's Island. A landing on Manhattan Island to his north would cut off his men completely. Mindful that he answered to Congress, Washington asked, "If we should be obliged to abandon this town, ought It to stand as Winter Quarters for the Enemy?" He was asking permission, as politely as he could, to fulfill the expectations of soldiers like Birge, Russell, and Bogardus.[11]

Washington explained both sides of the question: the British "would derive great conveniences from It on the one hand—and much property would be destroyed on the other." He urged haste: "It is an important question, but will admit of but little time for deliberation." The British assault force was coming, and "at present I dare say the Enemy mean to preserve It if they can." What if he could spoil their prize? Then he warned, "If Congress therefore should resolve upon the destruction of It," which he was suggesting as delicately as he could, "the Resolution should be a profound secret as the knowledge of It will make a Capital change in their plans."[12]

Military strategy called for secrecy. Although Washington did not say it, he had other reasons why he might ask for discretion. If Howe's warning of retaliation was real, then unless the rebels could evade responsibility for burning New York, Howe would burn more American towns in response. For the sake of the nation's reputation, Washington and Congress also had to adhere, at least outwardly, to the conventions of warfare. Less than two months had passed since Congress had announced the rebels' intention, in the Declaration of Independence, "to assume among the powers of the earth" an "equal station" with "a decent respect to the opinions of mankind." The new United States had to align themselves with the laws of war, or the rest of the world would dismiss them as rebellious criminals or backwoods ruffians, and they would deserve whatever mistreatment the Howes could dish out. If Congress were to authorize the burning of New York, then, the rebels had many reasons to keep it a "profound secret."[13]

As Washington waited for an answer from Congress, he turned to his senior officers for advice. Colonel Rufus Putnam, chief engineer, noted that the British could choose from several landing points between Manhattan and Throgs Neck. The British were keeping close track of the rebels' deployments, and they could easily overwhelm any of the Continental Army's divisions. The rebels had no time to build further defenses. Putnam argued, therefore, that the army should retreat northward: "I know that this Doctrenn gives up york to distru[c]tion and Exposes many other towns to be Ravaged by them But what are 10: or 20 towns to the grand object[?]" What was one city, or even ten or twenty, compared to the common cause?[14]

Colonel John Haslet of Delaware, a Scots Irish veteran of the Seven Years' War, concluded on September 4 that "the City is Indefensible"; he also believed that the city should have been "laid in Ashes" and a defense made farther north. "This kind of Devastation may be condemned as cruel," but it was worthwhile to sacrifice parts of America for the safety of the whole. It was foolish, however, to endanger the entire war effort "for the Preservation of N. York & its Invirons, all which deserve from every Honest American Political D[am]nation." Though he professed to "revere" Washington, Haslet was starting to doubt whether the general was the right man for the job: "wd. to Heaven Genl Lee were here is the Language of officers & men." Holding on to New York was causing Washington's popularity to slip.[15]

John Hancock, the president of Congress, replied to Washington the next day with permission to evacuate the city if necessary and an order for more reinforcements. At the same time, a committee of the whole specified that "Congress would have especial care taken, in case he should find it necessary to quit New York, that no damage be done to the said city by his troops, on their leaving it." Congress had "no doubt of being able to recover [New York], though the enemy should, for a time, obtain possession of it." This was wishful thinking, given the superiority of the Royal Navy; Washington and Greene had already pointed out the difficulties of someday retaking New York. Still, the civilian authority had made its wishes clear.[16]

Congress never forbade Washington from directly ordering (or secretly paying) someone to burn New York—the legislators only cautioned against a scenario wherein "his troops" did damage of their own accord when retreating from the city. Washington hardly needed the reminder to keep his men disciplined: his general orders had hammered away at this point for weeks. Thus, through its circumlocutions and passive voice, Congress left a rhetorical gap in its letter, giving Washington leeway to order the burning of New York, perhaps by someone other than "his troops." Maybe wide-eyed civilian zealots could do the job, or hirelings who were not too fastidious about other people's property, or his own men out of uniform. (Washington himself had said when he arrived in New York, "There is no distinguishing Citizens from Soldiers.") Congress could not directly countenance the burning of New York. Disavowing the act of incendiarism was crucial. It is impossible to know whether any secret orders accompanied the official missive from Congress; if any existed, either Washington and his clerks destroyed them, or the documents are otherwise lost to history. Nor is it possible to know whether Washington read between the lines. It is only certain that the official record called for "especial care . . . that no damage be done."[17]

The jaws of the British lion were closing around Washington. On September 4, the British took Blackwell's (now Roosevelt) Island in the East River, and the rebels began removing all excess stores above Kingsbridge, "that we may have resources left, If obliged to abandon this place." In reality, defending the city was no longer an option.[18]

The next day, Greene suggested to Washington that the only way to avoid "disgrace" was to retreat: "I would burn the City & subburbs." Greene could not justify jeopardizing the Continental Army to protect one island and its city, "no Objects for us" compared to "the General Interest of America." As a matter of morale, "the Country is struck with a pannick," and so "any Cappital loss at this time may ruin the cause." Besides, as Greene pointedly argued, two-thirds of the property in the city and suburbs belonged to Loyalists: "The sacrafice of the Vast Property," he wrote, should have no bearing on Washington's decision, because it would disproportionately hurt British sympathizers. It also made strategic sense. First, it would deny the British a secure barracks in the city, one that the Continentals could never recapture "without a superior Naval force to theirs." Second, it would also deprive the British of a market for trade and supplies, which would tempt farmers, craftsmen, and merchants throughout the area and cause their loyalties to waver. "All these Advantages would Result from the destruction of the City," Greene wrote, "And not one benefit can arise to us from its preservation that I can conceive off." Besides, once the British took the city, they could use it for their own ends and *still* decide to destroy it themselves. By destroying it now, while they still had the chance, the rebels would constrain the Howe brothers' options. Greene worried whether "my Zeal has led me to say more than I ought" but insisted he spoke not "from fear" but from "good Intentions" and "a cool and deliberate survey of our situation."[19]

Washington was persuaded by Greene's arguments, as he later admitted to his cousin: "To this end I applied to Congress, but was absolutely forbid." He appears to have interpreted Congress's resolution as an order not to burn the city, and he had no doubt they "will have cause to repent the Order." On September 6, he wrote to them (perhaps ruefully), "Perceiving It to be their Opinion and determination that no damage shall be done the City in case we are obliged to abandon It, I shall take every measure in my power to prevent It." He would try to prevent damage from happening (which allowed for the possibility that it might happen anyway). Most importantly, he would have deniability, and so would Congress. Having ostensibly settled the issue, Washington weighed his options for foiling the British advance, hoping "to baffle their efforts and counteract their Schemes." He summoned his generals for a war council on the morning of September 7.[20]

After "painfull . . . reflection," Washington and his council of war shared their concern "that all our Troops will not do their duty" when the attack came. Washington hated to "dispirit the Troops and enfeeble our Cause" by evacuating the city after putting so much effort into defending it. People would criticize him for retreating instead of fighting, and many Americans would become even more discouraged about the rebellion's chances, so a withdrawal might be politically catastrophic. Many of his own generals felt sure that Congress wanted the city "to be maintained at every hazard." Some argued for immediate evacuation, but the majority voted to hold on for a little longer. They decided to split their forces between the northern and southern ends of Manhattan, a risky deployment that filled them with anxiety. Washington concluded his report to Congress in rueful, almost petulant tones: "That the Enemy mean to winter in New York there can be no doubt—that with such an Armament they can drive us out is equally clear. The Congress having resolved that It should not be destroyed nothing seems to remain but to determine the time of their taking possession." Washington wrote like a man burdened by his terrible choices: retreating would humiliate him and his army, but he had no good options for holding the city. He was tempted by the idea of destroying the city behind him, like a beacon of defiance amid the gloom of defeat, but Congress was worried that the political cost would be too high.[21]

Sensing Washington's discomfort, Hancock clarified Congress's decision: "Their wish is to preserve N. York & leave the time of Evacuat[in]g it to yo[u]r Judgment." The new congressional resolution actually said nothing about preserving the city; Hancock inserted that line himself. Regardless, the civilian authorities signaled that Washington still had some freedom to make decisions. Meanwhile, at the request of the New York Provincial Convention, Washington sent the city's church bells to New Jersey, where smiths would melt them down and recast them as brass cannon. When the Great Fire began, the city was fatefully silent.[22]

Around the same time, Captain Frederick Mackenzie of the Royal Welch Fusiliers, a brigade major in Howe's army, eagerly awaited "something decisive against the Rebels." An assault somewhere near Harlem, he was sure, would cut off part of their army and strike fear into the remaining soldiers. "It is in our power at any time to drive them from New York, and take possession of it, but if we attacked them there, they might set fire to it, and once more slip out of our hands." The city was so valuable as winter quarters, supply depot, and harbor, "It is of very material consequence to prevent them from burning the town."[23]

Tench Tilghman, Washington's aide-de-camp and a close member of his military "family," wrote to his father about the exchange between Congress and Washington (fig. 5.1). Like Mackenzie, Tilghman's Loyalist father apparently thought that the potential destruction of New York City was entirely in Washington's hands, but Tench pointed out that Washington had reached out to Congress "for an explicit Answer on that head, and they have directed him by a Resolve to preserve the City at all Events, that is, if he was obliged to abandon not to suffer the Soldiery to do any damage." Again, perhaps Washington still had room to dispatch civilian saboteurs or spies: Tilghman seems to acknowledge that Congress primarily wanted Washington to avoid the *appearance* of Continental Army soldiers burning the city. "I never saw any Man so strictly observant of the preservation of private property," he said of Washington, noting his punishment of any infraction "that comes under his Observation" (which the Great Fire did not). Continuing, Tilghman wrote, "But I am sorry to say that most of his Officers do not keep up the same Discipline." This was almost a week before the rebels evacuated the city. Tilghman may have been privy to a plan in the works, so he may have preemptively been defending Washington against the charge of incendiarism by shifting blame to "his Officers." At minimum, Tilghman recognized that an element of the Continental Army was willing to take or damage property.[24]

Meanwhile, Admiral Howe kept trying to make peace overtures. He sent his highest-ranking prisoner, Major General John Sullivan, to Philadelphia with a proposal for a meeting. Congress, despite their skep-

Fig. 5.1. Although his father was a Loyalist, Tench
Tilghman (*right*) faithfully supported George Washington (*left*) as aide-de-camp from 1776 to the end of
the war. Charles Willson Peale, *Washington, Lafayette,
& Tilghman at Yorktown*, 1784, oil on canvas, MSA SC
1545-1120, Collection of the Maryland State Archives.

ticism, dispatched John Adams, Benjamin Franklin, and Edward Rutledge
to meet with the admiral on Staten Island on September 11. Lord Howe
asked Congress to renounce independence, in part because "ravaging
and destroying America would give him great pain and uneasiness." The
delegates refused, arguing that the "Towns destroyed" had helped make

the rebels irreconcilable, and returned to Philadelphia. One of Howe's captains later wrote that the British commanders delayed the attack on Manhattan, "an object of great consequence," until after these negotiations, partly because they "were desireous of shewing, to all the world, that nothing had been neglected to settle the matter without further bloodshed." Both sides were aware of the world's eyes on them; the Howes wanted to be seen as peacemakers. Washington was trying to show he could conduct the war with virtue. Regardless, the fruitless three-hour parley bought Washington a few more days to make his decision.[25]

Back on Manhattan, rebel officers knew a British landing was imminent. Colonel William Douglas, from his position at Rose Hill, considered the scattered army's vulnerability and wrote, "I fear this Island of NYork will Cost Amarica too much." General Greene and six other generals requested a new council of war. Before, the majority had urged Washington to hold the city a little longer. Now, on September 12, enough of them had changed their minds to vote ten to three in favor of immediate departure. They would try to maintain a defensive position in the heights of upper Manhattan and repulse the British from there. The records are silent as to whether the council discussed burning the city, but Washington did order the abandonment of the city's fortifications and the removal of the troops up the island.[26]

The three dissenting generals, Joseph Spencer, William Heath, and George Clinton (General Alexander McDougall called them "a fool, a knave, and an honest, obstinate man"), begged Washington to continue defending New York City. Their reasoning must have reminded Washington why he wanted to burn it in the first place. Clinton argued, "If possessed by the Enemy it furnishes them with a safe Harbour through the Winter for their Fleet Barracks & good Quarters for their troops," plus it would offer a haven for Loyalists and a beacon for new recruits. Heath believed that General Howe wanted New York City for "access to navigation . . . where He Can with Ease form His Magazines, fortify and Secure the Place for a Safe retreat," and as "an Assylum for his Sick & Wounded" and "winter Quarters." The city "gives the Enemy an unspeakable advantage, to Attack Differant States with great Ease & Advantage." With New York maintained by a small British garrison, Howe's forces would "ravage the Country" while the Royal Navy would "Infest our Sea Coast."[27]

Up on Mount Washington (later Washington Heights), the Continental Army camp was "filled with an Expectation that the City is soon to be given up to the English Army, which makes them very dull-spirited," as Fithian wrote in his diary on the thirteenth. "The lads wish to fight, & we see it written on the Sides of Houses, Tents &c—'Let us fly no more.'" The idea of retreating left a sour taste, but Fithian knew this sentiment was foolish: "where the Ships can carry the British Thunder, we must give Way."[28]

Clinton, Heath, and "the lads" were deluding themselves about the army's capacity to defend the city. The rebels had enough men, but they were spread too thinly on Manhattan Island and the mainland. Now that the British had landed on Montresor's Island (present-day Randall's Island), they could cross the East River anywhere from the Battery to Harlem Village. Washington thanked Congress for supporting his decision to retreat. "I could wish to maintain It, Because I know It to be of Importance, But I am fully convinced that It cannot be done." He hated to leave New York City to the enemy, but he needed his army more.[29]

Tensions ran high. The Loyalist Samuel Bayard Sr. later testified about a story he heard from Captain Sebastian Bauman of the New York Artillery. On the night of September 14, some men, apparently from Captain Thomas W. Foster's Massachusetts artillery company, set one or two houses in Pearl Street on fire. Bauman and his men helped extinguish the flames and then stayed awake most of the night trying to prevent the Massachusetts men "from setting the City on fire who intended to have effected it that Night."[30]

Lieutenant Colonel William Tudor, the judge advocate general, wrote to his father about the fire rumors the day before the army evacuated. "It is generally expected the City will be laid in Ashes before we quit it, but," he insisted, "the Supposition is groundless." This turned out to be true; the city did not burn until a week *after* the evacuation. Tudor added an afterthought: "And you may be assured it will never be done by General Washington's Order." Since this "groundless" rumor needed further assurance, perhaps it was not entirely groundless. Tudor knew more

Fig. 5.2. Washington occupied the summer house of the Loyalists Roger Morris and Mary Philipse in upper Manhattan from September 14 to October 21, 1776. Some depicted features, such as the portico and balustrade, may have been added later. George Hayward, "Col. Roger Morris' house, Washington's head quarters Sept. 1776 [. . .]," in *Manual of the Corporation of the City of New York,* ed. D. T. Valentine (1854), plate following p. 362, Miriam and Ira D. Wallach Division of Arts, Prints, and Photographs, New York Public Library.

about rebel soldiers' acts of criminality than anyone alive, but he was a Harvard graduate and a lawyer, and he hardly had the same perspective as the troops. Perhaps he had his suspicions about what might happen, and he wanted to absolve Washington in advance. At the same time, he was laid up with dysentery and may not have been privy to all of Washington's plans. Tudor's was the last letter from Washington's inner circle to discuss the idea of burning New York City.[31]

Sometime that night, Washington moved his headquarters to a mansion that had been vacated by its Loyalist owners: Colonel Roger Morris (a member of the New York Governor's Council) and his wife, born Mary Philipse. Atop what would later be called Coogan's Bluff above the Polo Grounds, the Morris-Jumel Mansion became the oldest surviving house in Manhattan (fig. 5.2). From the south portico, Washington had a marvelous view of the islands he had already lost, and the valuable city he was about to lose.[32]

The rumors in both armies said the rebels would burn the city. A few of his senior officers had encouraged him to do it, and Washington himself would have preferred to do it. Congress had publicly resolved that "no damage be done," and Washington publicly acknowledged their resolution. He may have glumly swallowed their directive, or not. Washington had also spent a summer surrounded by unruly soldiers and rebellious civilians. Some of them would remain in town as the army left.

The Loss of New York City

A s the sun rose on Sunday, September 15, five British warships floated in Kip's Bay on the east side of Manhattan (fig. 6.1). On the west side, three more of His Majesty's ships, the *Pearl,* the *Renown,* and the *Repulse,* sailed up the Hudson River at 7 a.m., as the chaplain Philip Fithian wrote, "to hinder us from removing our Stores, out of New-York." The Continental artillery at Paulus Hook opened fire, which the British ships and batteries returned. Watching from on board the *Eagle,* Ambrose Serle, Lord Howe's secretary, called it an "awful & grand" scene, "heightened by a most clear & delightful morning."[1]

Pastor Ewald Gustav Shewkirk of the city's Moravian church described a "cannonading which made the houses shake, and the sound of it was terrible"; he heard "Bricks flying about here & there & the Ball hiss thro' the streets." A cannonball smashed into the Dutch Reformed congregation's North Church. As the ball split apart, a fragment flew into a cellar kitchen, sending a Black woman fleeing to Shewkirk's chapel, where one of the families in his flock had already spent the night. "After some time the firing ceased," so he preached that morning "in all stillness." It was "the only service kept in the city": all the other civilians were hidden or gone.[2]

Washington stepped out of the Morris mansion and mounted his

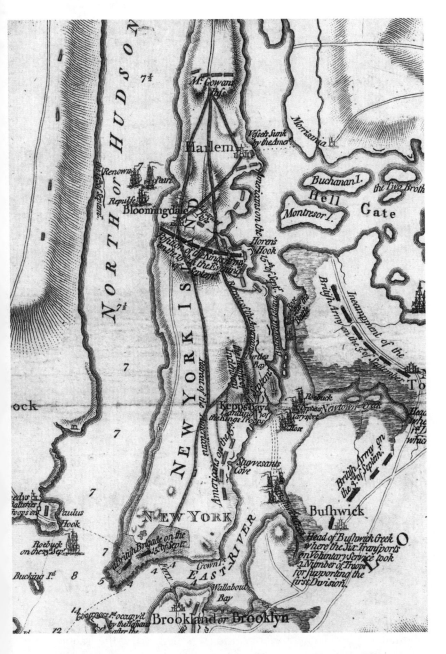

Fig. 6.1. This campaign map shows British warships and troops approaching as the rebel army retreated on September 15, 1776. Detail of William Faden, *A Plan of New York Island, [. . .] shewing also the landing of the British Army on New-York Island, and the taking of the city of New-York &c. on the 15th of September [. . .]* (London, 1776), Library of Congress, Geography and Map Division.

horse at 9 a.m. Some 3,500 of his men were in the city. The rest stretched thin across Manhattan Island, holding a long string of defensive posts as their comrades removed the rest of the guns and stores from the garrison.[3]

The British invasion force had awoken at 2 a.m., marched, and waited. By 10 a.m., the men were packed into a flotilla of eighty-four vessels in Newtown Creek, across from Kip's Bay. The Germans sang hymns. The Britons damned themselves and the rebels "with wonderful fervency." The current churned. From the *Carysfort,* the *Orpheus,* the *Phoenix,* the *Roebuck,* and the *Rose,* dozens of guns pointed toward the Connecticut troops onshore; as a Connecticut chaplain wrote, they stood "within musket Shot of our Entrenchments."[4]

Just before 11 a.m., the warships unleashed thunder—"so terrible and so incessant a Roar of Guns" that most of the men on both sides had never heard anything like it. For a full hour, the cannon fire flattened the rebels' breastworks and showered them with dirt. The first wave of British and German troops landed under the cover of smoke, virtually unopposed. Over the course of the day, 12,500 men would arrive; as they pushed the rebels northward up Manhattan, Shewkirk wrote, "there was a good deal of Slaughter."[5]

Among the rebels, their rawness and lack of discipline told. As one delegate to Congress put it, "They saw, they fled, not a single man faced his Enemy or fired his Gun." Nicholas Fish, a brigade major under General John Morin Scott, remarked that the cannonade "seemed to infuse a Panic thro' the whole of our Troops, especially the Connecticut Troops." Upon the approach of the British, "these dastardly sons of Cowardice deserted their Lines & fled in the greatest Disorder," which soon "infected those" on the west side of Manhattan, who broke and ran northward themselves. The officers and men convinced themselves that the British had three times their actual numbers. "Shame to *Connecticut* Valour," Fithian scolded. General Henry Knox was disgusted at the "rabble army" of "raggamuffins" who conducted such a "miserable disorderly retreat": Washington described them "running away in the most disgraceful and shamefull manner." Knox blamed their field officers, too, "a parcel of ignorant stupid men." General Thomas Mifflin ordered his guards to form along the width of northern Manhattan with fixed bayonets to prevent anyone but women and the infirm from fleeing farther north. The soldiers thronged the guard in a confused mass: "Some swore—some begged & pleaded—& some like timorous Children cry'd." Mifflin threatened to fire on them.[6]

The men blamed their officers. The British heard about a rebel general who hid in a "cellar among the women and children" in a nearby house; "upon being told his presence was required he made answer he could be of no use and might as well stay where he was." Joseph Plumb Martin, then a fifteen-year-old Connecticut private, remembered that he and his comrades at Kip's Bay could have shot at the British sailors, but they were told to hold their fire. Once the cannonade started, Martin took to his heels: "The demons of fear and disorder seemed to take full possession of all and everything that day." For some reason, they had been ordered to leave their packs behind. "The men were confused, being without officers to command them." He never forgot the artillery officer who detained him along the road that day when he was trying to bring a sick friend to safety. "Well," the rebel officer said, "if he dies the country will be rid of one who can do it no good."[7]

Benjamin Trumbull, the chaplain of Colonel William Douglas's regiment, agreed with Martin: "The men were blamed for retreating and even flying in these Circumstances, but I imag[in]e the Fault was Principally in the General Officers" for not properly arranging the defensive position and retreat. By fleeing, the soldiers had saved countless lives. The generals might despise disorder, but the men could see that sometimes it got results.[8]

The retreat revivified the tensions between New Englanders and the rest of the country. Andrew Hunter, another New Jersey chaplain, wrote that the rebels "had given up New York in a Manner not much to be applauded, chiefly on acct. of the Cowardice of the Eastern Troops." Colonel William Smallwood of Maryland was flabbergasted at the soldiers' cowardice: "I could wish the transactions of this day blotted out of the annals of America. Nothing appeared but fright, disgrace, and confusion." He singled out "the Connecticut troops—wretches who, however strange it may appear, from the Brigadier-General down to the private sentinel, were caned and whipped by the Generals Washington, [Israel] Putnam, and Mifflin, but even this indignity had no weight, they could not be brought to stand one shot."[9]

Smallwood was referring to Brigadier General Samuel Holden Parsons of Lyme, Connecticut. Parsons complained in turn that people like Adjutant General Joseph Reed were "blasting the Reputation of whole States" on a "daily" basis: "Every Measure is Used to create a Disaffection between the Northern and Southern Colonies." Why didn't they also mention the New York and Pennsylvania troops who had run away during the Battle of Long Island? "Yet every Misconduct of Officers and Soldiers in the NE Troops are painted in the worst Colours." John Adams later reflected that all of Washington's staff were arrogant mid-Atlantic and southern men who tended to think "disrespectfully of New England."[10]

That very day, Major General William Heath reported that about two hundred men of the Pennsylvania battalions mutinied and then left for home. They griped that they had not received blankets, clothes, particular rations, or their pay. They disliked "the Severe Duty of the Camp" and reminded Heath that "they were Volunteers." Their commanders had promised them they would be "used well" when they marched to war, but Pennsylvania had not held up its end of the bargain. Three days before, a regiment of New Jersey militia had deserted the Connecticut troops stationed on Paulus Hook.[11]

Colonel Douglas also defended himself against his "unjust" fellow officers who liked to "Stigmatise New England Troops," since those soldiers "are always at work and Stationed in the Most Dangerous Posts" with little support from anyone else. These New England soldiers must have seethed with shame and indignation. They expected better gratitude from the rest of the continent, when so many of them were risking their necks in the field. General Gold Selleck Silliman later told a congressional delegation that such "rancour & malice" would either drive New Englanders out of the army or get Reed and his fellow backbiters "killed."[12]

The British had taken the city. They could have taken many more prisoners, too; had their battalions pushed forward all the way to the Hudson River, they would have cut off thousands of fleeing rebel soldiers. Some historians have argued that such an aggressive strike would have been tactically unwise—the British generals did not know what kind of resistance they would face, and they may not have been confident in their own soldiers' discipline, so they waited until all their forces were ready before they advanced. It would take them another two months to expel the rest of the Continental Army from Manhattan Island.[13]

For all the rebels' supposed cowardice, the escape was impressive. General Israel Putnam of Preston, Connecticut, and his aide, Major Aaron Burr (then twenty years old) took responsibility for evacuating most of the 3,500 men still in the city. David Humphreys, an adjutant with the 2nd Connecticut militia regiment, recalled Putnam "flying, on his horse covered with foam," to spur men northward along the Hudson River. Burr warned them to retreat and avoid being "crammed into a dungeon, or hung like dogs." Some of the men the Continental Army left behind "staid out of Choice," probably as deserters but perhaps as spies or saboteurs.[14]

Captain Sebastian Bauman of the New York Artillery was one of the last to leave. The previous night, he and his men had kept a vigil trying to prevent a company of Massachusetts artillerists from setting the city on fire. "Take care of yourself," he said to the Loyalist Samuel Bayard Sr., because "the City will certainly be set on fire." Thinking he had been completely cut off from the rest of the Continental Army, Bauman and eighty others held the fort at Bayard's Hill until 4 p.m., with the British troops closing in. As they lugged two howitzers up the west side of Manhattan under cover of night, they discovered an abandoned boat and sent some of the men across the Hudson to Paulus Hook for help with the artillery pieces. Bauman also sent a corporal "in disguise" to the city to gather intelligence and look for another boat or raft. After an agonizing wait, a boat arrived to carry Bauman and the howitzers to New Jersey.[15]

Up in northern Manhattan, the men despaired. Fithian lamented, "We are a sinful Nation, O Lord. But is it written in thy Book concerning us that we must always fly before our Enemies?" Even before the retreat, the men were weak from illness and exhaustion. By the time the retreating troops reached camp, they were thirsty and hot. Already tired, they were drenched by an evening rain shower and then chilled by the wind

that blew through the lines. They had left behind their tents and baggage, and "their hearts sunk within them." Indeed, "the warmth of enthusiasm seemed to be extinguished."[16]

John Bowater, a British marine captain, had nothing but contempt
for the rebels: "They Evacuated the City in the Utmost precipitation,"
while "taking nothing with them but their fears." Serle marveled that the
rebels had put so much time and effort into fortifying New York, only to
abandon the city "in one short Hour, without making the least Defence
or any thing like a handsome Retreat." Perhaps "Regret" would have
motivated the rebels "to make some kind of Stand. But their Fears over-
powered their Resolution." Having lost New York City to the British, the
rebel soldiers and officers grew disappointed and ashamed. With high-
toned gentlemen berating them from all quarters, they felt the sting of
criticism.[17]

For better or worse, New York City had survived. The British general James Grant said later, "The Rebell Panic had saved [New York] from
Destruction." Dr. Peter Tappen reported the opposite reaction among
the rebels at Fort Montgomery: "Our week [weak] Friends in the Country where [were] much allarmed at our Leaving the City standing." A
rebel correspondent tried to put a good face on the decision: New York
"might have been destroyed, but as I heard a gentleman say, it is not
worth while to burn a barn, because rats *may* get possession of it."[18]

Still, there was plenty of scurrying in New York. Looters broke open
the remaining Continental stores and carried the provisions away. Boats
and rafts shuttled some of the remaining rebel soldiers and supplies back
and forth between the city and Paulus Hook, and men drowned in the
crossing. During the retreat, soldiers looted the Richmond Hill mansion
(Washington's former headquarters) and shattered all its glassware. That
night, "some of the inhabitants" filched gunpowder and "other Stores"
from the fortification on Bayard's Hill. The abandoned city was a place
of abandon, but what—and who—was left behind?[19]

A few British officers and marines rowed to the city that afternoon.
When Captain Henry Duncan of the *Eagle* stepped ashore, the crowd
gave him three cheers, hoisted him on their shoulders, carried him to
the fort, and gave him several more rounds of cheers; "men, women, and
children shaking me by the hand, and giving me their blessing, and cry-

ing out 'God save the King!'" Serle, describing these "overjoyed Bedlamites," wrote, "Nothing could equal the Expressions of Joy, shewn by the Inhabitants, upon the arrival of the King's officers among them." General Howe ordered Lieutenant Colonel Francis Smith's 5th Brigade to take possession of the city. They reached the Bowery at 7 p.m., so late that Captain Frederick Mackenzie (the brigade major) wrote, "Many of the Rebels who had not time to make their escape by daylight, and concealed themselves in the town," escaped up the west side of Manhattan.[20]

Captain Abraham Van Dyck, fifty-seven, was unable to make his escape. Most of his men fled with the rest of the rebel army, but he fell behind. "He being a heavy fat man," General Alexander McDougall later wrote, "became so fatigued in the retreat from the City of newyork, that he could not retire with that corps, and secreted himself in the Cedars between the City and Harlem." Now British troops had swarmed over the island and cut off Van Dyck's retreat. "Finding no prospect of escape," he turned around and "concealed himself in the City."[21]

Even before the troops arrived, Loyalist women claimed New York City for the Crown. One "pulled down the Rebel Standard" at Fort George at 4 p.m. and began "trampling . . . [it] under Foot with the most contemptuous Indignation." (One diarist specified that she was Irish, and a newspaper reported that she was the "wife of a gentleman of considerable property in the city.") Then the women tore the flag to pieces and raised the Union Jack instead. Serle turned to Lord Howe to congratulate him. "Thus this Town and its Environs, w[hi]ch these blustering Gentleman had taken such wonderful Pains to fortify, were given up in two or three Hours without any Defence, or the least appearance of a manly Resistance." Shewkirk added, "The city was now delivered from those Usurpers who had oppressed it for so long."[22]

Major Alured Clarke of the 54th Regiment remembered the moment. Either on September 15 or shortly afterward, he was walking through the city to determine suitable posts for sentries. Suddenly "he heard a cry of fire in a small street leading from Water Street to the East River near the Fly Market." It was "a small Wooden building in a Narrow Street & with many other wooden buildings about it," a perfect way to start a large conflagration. Although this small fire "was immediately extinguished," he also testified, "there was every appearance of the house being purposely set on fire, as he discovered the marks of a train of powder."[23]

British officers tried to curtail further chaos. Lord Howe ordered the *Mercury* and the *Fowey* "to lie close to the Town, to prevent the Transport Boats from going on Shore & plundering, w[hi]ch many of them appeared very ready to do." Most of the army remained stationed outside town (one rumor said it was because of the "epidemical fever" that afflicted two thousand of the inhabitants). The British and German troops, having left their baggage behind on Long Island, settled down for a "terribly cold" night that their fires could not banish. The soldiers ate their way through Manhattan's farms: a German lieutenant marveled, "Never before have so many geese, chickens, ducks, sheep, cattle, and pigs been slaughtered."[24]

The next morning, September 16, the redcoats tested the Continental Army's lines at Harlem Heights. Adjutant General Joseph Reed took note of the "insulting manner" in which the British "sounded their Bugle Horns as is usual after a Fox Chase." He added, "I never felt such a Sensation before, it seem'd to crown our Disgrace." Still, the rebels successfully repulsed the attack, and Private John Adlum remembered the battle "raising the spirits of our troops."[25]

Rumors of battlefield atrocities flew through the Continental Army camp (Burr called "most of them incredible and false"). A captain from Colonel John Durkee's Regiment said they "found near a Dozen" dead rebel soldiers "with their Heads split open by the Hessians." Fish wrote, "All our killed were shot thro' the Head, which induces . . . belief that they were first taken Prisoners, & then massacred." On the fifteenth, Lieutenant Bartholomew James of HMS *Orpheus* claimed that he "saw a Hessian sever a rebel's head from his body and clap it on a pole in the intrenchments." Presumably these allegations, as well as the deaths of admired officers like Thomas Knowlton of Ashford, Connecticut, "stimulated . . . the thirst of revenge" that Humphreys noticed at the Battle of Harlem Heights.[26]

Over the next week, British and German soldiers angered Americans further with their misbehavior. "Sad Complaints are made of the Hessians," Serle wrote, "who plunder all men, Friends of Government as well as Foes, indiscriminately." Lieutenant Loftus Cliffe of the 46th Regiment agreed: "The Houses of friends or foes are equally *damned*[,] *rebel Houses* especially if there's a good Cellar." From Manhattan he reported that these Hessian marauders were stealing all the horses and slaughtering all the oxen and sheep in reach, even milch cows.[27]

Catharena Clopper later testified to "the Conduct of Scotch & Hessian Troops" on September 16 and 18 at Nicholas Jones's Bloomingdale estate in upper Manhattan, a litany of "Plunder, Ravage & Devastation." She remembered British soldiers seizing the milk, butter, and pork, and the Jaegers killing a steer and seizing the cattle. Captain Andrew Lawrie of the 71st Regiment menaced Jones "with a drawn Knife, threatning to rip him Open" unless he delivered the key to the wine cellar. When Jones relented, the soldiers took possession of "Every Article of furniture, Plate &c together with the Wine." Rumors of plunder and atrocity spread. Some of the rebels—men and women alike—must have thought about taking revenge.[28]

Down in Philadelphia, delegates to Congress tried to argue that the loss of New York was predictable and no cause for discouragement. William Williams of Lebanon, Connecticut, told his father-in-law, Governor Jonathan Trumbull, that Congress had "directed that [New York] shod not be destroyed by Us on leaving it." In a section that was published a month later, Williams urged "every Soul that has one Sparck of Heavenly Fire" to "kindle it to a fervent Heat & expanded Blaze." Dr. Benjamin Rush of Pennsylvania acknowledged that "Affairs in New York" might look "melancholy," but the city would be like molasses left out to trap flies: "Genl. Howe will attract all the tories of New York & the adjacent states to his army where they will ripen as the tories of Boston did for banishment & destruction," while the rest of the "continent . . . will be purged of those rascals." Mary Silliman, the Connecticut general's wife, was glad he was "out of that dirty City," and she kept a stiff upper lip: "Let the regulars take your leavings and boast of their acquisition."[29]

Washington, however, could hardly hide his disappointment at the loss of New York City and his men's conduct during the retreat. Over the next few days, he continued to rail against his own soldiers' lack of discipline. From the Morris mansion on Harlem Heights, Washington ordered that any soldiers caught "carrying Plunder" should be "whipped on the spot." The next day, he called on his officers "to restrain every kind of abuse of private Property, whilst the abandoned and profligate part of our own Army . . . are by Rapine and Plunder, spreading Ruin and Terror wherever they go." Three days later, he still heard "Complaints that are hourly made of plundering both public and private property," and ordered the men to turn their tents and knapsacks inside out. A court-martial found an ensign guilty of plunder and cashiered him. Washington's orders from this week also promised that any fleeing soldiers "shall be instantly Shot down," and another court-martial sentenced a soldier to death for running away.[30]

The rebels kept singling out their New England comrades for blame. Tench Tilghman, Washington's aide-de-camp, bragged that Maryland and Virginia soldiers "are well officered and behave with as much regularity as possible, while the Eastern people are plundering everything that comes in their way." On September 18, a Connecticut captain was court-martialed for forging a pass to return home. As punishment for cowardice, the "Scoundrel" was dressed in women's clothes, given a wooden sword and musket, paraded through camp, and pelted with "Cow-dung and almost every Kind of Excrement." Few felt ennobled by the retreat from New York; New Englanders grew defensive about their reputation, and Washington had to make a special effort to smooth things over.[31]

In his letters to Congress, Washington complained bitterly about the attitudes of his men. The militia, "just dragged from the tender Scenes of domestick life," were undependable, untrustworthy, prone to illness, homesick to the point of desertion, "timid, and ready to fly from their own Shadows." He concluded, "Men accustomed to unbounded freedom, and no controul, cannot brooke the Restraint which is indispensably necessary to the good Order and Government of an Army; without which Licentiousness, & every kind of disorder triumphantly reign." When militia mixed with regular troops, they spread these disorders like diseases. It would take months to bring the army "to a proper degree of Subordination." Washington also complained of the "infamous" and "horrid practice" of plundering. His soldiers would sometimes threaten to burn a house to drive out the inhabitants and seize the goods, or burn a house to cover up an act of plunder. Without sufficient laws to restrain his men, Washington feared that the Continental cause would fall apart.[32]

On September 20, Congress finally responded by passing revised articles of war. One of the new regulations promised harsher punishments for any "officers and soldiers" who "shall maliciously destroy any property whatsoever belonging to the good people of the United States." The laws allowed exceptions, however: the "commander in chief" could direct soldiers to destroy Loyalist property. Other articles promised to execute cowards, runaways, or men who left their post to "plunder and pillage." Sentences of corporal punishment were increased from an upper limit of thirty-nine lashes to one hundred. The new regulations reached Continental Army headquarters after New York City was already on fire; still, they show the lawmakers' intentions. Washington could authorize his men to burn Loyalist property, but soldiers were warned—on pain of more whipping or even death—not to take such matters into their own hands.[33]

Some of these rebel troops—undisciplined, dispirited, and vengeful—apparently remained in New York City after the British took it. It is unknown whether they had orders to burn the city. With their officers gone, they may have been more inclined to do it themselves.

"Most of the loyal Inhabitants have fled," Captain Mackenzie wrote, "or been carried away from the town, so that numbers of the houses are empty." A returning Loyalist described New York as "a most dirty, desolate, and wretched place." Another writer marveled, "It is impossible to give a true description of the wretched situation in which the Rebels left this town; not a house in a hundred inhabited, all plundered of every thing, and full of rags, vermin, and all kinds of filth." Washington had ordered the evacuation of any remaining women, children, and the infirm on August 17, and some said this "looked suspicious." Most—but perhaps not all—of the remaining rebel soldiers had fled on September 15. Perhaps as few as two to five thousand people remained in the city when the British troops arrived.[34]

A significant number of them were Black: one slave owner fretted that Black New Yorkers "are Encouraged by some Secret Enemies to stay in the City, as they were seen to Muster in large Company's." Throughout the area, enslaved African Americans (14 percent of the city's population) took advantage of the armies' movements to slip loose from their chains, while free and enslaved Black men crossed enemy lines to provide intelligence to army officers. One provided aid to Captain Van Dyck, now in hiding at the Learys' livery stables on Cortlandt Street, across Broadway from his own inn. Van Dyck had shelter, but he still needed food. As a big man, he was instantly recognizable to the city's inhabitants, so he would risk capture if he ventured out himself. He enlisted a "Negro man," perhaps someone he claimed as property; since white people often ignored Black laborers, perhaps this man could wander through the city more invisibly amid the chaos of the British occupation.[35]

The Royal Marines took possession of Fort George on September 16 and raised the Union Jack (fig. 6.2). As the troops formed two lines along Broadway, "a great Concourse of People assembled round the Soldiers." People treated the event as a holiday, and no one went to work. Witnessing the cheering crowds, Serle wrote, "The Happiness of the Inhabitants upon the Occasion drives them about like madmen." Such was the "real Tyranny" they experienced under the rebels "that they are at a Loss how to enjoy their Release." Former strangers warmly shook hands with one another, and Pastor Shewkirk exulted, "An universal Joy was spread over all Countenances."[36]

English newspapers invited readers to envision the scene of British triumph: "Nothing could exceed the extravagant joy of the people left in new York on their release from the tyranny of the rebels.—They chaired some of the King's officers up and down the streets amidst shouts and acclamations." They would have rung bells, too, if the "New England rebels" had not taken them away. "I believe his Majesty's name was scarce ever so loudly or so affectionately shouted, as it was on this and the ensuing day, in the streets of New York." The enthusiasm echoed across England: Manchester, Wakefield, Halifax, Bradford, Derby, and Colne celebrated with bells, illuminations, bonfires, toasts, cannon salutes, and burning "American Chiefs" in effigy.[37]

The victors took in their new surroundings. Serle admired the city's "many good Houses . . . and several handsome Streets," such as Broadway and Queen Street. He noticed that the rebels had carried off all the

Fig. 6.2. This fictive European engraving conjures the British army marching through the streets of New York City. Franz Xaver Habermann, *L'Entré triumphale de troupes royales a Nouvelle Yorck,* [Augsburg, 1778?], Library of Congress, Prints and Photographs Division.

church bells, vital for sounding fire alarms. Other signs worried the British, too. Captain Mackenzie noticed that "many of the Rebels who were unable to make their escape yesterday, are now in the town, and as they have changed their dress it is extremely difficult to discover them." Perhaps some had taken their cues from Bauman's disguised corporal. Americans knew that people's clothes could easily disguise their true identity. Striving status seekers, con artists, gender nonconformists, rioters, deserters, and runaway slaves all took advantage of their ability to don disguises. In a civil war, this problem grew more fraught—it was hard to know whether a person was loyal or rebellious.[38]

Van Dyck may still have been wearing his grenadier uniform—a blue coat with red facings over a white waistcoat, breeches, and stockings. The British arrested him on September 16, angry at finding a Continental Army officer "secreted in a private House."[39]

There were other newcomers, too. Serle wrote, "Many of the loyal Inhabitants were returning with their Goods to the Town," with a touch of overconfidence. On the evening of the sixteenth, the New Jersey Loyalist Peter DuBois heard from a woman who had just left town that "a great many of the [rebel New] Yorkers had for some days before been Striping themselves of their Regimentals & puting on their Brown coats." She saw men she knew from the Second Battalion of New York—out of uniform. John Wetherhead, a Loyalist merchant, later complained of the army's "almost unpardonable want of Caution" for having "admitted without examination a promiscuous Number of Strangers into the City, many of whom were Spies."[40]

On September 16, Howe appointed General James Robertson as commandant of the town. Robertson was a natural choice: he had served twenty years in America, most of it in New York City, as a quartermaster general and barrack master general. He owned a town house on Broadway and had socialized with many of the city's prominent families. He, his fellow staff officers, and the aldermen William Waddell and George Brewerton now had to organize the emptied spaces of the army's new garrison: the officers needed residences, the men needed barracks, and other buildings were commandeered for prisoners, the sick and wounded, supplies, and provisions. There were dead bodies in cellars and other places that needed removal. Loyalists like the breeches maker and leather dresser Cornelius Ryan were appointed to "make a return of the stores and mark the Houses belonging to the Rebels (that they evacuated)."[41]

Serle noted how the British seized their enemies' homes—"as to the rebellious, the Quarter Master General . . . has marked G. R. [short for "Georgius Rex"] upon the Doors of their Houses, which are to serve for Habitations to the Army." The next day, September 20, Serle elaborated: "The People begin to return to their Dwellings, except those who deserted them in Rebellion, of w[hi]ch, it must be owned [i.e., admitted], there are many." Much as the rebel authorities had begun confiscating the property of Loyalists, so the British sequestered rebels' homes. Amid the chaos of the new occupation, these property markings were far from precise: "Many [houses] indeed were marked by persons who had no order to do so, and did it perhaps to one or the other from some personal resentment." Shewkirk learned that several of his congregants had their houses erroneously marked, and he hastened to intercede with army officers on the families' behalf. Their marks were "rubb'd off," but he did not know by whom.[42]

As they began settling into the city, the British army committed fresh provocations. The provost marshal imprisoned rebel soldiers at "Liberty House" (a former meeting place for the Sons of Liberty) and the Provost (one of the city's prisons), as well as the Old North Dutch and Brick Presbyterian churches. Religious Dissenters must have been reminded of the damage the British soldiers had done to Congregationalist meetinghouses in Boston.[43]

The British found fresh evidence of the rebels' plans to burn New York. The merchants Edward Laight and Henry Law each recalled that they returned to Manhattan on the sixteenth. While "walking thro' the City," Laight "discovered Combustibles in many parts of it." John Burns also remembered finding combustibles "in great quantities in many parts of the City, before the fire particularly Dock Street New Street & Broad Street concealed in different parts of the houses." Law, recalling the rebels' threats (from back in May) to burn the city and "observing many stragglers lurking about in the City whom he did not know, he did not think it safe to lodge on shore," so he slept aboard the schooner *Alert,* "lying at a Wharf near the New Slip." William Backhouse, a Quaker merchant, also moved "his effects from the City" because he had heard the rebels' threats to set the town on fire and was afraid they meant it.[44]

The city was poorly protected from fire. Even before the British occupation, more than a third of the firemen had left town or enlisted in rebel military companies. General Robertson tried to cobble together a firefighting service and a night watch with the aldermen and enginemen who remained. Around September 17, he appointed John Baltus Dash "to take charge of the Fire-Engines." Over the next few days, Dash observed the other people who remained in town after the rebels' evacuation. He was so convinced some of them would set the city on fire that on September 20, "he dug a hole in his yard & buried his most valuable effects." New York's ranking firefighter knew enough to be frightened.[45]

The British commanders started to relax, thinking the danger had passed. On September 17, Shewkirk remembered, "The fear one had of the city's being destroyed by fire subsided, and the inhabitants thought themselves now pretty secure; little thinking that destruction was so near." One New York Loyalist, whose home had been plundered by the rebels, tried to shake off the loss: "I flattered myself that the City would soon be peopled again, and that Matters would speedily be restored to their former State." The inhabitants told one another that General Howe, having heard the rumors of the intention to burn New York City, had threatened to retaliate by laying waste to Connecticut; for the next few days, they assured themselves that the city might be safe from saboteurs after all.[46]

The British let down their guard in spite of other warning signs. The regular workings of the city had not yet returned to stability. The city had no bells to sound an alarm, and the firefighting equipment was in disarray. Hundreds of buildings stood empty, and people were marking their neighbors' houses for sequestration out of spite. The rebels were smarting from a humiliating defeat and gnashing their teeth over rumors of bad behavior by the British army. Not all the rebel soldiers, it seemed, had fled—and people had no way of knowing whether all the city's new arrivals were loyal to the king. There was a sense that anything could happen.[47]

As darkness enveloped the city on September 20, a strong wind began blowing from the south and southeast.[48]

William Shipman, a Loyalist cashier, walked past a small tavern on Whitehall Slip where postriders and other travelers used to drink while waiting for the ferry. He "saw there several Sailors women & others . . . some of whom were drunk, and a fire in the Chimney." Ann Lynch hazily recalled something similar: an old man (or maybe a couple of soldiers?) and two women. She couldn't remember whether they were sober or drinking between two piles of lumber, whether an orderly sergeant chased them off, or whether they wandered into a shed behind the tavern at 9 p.m., holding a candle. At the time, neither Shipman nor Lynch thought anything more of it.[49]

The Great Fire

WHEN civil Discord rais'd her flaming brand,

And red Rebellion scourg'd the guilty land,

What dismal scenes and complicated woe

Arose to view!—Who saw them only know.[1]

James Wells, a fifty-three-year-old shopkeeper, awoke shortly before midnight. His dog was trying to pull him out of bed. Wells got up, left his house in Little Dock Street near Coenties Dock, and ran about a hundred yards toward Whitehall Slip (fig. 7.1). From sixty yards away, he heard a noise and saw a building on fire—a wooden shed, sandwiched between the ferry house on Whitehall Slip and Hilyard's tavern. The fire had started to consume the boards on the eastern side of the shed, next to the tavern, and Wells believed the fire was then small enough that he could have put it out with a little help. He went through the back doors, which were open, and saw "a barrel with bottles in it burnt almost down to the bottom"—evidence, he later concluded, of a drunken party and a misplaced candle. Soon after, Wells was joined by a Loyalist officer. No one else came in time. Wells saw the flames jump

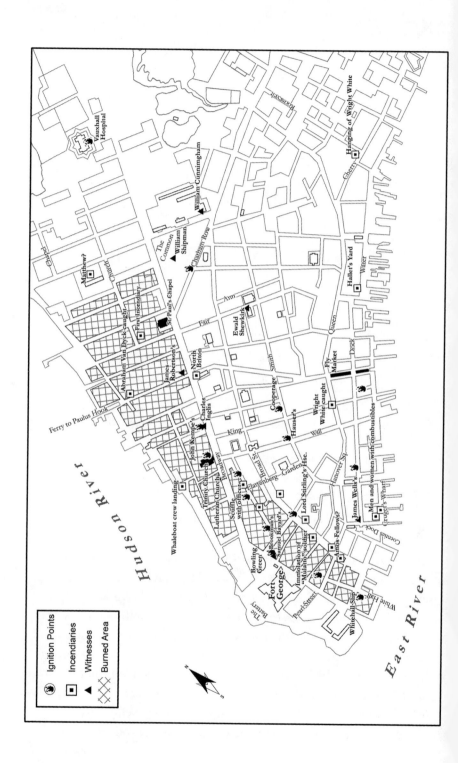

to another building and then begin spreading so fast that no one could have extinguished it. Years afterward, Wells still believed that it had all been a terrible accident, although he was only one observer among many.[2]

> Sudden I start—what means that dismal cry?
> "Fire! fire! awake, behold destruction nigh!"
> To the high roof in trembling doubt I flew—
> The dreary prospect open'd on my view.[3]

Joseph Chew, a Virginia-born Loyalist, was sleeping aboard the *Earl of Suffolk*, a transport ship, anchored close to Whitehall Slip at the southern tip of Manhattan (see fig. 3.1). The cry of fire woke him sometime after 1 a.m.; when he got above decks, he saw a house on fire on the Whitehall dock. Chew hopped in a boat to go ashore, but a lieutenant rowed up and ordered him back aboard ship. The *Earl of Suffolk* was so close that the lieutenant asked the ship's captain to move it farther away. Soon after this, Chew saw an adjacent house catch fire, and shortly afterward he saw a light at a high house in Wynkoop Street, two hundred yards away. The light flickered on and off a few times, and then a fire broke out in the upper chimney, followed four minutes later by the roof. This looked like a separate ignition, unrelated to the original fire. Chew thought the fire had been set on purpose, and he said so at the time to the other people on board the transport.[4]

> Let faithful memory exert her power
> To paint the horrors of that luckless hour.[5]

Fig. 7.1 (*opposite*). Map of the Great Fire of New York, Sept. 21, 1776, and combustibles found. "Ignition Points" symbols refer to locations where witnesses saw fires begin or found combustibles. "Incendiaries" symbols refer to locations where witnesses saw people starting fires, carrying combustibles, or interfering with firefighting efforts. Contemporary mapmakers designated a Burned Area as shown, but incendiary events were taking place elsewhere in the city. Some locations are approximate because witnesses named only the street, not a precise location.

These blazing houses grew to become a massive urban fire, and amid the blistering heat and confusion, no one had time to think. Only later did witnesses have an opportunity to testify, speak, or write down their reasoning about what they had seen. By then they would draw inferences from their preconceptions, observations, and recent memories, and from comparing notes with other witnesses. They tried to understand what had happened and why. Some, like Wells and Chew, recalled their stories years later before the 1783 investigators. Others recorded their memories as soon as they retired to their desks, or within a few days.

These accounts unfold imprecisely and imperfectly. Even a simple question like "when did the fire start?" yields a dozen different answers. For example, the frigate *Orpheus* was anchored in the East River; its captain, master, and lieutenant separately logged the fire's outbreak at midnight, 12:30, and 1 a.m. From Long Island, northern Manhattan, Staten Island, and dozens of ships in the harbor, other observers recalled the fire's outbreak as early as 10 p.m. on September 20 and as late as 3 a.m. on September 21. These outliers aside, almost everyone else agreed—like the officers of the *Orpheus*—that the fire began sometime between midnight and 1 a.m.[6]

Alderman William Waddell remembered that a sergeant called him up from the main guard at about midnight. Around the same time, the officers of the *Experiment* in Gravesend Bay described "the Rays of a Immense Fire" and "a large body of flames rising Over the City of New York and frequent gushes of fire." Andrew Elliot's suburban house in the Bowery served as the headquarters of the British army's 5th Brigade; the sentry there woke the brigade major, Captain Frederick Mackenzie, at 1 a.m. Mackenzie looked out the window; seeing "an immense Column of fire & smoke," he dressed and ran the two miles into town. When he arrived, Trinity Church was already on fire. By 1:30, most of the city's other residents had leaped from their beds. Many of the ships near Long Island reported seeing the fire even later, around 2 a.m., which is probably when the fire was unmistakably visible from any vantage point.[7]

Even more importantly, witnesses disagreed about whether the fire started in one place or many. William Shipman, the Loyalist cashier, remembered waking at the cry of fire around 1 a.m. Immediately he thought of the carousing women and sailors that he had seen the night before (a tavern keeper later called them "men and women of bad character"), so he ran to the small tavern on Whitehall Slip. Sure enough, he found the place on fire, but—as he, Wells, and the firefighter John Burns later testified—the flames had not yet spread anywhere else.[8]

Other witnesses, however, saw separate fires appear in an instant. An artillery colonel, rousted from his bed at 1:30, "found the city was in flames in two places." From the roof of the Provost on the northeast corner of the Common, the infamous jailer William Cunningham remembered that he "saw a fire in five different places": two at Whitehall, one near New Street, and two behind General James Robertson's house on Broadway. Captain Mackenzie believed that the fire broke out "in three different places in the South, and windward part of the town." With Trinity Church aflame long before anything near it, he had no doubt "that it was set on fire wilfully." George Tripp, keeping watch aboard the *Eagle* off Bedlow's Island, remembered that "he saw the fire break out suddenly in two or three different places distant from each other nearly at the same time," so far away that he didn't think the fire could have made the leap on its own; instead "they broke out independent of each other." Ship captains and army officers—even rebels at Harlem Heights and Paulus Hook, New Jersey—also saw the fire ignite in three, four, five, or six places at once or reported multiple outbreaks.[9]

Some believed the Great Fire had even more points of origin. Colonel Loammi Baldwin of Massachusetts heard reports from rebel encampments in New Jersey that the fire broke out in fifteen different places simultaneously; the master of the transport *Dorothy* reported twenty different blazes at midnight; another account said there were fifty outbreaks. A Hessian lieutenant went even further: "At midnight the flames broke out everywhere." Once begun, the fire seemed to have originated from every direction at once.[10]

Two days after the fire, Governor William Tryon offered his theory that the fire was set by several incendiaries: "The fire broke out in sundry places nearly at the same time, but was first discovered at White Hall Stairs." Tryon grafted together pieces of the story in a way that made the most sense to him, but many eyewitnesses corroborated his theory.[11]

The engine's roar—the carman's rattling wheel—
The fireman's cry, the Soldier's glittering steel—
Grief at each heart, in every face amaze,
The town all uproar, and the heavens ablaze.[12]

If a fire of this magnitude is not stopped in time, it produces even more heat, overwhelming people's capacity to stop it. Had New Yorkers reached these fires quickly enough, perhaps they could have averted disaster. Unfortunately, most of the town's inhabitants were gone. The British garrison may also have borne some of the blame; Major Carl Baurmeister, the Germans' adjutant general, criticized the "carelessness" and "inadequacy, of the watch." By the time Captain Mackenzie had run to town from the Bowery, the people on the scene seemed to think the fire was too large to be stopped.[13]

In peacetime, constables and night watchmen could have sounded the alarm, but in May 1776, the city government had reduced the watch to only four men and stowed away the city's lamps. Nor could the citizens sound the alarm in time, because the rebels had taken the city's church bells to recast them into cannon. Governor Tryon believed the rebels had intended "to prevent the alarm being given by ringing of the Bells before the fire should get a head beyond the reach of Engines and Buckets." To Tryon, this proved that Washington had authorized the fire. The Reverend Charles Inglis agreed that since the rebels had previously planned to destroy the city, they had removed the bells, in part "to prevent notice being given speedily . . . when it began." Even if the bells had clamored, however, there was no one to answer the call. As Wells testified, "Most of the firemen were absent from the City," and the remaining "People present at the fire" were "mostly strangers unacquainted with the business." The city's disruption had become dysfunction.[14]

Still, a skeleton crew of firefighters rushed to the scene. Alderman William Waddell, who had been overseeing fire prevention efforts since the British landing, "exerted himself during the Night" on horseback to help fight the fire (see fig. 7.2). John Baltus Dash, who had charge of the city's twelve fire engines, heard the alarm between 1 and 2 a.m. and brought the city's machines to Whitehall Slip as quickly as he could. Soon he was already hearing of a separate fire, at a house farther up the Hudson River,

Fig. 7.2. This British drawing shows a fire engine crew in action. Thomas Rowlandson, *The Arrival of the Fire Engine*, n.d., watercolor with pen and ink over graphite on paper, Yale Center for British Art, Paul Mellon Collection.

behind the Trinity Church rector's house. By the time his colleague engine-master Jeronymus Alstyne arrived, the fire "had reached from Whitehall nearly to the bridge in Dock S^t." The Loyalist merchant Edward Laight also found himself at Whitehall among the engines, when "it was soon observed by some persons coming up, that it was in vain to attempt to extinguish the fire as it had broke out in two places in Beaver Street." Laight "soon after saw many houses on fire in other parts of the City."[15]

Distressingly, the firefighters found themselves unable to do their job, because, as Chew and others noted, "many of the Pumps & Buckets had been rendered useless"—not just broken but in some cases deliberately cut. Henry Law, captain of the port of New York, saw two such pumps, one in Beaver Street. Dash and his firemen found several more. John Burns, another engine-master, "found most of the pumps much out of order, the handles & spears broke & taken out," so the firefighters had to rely on "the River & private Wells & Cisterns" for water.[16]

The engines also failed them: on Alstyne's engine, "the Key was twice put out of its place," which disrupted its proper functioning. He was unsure "whether it was purposely done" and acknowledged that the scarcity of firemen made it difficult to keep the engine running properly. Captain Mackenzie lamented "the bad state of the Engines, a want of buckets, and a Scarcity of Water," and others noted that the rebels had removed, hidden, or damaged many of the fire buckets. Eventually firefighters found sources of water and buckets to carry it, but the initial delay was devastating.[17]

'Twas night—no friendly star appear'd on high,
Tumultuous clouds involv'd the sullen sky.[18]

Alstyne was uncertain how the fire started, but he thought the "violence of the wind" helped spread it; the Reverend Benjamin Moore recalled that the wind was "moderate" when the fire first began, "but increased as the fire spread." A Hessian lieutenant believed that "the rebels set fire to a number of places in New York," and "a strong wind helped their plan." The fury of the gusts created perfect conditions for an "irresistible," unstoppable fire.[19]

Enormous ladders scale the tottering wall;
The lofty roofs in smoking ruins fall;
Vast flakes of fire before the tempest fly,
And tinge with blood the sailing clouds on high.[20]

The wind remained the key factor in helping the fire to spread, perhaps giving a false appearance of multiple ignitions. Captain Mackenzie saw the flames spread "by means of the burning flakes of the Shingles, which being light, were carried by the wind." Modern fire scientists call this "spotting ignition" or "roof-to-roof spread." The city's wooden roofs spat wisps of fire toward the north, from housetop to housetop. Colonial New Yorkers had failed to mandate the use of slate tiling and stone walls; this failure now rendered the city a tinderbox of thin cedar shingles that made the fire float aloft, out of reach, and onto the roofs of buildings whose inhabitants had left the city.[21]

Several witnesses believed this was how Trinity Church caught fire, sometime between 1 and 3 a.m. The Loyalist merchant Andrew Kerr remembered "Sparks that fell upon it," perhaps from 1,200 feet away, and Major Alured Clarke of the 54th Regiment "saw flakes of fire fall." Although both believed the city was "designedly set on fire," they thought the church had caught fire "by accident." Others watched the roof catch fire in several places and concluded that someone had targeted the church deliberately. Early in the night, Dr. John Mervin Nooth, looking through a spyglass, saw clearly "a man upon the top of Trinity Church with a firebrand or torch in his hand, going backward & forward upon the Roof with great rapidity." He soon saw the roof catch fire in several places, while the main fire was still confined to Whitehall Slip, and the wind was blowing a different way. Aboard the *Earl of Suffolk,* someone yelled, "They are now setting fire to Trinity Church." Once begun, the church burned quickly. Decades later, a resident remembered it as "an amazing blaze, and it soon became out of human power to extinguish" it. The roof was so steep that no one dared to climb it.[22]

The errant firebirds that flew about the city, in other words, were not the only harbingers of devastation. Captain John Thompson, who had lodged in the city, also saw "the town . . . on fire in different parts at the same instant and the fire spreading in a different direction from that which it received from a strong gale," which he attributed to "the Villainy of the Rebels." As a young Hessian grenadier wrote, "At one place it was extinguished but then was set again in another place, by one here and then by another there."[23]

The Reverend Inglis remembered running down Broadway (this was sometime after 2 a.m.) to the house where Attorney General John Tabor Kempe lived, on the corner of Stone Street, joining a crowd of soldiers and civilians. (By this time, two regiments from the 5th Brigade, including the 43rd Regiment, had been ordered into town.) At that point, "although the Fire raged violently," it was mostly concentrated near Whitehall and had not yet reached the houses of David Clarkson or Ann Heathcote DeLancey, "which were directly in its Way." The wind was blowing from the southeast, or south-southeast, throwing sparks in the direction of the battery, Pearl Street, and Fort George. Yet suddenly, as Inglis stood there, "Fire was discovered on the Roof of M^r. Kempe's

House, though out of the Line of the Sparks which were carried from the burning Houses." The fire emerged "as a faint, glimmering Flame," probably from a trapdoor in Kempe's roof. To Inglis, too, this suggested rebel saboteurs at work.[24]

Summoning his authority as a clergyman, Inglis "called several Soldiers & Citizens to his Assistance." To his dismay, a nearby pump was missing its bolt. He scavenged a house for a fireplace shovel and gave it to a soldier, telling him to break off the blade and use the handle as a bolt. Inglis then led a party to try "to force open the Doors to Kempe's house "but found the Doors both in Front & Rear so well secured that they could not get in." All this transpired over the course of a few minutes— not more than fifteen—when suddenly Inglis heard that "two Houses were on Fire in New Street," which was even farther out of the way. (William Cunningham remembered seeing this New Street fire as well.) Again, Inglis thought the implication was clear: "The City was set on Fire on Purpose."[25]

Inglis was now "so fully persuaded of the City's being set on Fire by Design" that he ran up Broadway to the home of General Robertson, the commandant of the city. Inglis warned Robertson "that if speedy & vigorous Exertions were not used, the whole City must be consumed." Inglis then went farther uptown to alert the sextons of the Anglican churches. He helped save St. Paul's Chapel and King's College by sending bucket brigades onto the roofs (fig. 7.3); Dash remembered leading the effort to preserve St. Paul's, where the flat roof and balustrade gave the firefighters enough of a footing to extinguish the fire from above.[26]

Robertson now took command of the army's efforts. The fire started to fork in two directions, a devil's tongue. One course of flames began roaring up the west side of Broadway, toward Robertson's own house, and he "saw People running to try to save [that] part of the Town." The earl of Dunmore, a fellow Scotsman and former New York governor, offered to save Robertson's house with one of the fire engines. Unfortunately, another course of flames near William Smith Jr.'s house at Flattenberg Hill "threaten'd immediate destruction to all the King's Magazines and Ships," and Robertson saw that "the few People and Water-Engines then in Town were scarcely sufficient to stop the torrent of Flames." At this point he decided that dividing the firefighters "would be fatal," so he "order'd away

Fig. 7.3. Trinity Church archivists speculate that this leather
fire bucket, now missing its handle, might have been used
to save St. Paul's Chapel during the Great Fire of 1776.
In other parts of the city, witnesses reported people
cutting the handles of buckets. St. Paul's Chapel fire
bucket, 1768, Trinity Wall Street Archives.

the Engine from his own House, and brought all the People with it, to
unite in saving the King's Magazines, & Ships." The engines prevented the
fire from heading east. Instead the fire went on to consume Robertson's
house; he had sacrificed his own property for the king's interest. General
Howe praised Robertson's leadership of the firefighting efforts.[27]

Out in the harbor, the men of the Royal Navy had also noticed that the fire threatened the ships near the wharves. "For a long time," wrote Captain Andrew Snape Hamond of the *Roebuck,* the fire "burnt with so much fury that there were little hopes of saving any part of the City, and even a number of the Transports that were got to the Keys were looked upon to be in great danger." At 2:30 a.m., Admiral Howe signaled for all the ships' lieutenants; any men-of-war close to hand were ordered to send their boats ashore to Manhattan. The *Eagle* dispatched its yawl, launch, and flat boats; the *Preston* sent an officer aboard its cutter; the *Renown* sent its barge with another officer; the *Roebuck* sent its boats and engine; the *Jersey* and *Tartar* sent their boats. Some of the boats aided the merchant ships, making sure they got away from the wharves "and out of danger." Others brought officers and men ashore "to Assist in Saveing the Town" or "assist in extinguishing the Fire." Captain Mackenzie noted that "a great number of Seamen from the Fleet were sent on shore under proper officers by order of Lord Howe, to give assistance."[28]

Nevertheless, the fire kept getting more intense. The master's log of the *Preston* recorded that at 4 a.m., the conflagration had "greatly Increased and [was] Burning with great Violence." Although thousands of British soldiers were stationed farther north on the island, General Robertson, his staff, and the regiments from the 5th Brigade seem to have been on their own for most of the night. "No assistance could be sent from the Army 'till after daybreak, as the General [Howe] was apprehensive the Rebels had some design of attacking the Army." Sometime around "daybreak the Brigade of Guards came in from Camp" to assist with firefighting efforts. Some or all of the sailors returned to their ships around the same time.[29]

The servicemen inspired the townspeople, "who, giving all over for lost, at first seemed only to look on with astonishment." Then, "at last being rouzed by the Activity of the Sailors & Soldiers" who were "pulling down Houses to make breaks in the fire, They set heartily to work." When throwing more water on the fire proved fruitless, firefighters resorted to the only sure way to prevent a large fire from spreading: by tearing down even more houses. Mackenzie wrote that "the Soldiers & Seamen were particularly active and useful" at pulling down these buildings; a German lieutenant concluded that these men "prevented the entire city from being laid in ashes." A petty officer from the *Eagle* bought £3.4s. worth of liquor for the sailors who helped pull down houses; the enginemen and others drank another £9.6.8 worth.[30]

> The sick creep forth with feeble steps and slow,
> The old, the young, in mixt confusion go.[31]

Captain Mackenzie did his best to describe the Great Fire in his diary:

> It is almost impossible to conceive a Scene of more horror and distress than the above. The Sick, The Aged, Women, and Children, half naked were seen going they knew not where, and taking refuge in houses which were at a distance from the fire, but from whence they were in several instances driven a second and even a third time by the devouring element, and at last in a state of despair laying themselves down on the Common. The terror was encreased by the horrid noise of the burning and falling houses, the pulling down of such wooden buildings as served to conduct the fire, . . . the rattling of above 100 waggons, sent in from the Army, and which were constantly employed in Conveying to the Common such goods and effects as could be saved;—The Confused voices of so many men, the Shrieks and cries of the Women and children, the seeing the fire break out unexpectedly in places at a distance, which manifested a design of totally destroying the City, with numberless other circumstances of private misery and distress, made this one of the most tremendous and affecting Scenes I ever beheld.[32]

The Reverend Ewald Shewkirk, alone at his house when the fire started, was "struck, when he saw the whole air red." The fifty-one-year-old Moravian pastor raced "about the fire from the Beginning to the End & help'd what I could, till I could hardly walk any more my feet being so sore." He went into the streets and found parishioners, including a mother and her small children, and gave them shelter in his residence. Other parishioners brought their worldly goods with them, cramming them into his home. Shewkirk carried buckets sloshing with water. When the fire reached a house on the corner, making his neighbors "much frightened," he fetched the church's ladders so that firefighters could carry up their buckets: they saved the house and perhaps the whole block. Shewkirk also endeavored "to be of some Comfort to our Neighbours, who cried for fear especially the Women & asked me frequently whether I thought the fire would come our Street too."[33]

> With ruin leagued the flaming fury rode,
> And seiz'd, relentless, on the house of God.
> . . . .
> O'er the high spire the blazing mischief flies
> In awful glory streaming to the skies;
> A dreadful beacon that proclaim'd afar
> The wasteful vengeance of intestine war.[34]

While "the vigorous efforts" of the men and their officers were appreciated, fighting the fire was also a team effort by people of goodwill on the ground: "By the industry of all the people the fire was put out." Nevertheless, "The Fire instantly spread and raged with inconceivable Violence," defying all efforts at suppression. "If one was in one street and looked about, it broke out already again in another street above"; from Fair Street, the Reverend Shewkirk described the path of the fire in terrifying detail: "The wind was pretty high from southeast, and drove the flames to the northwest. It broke out about White Hall; destroyed a part of Broad street, Stone street, Beaver street, the Broadway, and then the streets going to the North River, and all along the North river as far as the King's College," a wing of which suffered damage.[35]

The chaplain of Colonel John Durkee's regiment outlined a similar progression from his vantage point at Paulus Hook, New Jersey: "The fire began at the South East end of the city, a little East of the grand battery, it was spread by a strong South wind, first on the East River, and then Northward, across the Broad Way, opposite to the Old English Church. . . . From thence it consumed all before it, between Broad-Way and the North River, near to the college." Aboard the *Eagle*, Ambrose Serle said the "Flames . . . extended in a Line for almost the Length of a mile." From northern Manhattan, General Hugh, Earl Percy, wrote, "It seemed for a long time to threaten the Destruction of the whole Town."[36]

Captain Mackenzie continued watching in awe: "The appearance of the Trinity Church, when completely in flames was a very grand sight, for the Spire being entirely framed of wood and covered with Shingles, a lofty Pyramid of fire appeared, and as soon as the Shingles were burnt away the frame appeared with every separate piece of timber burning, until the principal timbers were burnt through, when the whole fell with a great noise." The fire had altered the Manhattan skyline, making a statement visible for miles around.[37]

As the fire grew, witnesses could also see it at a distance—even as far as New Haven, seventy miles away. The fire turned the night sky as bright as daylight. On the other side of the lines at Harlem Heights, Alexander Graydon was part of the Continental Army's picket guard; although a hill blocked his view, "the heavens appeared in flames." Witnesses at a distance were unsure what to think. From the *Carysfort,* off Bushwick Creek, Captain Robert Fanshawe thought he "heard several Great Guns & small Arms."[38]

> While some whose hearts with rebel fury glow,
> In secret triumph at their neighbour's woe.[39]

People in the streets of New York City made the firefighters' efforts even harder (fig. 7.4). "Some people," a Hessian officer wrote, "refused to be helpful." Firefighters and soldiers recalled people cutting the handles of fire buckets, sometimes while standing in a bucket brigade. A newspaper described "some Fellows destroying a Chain of Buckets," and the master of the *Dorothy* transport reported almost comical forms of sabotage: "The rebels cut off the straps from the leather buckets; others, under pretence of assisting, would bring water from a distance, and the instant they came near the engines would purposely fall down and spill it." Down near Whitehall when the fire first began, Edward Laight thought he remembered seeing "some person wresting" the fire engine's pipe from Jeronymus Alstyne's hands. The 1st Brigade of Hessians heard that "arsonists cut the towing cables [of the fire engines] to pieces" while the fire

Fig. 7.4. This European print, derived from British newspaper stories, conjures the Great Fire with distressed civilians and burning churches. British soldiers are killing incendiaries while Black men carry possessions to safety. When this *vue d'optique* was lit from the back, the flames would have glowed. Franz Xaver Habermann, *Representation du feu terrible a Nouvelle Yorck,* [1778?], Eno Collection of New York City Views, Miriam and Ira D. Wallach Division of Art, Prints, and Photographs, New York Public Library.

was being fought. He also heard that some malcontents were throwing projectiles at the British sailors who "were not deterred by stones and glowing coals." Some onlookers contented themselves with jeering the firefighters; Loftus Cliffe reported, "The Villains had the audacity to cry out in the Streets *cursed be he who puts it out* in the face of the Army."[40]

> With matches arm'd the lurking villains raise
> The greedy flames, and glory in the blaze.[41]

The firefighters, soldiers, and sailors also said they found men and women starting fires and carrying combustible materials. They apprehended culprits and hauled them to prison. Others—a few? several?—were executed on the spot, stabbed with bayonets or tossed into burning houses. As the fire spread, a roaring heat radiated until the skin began to prickle, driving people farther away. Breathing gave way to coughing. Odors assailed the nose: woodsmoke, mostly, but also acrid and nauseating smells: turpentine, pine resin, sulfur, and burning flesh.

> Wide and more wide the flaming torrents roll,
> No art can check them, and no force controul.[42]

Samuel Bayard Sr. thought his house was safe. He watched from atop his three-story home in Broadway as the wind blew violently, raining sparks down on the streetscape below. The nearest flaming house was a hundred yards away; he still had time to run. He went downstairs, when suddenly, looking out a ground-floor window between the front and back parlor, he saw the lower part of his neighbor Brookman's house on fire. There was no way, Bayard later concluded, that the bottom floor of Brookman's three-story house had caught fire from a falling spark. Bayard's own house was only ten inches away on that side, and the gutters were almost touching. To Bayard's dismay, "in a very short time" the lower part of his own house was on fire. Brookman was long gone; during the Continental Army's occupation, his house had quartered Thomas Waite Foster's artillery company. Bayard concluded that the fire could not have been accidental; he speculated that hidden arsonists might have used the artillerists' portfires, or incendiary fuses, to start the fire.[43]

As the sun rose, Mackenzie was sitting in the doorway of the parsonage for St. Paul's Chapel. The fire was raging to his west, when suddenly a house burst into flames to the east, in Chatham Row (now Park Row, the southern edge of City Hall Park). It was four or five houses away, "so far distant from the houses before on fire and the direction of the wind such" that it must have been set purposely. Some "soldiers . . . [threw] off the roof of the house" and extinguished the fire; in the garret they found a man they thought was an arsonist: "They were much exasperated," Mackenzie recalled, "& if not prevented, would in all probability have put the man to death." Instead they carted him off to the Provost.[44]

> To neighbouring fields the weeping crouds retire,
> From thieves to guard the reliques of the fire.
> No friendly roof to mitigate their woe,
> On the cold earth their weary limbs they throw;[45]

A German lieutenant wrote that New Yorkers "were fortunate to save their lives" but were startled too quickly from sleep to save their possessions. Captain Thompson felt similarly: "In making my escape the burning cinders flew about me." He continued, "The flames were so fierce and rapid" that "few effects escaped this fury in the houses which suffered."[46]

It was a carnival of miseries; a disaster like this always has knock-on effects. Opportunists stole furniture and other movable goods before their owners could get them to safety. Some of these thieves belonged to the Royal Navy: although "the sailors from the fleet did the best work" fighting the fire, a German officer heard that they "rewarded themselves for their labors by plundering other houses which had not burned." Captain Mackenzie, on the other hand, insisted that the men had behaved under proper order and discipline.[47]

> For twelve long hours, with unabated force,
> The angry Dæmon held his vengeful course;[48]

The whole city might have been ravaged, but for a lucky change in the weather. A couple of times during the night, the Reverend Shewkirk thought the wind might have shifted to the west, which would have been devastating; instead, as he wrote to a friend, "God was pleased to stay the flames." (The Connecticut chaplain at Paulus Hook put it differently: "Had not the wind as it veered to the West, died away, the remainder of that nest of vipers would have been destroyed.") Governor Tryon and others affirmed that "a sudden change in the wind" had saved the city; the gusts tapered off around eight in the morning. Fireman Burns recalled a bit of rain, which would also have helped. Thus the firefighting sailors, soldiers, and civilians got the fire under control, but only "with the utmost difficulty," as Captain John Bowater wrote. Luckily, none of the firefighters died trying to save New York.[49]

By 11 a.m., the British forces and local firefighters finally stopped the fire "by preventing it from crossing the Broad-way at the North part of the town," Captain Mackenzie wrote. By noon "it was so far got under that there was no danger" of its spreading farther, and the firefighters concentrated on putting out the still-burning buildings. Shewkirk said the blaze had "raged X or XI hours with the greatest fury."[50]

Though the fire had slowed down, "everything was in confusion and the garrison had difficulty restoring order." Finally, "at four in the evening the fire was entirely extinguished." From the army camps, a Hessian brigade reported, "This afternoon we saw absolutely no more smoke, and furthermore heard nothing; indeed the fire must now have been fully quenched."[51]

> When seats of grandeur, and the poor man's cell
> In ruin indistinct together fell.
> . . . .
> One vast extent of desolation round,
> And ruins pil'd on ruins press'd the smoking ground.
> Come, meek-ey'd Pity! view a scene like this,
> And mourn th' uncertainty of earthly bliss![52]

The fire had spared the shipping, barracks, warehouses, and most of the city's public buildings, but the destruction was still staggering. Major Baurmeister remarked, "New York in this state of desolation is a horrible sight," and Lieutenant William Carter of the 40th Foot proclaimed, "The once beautiful city of New York is now nearly a heap of rubbish." One New Yorker wrote, "Our Distresses were great before, but this Calamity has encreased them tenfold. Thousands are hereby reduced to Beggary."[53]

Henry Strachey had sailed to America to negotiate peace; instead he bore witness to "this Calamity, which was by far the most shocking Scene I ever beheld, though I saw it only from Ship board at the distance of about Two Miles." He told his wife it was "the most melancholly Catastrophe that ever came within my View."[54]

Firebrands

One wretch discover'd through the shades of night
The centinels seize, and drag him forth to light.
In sore dismay I saw the miscreant stand,
Hell in his heart, and sulphur in his hand.

. . . .

The astonish'd villain through the gazing throng
The soldiers drew with bitter oaths along,
And plung'd where flames with hottest fury rise,
He writhes in torment, shrieks aloud, and dies.[1]

The soldiers and inhabitants found incendiaries everywhere. They were "caught . . . in the very act of setting fire to the inside of empty houses at a distance from the fire." Witnesses chased some men holding torches or found combustibles on them. They saw others "cutting the handles of the fire buckets" or otherwise obstructing firefighters. The Reverend Charles Inglis remembered hearing "that Persons had been repeatedly detected in the Act of setting Fire to Houses" as the fire raged through the night and the next morning.[2]

British and Loyalist authorities sent dozens of suspected incendiaries to prison. They also executed some of them on the spot. The people who set fires were a mix of rebel soldiers and civilians, men and women, including at least one mixed-race soldier. They had concealed themselves in town, mingled among the Loyalists, or rowed over from New Jersey. They emerged from the margins and set fire to a city. Their adventures reflect the secrecy of their work, conflicting accounts, witnesses' confusion, and the fact that some of them were killed on the spot. Although these stories were later forgotten, we can piece them together to reveal the perpetrators' means, motives, and opportunities. Together, these stories may even reveal something about the untold scope of a radical revolutionary movement.

"The First Incendiary"

Sometime after 2 a.m., the 43rd Regiment of Foot left their barracks at Lispenard's Brewery and responded to the fire. Private George Kerr found five men and a woman, a cupboard with a keg full of gunpowder, and a bundle of matches in a house behind St. Paul's Chapel. The men claimed that these items were normally kept in the cupboard, even in peacetime. Henry Strachey told a similar story: "One Woman was caught with a Match, and her hands all over Gunpowder which she had been kneading into balls." Kerr said he seized them along with their materials to bring them to the Provost jail. The woman "cried & offered me money to let them go." She hoped he would look the other way. Kerr took the money and gave no testimony about what happened next, but a London newspaper offers further details: "The first Incendiary who fell into the Hands of the Troops was a *Woman*, provided with Matches and Combustibles; but . . . her Sex availed her little, for without Ceremony, she was tossed into the Flames by the soldiers" (fig. 8.1).[3]

Women had become political rebels and participated in auxiliary military activities once the war began. Men sometimes criticized women for being "disorderly" and immodest, drove them from their homes, and

Fig. 8.1. Based on British newspaper accounts, this image shows women burning New York. A British officer stops one woman from stabbing herself in despair. Jean-Jacques-François Le Barbier (artist) and Louis Michel Halbou (engraver), *Incendie de New-York,* in *Essais historiques et politiques sur les Anglo-Américains,* by Michel-René Hilliard d'Auberteuil, book 2, vol. 2 (Brussels, 1782), plate following p. 20, courtesy of the John Carter Brown Library.

assaulted or even killed them; but they also sometimes admired women's wartime heroism. Edmund Burke, for instance, stood on the floor of Parliament and portrayed the first Incendiary as valorous: "This miserable being was found in a cellar, with her visage besmeared and smutted over, with every mark of rage, despair, resolution, and the most *exalted heroism, buried* in combustibles, in order to fire New-York, and perish in its *ashes.*"[4]

This woman might have belonged to the Continental Army as a camp follower and cared little for the city's property. Or she might have been an active rebel from New York City. Since Kerr discovered her in the neighborhood behind St. Paul's, she may have come from the world of disorderly houses, prostitution, theft, and criminal violence. Perhaps she was a counterpart of Lorenda Holmes; she saw herself as defending her hometown and chose, like the rebellious men around her, to burn houses before they fell into enemy hands.[5]

Executing Suspects

British soldiers and sailors, as well as New Yorkers, killed other suspects that night. Governor William Tryon reported as many as eight "detected in their hellish design." Some were thrown to the flames; others were stabbed to death. British army reports were vague about the number of "suspicious persons" who "were now and again thrown into the flames." Death by fire was an extreme punishment, normally reserved for arsonists and traitors. At that moment, however, the bonds of authority were loose and civic institutions were mostly inoperable. The Continental Army had retreated, the British army had recently occupied the city, and Loyalists had only begun to return. This unstable scenario gave license for British soldiers and sailors to punish incendiaries—including a woman—in ways they might not otherwise have done.[6]

The British professed to adhere to the laws of war, and Emer de Vattel's *The Law of Nations* counseled restrained treatment of prisoners and civilians, but "incendiaries . . . may be exterminated wherever they are seized." As for the woman caught behind St. Paul's, normally it was "a maxim of justice and humanity" not to mistreat women and other noncombatants, "but if the women wish to be spared altogether, they must confine themselves to the occupations peculiar to their own sex, and not meddle with those of men by taking up arms." The redcoats' summary executions were politically risky: in a civil war among Britons, the broader public might frown on such killings. British officers themselves had few moral qualms about killing incendiaries, since, after all, the "enraged soldiery . . . threw them into the midst of those flames which they had kindled for the destruction of others." Lieutenant Bartholomew James gave a similar verdict: "Such was the consequence attending those unhappy villains who so far succeeded in their wishes as to destroy the property of individuals."[7]

The men of the British forces argued that they had showed admirable restraint, given the circumstances. Yes, some soldiers, sailors, and the "enraged Populace" had committed summary executions, and the public might find this regrettable, but officers and gentlemen on the scene had also interceded "with some difficulty" to prevent more deaths. General James Robertson, for instance, "rescued two of those Incendiaries from the enraged Populace, who had otherwise consigned them to the Flames, and reserved them for the Hand of deliberate Justice."[8]

Most of the alleged incendiaries were imprisoned rather than killed. The HMS *Experiment*'s logs refer to "a party of Marines Guarding the Rebel Prisoners," under command of their officers. James Wells, the Loyalist shopkeeper, rescued a suspect from "some Sailors" and handed him over to Lieutenant Colonel William Shirreff. Not everyone approved of the officers' coolheadedness: Lieutenant Loftus Cliffe complained about the incendiaries "who were saved from the fury of the inraged Soldiery and Sailors by the too great Lenity of Col: Sheriff." Cliffe hoped they would "meet their Deserts" the next day.[9]

At the Oswego Market in Broadway, near General Robertson's house, privates John Cochran and Lee Ashton of the 43rd Regiment spotted "a short old man," a "North Briton," wearing a brown coat and a round hat. He had "a bundle of matches under his arm," and he tried to run. Ashton confessed that he and another soldier with blue facings "push'd him into the flames," and "whether he was burnt to death or escaped I do not know." The fireman John Baltus Dash saw it happen: the soldiers and sailors dragged the man from a house and threw him into the fire "in their rage & resentment." Somehow Ashton's victim lived: Dash and the regiment's surgeon, Donald McIntyre, remembered him being "rescued from the violence of the Soldiers by an Officer [probably Captain Charles McLean] & sent to the Provost." Later, when McIntyre knocked down a troublemaker in New Street, the man offered to show him a rebel officer in hiding.[10]

Some of the incendiaries confessed, while others shouted their denials. "A Fellow was seized, just about to set Fire to the College, who acknowledged he was employed for the Purpose." This may have been "Matthew," a servant who worked for King's College; the Reverend Inglis and others later applied to General Howe to have him released, "but the General could not be persuaded that he was innocent," and by March 1777, "he died in the Gaol."[11]

Samuel Handleigh described a man wailing that he had been "totally ruined" by the fire, but it turned out that the man had matches on him, "with which the Villain had himself set Fire to three Houses." As a result, "he was pinked with a Bayonet, and otherwise punished for his Villainy."[12]

Another man was caught setting fires and "had to flee." He "called back during his flight that if he could not carry out his intent, he would still find opportunity later to set fire in the city." Lieutenant Johann Henrich von Bardeleben, a Hessian officer, was aghast. "The evil intentions of this nation cannot be described."[13]

A Hessian brigade journal noted "a scoundrel, honored by Congress with the name of Colonel," who "was captured, along with [his] . . . commission." This unnamed colonel had on his person written orders of the plot to burn New York City, in the handwriting of General John Morin Scott, a delegate to the New York Provincial Convention. The colonel commanded forty men who had waited in abandoned houses, "adequately furnished with all the flammable materials." Major Carl Baurmeister, adjutant general of the Hessian troops, also mentioned a colonel leading forty men, probably based on the same intelligence, although his details differ.[14]

Could there have been as many as forty incendiaries? The Reverend Inglis later told another story with that number. At some point during the war, a Boston privateer captured the Loyalist James Devereux. Three of the sailors taunted him, claiming to have been "part of forty Seamen from Boston & Marble Head, who had been left in the City of New York, when it was evacuated by the Continental Army, for the Purpose of setting it on Fire." They even named the places where they had hidden in town. Devereux, however, was too afraid to testify to these facts before a magistrate, since "he followed the Sea as his Occupation" and feared retribution.[15]

Many attributed the fire to rebel officers who had hidden in town. The woman who talked to Peter DuBois had observed these spies before the fire. After the British occupied the city, "these Scoundrels passed amongst them unsuspected." They may have mingled among the Loyalists, wearing a "particular cockade" in their hats that marked them as friends of government. Or they may have posed as Continental Army deserters who had turned their coats. Governor William Tryon, who believed "Mr. Washington was privy to this villainous act," reported, "Some Officers of his army were found concealed in the City, supposed for this devillish purpose." Some had names that can be positively identified.[16]

The British found an officers' commission from Congress in the pocket of Richard Brown, "who was detected in setting fire to some of the houses in New-York," before putting him to death. Brown was a Pennsylvania rifle company captain who had supposedly been captured along with much of his regiment at the Battle of Long Island on August 27. If the British really found him on September 21, it implies that Brown broke parole sometime after his capture.[17]

Another London paper accused "one William Smith, an Officer in a New England Regiment, who was taken with a Match in his Hand, and sacrificed on the Spot to the Fury of the Soldiers." Samuel Curwen, a Massachusetts Loyalist in London, identified "Smith" as the brother of Abigail Adams; while Captain Smith's whereabouts in September 1776 are not precisely known (his sister indicated on September 29 that she hadn't heard from him in a while), he did survive the night. He lived another eleven years, suffering from alcoholism, poverty, and his family's condescension. The prospect of John Adams's ne'er-do-well brother-in-law as a skulking fire starter is tantalizing, but the evidence is far too flimsy.[18]

We find little consistency among these stories, most of which are difficult to corroborate. But the British thought they had uncovered a pattern of rebel soldiers and officers under orders, setting house fires. The rebels used disguises and denials to try to hide what they were doing, but the British believed they had caught them dead to rights and put some of them to death.

Abraham Van Dyck and His "Betrayer"

On the morning of September 21, a "Negro man . . . accosted" Lieutenant John Innes of the Royal Artillery "in the Street" and offered to "show him a Man that set fire to the City." Innes followed the informant to Leary's house, searched it, and found Abraham Van Dyck, "secreted in a Closet of one of the Bed-Chambers, which a young Lady endeavored to prevent his going into." Innes's story comes from the 1783 testimony of Major Stephen Payne Adye, another artillerist as well as deputy judge advocate general in the British army. At that moment in the 1783 hearings, Brigadier General William Martin (one of the investigating officers) piped up, recalling that he remembered Innes—one of his subordinates— telling the same story; he also recalled that he "saw this Man Vandyke soon after going by to the Provost under Guard."[19]

The firefighter John Burns told a slightly different story to the 1783 investigators and also pinpointed the timing of Van Dyck's arrest to September 21: "I particularly remember that one Ab. Vandyke a Captain of Grenadiers in the American service was found on the morning of the fire hid in the Leary's stables. . . . I saw him taken out of these Stables when I was assisting in pulling them down to stop the progress of the fire." This would have been a dramatic scene: Van Dyck cowering in the stables as firemen tore down the walls around him.[20]

The British had supposedly captured Van Dyck on September 16, so why did he appear in a closet or a stable five days later? General Alexander McDougall of the rebel army echoed Innes's story, writing that "the Negro, who brought him victuals betrayed him; after the Fire." It is also significant to consider the motivations of the "Negro man" who was accusing Van Dyck of incendiarism. British-occupied New York offered new avenues for Black opportunity, and this man had decided to stand with the firefighters instead of the fire starters. In New York's civilian courts, an enslaved person could not testify against a white person, but in the midst of the fire, he offered up Van Dyck.[21]

If Van Dyck was innocent, then the "Negro man" was seizing a different opportunity—to falsely accuse a white person who may have mistreated him or claimed to own him. The nature of the so-called betrayal is unclear: was he betraying Van Dyck's crime, or just his hiding spot, or whites' expectation that Black people ought to serve faithfully? We have no way to know for sure, but the unstable environment of the British occupation opened new possibilities.[22]

This "Negro man" must have noted the inhumane treatment that white Americans meted out to people like him. Black people had resisted enslavement in countless ways, but the American Revolution was the first time when thousands of African Americans disrupted the plantation system all at once. They petitioned for emancipation. They ran from their enslavers or bargained for their manumission. They took up arms for one side or the other. They argued for recompense and recognition. They called for freedom by throwing whites' rhetoric in their faces.[23]

Van Dyck, a man who had played host to a leopard, was found sleeping among horse manure. His army had left him behind, and his hometown was now enemy territory. To venture out would mean prison. To sustain his great girth, he had to depend on this "Negro man." Van Dyck assumed he could order this man about, but instead this Black man turned him over to the British. Van Dyck somehow conveyed to McDougall, his superior officer, that he felt "betrayed." He was claiming innocence, to be sure, but he also signaled his belief that Black New Yorkers were supposed to know their place.

Van Dyck's Black victualler did not share this assumption and instead seized the chance to switch and fight. He seems to have exacted a bit of revenge against the injustices of the slave system: he exposed Van Dyck as a guilty man—or framed him despite his innocence.

Amos Fellows

Private John Grundy of the 43rd remembered being "sent . . . to observe & detect any persons they might find setting fire to any part of the City." Then he heard, "*Soldiers Soldiers there is a man setting fire to the town, seize him[!]*." Grundy saw a man near the Exchange with "a burning torch in his hand . . . holding it up against the Roof of a Shed." He chased him to a boat near the Fly Market, where the man was offering to pay bystanders to row him off the island. As he testified in 1783, Grundy recalled the man's white cap and his wallet full of pewter (perhaps coins). He took him to the British main guard and later identified him again at the Provost.[24]

The runner may have been Amos Fellows. Fellows had moved to Tolland, Connecticut, as a teenager, where he met and married Abigail Lothrop. The town's headstones reveal his life's tragedies: he buried Ruth, age two, in 1753, and then Ichabod, age six, and Stephen, age five, a few months apart in 1759. Abigail herself passed away at the age of forty-one on June 25, 1773, leaving Amos alone with their surviving son, Isaac. The men of northern Tolland elected Amos as their militia captain in February 1775, and they responded to the Lexington Alarm on April 19. By September 1776, as a captain in Connecticut's 22nd Regiment of militia, he was forty-seven years old.[25]

Grundy's story resembles newspaper accounts from 1776: "A New-England Man" with a captain's commission, £500, and bundles of matches, or a slain man with a New England promissory note "as a reward." Joshua Loring was a Massachusetts Loyalist serving as the British army's commissary general of prisoners, who later reported what he had heard from General Robertson: Amos Fellows had "lurk't in Town after the Enemy had left it, never offering to give himself up." Then, "when the Town was set on fire, he was seen runing out of a house at a distannce from the fire, which immediately blazed out." A sergeant "followed him down to the ferry Stairs, and caught him while offering a large Sum of money for a Boat to carry him over the Water." The pocketful of cash, common to both stories, confirmed British suspicions that the rebels would stoop to treason and incendiarism for the basest of reasons. General Robertson was "fully convinced" that Captain Fellows "was One of those who set fire to the Town." He too may have been captured, as Loring said, on the twenty-first.[26]

The Motley Crew

The lawyer John Le Chevalier Roome testified before the British investigating commission in 1783. The rebels had arrested him for his Crown loyalties on May 13, 1776, and eventually transferred him to a jail in Norwich, Connecticut. In mid-December, the rebels let Roome roam freely around Norwich on parole. He soon ran into one of the town's leading rebel officers, Colonel John Durkee, who was home recruiting men for a new regiment. Durkee had been "second in command at Paulus hook [New Jersey] at the time of that fire." He told Roome that at 8 p.m. on September 20, 1776, the rebels there sent eight men in a whaleboat across the Hudson River, "one of which was a Mulatto, with directions to land behind Trinity Church among the Stink Weeds." Roome "understood" from this story that the expedition's "design" was "to set fire to the city." The remaining men on Paulus Hook squinted across the vast expanse of the river and "anxiously" awaited the boat's return. Durkee remembered seeing that "the fire had broke out in several places." The "boat returned" at 10 (a.m.?), but the expedition had suffered casualties: "Six of the men only returned in the boat, the other two one of which was the Mulatto it was afterwards found, were thrown into the fire & burnt to death, the Mulatto into Aime's house in Broad Street." Roome heard Durkee tell this story "frequently." When the lawyer returned to New York in March 1777, he reported it to British officials.[27]

Durkee had a storied career leading men of color as well as radicals. As a young lieutenant during the Seven Years' War, his company had many soldiers of color. He was an innholder and merchant in New London County, the center of Connecticut's radicalism—a hotbed of religious enthusiasm, smuggling, effigy burning, nonimportation, military procurement, and privateering: the "Genius of the Town is a restless, discontented spirit." The Trumbull, Huntington, Parsons, and Putnam families helped lead the local rebellion and had strong cultural connections to northern towns like Ashford, Coventry, Tolland, and Windham. Durkee led a crowd of five hundred to personally compel the colony's appointed stamp officer to resign in 1765 and then became Connecticut's corresponding secretary for the Sons of Liberty. He served a term as an assemblyman; then he helped lead the Connecticut settlers to Pennsylvania's Wyoming Valley, making alliances with local Scots Irish settlers; during a conflict with the Penn proprietors, he spent almost two years in a Philadelphia jail for rioting. Then, in May 1775, he had marched with Mohegan and white men to the hills around Boston and fought at Bunker

Hill; in August, he asked his wife to make a dozen shirts for "the Indians" in his unit. Later, in 1780, he headed a company with at least eighteen Black and Mohegan men, all short levies in his 4th Regiment.[28]

Roome's testimony about a mixed-race man is striking—a suggestion that a multiracial "motley crew" helped to burn New York. Since most of Durkee's regiment came from New London County, some were almost certainly of Native American or African descent or both. The county was a locus for people of color, containing around one-third of the colony's total nonwhite population and half of its Native Americans. Preston (adjacent to Norwich) was "a sort of crossroads between the Mohegan, Pequot, Nipmuc, and Narragansett homelands." The town of New London was an important node of the Caribbean trade, including the slave trade, as well as a center of whaling for men of all hues.[29]

Black people came to understand the American Revolution as a potential opportunity for freedom, one way or another, and some chose to fight alongside the rebels. In New England, many soldiers of color joined up as early as April 19, 1775. George Washington, some of his officers, and members of Congress expressed a prejudicial discomfort toward nonwhite soldiers and even tried to stop their recruitment, yet the free Black veterans of 1775 advocated for themselves, and Congress permitted them to reenlist. Many Black Americans, like the "Negro Man" from Van Dyck's story, felt little allegiance to property-owning rebels— in fact, the "Stink Weeds" behind Trinity Church were not far from John Hughson's tavern and Gerardus Comfort's well, where blacks and whites had allegedly gathered in 1741 to conduct Coromantee rituals and plot arson as a form of resistance. For Black soldiers during the Revolutionary War, however, the call for equality in the Declaration of Independence apparently dovetailed with the fight to abolish slavery. The five thousand men of color who fought for American independence were fewer than the tens of thousands of Black people (mostly from the mid-Atlantic and South) who ran away from their enslavers and supported the British cause. While these Black Americans mostly relied on the British army for emancipation, serving in the Continental Army provided the readiest avenue to freedom for Black New Englanders.[30]

In September 1776, according to Roome, the Paulus Hook encampment included an anonymous private of mixed heritage. The risks of military service were great; the mortality rate of Connecticut Indians who served in the Seven Years' War was between 45 and 75 percent. Despite whatever skills he possessed and the occasional advantages granted to light-skinned individuals, this "Mulatto" may have seen soldiering as his best option, given the limited opportunities for people of color: Connecticut's white citizens had been dispossessing the Indians of their land and arrogating control of Black labor, and many northeastern native groups excluded mixed-race people from certain land rights. This man may nonetheless have seen Revolutionary War service as an opportunity to contribute to his community, advance himself, prove his masculinity—like any other soldier—and perhaps reach for greater social and economic freedom.[31]

The three hundred men of the 20th Continental Regiment watched the fire from across the Hudson River while their whaleboat detachment committed a risky and radical act on behalf of the rebel cause. The soldiers at Paulus Hook "gave three cheers" when the steeple of Trinity Church fell in an "awfully grand" blaze.[32]

Our record of this tale comes from Roome's secondhand account, seven years later, and it is the only evidence of a mixed-race perpetrator; yet there is some corroboration for the incendiaries' expedition. At least three contemporary accounts from September 1776 attested that a group of rebels rowed across the Hudson River to set fire to the city. The captain of His Majesty's bomb vessel *Thunder* recorded in his ship's log that the fire "was Occasioned by the Rebels that came in the night from the Jersey Shore some on [of] them were put to Death on the spot." Ensign Wilhelm Freyenhagen of the Hessian von Donop regiment wrote, "Last night a boat coming from the Jersey side set fires and about 300 houses burned." While it is not clear how these officers knew this, their accounts are closer to the event than Roome's.[33]

Since the muster rolls for Durkee's regiment in 1776 do not survive, it is exceedingly difficult to identify the two slain crew members. A Virginia Loyalist who was passing through Paulus Hook on September 8 recoiled at the smell of the "Yankee men, the nastiest Devils in creation"; they were "numerous, but ragged, dirty, sickly, and ill-disciplined." Two of these "Devils" may have perished on the night of September 21.[34]

Twenty-five-year-old John Cary, a white man from Windham, responded to the Lexington Alarm on April 19, 1775, and served in General Israel Putnam's 3rd Regiment; Durkee commanded a multiracial company in this regiment and later became its lieutenant colonel. Cary's older brother Jonathan took possession of his effects on September 22, 1776. This was a routine practice soon after a soldier died, but no major military actions had been fought since September 16. Cary might have died from illness, an accident, or a lingering injury, but his date of death is still suggestive.[35]

Several soldiers of color from New London County were also recorded as dead or missing during the tumultuous week of September 15 to 22. The records do not identify any of them as the slain incendiary, but their names—Charles Scadoab, Fontain Quamono, and Robert Ashbo—may be worth further scrutiny.[36]

Whoever the slain incendiaries were, Roome reported that only six of the boatmen returned to their cheering comrades and joined the retreat from Paulus Hook on September 23. It is difficult to guess why Durkee would have bragged about this clandestine expedition while talking to a committed Loyalist from New York. Apparently he was proud of having sent these men to burn New York City. As a crowd leader himself, the Connecticut colonel may well have regarded these men as heroes, but apart from Roome's testimony, their deeds went unsung.[37]

Wright White

The Loyalist carpenter Wright White was seen cutting the handles of fire buckets. Then, perhaps by accident, he slashed a woman's arm as she carried water to the fire engines. The story grew more lurid in the telling. Did White "knock a feeble old woman down" and break her arm with a sledgehammer? Did he sever her arm completely while she was trying to save her house? Was the woman White's wife, and was he trying to burn his own house? Were she and their five children begging him to "refrain from this murderous arson"? Is that when he slashed at her? Did she die from her injury?[38]

What happened next was clearer: when White's knife drew blood, "This provoked the Spectators to Such a Degree" that they set upon him. Soldiers ran him through with their bayonets. The sailors hanged him "without ceremony" by the neck. Then they hung his corpse by the heels from a signpost at the corner of Cherry and Roosevelt Streets.[39]

Major Baurmeister assumed that White was a "fanatical rebel," but other accounts contradicted him. A rebel newspaper called him a "poor tory shipwright" who fell victim to the soldiers' "inhumanity." The Reverend Ewald Shewkirk, a more reliable source, reflected that "he was always against the Rebellion." People familiar with his loyalties "cannot account" for his actions, "unless he was drunk, as they suppose he was," having recently become addicted to alcohol.[40]

The experiences of living in New York City over the past two years had not been easy, especially for Loyalists like Theophilus Hardenbrook and Wright White. On the night of September 21, White saw, perhaps with bloodshot eyes, his city on fire, and he started slashing leather bucket handles, rendering them unusable. When a woman (maybe his wife) tried to stop him, his knife cut her arm. Maybe he suddenly decided to join the rebellion by sabotaging efforts to save the city; more likely, the Revolution had finally driven him mad.

Many later argued that the Great Fire of New York was a devastating accident exacerbated by madness and thoughtless vengeance. If so, the British soldiers' murderous mistake compounded the tragedy.

Combustibles

Joseph Chew came ashore at dawn on the twenty-first to help extinguish the fire; later that morning, he remembered waiting at Cruger's Wharf to return to his transport ship. He watched as a sailor found "two bundles of white Cedar Matches" under a warehouse or store. The bundles contained fifty-five matches, each eighteen inches long and dipped in brimstone and rosin (fig. 8.2). Henry Law, the captain of the port, also remembered seeing "several Men & Women" with "a large quantity of Cumbustibles in the Stores on Cruger's Wharf." As the sailors "dragged" them away, he noticed that "two of the women had matches in their Arms."[41]

The variety of accelerants and combustibles that the British uncovered was also astonishing: Captain Henry Duncan described matches made of "lath wood, split in small slips, tarred and brimstoned." General

Fig. 8.2. This London image shows the matches used during the early modern period. Marcellus Laroon (artist) and Pierce Tempest (printmaker), "Any card matches or save-alls," in *The Cryes of the City of London: Drawne after the Life* (1688; London, 1733), courtesy of The Lewis Walpole Library, Yale University.

William Howe reported "matches and combustibles that had been prepared with great art and ingenuity." The statesman Henry Strachey noted that "Bundles of Straw, Matches of Pitch and Brimstone, and Trains of Gun powder, were concealed in the Buildings." Serle described men "caught with Matches, and Fire-balls about them." Captain Duncan also wrote that the rebels had stashed "tow and all manner of combustibles . . . in different parts of the city" to serve as kindling. All these discoveries added to the keg full of gunpowder and the bundle of matches in the house behind St. Paul's, the bundle of matches under the arm of the man near Oswego Market, and the burning torch (or bundle of matches?) somewhere near the Fly Market.[42]

Witnesses remembered prisoners being taken to City Hall who were caught with combustibles on them. Captain Lieutenant Archibald Robertson, an engineer, said that "Rebels" were caught "with faggots dipp'd in Brimstone." An artillery colonel described "villains" who "were detected in setting fire to houses with port-fires and light balls, dipped bavins, tar-barrels, &c." Captain William Leslie mentioned "several People . . . with lighted Torches." These "Skulking" incendiaries had concealed some materials beneath their clothes or in their pockets or were found holding them—sometimes bundles of matches in tubs or barrels.[43]

The British also caught people inside buildings along with these combustibles. Lieutenant Loftus Cliffe compared them to "Guy Faux of old concealed with Combustables & Powder in under Cellars." Wells, the shopkeeper, remembered "some Sailors" escorting a "shabbily dressed" prisoner; they had found the man in a cellar with a barrel of gunpowder and lashed it to his shoulder. Wells rescued the man and delivered him to British officers.[44]

Other witnesses noted the discovery of unattended combustibles concealed in houses. Sergeant John Norton from the 43rd Regiment, for instance, remembered entering a Chatham Row house with its roof on fire—he found combustible materials in the garret, but these apparently had not been ignited. The Reverend Inglis recalled hearing "that Bundles of Matches & other Combustibles were found in many Houses, & in different Parts of the City, with Design, as was supposed, to promote & increase the Conflagration." The British tallied these combustibles alongside the ones they had uncovered before the fire began.[45]

A few people suggested an innocent explanation for all the flammable stuff lying around. The rebels may have left military stores throughout the city when they evacuated; William Shipman guessed in 1783 that the matches he saw after the fire had "been originally prepared for fire rafts." Alderman William Waddell remembered, "Some Persons were taken up having matches about them, which he supposes they had taken from the stores from mere motives of curiosity, without any design of doing mischief with them." When caught with flammable materials, suspects claimed that they were trying to bring them to safety, away from

Fig. 8.3. This satire shows Joseph Priestly and Thomas Paine, radical
supporters of the American and French Revolutions, plotting with
the Devil amid an array of phosphorous, gunpowder, brimstone, and
bundles of matches. Isaac Cruikshank, "The Friends of the People,"
(London, 1792), American Philosophical Society.

their places of residence. For many civilians on the scene, this was true.
For instance, the Loyalist shipwright Joseph Totten remembered finding
his former governor, Lord Dunmore, holding a "bundle of Matches" that
"he had taken out of a barrel of Combustibles"—but Dunmore was hardly
a suspect. Although a handful of witnesses recalled these explanations
in 1783, most British and Loyalist witnesses in 1776 judged that these
portfires, gunpowder, and rosin-coated matches had a nefarious purpose
(fig. 8.3).[46]

After the fire, parties of loyal citizens searched the remaining
houses for "forbidden Materials" and uncovered more signs of sabotage.
The fireman Jeronymus Alstyne "found several matches in Mr. [Joseph?]

Hallett's yard in Water-Street, lying carelessly about, which we threw over the Dock." James Wells, leading another group, discovered a sixty-pound bundle of matches on the second story of a house on the east side of Broad Street, between Prince and Garden. A woman there told them that those matches were usually sold to privateering adventurers. William Hervey found "a Cartridge of Powder . . . with a Straw bed laid over it & a large train of powder leading from it down to the back door in the yard," in a house owned by one "Hauser" in Smith Street, near the statue of William Pitt. The search parties brought the evidence to City Hall and to the Provost. Major Stephen Kemble noted the "Combustibles, Matches, &c. having been found in Houses since [the fire], hid under stairways, and ready for another Conflagration." He concluded, "It is not to be doubted; but it was done by design."[47]

The search parties did not catch everything. A few days after the fire, Chew visited a cooperage in Smith Street; after the cooper took a parcel of shavings out of a large barrel, Chew saw that the barrel was "close packed with Matches made of Walnut about 18 inches long & cover'd at both ends with brimstone & rosin." The cooper claimed he had taken over the shop only the day before and did not know who the shop's proprietor was. Later in 1776, Dr. John Mervin Nooth remembered the day it finally became chilly enough to build a fire in the hearth at the Vauxhall hospital. Some "combustibles concealed in one of the Chimneys" exploded, blasting the firewood "into the Room, with some violence." The fire was not yet done with New York.[48]

Conclusion

As navy lieutenant Bartholomew James recalled, "The chief of those concerned in this business was detected, hung up by the heels, and their brains knocked out with the soldiers' muskets, while others were thrown into the flames and consumed with the houses." The British believed their soldiers had righteously slain several deserving incendiaries—inveterate enemies of the Crown—but Wright White, a drunken Loyalist, did not fit that description. The soldiers' and sailors' blood was up, so perhaps their mistake is understandable, even as their deadly error undermines their credibility as accusers. Their murder was unreasoning—and unreasonable. White was known around town, and his death was frightful and memorable. He seems to have been a tragic victim of alcohol, trauma, and a chaotic misunderstanding. As for the others killed at the scene, they either helped to burn New York City or were caught in the wrong place at the wrong time. Soldiers, sailors, and crowds misinterpreted their frightened actions as malice; a lawyer might ask whether their furtive movements warranted reasonable suspicion.[49]

Most of the alleged perpetrators remain anonymous. No one recognized the captain from Connecticut or the sailor from Massachusetts—not the locals, and certainly not the British soldiers and sailors who had recently stepped ashore. Saboteurs, who understood arson as a tool of radical rebellion, moved freely behind enemy lines. If white men assumed that women and nonwhites had more limited capacities, then the particular ability of a female or "Mulatto" saboteur to exploit those assumptions was exactly what made them dangerous. Such people were accustomed to moving around the city at its margins.[50]

New Yorkers, soldiers, and sailors chased suspects with unfamiliar faces. For the most part, we do not know the incendiaries' names, because they evaded capture or suffered a quick death. So it is difficult to say who they were, what they believed, or what they were doing before the fire. Some of the witnesses' stories look like rumors: vague guesses ("Smith" and "Brown") or reflexive attempts to blame Washington and his officers. The witnesses' judgment may also have been flawed. Finally, the sources suggest that many of the incendiaries were anonymous because of their humble background: they were laborers, rank-and-file soldiers, women, and people of color who were beneath the writers' notice. The lives of people like them and the discontent that animated them reveal aspects of the Revolution that might otherwise be "smutted over."

Although the witnesses' conclusions may have been murky, ample evidence points to incendiary materials in multiple locations and to people who appeared to be using these materials to burn New York. However imperfect the evidence, there is too much of it to ignore the apparent fact that incendiaries deliberately ignited the Great Fire.

Surveying the Wreckage

Two days after the fire began, stray fires still flickered down by the Hudson River; "Only after three days was it possible to quench the coals." Stephen Allen recalled, "For several days . . . the city was enveloped in a cloud of smoke scarcely penetrated by the rays of the sun." Then nine years old, he explored the ruins with his brother. "So dense was the atmosphere with the smoke," he recalled, "we were compelled to cover our faces with silk handkerchiefs . . . to breathe this disagreeable air."[1]

Captain John Thompson commented on the city's "melancholy spectacle": he guessed that only five hundred people remained in town, where "most of the houses are shut up as at midnight." The fire and its "ruins" would "mark in characters dismal enough what kind of spirit that is which goes under the name of American virtue and patriotism," he wrote. "Indeed these mad & wicked people seem to be heaping one pile of iniquity upon another and are accumulating a mass which I should conceive must one day fall with dreadful ruin on their own heads." He thought that even if the soldiers had not caught the incendiaries in the act, there would still be "indubitable proofs" of the rebels' guilt, such as their previous threats or the fire's pattern of multiple outbreaks.[2]

Lieutenant Loftus Cliffe walked among the smoking wreckage on September 22 and felt "low spirited from my Curiosity, the gloomy prospect the Town affords would affect even a Hessian." Women and the infirm huddled in the city's "poorer houses" now that the fire had left so many of them "inhabitants of the Streets." Soldiers and sailors stole whatever humble items the inhabitants might have tried to rescue. "I can not paint the Misery a very pretty Town . . . is now reduced to, where once Peace & Plenty smiled in every countenance," Cliffe wrote. On his way back to camp, he spotted the corpse of the Connecticut captain Nathan Hale, with a wooden effigy of George Washington hanging beside him. Hale had confessed to being a rebel spy, and the British executed him on September 22. He had not reached Manhattan when the fire began, but some historians have argued that the British were so angry about the fire that they made a scapegoat of him.[3]

Hale may not have been involved, but local Loyalists still blamed the rebels for starting the fire. Jeronymus Alstyne, who helped fight the blaze, concluded in 1783 that the wind had hastened its spread, but he still testified that New York "might have been set on fire by the Americans," just "as they burnt the barns & Grain as they retreated on Long Island." His colleague John Baltus Dash was more certain: "From his own long experience & observation at many different fires," he did not think that the fire had been transmitted by flaming brands, "but verily believes that it was purposely set on fire in different places." The Reverend Shewkirk, another witness, also understood all the factors that had hampered firefighting, but he believed there was "great reason to think that the fire was caused or promoted by some men lost to humanity & hired perhaps for such an hellish design."[4]

The brigade major Captain Frederick Mackenzie, an eyewitness almost from the beginning, declared in his diary, "It is beyond a doubt that the town was designedly set on fire," either by rebel soldiers who had concealed themselves on September 15 "or by some Villains left behind for the purpose." He recalled the summer rumors that the rebels had said "they would burn it, sooner than it should become a nest for Tories," while the most radical insisted that "they would set fire to their own houses sooner than they should be occupied by The King's troops." Among British army officers, the consensus was overwhelming that the burning of New York was a "concerted Plan," showing "what an infamous set the Rebels are," and not merely an accident or a senseless crime.[5]

Naval officers came to the same conclusion. "It was evident from many circumstances," declared Captain Duncan of the *Eagle*, "that the city was maliciously set on fire." In particular, "the proof seemed very plain" against the incendiaries the British seized.[6]

The Reverend Thomas Lewis O'Beirne preached a sermon at St. Paul's Chapel on Sunday, September 22. The firefighters had saved the building, and it still stood in 2001 when relief workers in the aftermath of 9/11 used it as a place of rest and recovery. In 1776, the building was at the edge of ash and chaos for the first time. O'Beirne was chaplain to Admiral Howe. On that smoky Sabbath, O'Beirne tried to channel the feelings of his Loyalist listeners, who had "just escaped" from the rebel occupation and were "congratulating your Friends on your mutual Deliverance," only "to awake at the Midnight Hour and find your City in Flames." O'Beirne noted the calculation and deception of the rebel incendiaries: "Ye saw the treacherous Adherents of these pretended Guardians of your Rights and Possessions," who returned to the city under false pretenses and lit it on fire.[7]

The accusations of British officers and Loyalists might seem to be overblown products of prejudice and paranoia—the natural outcome of the rumors that had circulated throughout the summer—but they also match previous statements by Charles Lee, Nathanael Greene, and Washington himself.

The British blamed the fire on rebel incendiaries with real political motivations. A correspondent to a London newspaper specified that "some great ones among the Rebels" had planned the fire, while "the poor Wretches who did the Business were only their Tools." The writer accused New Englanders left behind by the Continental Army of setting the fire near the Hudson River, "in a Part of the Town where the labouring People lived." A few other observers also implied that poorer New Yorkers had done the deed. James Wells recalled that eight months before the fire, burning the city "had been frequently threatened by the lower Class of people." Several army officers emphasized that the fire had struck the "superb" houses in "the best Part" of the city or "the most elegant Part of the Town." The recurring nightmare of the genteel had come to life: people of lesser means (the spirit of the New England "levellers" at last?) had taken up the torch to deprive wealthier people of their property.[8]

"Good God what a sight," wrote Dr. Samuel Clossy, a King's College professor, surveying the blighted city; "800 Chimnies standing without an house, the old Church destroyed, all the suburbs torn to pieces the remaining houses mostly wrecked, a few dispirited remnants of the old populace." The congregations of Trinity Church, the Lutheran Church, and (some said) a secret Catholic enclave would need new places to worship. "The old Church awful & majestic in Ruins," wrote the Reverend John Milner, was "silently reproaching the infernal monsters" whose "impious rage" had led them to burn it.[9]

No one could agree on how much of the city had been consumed: some said as few as two hundred buildings, Captain Mackenzie estimated 600 houses, the Reverend Charles Inglis said a thousand, and the press gave even larger figures, up to 1,500 or 1,600. Several witnesses said that as much as a third of the city had burned, while others guessed a quarter or a fifth or a sixth. The maps suggest that forty-five and a half acres had burned: no less than an eighth, or perhaps more than a fifth, of the city (figs. 9.1, 9.2). In a town with a prewar population of twenty-five thousand, that meant that at least three thousand—probably around five thousand—people were now homeless.[10]

Had the wind and firefighters not foiled their plans, the incendiaries probably hoped to burn the ships and the commercial district on the East River. Nevertheless, the fire damaged other targets: the customs house (with all its books and papers, as well as the collector's private papers), the city's principal Anglican church and its estate, as well as the fine mansions of lower Broadway.[11]

Officials never calculated the total monetary cost of the fire. A Hessian journal estimated a million thalers, or about £225,000. The leading ministers of Trinity Church estimated its losses at £25,000 or perhaps even £40,000: this figure included a £850 organ, the church, rector's house, charity school, and two hundred houses on church grounds, but it did not include lost income from rent that the displaced tenants were now "unable to pay."[12]

Then as now, people envied and admired the city's grandest homes,

Fig. 9.1. British officers commissioned new surveys of New York City to account for the portion of the city that had burned. Detail of Claude J. Sauthier, "Plan of the City of New-York as it was when his Majesty's Forces took Possession of it in 1776. Showing [. . .] the part of the City which burnt the same year by a red colour and dott'd lines," October 1776, Collection of the Duke of Northumberland at Alnwick Castle, D2M: IV.8.

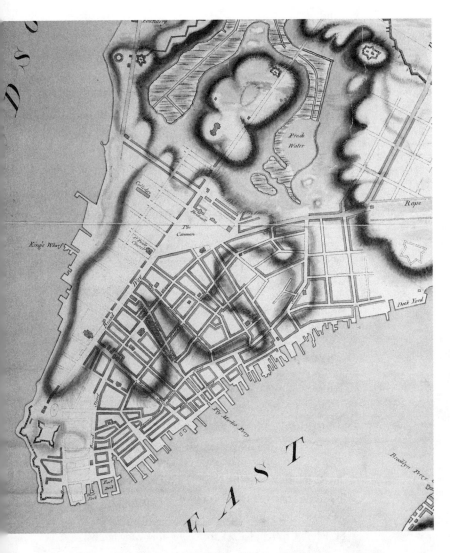

Fig. 9.2. This map depicts entire blocks being erased by the Great Fire.
Detail of Samuel Holland, *Plan of the City of New York and Environs*,
[1776–81?], from the collections of the New York State Library,
Manuscripts and Special Collections, Albany, New York.

Fig. 9.3. An image of St. Paul's Chapel from after
the Revolution, with the steeple added in 1794; the
building survived the Great Fire. John Anderson
(artist) and John Scoles (engraver), "A View of
St. Paul's Church, New York," *New York Magazine*
6 (Oct. 1795): 577, Library of Congress, Rare
Book and Special Collections Division.

and extant accounts tend to focus on wealthy people's property. So many
Broadway mansions had burned that witnesses emphasized the lonely
survivors, "preserved as by Miracle": St. Paul's Chapel (fig. 9.3) and Hull's
tavern, John Cortlandt's sugarhouse and dwelling house, along with the
houses of Thomas Randall, Archibald Kennedy, Jonathan Mallet, and

the Reade, Jones, Axtell, and Rutherford families. On the other hand, General Robertson, John Watts, Colonel Roger Morris, Colonel William Bayard, David Johnson, John Wetherhead, Richard Harrison, William Smith Jr., and Samuel Bayard were "the greatest Sufferers."[13]

In O'Beirne's sermon, he noted that "so many Families once blessed with Comfort and Affluence" were "turned out on the World, naked, helpless, and stripped of their All." General James Grant estimated that the fire had claimed "a sixth part of the Town in quantity" and "at least a fourth in Quality." Colonel Carl von Donop specifically noted "General Robertson's own handsome dwelling-house" along with "about eighty right good houses, which for the most part had belonged to persons of distinction," out of six hundred houses total. If such houses with their goods were worth £1,000 on average, then the cumulative loss was £80,000 in addition to the city's more modest homes. Robertson himself believed that his firefighting efforts had saved the Crown £200,000 worth of ships and stores (all the more valuable during wartime), only to personally lose £2,000 when his own house burned.[14]

The fire was indiscriminate, destroying homes of the haughty and humble alike. Governor Tryon found it "afflicting to view the wretched and miserable inhabitants who have lost their all, and numbers of reputable shop keepers that are reduced to beggary, and many in want for their families of the necessaries of life." Attorney General John Tabor Kempe lost his house and remarked that he would take a larger financial hit from "the Ruin of some of my Debtors by the Fire." Cornelius Ryan lost two houses on Broadway and another in back, valued at £620 (New York currency), not to mention furniture worth £65 and wool, sheepskins, and deerskins worth more than £130. The Reverend Bernard Michael Houseal of Trinity Lutheran Church lost £665 in furniture, books, and scientific instruments when his parsonage burned, "kindled by the cruel Hands of wicked Incendiaries." Many of the tenants' houses on Trinity Church lands had been built by the carpenters and laborers who lived there.[15]

British officers were relieved that the fire had not achieved the rebels' goal of "distressing us" militarily, but the fire still damaged morale and caused widespread bankruptcies and deprivation, with "many unhappy individuals among the inhabitants." As another correspondent confirmed,

"This infernal Scheme was confessedly executed to prevent the King's Troops from having any Benefit by the City, and to distress the Friends of government." He apologized for his incoherent letter and explained that he had been "interrupted at least fifty Times with Complaints from the Distressed" while writing it, "besides being in the utmost Agitation of Mind."[16]

Greene had guessed that the Loyalists owned two-thirds of the property, but people of all political persuasions grieved for their homes and possessions. Major Francis Hutcheson lamented that it was "chiefly the friends of Govern[ment] who have Suffered," yet the rebels' friends suffered, too. Thomas Petit, doorkeeper to the New York Convention, begged legislators for a raise because he "has been so unfortunate as to have a house Burnt in the late fier at New York which was nearly his all."[17]

Much of this distress came in the form of crowding. Although the city seemed to be "a deserted Place," a German lieutenant wrote that "the worst houses were occupied and there was almost nothing unoccupied." Within months, the city swelled with 11,000 civilians, 14,000 British and Hessian troops, and 5,000 prisoners of war; this was 5,000 more people than the city's prewar population, but with the housing capacity reduced by 12 to 22 percent. Even accounts that tried to minimize the fire's damage noted its consequences for garrisoning the troops. "The part of New York that is burnt is the old town, which is the least valuable," one London paper reported, "except affording tolerable barracks for the soldiers." The British army almost put four hundred prisoners of war in Shewkirk's church, telling him, "It was a spacious Building & they did not know where to put all the People, especially since the fire destroyed so many houses."[18]

The immediate military impact of the Great Fire was minimal. The British had intended to assault Paulus Hook, New Jersey, but "deferred on account of this vast Conflagration, most of our Soldiers being engaged in extinguishing the Fire." The fire only slowed them down by two days, and the British took the post without opposition on September 23.[19]

Instead the incendiaries appeared to have nastier ambitions in mind: to disrupt military capacity, to destroy property, and possibly to take lives, both military and civilian. As wanton destruction with no immediate tactical purpose, the fire was an "atrocious crime," and Major Baurmeister was shocked that the rebels believed it "fully justifiable in times of war." The rebels were evidently pursuing a maximally destructive scorched-earth policy, a variation on what later generations would call "total war." The incendiaries had not just planned on property destruction but also attempted murder, Crown supporters said. Lieutenant Loftus Cliffe concluded, "Their Design was to destroy the Town, Troops and Shipping who had now moored close to the Docks," many of which had gunpowder aboard. The incendiaries' plan was to start at the commercial district and then "go thro' the whole town if they had not been timely prevented." An Irish newspaper envisioned a gruesome sort of slaughter: "The design of setting fire to the town was to burn the troops who were in it." Captain Andrew Snape Hamond agreed: "They just gave time for the Houses to be filled from the Fleet & Army," for the British to haul some of their stores ashore, and for Loyalist civilians to return to their homes—then the incendiaries "took the opportunity of a windy dark night, and set the Town on fire." No evidence indicates that the fire claimed lives (except those of suspected incendiaries), but Crown supporters were still horrified by the rebels' apparent intentions.[20]

The incendiaries' religious motivation was also apparent. Governor William Tryon concluded, "It really seems the conflagration was directed against the interest of the Church." The Reverend Inglis agreed: "The church corporation had suffered prodigiously, as was evidently intended." These accusations drew on assumptions that the American rebellion was "a religious War" that had "been fomented by Presbyterian Preachers, with a View to the Extirpation of the Church of England from the Colonies," as Ambrose Serle insisted. A London newspaper blamed Congregationalists for burning "Poor Trinity Church, a principal Object of Republican, Independent Malice," by setting it on fire in three places, and another joked that the rebels, not content with trying to starve British soldiers in Boston, now wanted to "prevent them from *praying*" in New York. Jonathan Boucher, an Anglican minister who had been friendly with Washington before fleeing to London as a Loyalist, observed that "not a single [Dissenter] Meeting House &c was touch'd. This needs no Comment." To Anglicans, the burning of Trinity Church was a tragedy and a sacrilege. It felt like treason.[21]

"The New England People," Serle insisted, "are maintained to be at the Bottom of this Plot, which they have long since threatened to put into Execution." General Grant agreed: "The Yorkers are Convinced that the New England Men sett Fire to the Town, they will never forgive them." British and Loyalist newspapers blamed "New-England Saints," "New-England Incendiaries," and "new England miscreants" or singled out a "New England Captain." One correspondent concluded, "They all prove to be of that detestable Fraternity the Fanaticks, which has been nestling the last hundred Years in the Eastern Provinces of America." The writer argued, "This Conflagration proves, that the old Republican Plan was to drive every Member of the Constitutional Church of England out of the Colonies."[22]

As Captain William Bamford took in the ruins of New York City, he thought about the rebels who had been deluded into rebellion by "a few wicked designing men." He wondered whether the Great Fire "may open their eyes that they may see their error" and give up on the idea of independence. He could not help but blame New Englanders: "I fear the old Hatred for Kings & the seeds of sedition are so thickly sown among them, that it must be thrash'd out of them. . . . New England has poyson'd the Whole."[23]

New Englanders made up most of the Continental forces in 1776, and so for many Crown supporters, "New Englanders" was shorthand for "rebels." The phrase betrayed Britain's wishful assumption that true Americans remained loyal to the Crown, while the rebels were a narrow, largely regional faction of fanatical Congregationalists. General Grant wondered "whether they did it from Enthusiastick Zeal, or from the promise of Reward." The incendiaries had served the rebel cause, either for spiritual reasons or for hire.[24]

Some Crown supporters said the incendiaries were outsiders looking to destroy a commercial rival. One naval officer argued, "This infamous business has been meditated a long time by the Bostonians and Philadelphians, who have always envied the trade and situation of this place." New York's Loyalist paper agreed: it was New Englanders' "inveterate Malice against the Trade and Prosperity of this Colony."[25]

Whatever the Crown supporters' preconceptions, the incendiaries may have had radical motives beyond mercenary greed or religious

"Zeal." Some civilians and soldiers had expressed animus toward Loyalists, wealthy people, the Church of England, the marauding British army, and even the rebel army's own martinets. The Continental Army had men who did not shy away from sowing chaos, disobeying orders, and using irregular methods of war. Some of these men may have ranked as high as captain. Radical actors were willing to consider radical methods, including the deployment of women and nonwhites as saboteurs. Female and mixed-race incendiaries may have had their own notions of their role and status in the new United States, and spectacular disruption may have looked like the best way to achieve their goals.

A New York Loyalist urged readers to behold "the Miscreants who thus wantonly sport with the Lives, Property, and Happiness of their Fellow Creatures, and unfeelingly doom them to inevitable Ruin." The fire's victims were angry at the ruin that the fire had made of their city, and they were hungry for justice. British soldiers and sailors had already executed several incendiaries on the spot. Now, in the aftermath of the fire, many sufferers, soldiers, and Crown supporters fantasized about punishing the rebels for their crimes.[26]

T • E • N

The Commandant's Conundrum

Wright White's family and neighbors had to avert their eyes from his punctured corpse, hanging by its heels from a signpost. Stephen Allen still remembered it almost fifty years later: "It continued a spectacle of horror to those in the vicinity and a warning to the multitude that such would be their fate, if they attempted to murmur or complain of the treatment they were receiving from the invaders." According to Allen, some ardent Loyalists grimly accepted the display, hoping it would terrify any New Yorkers who still had rebel sympathies. Allen, who later became mayor of New York City, remembered the Loyalists nursing a sense of vengeance in the aftermath of the fire.[1]

British military officers were just as angry. General William Howe wrote, "A most horrid attempt was made by a number of wretches to burn the town of New-York, in which they succeeded too well." He included in his official report that his angry soldiers had discovered combustibles throughout the city and executed some incendiaries. Knowing that his reports were published, he must not have feared public disapproval.[2]

The fire showed the Reverend Inglis that the rebels were "enemies of peace." Captain Andrew Snape Hamond of the *Roebuck* grumbled that the British were waging a war on "unequal terms; whilst we are treating them with openness & generosity, they are daily practising every kind of Art treachery & cruelty to destroy us." The rebels would sacrifice anything and everything, it seemed, for their cause. In Hamond's mind, the time for magnanimity had passed. Perhaps Allen was right to think that the hanging corpse of Wright White was General Howe's gruesome way of warning New Yorkers that they had gone too far.[3]

Yet in his sermon the day after the fire, the Reverend Thomas Lewis O'Beirne, a close ally of the Howes, preached a message of reconciliation. The rebel incendiaries were "treacherous" and unreasonable, and Loyalists needed to watch out for their tricks, but he urged his listeners to "let a Reciprocation of Kindness and Humanity distinguish you in this Season of Distress." As a minister of God, O'Beirne did not want to further stoke the hostility between the two sides.[4]

New Yorkers choked with grief and jumped from frayed nerves. General Howe had his men search for any incendiaries who might still be lurking in the city, ready to finish the job they had started. Through tears and smoke, Francis Panton, along with several others, patrolled the city for further signs of disturbance. One of the patrollers entered the rebel general Lord Stirling's house in Broad Street and searched it "to see if any Villains had concealed themselves there." Suddenly a man rushed out the door, flew past Panton, and swore that "*he would do it yet*," meaning he would set fire to the house. A sentry standing nearby aimed and snapped his musket, but it misfired, and the man ran off. Henry Strachey also noted further "attempts" of incendiarism, but these were "defeated, and the Villains secured." People kept uncovering more caches of combustible material, too.[5]

Captain Nisbet Balfour, Howe's aide-de-camp, arrived in London on November 2 and had an audience with the king. His Majesty was thrilled with the report on the taking of New York, further validating the king's decision to bestow a knighthood on Howe for his victory at Long Island. Lord George Germain wrote, "The Attempt which was made to burn the Town of New York might well exasperate the Troops. I trust that an Apprehension of condign Punishment will deter the infatuated Wretches from persevering in their Resolutions" to burn the city. He was hinting, perhaps, that he approved of the summary executions as a deterrent. Germain expressed his hope that Howe's "Inquiry . . . will serve to discover the Original Promoters & Abettors of the villainous design." But by the time this reply reached Howe in December, it was far too late.[6]

In Parliament, Opposition member Edmund Burke accused the king's ministry of creating "this unhappy situation . . . by a succession of acts of tyranny." He listed a few of the rebels' grievances and concluded, "This it is that has *burnt* the noble city of New-York; that has planted the bayonet . . . in the bosom of the city, where alone your wretched Government once boasted the only friends she could number in America." According to the minority party in Parliament, British policy had so alienated Americans that the ministry had no one but themselves to blame for the destruction of New York City.[7]

General Howe was focused on expunging George Washington from northern Manhattan, so it fell to General James Robertson to ensure the city's safety. Two days after the fire, on September 23, he issued a proclamation: first, the circumstances of the fire "afford too fatal a Proof of an Intention to destroy this City." Robertson was concerned that the rebels would finish the job: "To prevent the Execution of such a hellish Design," he imposed an 8 p.m. curfew and required an updated census of every household, including people who returned to the city in the future. He declared, "Every Householder is to be answerable for the Conduct of the Persons in his House." Anyone who refused to comply "will be considered as bad Subjects and bad Citizens." Governor Tryon enthusiastically reported that he and Robertson were pursuing "every measure . . . to establish such regulations and police as may ensure its future security." A week later, Mackenzie wrote that the commandant had detailed more than 250 men to guard the city, anticipating "that some Villains may be employed by the Enemy to burn the remainder of New York."[8]

Robertson had to decide whether to make examples of more incendiaries. Thus far, the British had only pursued the rough and sloppy justice of summary executions, but they had also taken prisoners. Initially, there were perhaps fewer than twenty, but soon there were many more, Colonel Carl von Donop wrote, "who were suspected of complicity in the wicked business." By September 24, at least a hundred people were "confined upon Suspicion," some for having helped to set fires, the rest for otherwise "aiding in the Rebellion." Charles Stedman recalled "between one and two hundred men and old women" being imprisoned for setting the fire. There was no way to know the number of incendiaries, but the British worried that they were legion. A rebel newspaper claimed, "Many hundreds of innocent persons . . . were taken up and confined . . . on suspicions, arising from the side they had taken in the present struggle, or imputations of unfriendly tory neighbors." The fire seems to have prompted Howe and Robertson to round up anyone with questionable loyalties.[9]

General Howe sent Major Stephen Payne Adye, the deputy judge advocate general, to "consult" with General Robertson a few days after the fire about "proper measures for discovering the persons who set fire to the City." Adye and Robertson now had to decide on the best means to fulfill their duty. Their fellow officers and the city's remaining inhabitants were outraged about the fire. The soldiers had already killed a few people on the spot, and their officers might still have to account for those killings. Adye and Robertson must have suspected that the public would be ambivalent about the soldiers' violent acts, which may have led the two men to be cautious about pursuing further justice.[10]

The British had rounded up hundreds of people under chaotic circumstances. An English newspaper floated a rumor "that about 100 of the incendiaries were taken, and reserved for some exemplary punishment," but the example never materialized. Adye and Robertson could have tried the suspects in military courts, but they also knew that the Howes wanted to restore North America to imperial control, and that this would require them to cultivate popular allegiance. The British would have to be careful, therefore, about sentencing the accused incendiaries too hastily and harshly.[11]

The imprisoned suspects could barely breathe in the Provost's twelve cells and three basement vaults (fig. 10.1). Adye remembered fewer people, "about forty in Number," which may indicate that more than a hundred suspects had already been released by the time he began his interviews. The tavern keeper David Grim later recalled that after "several of

PROVOST, OR NEW JAIL, NOW HALL OF RECORDS, PARK, N.

Fig. 10.1. William Cunningham, provost marshal, observed the fire from the top of this building. The British examined accused incendiaries there and imprisoned some, including Amos Fellows and Abraham Van Dyck. "Provost, or New Jail, now Hall of Records, Park, N.," *Frank Leslie's New York Journal,* new ser., 4, no. 2 (Aug. 1856): 105, Emmet Collection, Miriam and Ira D. Wallach Division of Art, Prints, and Photographs, New York Public Library.

the citizens were sent to the provost guard, for examination, some of them remained there two or three days, until they could give satisfactory evidence of their loyalty."[12]

The Reverend Benjamin Moore remembered that one Whaley, the sexton of Trinity Church, was not suspected of taking part in the destruction, but he was still arrested on the twenty-first for his general disloyalty to the Crown and then "released" on account of "his general good Character." (Moore had been unsettled when he found the church's rear door open and unlocked during the fire, and he believed the fire was deliberate.) The Reverend Shewkirk wrote that even though one of his parishioners ("our old Conrad") was "taken up on Suspicion to have had a hand in the fire . . . or else to have been aiding in the Rebellion," the British quickly discharged most of the prisoners.[13]

Alderman William Waddell had caught the baker Samuel Charlotte with a "large fire ladder made use of at the fire" that he had "taken away & secreted in a narrow Street leading from John Street." Waddell had Charlotte "committed to the Provost" and offered him "a reward of 50 Guineas & his Majesty's Pardon" if "he would discover what he knew respecting the fire." Charlotte was initially willing, but when Waddell examined him further, Charlotte "said he knew nothing about the matter" and "declared he carried the ladder alone," even after Waddell pointed out that the ladder required six to eight men to lift it. Waddell never knew "what became of this Man Charlotte" or "whether he was ever brought to trial."[14]

The prisoners' caretaker was the notoriously brutal provost marshal William Cunningham. "They were of various descriptions," Cunningham recalled, "& many of them dres'd like Seamen." By September 25, Strachey believed that the alleged incendiaries "are now in a course of Trial, by which it is hoped the Contrivers will be discovered—though They may at present be out of our Reach." The next day, a memorandum went out from headquarters: "All Persons who can give any information of the incendiary's who set New York on fire are to wait upon Gen[l]. Robertson early tomorrow Morn[g]. for that purpose." Three men led the investigation: Adye, Robertson, and Robertson's aide-de-camp, Major James Wemyss.[15]

Adye, by himself and with Robertson, spent several days querying the guards and other soldiers from the regiments "who were present at the fire." Then he visited the Provost jail, accompanied by those soldiers, to examine the prisoners. They were "paraded in the Room," and as soldiers pointed out suspects, Adye pulled them aside for further questioning. Yet the prisoners had already found a way to confound these witnesses: according to Captain Andrew Snape Hamond of the *Roebuck,* "by changing cloathes with each other, They were so altered that the next day their accusers did not know them, and the greatest part escaped punishment for want of Evidence." Claiming mistaken identity was a classic tactic for criminal defendants, which was useful in a scenario where the soldiers did not know the American colonists.[16]

The goal of Adye's inquiry, like most eighteenth-century examinations of this type, was to extract confessions. Captain Francis, Lord Rawdon previously stated that some of the captured incendiaries had already confessed to having been "left in the town" for the "purpose" of setting it on fire. If so, they did not share these confessions with Adye. Instead, "They all denied their being any way concerned in it," as Cunningham recalled. The prisoners who had been caught with combustible materials claimed "they were removing them from the places where they lived" and trying to keep their own homes out of danger.[17]

It was like the unloading of smuggled goods or the *Gaspée* riot or the Boston Tea Party all over again: another overt crime with covert perpetrators. The incendiaries had disposed of their neighbors' property as they saw fit. Now, as a community, they stood together: the prisoners refused to inform on whoever had done the deed. From British authorities' perspective, these were outrageous acts of treason. Adye must have thought that the city seemed devoid of reliable witnesses, just as the whole continent seemed devoid of reliable subjects.[18]

Some of the accused may have stood before a formal court-martial. On September 27, General Howe ordered Lieutenant Colonel John Gunning of the 43rd Regiment to hold a court-martial three days later to decide the fate of several prisoners in the custody of the British army. British soldiers stood accused of various crimes during the campaign around New York harbor; these soldiers and other retainers to the army faced charges of rape, housebreaking, desertion, plunder, and horse theft.[19]

No evidence indicates that any British soldiers were tried for arson. The investigating committee of 1783 asked Adye whether the evidence pointed to the British troops setting the city on fire, either accidentally or on purpose. Adye answered cautiously but decisively: "As far as his recollection of a transaction of seven years standing will carry him there was no appearance in the course of that trial, that the British Troops were concerned directly or indirectly in setting fire to the City." Furthermore,

Adye thought the whole idea defied logic: "Nor did it seem probable to him . . . that those who were to seek shelter in that City the ensuing winter should be concerned in setting it on fire." Still, the question had come up: "There was a particular scrutiny at the trial to discover whether this event had taken place from motives of plunder, on the part of the British Troop, but nothing of that kind appeared." Over the years, Adye had meted out justice to hundreds of disobedient men in uniform: his *Treatise on Courts Martial* called them "miserable wretches" who were "frequently guilty of crimes that bring disgrace upon the profession." So while he had no illusions about British soldiers' discipline and behavior, he also had no reason to think that any redcoats had burned the city on September 21 out of malice.[20]

If not a court-martial, the British apparently held some other court of inquiry. Adye recalled two of the defendants: "one a grey-headed old Scotch Man" (probably the old "North Briton" that other witnesses had seen captured at Oswego Market) and "the other apparently a foreigner." Before the inquest, Adye had examined them individually and together and offered them pardons if they would tell him about the plot to burn the city and the identities of the plotters; Adye recalled "there was reason to suppose" such a conspiracy "had been formed." Both of the accused men said they were innocent and knew of no such "combination." Even with a full pardon dangling before them, no one was talking. Either they were innocent, or they felt confident they could evade punishment, or they preferred to face justice (perhaps a hanging) without naming accomplices. If they were gambling on an acquittal, they bet right. "The witnesses widely differed with respect to the identity" of the prisoners, and "these Prisoners were afterwards released from the Provost."[21]

For most of the suspects, the trials ended swiftly. They all denied any involvement, and there was not enough evidence for a conviction, least of all a capital conviction. Mayor Allen remembered the "Tories" howling for vengeance, but many civilians might have been inclined to show mercy to defendants whose guilt was uncertain. Absent a confession and written evidence, as in Nathan Hale's case, it was tricky to distinguish soldiers, spies, and civilians. Even people caught with incendiary materials might have been carrying them away for safety.

Howe and Robertson both believed that the rebels had set the city on fire, but they could not start sentencing British subjects (however dis-affected) to hang, based on shaky evidence, without alienating the pop-ulation of New York, whom they were now charged with governing. As a result, Cunningham recalled, "all but a few . . . were dismiss'd," with no more than six prisoners remaining. Cunningham drew up a list of them, but his papers were lost aboard the HMS *Swan* on its way to Georgia, in January 1780.[22]

The British army's lenient treatment of these prisoners baffled Loy-alist civilians. In February 1778, one wrote, "Not one Example has been yet made of two hundred, confined for burning this City. And I have reason to presume that most of them are now released." The merchant William Bayard complained around the same time that "one Who had the Greatest hand In the Destruction of this City" was "Paradding thro this Town," proclaiming himself a Loyalist. Rebel newspapers and pa-triotic historians smugly concluded, therefore, that the British could not prove an act of deliberate incendiarism. Justice Thomas Jones later tried to explain: "In the hurry, no affidavits could be taken or even memoran-dums made," so it was impossible to bring charges.[23]

Evidence from these trials does not survive, apart from Adye's own recollection: "It appeared to him from the whole course of the testimony, that many of the houses were purposely set on fire, as it was proved that the fire broke out in parts of the City very distant from each other nearly at the same time." Since Adye was certain the British troops were not responsible, he concluded that rebel sympathizers had set the fire.[24]

Robertson decided, regardless, that the summary executions on September 21 had been enough to make an example. Rather than pro-long imperfect trials amid a climate of mistrust and doubt, he appar-ently concluded that the destroyers of New York had received as much punishment—aside from further imprisonment—as he could realisti-cally secure. Most of the civilian prisoners apparently went free, and the army and townspeople resolved to be more vigilant about fires in the future. Robertson's reasons are a mystery because the British army never made the trial records public: "The opinion & proceedings of the Court were forwarded in the usual manner to the Commander in Chief," Adye remembered, yet "the opinion of that Court was never made known to

the Army nor their proceedings returned as is the custom to the Judge
Advocates Office." Furthermore, aside from the Scotsman and the "foreigner," none of the other fire suspects "were ever brought to trial." The
lack of successful prosecutions would seem to exonerate the suspects;
one could argue that the British made a deadly rush to judgment followed by a sheepish decision not to pursue the matter further. Yet this
is reading backward from the muddled outcome. While arson has always been a difficult crime to prove, the on-scene reports (and subsequent detailed recollections) about the alleged perpetrators cannot be
wholly dismissed.[25]

An unknown number of suspects languished in jail for months
and years. None of these alleged incendiaries faced criminal trials, since
civilian courts were suspended. Instead the British apparently identified
the remaining fire starters as rebel soldiers and officers, who could potentially be exchanged for British captives. The British army exercised a
great deal of latitude in its treatment of military prisoners; the British
were constrained only by the possibility of retaliation and the dictates
of humanity. On November 20, Captain Mackenzie worried about captive rebel officers walking around on parole, since "it is perfectly easy for
them to set fire to the remainder of the town; and as we know they would
not scruple to commit an act of that nature." Having identified Captain
Abraham Van Dyck of New York and Captain Amos Fellows of Connecticut as officers and incendiaries, Howe and Robertson kept them
confined.[26]

The British may also have imprisoned some enlisted men whom
they suspected of setting the fire; as bad as prison conditions were for
rebel officers, they were even worse for rank-and-file soldiers. An officer
of Van Dyck's regiment reported in January 1777 that "the privates who
were prisoners in the city of New-York were uniformly treated with
great inhumanity; that they were kept in a starving condition, without
fuel or the common necessaries of life"; from illness and "hard usage," he
had heard that their mortality rate since the Battle of Long Island was a
woeful 50 percent. Another of Van Dyck's fellow officers described the
prisoners' bodies being "thrown into a hole promiscuously together"
without funeral rites. Since these soldiers were so often "releas'd from

their miserable confinement by Death," their names might not appear in the historical record. Some of the accused incendiaries may have died in prison without ever standing trial, their names lost to history.[27]

Stephen Allen's ancient memory of vengeful "invaders" may have sounded patriotic to his own ears in 1825, but he also remembered that White's body was taken down after "several days and until putrefaction had commenced . . . by an order from the Commander-in-Chief." Although local Loyalists continued to mutter darkly about executing anyone else who might try to burn the city, the British garrison did not hang anyone else for the Great Fire, at least not in New York. There would be no more corpses on display.[28]

It is unclear why Howe never publicized the court's findings and why he held on to the trial records instead of returning them to the judge advocate general's office. Had Howe followed protocol, historians could have read the court proceedings in the British National Archives. Instead Howe either discarded the records or filed them with his private papers, which would have burned with the rest of the library at Westport House, Ireland, in 1826.[29]

Perhaps the trial did implicate rebel sympathizers, but Howe, as peace commissioner, did not want to heighten tensions among Americans. Henry Strachey, who was secretary for the Howe brothers' peace commission, wrote in the aftermath of the fire, "The Infatuation is inscrutable. I have read somewhere, and I begin to think it possible, that a whole Country as well as an Individual may be struck with Lunacy." Although the fire revealed the "very diabolical Cast" of the American people, the Howes seemed disinclined to mete out harsh punishments for a people who were not in their right mind.[30]

The trial records may have indicated, contrary to Adye's recollection, that British soldiers or sailors had set New York aflame. While we have no reason to believe this, such evidence might have motivated Howe to bury the records. The depositions would also have publicized the summary executions committed by British soldiers and sailors on the scene. These killings may have been legitimate under Vattel's laws of war, but they might not withstand scrutiny in the court of public opinion. One English newspaper fulminated "that the soldiers (contrary to the General's positive orders) were guilty of a piece of great barbarity," for throwing the incendiaries into the flames, and another thought it was "rash" to execute people without trial.[31]

Finally, Howe had a war to wage, and he could not get bogged down in a politically controversial prosecution using the muddled evidence before him. Besides, the fire had occurred on his watch. He had not prevented it. His best option was to control the narrative of the fire in his official correspondence. After that, he moved on, in pursuit of Washington.

The Howes' apparent decision also accorded with their approach to war and peace. After the British occupation and the fire, the first newspaper to appear in New York City published two proclamations the Howes made on July 14 and September 19. They offered pardons to anyone who promoted the restoration of government and even hinted that the king might reconsider colonial grievances. Would Americans prefer to "offer up their Lives as a Sacrifice to the unjust and precarious Cause" of the rebels, or "accept the Blessings of Peace, and be secured in a free Enjoyment of their *Liberty* and *Properties*"? Hundreds of Loyalists did declare their allegiance, welcomed the Howes, and praised their "well known Humanity" and "tender Regard . . . for the Welfare of America." The Howes may have hoped that New York City had become a beacon of loyalty.[32]

In another proclamation of November 30, authored by Strachey, the Howes declared that anyone taking an oath of loyalty before a British official could "obtain a full and free Pardon of all Treasons and Misprisions of Treasons, by him heretofore committed or done," echoing their previous offers. With such generous terms of clemency, the Howes revealed their goals: "that Peace may be restored, a speedy Remission of past Offences quiet the Apprehensions of the Guilty, and all the Inhabitants of the said Colonies be enabled to reap the Benefit of His Majesty's paternal Goodness" in the retention of their property, commerce, and rights. During the fall of 1776, the Howes were inclined to show mercy, even toward traitors. Their decision turned out to be unpopular, because it did little to induce defections but still alienated Americans who had demonstrated their loyalty to the Crown from the outset.[33]

The proclamations also show that the Howes were willing to bend

over backward to make New York the headquarters of peace and reconciliation. Prosecuting the war on the battlefield was considered honorable, however grim, but executing suspects worked against the goal of
reconciling the colonies. The Howes believed that their overwhelming
victories, a magnanimous disposition, and the resurrected wisdom of
the American people would cure the infatuation and restore the colonies to their allegiance. They didn't grasp the powerful effect of property
destruction on public opinion, so they failed to use the Great Fire to
rally Americans against the rebellion.

In 1776, the rebels were losing most of the battles, but not the war
of words. One of Philadelphia's rebel newspapers boasted about the accused incendiaries: "No evidence could be met with against any of them,
and they were dismissed." The rebels, meanwhile, blamed the Great Fire
on drunken British seamen, focused on the careless murder of Wright
White, and marveled at the power of the wind. In this way, the Great
Fire became an ambiguous accident.[34]

The Story of the Fire Takes Shape

T he fire briefly lifted the rebels' morale, taking the sting out of the loss of New York. In the early morning of September 21, 1776, Major John Lamb of the Continental Army was standing on the quarterdeck of a British transport; he was about to be paroled to New Jersey. As his native city burned, he rubbed his hands and called it "a glorious sight!" When the ship's captain wondered at Lamb's reaction, he replied, "Let the whole perish rather than the city should afford quarters to the enemy."[1]

Many rebels shared Lamb's jubilation. Cheers sounded from the Continental Army encampments up and down the Hudson Valley. In the English Neighborhood (now Englewood Cliffs), New Jersey, the army camp "exulted on the News of the Conflagration." Dr. Peter Tappen at Fort Montgomery called it "joyfull news." When word reached Crown Point, Lieutenant Colonel Thomas Hartley wrote, "I hope we shall have intelligence that the rest of that nest of Tories, and sink of *American* villany, has shared the same fate. That cursed town from first to last has been ruinous to the common cause."[2]

Amid the celebration, it was tough to get reliable intelligence. Aboard British prison ships in the harbor, even after seeing the sky lit up at 1 a.m., the men could not believe the city was on fire. From Kingsbridge, Colonel Isaac Nicoll initially assumed the fire was in Harlem. In

New Brunswick, New Jersey, Colonel Samuel Patterson was "without doubt" that the British had burned the city, "although some, not with us, want to say we did it—absurd." Rumors took flight: Dr. Tappen heard that a French fleet was anchored near Sandy Hook, New Jersey, which had spooked the British into burning the city. From Harlem Heights, General Gold Selleck Silliman of Connecticut heard that "it must be the regulars who fired it, and why they should do it I can't conceive," unless they were withdrawing. These rebel officers knew that the British intended to occupy New York City and use it as a base: strategically, it made no sense for the king's men to burn the city unless they were leaving in a hurry.[3]

The chaplain Benjamin Trumbull and the New York general George Clinton noted that the city "took fire in various Places" or "broke out in sundry Places at the same Time," and other rebel officers understood right away that this was their comrades' work: from Harlem, Fithian awoke at 3 a.m. and saw the blaze: "Many suppose it must be New-York set on Fire by some of our zealous Whiggs." Colonel Loammi Baldwin of Massachusetts was at Stratford, Connecticut, when he heard that the fire had broken out in twelve or fifteen places at once. He concluded that the incendiaries had strategically waited for the British to settle in garrison before enacting rebel military "Pollicy" by burning the city. He also wrote (though his wording was ambiguous) that the rebels would have burned the whole city, but they ran out of time.[4]

A few days later, militia lieutenant Benjamin Bogardus wrote, "New york is 1/3 of it burnt Down, it is said by our own people." On the prison ships, the rebels heard that the fire was "supposed to have been started by our people who remained," though Lieutenant Jabez Fitch later called these "false & Futile Representations" by the British. Still, according to one of General James Robertson's informants (a "man of credibility"), the Connecticut general Samuel Holden Parsons said "that it was ridiculous to deny that the City of New York was set on fire" by the rebels, "as it was a matter of general notoriety." Israel Evans, a Continental Army chaplain from Chester County, Pennsylvania, later told the Loyalist William Smith Jr. that most people in the Continental Army camp were "pleased" with the fire and attributed it to rebels "fired with an enthusiastic Resentment."[5]

Robert Ogden, a rebel leader in Elizabethtown, New Jersey, did not know whether the executions of incendiaries were "just or unjust," and concluded, "The great day will decide." Trumbull was more certain that "evil minded Persons left in the City" had set the fire; "6 or Seven it is said have been put to Death for it." General Silliman initially assumed that British soldiers had burned the city but changed his mind a few days later: "I believe it was not the regulars, but some of our own people in the city that set it on fire, for they executed several of our friends there for it the next day."[6]

Here was a paradox for the rebels: could "evil minded Persons" have been "our own people"? One way to resolve the dilemma was to shape Americans' emotional response to the news. Up in Albany, Ensign John Lansing (General Philip Schuyler's secretary) heard a false report from Kingsbridge that General William Howe had ordered "six persons who were detected in setting Fire to the Town to be hanged." These officers wanted to distract people from their despair over the loss of New York and head off doubts about the wisdom of burning it. Instead of speculating about the fire's origins, they stoked outrage at the British soldiers' treatment of their "friends" in town. The rebels sought to avoid blame for the fire so that they could continue to claim that their side was fighting a more just war.[7]

The rebels' public opinion strategy originated with George Washington and his adjutant general Colonel Joseph Reed, who began putting a plan into action once they received formal intelligence about the Great Fire. Howe's aide-de-camp Captain John Montresor carried a letter through the lines to Harlem Heights under a flag of truce; Washington read it on the evening of the twenty-second. While the letter said nothing about the fire, Howe still charged the Continental Army with two misdeeds. First, he condemned "the ill Treatment" that British officers suffered in New England jails. Second, he enclosed a musket "Ball cut and fixed to the Ends of a Nail," one of several the British had found in the abandoned rebel encampments (fig. 11.1). This type of "mutilated" ammunition was designed to rip untreatable wounds in the bodies of victims, but Howe trusted that Washington was ignorant of "such unwarrantable and malicious practices." Separate from the written letter, Montresor told a few officers about Nathan Hale's last words and execu-

Fig. 11.1. These mutilated bullets were found along with British military buttons at an archaeological site in northern Manhattan; the middle one resembles the type of bullet that General William Howe accused Washington's men of using. From "Framed set of musket balls (23), 1760–1783," lead, iron; overall 1½ × ⅞ inches, Gift of the Washington Headquarters Association, Daughters of the American Revolution, New-York Historical Society, 1947.283a-w. Photography © New-York Historical Society.

tion earlier that day. He also told Colonel Reed two key things about the Great Fire: that the British had caught rebels setting fire to the city, and the British had summarily executed them.[8]

The two opposing commanders now faced a sensitive predicament. Although Howe had supposedly threatened Washington with retaliation if he destroyed New York, neither man actually wanted the American rebellion—a civil war—to succumb to *lex talionis* (the law of retaliation). Both wanted to fight a war of honor that had a chance of peaceful resolution. If their own troops began taking an eye for an eye, then that would mean targeting officers, using brutal tactics, mistreating prisoners, plundering and destroying civilian property, assaulting noncombatants, and desecrating corpses. It would lead to the type of warfare that Europeans and their colonists practiced when fighting indigenous people, but mostly avoided when fighting one another. Already both sides were accusing each other of misconduct, because neither commander had full control of his subordinates or allied civilians. Howe and Washington could only call for civilized warfare, insist on discipline, and make examples of a few offenders. Taking responsibility was a double-edged sword, because the other side could seize upon it as an admission of misdeed and thereby justify an act of revenge. Both sides, therefore, denied any knowledge of their compatriots' atrocities and expressed abhorrence for them.[9]

Washington worried about public opinion. The new United States had several audiences for everything they did: they had to reassure their friends, persuade neutrals and the disaffected, and dispirit the Loyalists. In Great Britain, they wanted the public to condemn Parliament's suppression of the rebellion. The rebels also had to entice European powers to provide manpower, materials, and diplomatic recognition. Rebel leaders had heard the rumors that their own soldiers had planned to burn New York City as soon as the British occupied it. They had seriously considered the option themselves. Now that it had happened, the last thing they wanted was for the public to connect the dots and conclude that the rebels had done exactly what they said they were going to do.[10]

Colonel Reed, at Washington's side, reported news of the fire to his wife on September 22 but claimed that "we are quite at a loss" to know how the fire came about. "There was a resolve in Congress against our injuring it," he wrote; therefore, "we neither set it on fire or made any preparations for the purpose." Reed quickly pointed to Washington's promise to Congress that no damage would be done to the city upon evacuation. He was confident that the Continental Army could successfully escape blame, but he still worried: "I make no doubt it will be charged to us." Reed himself had advocated for the destruction of the city as early as August 4.[11]

Washington saw that Howe was beginning to grumble about the rebels' violations of the laws of war: the rebels were mistreating prisoners and doctoring their ammunition. Had Montresor also made a pointed accusation about the fire? Tench Tilghman, Washington's aide-de-camp, confessed uncertainty about the fire's origins but insisted: "If it was done designedly, it was without the knowledge or Approbation of any commanding officer in this Army, and indeed so much time had elapsed between our quitting the City and the fire, that it can never be

fairly attributed to the Army." Tilghman believed that the rebels' departure from the city provided an alibi. He also specified, "Every man belonging to the Army who remained in or were found near the City were
made close prisoners." Although Tilghman stressed that Washington
would never have disobeyed Congress, he had also previously warned
that other officers might not be "so strictly observant of the preservation
of private property." If anyone were to call them to account, Washington's intimates were ready to blame unscrupulous subordinates.[12]

Washington gave Montresor a letter for Howe, saying that he had
no certain knowledge of the allegations: "The information you have
rec[eive]d concerning the ill treatment of your officers, I would fain
hope, is not generally well founded"; as to the doctored musket ball, this
"was the first of the kind I ever saw or heard of; you may depend the
contrivance is highly abhorred by me, and every measure shall be taken
to prevent so wicked & infamous a practice being adopted in this army."
Washington promised "every exercise of humanity" possible. He knew
his honor was at stake. Perhaps he was grateful that he did not have to
answer for the cause of the Great Fire or call Howe to account for the
executions of the alleged incendiaries. The two generals set these issues
aside, at least in their surviving correspondence with each other.[13]

Washington did discuss the Great Fire with other rebel leaders. He
was tense, and terse. First, he reported to Congress that the fire had
begun around 11 p.m. or midnight near St. Paul's Church and "continued
to burn pretty rapidly." Like Reed, he wrote, "I have not been Informed
how the Accident happened, nor received any certain account of the
damage." How could any rebel be sure of accounts by the British soldiers,
sailors, and Loyalists who were on the scene? The rebels urged their followers to distrust their enemies' accounts as prejudicial.[14]

In a longer letter to Governor Jonathan Trumbull of Connecticut,
Washington repeated, "By what means it happened we do not know; but
. . . [Montresor] informed Colo. Reed that several of our Countrymen
had been punished with various deaths on account of it. Some by hanging, others by burning & c. alledging that they were apprehended when
committing the fact." Montresor had *alleged* that Americans had been
burning New York City, but the British had *in fact* executed them regardless of their guilt. As to the cause of the fire, Washington claimed he

had no information. Whether he was sincere or not, by emphasizing the summary executions in his letters to Continental and state officials, he took a dangerous accusation and turned it around on the British: they had killed several Americans based on mere suspicion.[15]

Washington was drawing a diagram for Congress and Governor Trumbull, showing them which parts of the story to emphasize. Continental leaders had to secure public approval if the republic were to survive. Faced with the widespread belief that he had ordered rebels to burn the city, Washington needed to protect his reputation, the army's reputation, and the reputation of the new nation. He may well have anticipated that the burning of New York would be politically unpopular and call the efficacy and ethics of the rebel movement into question. He and his allies would need to tell a story that better suited popular ideals.[16]

Tilghman knew what to do. "Many Acts of barbarous cruelty were committed upon poor creatures who were perhaps flying from the flames," he wrote his father. The British soldiers and sailors presumed the guilt of any civilian they came across, "and burnt and cut to pieces many." Eager to absolve Washington from guilt for the fire, Tilghman also gave the enemy's officers the benefit of the doubt: "This I am sure was not by Order." If Montresor described his fellow officers' rescuing some of the perpetrators, then Tilghman may have taken a fellow gentleman at his word. Still, Tilghman also offered the much more vivid details about the soldiers' indiscriminate cruelty. It is also not clear what he meant when he concluded, "Some were executed the next day upon good Grounds."[17]

The British undoubtedly threw alleged incendiaries into the flames and hanged at least one person by his heels. Continental officers and their allies took advantage of the unclear information from New York and invented new aspects to the story. Some, like Dr. Tappen, accused the British of burning the city, but the British felt they could easily refute this. General Hugh, Earl Percy, was relieved that the king's men had caught rebel perpetrators because it would exonerate the British soldiers: "Luckily sever[al] of the Person[s] employed for this diabolical Purpose, were caught in the very fact, otherwise I have no doubt but they [the rebels] coud have laid it upon us; for they never scruple telling an Untruth if it can serve their Cause."[18]

Percy turned out to be both too optimistic and exactly right: the

rebels were quick to lie about the fire. The day after Percy wrote his letter, Lieutenant John Richardson of Chester County, Pennsylvania, wrote
that he had heard about the fire from British deserters who said (falsely)
that most of the city was burned and (uncertainly) that it was "supos'd to
be done by our people," that is, the rebels. Then he reported intelligence
that supposedly came through Montresor and General Israel Putnam:
"During the fire the[y] Caught a Number of our people who they had
prisoners & threw them into the Flames & if they met an American
coming out of a house they imediately Cut his throat & several others
they tyed up by the Heels & cut them from ear to Ear." After mentioning
the hanging of Nathan Hale, Richardson wrote that the British "have
murdered a great many Women likewise & have taken up allmost eviry
person in [New] York & intend to Execute a great Numbr." He blamed
the Hessians: they "have plundred eviry One without Distinction or
regard to Whig & Tory." This was the fully caricaturized version of the
rumors from Washington's camp: throat slitting, upside-down hangings,
murdered women, mass executions, and the indiscriminate plunder of
civilians.[19]

John Sloss Hobart was not quite as lurid. Hobart represented Suffolk County in the New York Provincial Convention, but he had grown
up as the son of a minister in Fairfield, Connecticut, listening to his father's arguments that the Church of England was tyrannical, arbitrary,
a threat to Congregationalism, and productive of "open Irreligion and
undisguised Prophaneness." The younger Hobart reported to the convention on September 25 that he had seen Washington the previous evening. He described the extent of the fire's damage and advanced a theory:
"The most rational conjecture we can make for the cause of the fire, is,
that the [British] army, having been promised the plunder of the town
in case of conquest, and finding from their late repulse [the Battle of
Harlem Heights] that such an event is rather too far distant for their
impatience, have set fire to the town in order to facilitate their views." By
Hobart's reckoning, disobedient soldiers—*on the British side*—had set
the fire. "General Howe disclaims any knowledge of the matter until the
city was in flames, and in order to evince his sincerity, we are told he
threw several persons suspected of being concerned into the flames; several others were hanging up by the heels and afterwards had their throats

cut, this we suppose has been done in order to take the odium of such a crime from the [British] army."[20]

Hobart was alleging something flagrant and outrageous, especially because he himself had been dispatched by the Provincial Convention to oversee scorched-earth tactics on Long Island (and was simultaneously concealing the fact that so many Long Islanders were eagerly joining the British). Where Richardson mentioned the possibility of a rebel act and then buried an uncertain allegation among a series of British crimes, Hobart aggressively recast the fire as a British "crime," which the British general had then blamed on the rebels to cover for his own men. The British had not only meted out a gruesome execution to Wright White but also cut the throats of other alleged perpetrators as their bodies swung. Howe's denials looked suspicious to Hobart, even though Washington himself also denied any knowledge. Hobart was playing to the prejudices of his colleagues and their animus against British forces, giving them tools of public opinion that they could propagate to the broader population.[21]

Three days later, Colonel Jedediah Huntington of Norwich, Connecticut, reported a similar rumor to his father: "About one Third of the City of N York was consumed with Fire. unheard of Barbarities were committed by the Kings Troops at that Time upon any of the Citizens who came in their Way. some it is said were thrown into the Flames others tyed up by the Legs & their Throats cut, this they pretend is necessary to deter others from firing Houses, as they suppose the Citizens set Fire to the City." On the same day, Colonel Baldwin, who had arrived at Fort Constitution (later Fort Lee), New Jersey, amended his earlier report: "We are Ignorant how the fire took in the City . . . but the Enemy hung 4 or 5 persons up by the heals and Cut their throats at a Venture or Suspision they were the Cause." Although Huntington and Baldwin did not accuse British soldiers of setting the fire, they stressed the summary executions that their enemies had committed.[22]

Members of Congress received similar reports. William Hooper, a Boston-born delegate from North Carolina, wrote, "To what accident it is to be ascribed I know not." He tentatively advanced a theory about possible culprits: "It is reported, I know not with what truth, that Howe who is obliged now and then to condescend to humour the Hessians gave them one day to rejoice & riot & that in the heat of their festivity they made a Bonfire of the City. So says Rumour." Hooper also noted, "Others with less probability ascribe it to our forces who were 9 Miles distant from it at the time." Like Tilghman, Hooper believed that the Continental Army's distance from New York City absolved it of responsibility. Hooper preferred to spread the devilish tale about the riotous Hessians or at least call the fire an unknowable accident. In another letter, he wrote, "Some accounts attribute this Calamity to Genl Howe's orders while others with greater probability ascribe it to accident or the ungovernable Brutality to those Men monsters the Hessians," but he also conceded, "General Howe in full possession surely would not be mad enough to burn his house over his own head." New York's congressional delegates, meanwhile, were ambiguous about who had done it: "Brookland on Long Island is Burnt as well as the City of N. York Without doubt on purpose."[23]

The rebels hatched a two-step plan to deflect blame for incendiarism: first, as a British naval officer wrote, "they would not put it in execution until our troops were in possession," and then they "would swear to their sc[oundre]l friends in England, that we burnt the town." Like Percy, this writer knew the rebels would lie about the fire—just as they had lied about the burning of Norfolk. Ironically, Hooper and his colleague were simultaneously writing to North Carolina's Council of Safety with Congress's viewpoint so that "you may not be alarmed with false rumors" and they could counteract "the misrepresentations of wicked men who are . . . striving to dispirit the good friends of America by falsehood and exaggeration." The rebel leadership understood the importance of boosting the morale of the nascent United States. They dismissed tales that reflected poorly on Congress and Washington as false rumors and wicked misrepresentations.[24]

The rebels didn't necessarily have a unified strategy of propagating disinformation, but they didn't need one. They merely had to make space for questionable information. They had already disrupted British communication networks by destroying unfriendly pamphlets and even printing presses; they had also run several unfriendly printers out of town. They tried to ensure that good news would lift their allies' morale and dampen the Loyalists' while distracting the public from bad news.

After the fire, Dr. Tappen boasted, "No doubt it will have a glorious Effect upon the tories, the worst Enemies. They were Exceedingly Rejoyced at the news of our army Evacuating the town," but the fire had now blackened the Loyalists' triumph. Looked at the right way, the Great Fire could show Americans that the British government could not secure its victories or protect its allies.[25]

The Loyalists also clutched at favorable news because public opinion still seemed to be within their grasp. The Reverend Robert Boucher Nicholls believed that the British army's "late success . . . will dispirit the rebel forces." The rebel army was "sickly, disunited, thinned by desertions, and in want of many articles," so he hoped that a British victory, though difficult, was possible. The Declaration of Independence, the rebels' refusal to negotiate with the Howes, "as well as the wickedly setting fire to this Town, shew that we have much obstinacy and malice yet to deal with."[26]

The Loyalists tried to use the Great Fire to mobilize public opinion. The Reverend O'Beirne published his sermon a few weeks after the fire; he noted the irony of rebel incendiaries who "came to rescue you from Tyranny and Oppression, armed with Firebrands." General James Grant wrote, "The Yorkers are Convinced that the New England Men sett Fire to the Town," and "they will never forgive them." He added, "We may expect more good from their hatred to the Yankees, than from their Affection to us, in which I have no Confidence." An Edinburgh newspaper shared another officer's outrage: "As we left Boston without burning it, they can have no excuse for their villany. It is by no means the method to gain friends to their cause, but rather serves to show the rancour and malice of their hearts." Other newspapers reported that the fire had pushed neutral New Yorkers into the arms of the British. Crown supporters hoped that Americans would regard the Great Fire as a deliberate, uncivilized act.[27]

Many blamed Washington by name. "General Washington, & the Heads of the Rebels, took great pains in making a publick denial of their being accessary to this disaster," wrote Captain Andrew Snape Hamond, "but nobody believed them: as every circumstance that was discovered tended to prove that there had been people hired for the purpose." A Loyalist wrote that the captured "wretches" carried lit matches and "orders of Washington to execute the Horrid Deed." Lieutenant Loftus Cliffe concluded, "Oh Washington what have you to answer for!"[28]

Captain William Glanville Evelyn, who had once fantasized about the British burning American cities, now wondered, "What will the abettors of the American Rebellion say, when they hear that a few nights after their friends had abandoned New York, the emissaries of General Washington, or those left in town for that purpose, with fanatic rage set it on fire in three places." He added, "*They* may dignify it with the name of heroism and virtue, but to *us* it will ever appear the excess of villainy even in the virtuous Mr. Washington." Comparing Washington's evacuation of New York to Howe's evacuation of Boston, Evelyn decided, "It must strongly mark the different characters of the two nations," as well as their leaders. Evelyn hoped that people would understand who fought more honorably, and whose cause had greater justice, but he never found out: he was mortally wounded at the battle of Pell's Point on October 18.[29]

Hamond and Evelyn imagined public conversation flowing freely through America, between the two warring camps. Although getting good intelligence across enemy lines was difficult, information did slip in and out of occupied New York. Communication by word of mouth—like Montresor talking with Washington's officers—was still vital in the eighteenth century, as were written correspondence and printed news. Messengers, letter writers, and printers shaped public conversation by selecting what items to share (and usually offering a point of view). Ambrose Serle, secretary to Lord Howe, was particularly fascinated by newspapers' power to magnify the shaping of opinion: "One is astonished to see with what Avidity they are sought after, and how implicitly they are believed, by the great Bulk of the People," he wrote. Before the war, New York City was one of the rare places in the colonies where people read different papers; most colonists read only a single paper or confined themselves to one they trusted, if they read the news at all. Once the rebellion began, "The Congress saw the Necessity of securing this Advantage entirely to themselves," Serle wrote, by coordinating political messages and censoring contrary publications. As a result, most of the newspapers that Americans read in parlors and taverns in 1776 were sympathetic to the rebel cause. Readers tended to be more skeptical of sources that did not share their political beliefs. Because friendly newspapers reprinted items from one another and disparaged unfriendly reprints as false, American printers aspired to shape a national and international conversation, not just influence a few hundred local readers. From the Stamp Act crisis to the Boston Massacre to the battles of Lexington and Concord, rebel leaders became experts at painting their allies as innocent, imperial officials as deceivers, and the redcoats as monsters.[30]

In Newark, New Jersey, the New York printer Hugh Gaine was temporarily operating his press among the rebels. He set his type on the twenty-first, in time to report, "About 3 o'clock this morning, a most dreadful fire was discovered from the heights back of this town, which upon the appearance of day light was supposed to be the city of New York in flames."[31]

Four days later, the press still had little information; most newspapers issued only once a week and had not received the news in time. Philadelphia papers had a few dispatches. One, from Harlem, noted that a steeple had gone "missing" from the horizon. Another, from Washington's headquarters, said the fire "consumed all that part of the city near the North-River." A writer from New Brunswick, New Jersey, reported, "Almost all Broadway was burnt on Friday night, how or by whom set on fire is unknown, as we have no particulars. The city was on fire at two different Places." The New Brunswick account hinted at two separate ignitions but left this unclear.[32]

News about the fire kept spreading, changing, and stirring up emotions. On September 28, Gaine had published the first local story of the Great Fire. He noted "many and different reports concerning that melancholy affair, the most authentic of which, we believe is as follows. . . . That the fire originated at or near Whitehall, soon extended to the Exchange," and then followed a linear path up Broad Street and then across Broadway. Though Gaine appeared to use disinterested language, the article stated that the fire had a single origin point, and all other devastation was due to the fire's unchecked transmission from building to building. "The cause of the fire is no[t] known. We imagine about a 6th part of the whole city is destroyed, and many families have lost their All."

His account was reprinted in all four of Philadelphia's rebel newspapers, all four Connecticut papers, at least one Maryland paper, and both Virginia papers.[33]

This rebel account spread from southern New England to the Chesapeake. Crown supporters, now that they controlled an American city, tried to counter with their own version. On September 25, Governor William Tryon prevailed on Serle and the Reverend Charles Inglis "to undertake the management of the Political Part in the News Paper about to be published." Both men fervently supported the British Empire and the Church of England. Inglis had been present at the fire, while Serle had watched from on board the *Eagle*.[34]

Inglis and Serle offered the British perspective in the New York City edition of the *New-York Gazette and the Weekly Mercury* of September 30. "On Saturday the 21st Instant, we had a terrible Fire in this City, which consumed about *One Thousand* Houses, or nearly a *fourth* of the whole City." The article offered "the best Account we can collect of this melancholy Event." The fire, they wrote, began near Whitehall Slip "and was discovered between 12 and 1 o'Clock in the Morning," but "a few Minutes after the Fire was discovered at White Hall, it was observed to break out in five or six other Places, at a considerable Distance." The differences between their account and Gaine's are apparent.[35]

The piece praised General Robertson and Admiral Howe for dispatching men to assist with firefighting and the soldiers and sailors who "greatly exerted themselves, often with the utmost Hazard." Though "held up as our Enemies," they had "gallantly stept forth" and risked their lives to save the city. The writer hoped Americans would recognize their true guardians.

The *Gazette* emphasized how close the city had come to destruction: the town was depopulated, and the water pumps and fire engines were in disarray. The Continental Army had removed the city's bells, making it impossible to sound an effective alarm. The paper noted "the Time and Place of the Fire's breaking out, when the Wind was South," the multiple points of ignition, and "so many Incendiaries being caught in the very Fact of setting Fire to Houses." Such facts "clearly evince beyond the Possibility of Doubt, that this diabolical Affair was the Result of a preconcerted, deliberate Scheme." The article pointedly mentioned the "several Persons" who "were discovered with large Bundles of Matches, dipped in melted Rosin and Brimstone, and attempting to set Fire to the Houses." One was a Continental Army captain from New England with £500 on him. The account concluded, "The Persons who called themselves our Friends and Protectors, were the Perpetrators of this atrocious Deed."

The account made the British army look merciful: the British "secured" the alleged incendiaries, and Robertson personally "rescued two . . . from the enraged Populace, who had otherwise consigned them to the Flames, and reserved them for the Hand of deliberate justice." To everyone present, "it manifestly appeared that the City was designedly set on Fire." In its vivid tale of atrocity, the newspaper seems to have stretched at least one fact: "Several Women and Children perished in the Fire," and though no corroborating evidence exists for this claim (other than the reports of female perpetrators), the author no doubt accurately channeled "their Shrieks, joined to the roaring of the Flames, the Crash of falling Houses, and the wide spread Ruin which every where appeared," which "formed a Scene of Horror great beyond Description."

A week later, the same paper declared, "The savage burning of this City by the New-England Incendiaries, will be a lasting Monument of their inveterate Malice against the Trade and Prosperity of this Colony, as well as their rooted Disaffection to British Law and Government." The paper added further evidence that the rebels had set the fire: "They had long threatened the Performance of this villainous Deed." Pressing the point, the paper mocked the "heedless Credulity" of New York City's property-holding rebels who had earned such a poor "Return" on their investments. At least ten rebel newspapers printed this item: printers probably preferred it to the previous issue's for three reasons: first, it avoided scathing language and offered less evidence, so its accusations seemed more petulant; second, the item limited its accusations to generic "Incendiaries" instead of the Continental Army; and third, it criticized wealthy New Yorkers, which was music to New Englanders' ears.[36]

Two rebel newspapers hinted that the fire might have been deliberate. A correspondent to New Haven's newspaper gave the fire a single point of origin but also wrote, "Opinions are various whether it was accidental or not." (Meanwhile, readers who glanced to their left would see an opinion piece from London criticizing the shameful burning of Falmouth.) A rebel "Gentleman" in Washington's camp wrote to New London, "*We hear that it was seen to take Fire in twelve different Places at nearly the same Time.*" The same issue also printed a false rumor that the British fleet was sailing forth to burn more American seaports. Even in papers that questioned whether the fire was accidental, the British still came off as destructive.[37]

Rebel newspapers discouraged their readers from believing reports that were unfavorable to their side. The *Courant* of Hartford, Connecticut, warned, "Many false accounts of transactions in our armies, are by one means or other, published in gazettes, &c. at a distance, some of which are prejudicial to the common cause." The authors offered a Connecticut chaplain's perspective as a corrective. Then New London's *Gazette* reprinted an unfavorable item from Serle and Inglis's press about rebel casualties. "Our Readers will very much Question the Truth of the above Account." The Reverend Ezra Stiles, too, called Inglis and Serle's paper "a Mixture of Truth & Lies." Years later, a rebel pamphlet criticized Inglis for "the many false and scurrilous pieces you wrote and published." The rebels warned their readers not to trust their enemies' interpretation of events.[38]

To counteract the Crown's edition of the *New-York Gazette*, the rebellion's leaders tried to create versions of the Great Fire that were both more memorable than Gaine's initial report and more advantageous to their cause. Army officers and newspaper printers worked together to spread disinformation. Colonel Henry Jackson of Boston regularly corresponded with his friend Colonel Henry Knox, Washington's chief artillerist. On October 2, Jackson wrote, "I have Publish'd in this day['s] Paper what you desire." That week, Boston's *Independent Chronicle* printed a September 25 letter from a rebel officer at Harlem Heights (perhaps Knox himself) stating that New York City "was purposely fired by some private persons," which, significantly, freed the army from blame. "Since this fire, the enemy have practiced some inhuman cruelties on the unfortunate wretches they have in their power, under pretence of their being concerned in the plot." The city was not under the rebels' control, but the captured incendiaries *were* under British power, and what did they do? "They have hanged numbers by the feet, and then cut their throats!"

Furthermore, General Howe was allowing the Hessians to keep "plundering" the New York area because he was afraid that they would otherwise stage "a general mutiny." Knox and Jackson were offering exaggerations just like Richardson's, Hobart's, and Hooper's.[39]

Jackson was pleased to report that Knox's article had done its job: "The People here are much Alarm'd, about the burning hang'g & Cut'g the Throats of some of our People." The letter from Washington's headquarters acted in concert with other sources of information (or disinformation): "There is Severall Letter's come by the Post that give the same Acct: of the matter—which makes People believe the truth of it." Five Rhode Island and Connecticut newspapers reprinted the *Chronicle* item, two weeks before any New England papers reprinted Serle and Inglis's *New-York Gazette* account blaming the rebels. Any New Englander who relied on newspapers therefore heard about British and Hessian atrocities before hearing any suggestion that the rebels had burned New York.[40]

John Gill's *Continental Journal* in Boston simultaneously printed more letters from the rebels' encampment. "Our friends were immediately suspected," and according to Montresor, "those that were found on or near the spot were pitched into the conflagration: some hanged by the heels and others by their necks, with their throats cut. Inhuman barbarity!" This letter spread to at least eight more New England papers, usually instead of Gaine's more even-keeled account. Then New Englanders shared a more lurid description: "The Hessians are a barbarous savage race of mortals," said this account. "Men, women and children were thrown into the fire the night the city was burnt; women hung up by their heels with their throats and mouths cut from ear to ear." Rebels now rallied around a disinformation campaign that played to their prejudices. America's newspapers were filled with monsters, from slave uprisings to Hessian marauders, and the rebels wanted to make sure all those monsters were enemies of independence. These accounts, therefore, did not cheer the burning of New York, as John Lamb had done; instead they tried to ensure that the true villains of the Great Fire were the British.[41]

As the fight for public opinion raged, Americans had to rely on hearsay and newspapers. The Inglis and Serle newspaper remarked on "the Absurdities and Falsehoods with which the Leaders of the present

Rebellion endeavour to keep up the Spirits and Opposition of their de-luded Followers!" Even John Varick Jr., a rebel medical student, had to admit, "The News is so various, & opposite at Times, that it requires a great Deal of Sagacity to obtain certain Inteligence, as the Stories are told in favour of the Party the Informer most espouses." Varick was intro-spective about what he read, but many other Americans probably took comfort in the rebel-friendly information they received.[42]

Boston newspapers called the vengeful British troops "inhuman," a word that appears in another important account of the Great Fire. The congressional Committee of Secret Correspondence sent an intelligence report on October 1 from Philadelphia. Its members were Benjamin Franklin and the Liverpool-born merchant Robert Morris, and they were writing to Silas Deane, the rebels' secret envoy in Paris. Their let-ter gave the rebels an opportunity to explain the Great Fire to potential French allies. They knew most European news about the war came from the British press, so they worried that General Howe's successes would be inflated and "the conduct of our people . . . will be misrepresented as ten times worse than the reality." They tried to put a good face on the defeat at Long Island and emphasized Washington's escape from Brook-lyn (a "master Stroke") and his small victory at Harlem Heights. They took their cues about the fire from Washington's report: "The Enemy charged some stragglers of our people that happened to be in New York with having set the City on Fire designedly." Franklin and Morris essen-tially admitted that rebel soldiers or officers had been left behind in New York City. After the fire began, the British "exercise[d] some inhuman Crueltys on those poor Wretches that were in their power." Their victims were innocent ("some stragglers," "poor Wretches"), and the British de-served censure for executing blameless victims.[43]

Congress was aware of British suspicions about the Great Fire: "They will no doubt endeavour to throw the odium of such a measure on us, but in this they will fail." Franklin and Morris sounded quite proud of the rebels' ability to evade blame for the fire: they pointed to the corre-spondence between Washington and Hancock while the rebels still held the city ("it was in his power to do as he pleased with it"). They acknowl-edged that many of Washington's officers had advised him to burn the city, "but Congress Resolved that it should be evacuated and left unhurt as they had no doubt of being able to take it back at a future day." In conclusion, "This will convince all the World we had no desire to burn Towns or destroy Citys but that we left such Meritorious works to grace the History of our Enemies." This was the extra twist to the argument: Franklin had railed at the British for destroying towns for more than a year, and he would continue singing this refrain until the end of the war. To maintain the moral high ground, he and Morris worked to silence any suggestion that the rebels had burned New York City and encouraged Deane to draw French attention to British acts of devastation.[44]

A few weeks later, still headquartered in upper Manhattan, Washington wrote the letter to his cousin lamenting that he had obeyed Congress by declining to put New York City to the torch. The British would keep their "warm & comfortable Barracks" for the winter while attacking the Continentals anywhere the Howes might choose. Now it would be "next to impossible for us to dispossess them of it again." Reflecting on his failed defense of New York City, Washington wished he had destroyed it, predicting that Congress would regret its order: "To this end I applied to Congress, but was absolutely forbid." Washington professed to have been clear on this point. Although his surviving correspondence with Congress does not quite rise to the level of his being "absolutely forbid," *after* the fire he had to affirm to his family at Mount Vernon that his orders from Congress had been clear. Private letters like this were often shared and therefore had the power to influence public perceptions of the war.[45]

Washington had been forbidden to burn the city "before I quitted it"; the fire did not occur, as Tilghman wrote, until "time had elapsed" after "our quitting the City," and therefore, they hoped, "it can never be fairly attributed to the Army." Yet in Washington's same letter to his cousin, almost as an afterthought, he wrote, "In speaking of New York, I had forgot to mention that Providence—or some good honest Fellow, has done more for us than we were disposed to do for ourselves, as near One fourth of the City is supposed to be consumed. however enough of it remains to answer their purposes." Washington was annoyed with Congress, but he took some bitter satisfaction from the notion that someone—maybe God himself—also thought it was a good idea to burn New York. Washington could not officially condone the destruction of the city, but he could acknowledge that a "good honest Fellow" had done what was necessary for the Continental cause.[46]

William Smith Jr., a Loyalist New Yorker, had heard from Evans that the rebels were ignoring "all Complaints of the Sufferers" and rationalizing the Great Fire. Since the British might burn the rest of the town anyway, the rebels believed "the Perpetrators" of the Great Fire "deserve little or no Censure." Smith predicted that the rebels "would probably one Day defend & justify" the burning of New York City even as they "magnified" similar acts by British and Hessian troops "as the most atrocious Wickedness." Over in England, some allies of the American Revolution did justify the fire as a scorched-earth tactic and as vengeance for British acts of destruction. The rebel leadership couldn't make such an argument publicly, so they didn't. Instead, Washington and Congress simply denied that rebel sympathizers had burned New York City. They criticized the British army's prior acts of devastation in New England and the brutal violence it committed on the night of September 21. Tilghman, Hooper, Franklin, and Morris vindicated the rebels, since New York City did not catch fire while it was under Washington's control. What happened under a British flag, they argued, was the king's responsibility. They argued that the fire was either a deliberate British act, or the fault of British carelessness, or pure accident. It would be difficult for anyone to prove otherwise.[47]

Meanwhile, the 1776 campaign was going dreadfully for the rebels (fig. 11.2). After its defeats in Canada, Long Island, and Manhattan, the Continental Army retreated all the way through New Jersey. Reports of the soldiers' cowardice at the Battle of Kip's Bay had spread across the continent. By the end of October, triumphant Loyalists were becoming "Imprudent." Serle was optimistic that the Howes' success "has made Impressions of Despondency, too powerful for the Machinations of the Congress to remove." Rebel morale was low, and the inspiring victories at Trenton and Princeton were yet to come. Remarking that "a Shudder went thro' the Continent in Oct. & Nov.," Stiles wrote, "I hope God will uphold the Spirits of the pple & prevent a spirit of Intimidation & Dispair spreading thro' the Land." The rebels focused on Washington's lucky escape from Howe's clutches. They scoffed that the king's slow capture of New York City was insignificant or even ruinous to Britain. Indepen-

Fig. 11.2. This satire depicts Lord North, prime
minister, announcing the success of the British
campaign in New York; America is depicted as
a distraught woman in a liberty cap. "News
from America, or the Patriots in the dumps,"
London Magazine 45 (Nov. 1776): 599, Library
of Congress, Prints and Photographs Division.

dence was still relatively new, and the rebels still had to convince Americans that the cause was viable and honorable. The Great Fire might still
cheapen the rebels' hopes for a moral victory.[48]

The rebels had not entirely avoided blame for the Great Fire. William Bradford's *Pennsylvania Journal* of November 20, 1776, tried to refute Inglis and Serle's *Gazette*, which was "under the direction of Lord

and General Howe." The *Gazette* had raised "Slanderous reports" that the Great Fire "was the clandestine act of the friends of America" and had tried "to impute it to New-England men," but the *Journal* had other ideas. "The probable cause now assigned by all is, that Lord Howe having let his seamen go ashore for a day's frolic, they in their drunken revels, carelessly set an house on fire at the White-Hall slip, and that a high wind easily spread it through a town, void, in a great degree of inhabitants." Although no German regiments were stationed in the city on September 21, the *Journal* also blamed "the inhumanity and licentiousness of the Hessians" for killing Wright White, "a poor tory shipwright." The British imprisoned "innocent persons" and then released them after finding "no evidence." Newspaper publishers still worried about the reputation of the Continental Army and its leadership.[49]

Fithian, Baldwin, Bogardus, and Silliman speculated that their allies had set the fire to spite the British army. They may well have made these claims without any direct knowledge, but there is still value in the judgments they made before newspapers began blanketing America's taverns. Parsons and Evans both said (according to Loyalist sources) that "the Generality" of American rebels believed that their own allies had set the fire. William Smith Jr. also heard from a fellow Loyalist that General Israel Putnam "was heard to exult that the Scheme was effected," and that multiple witnesses could confirm hearing the former legislator Volkert P. Douw say that the New York Provincial Convention had left a thousand men in town with permission to burn the city. Some newspapers also entertained the possibility that the fire had been deliberate.[50]

Perhaps all of this was speculation and hearsay—embers of doubt that were smothered by the subsequent disinformation campaign. These rebels' statements, however, look remarkably different from the accounts that emerged from Washington's headquarters and from Congress, with good reason. The rebel leadership preferred to keep control of public opinion. "So many falsehoods have been propagated," Thomas Jefferson wrote, "that nothing now is beleived unless coming from Congress or camp." People had become "lethargick" from the lack of reliable intelligence. Congress and Washington's inner circle took advantage of public apathy to influence people's perceptions about the Great Fire. Henry Jackson, for instance, had published what Knox desired, while supportive bits of misinformation had encouraged people to believe it as truth. Rebel leaders pointed to Washington's prior correspondence with Congress and his orders not to let his soldiers burn the city before he left it. They reminded readers that Continental forces had departed the city six days before the fire. They suggested an airborne trajectory for the fire's course. They emphasized British atrocities. They managed to dispel the suggestion that the rebels had set the fire.[51]

The Loyalists and the British, meanwhile, insisted—with hardly any dissent—that the rebels had burned New York City. To their frustration, they found that the rebels' savvy manipulation of public opinion drowned out their claims.

The Fates of Three Captains

O utside New York City, the Great Fire had begun to fade from many people's minds. Yet for the accused incendiaries whom the British had imprisoned, the ordeal continued. And in June 1777, another incendiary stepped forward to meet his fate. Their stories reveal more about the fire's origins and some of the forgotten people who fought in the Revolutionary War.

Amos Fellows

The friends of Captain Amos Fellows, imprisoned at City Hall, denied that he had anything to do with the fire. Governor Jonathan Trumbull of Connecticut told Washington that the redcoats imprisoned Fellows on September 15. Jabez Fitch of Norwich, Connecticut, captured at the Battle of Long Island two weeks before, also said Fellows "had been made Prisoner on our Armys Retreat from N. York." Fitch believed that Fellows's close confinement was "under pretence that he had been somehow susspected of having been concerned in the late fire." Trumbull said the same. Had Fellows helped to destroy New York? Prison conditions were so harsh that this was a matter of life and death.[1]

On January 20, 1777, Lieutenant Isaac Fellows went to New York City under a flag of truce to beg for his brother's life. The week before,

Trumbull had written to Washington with some urgency about Amos, who "has suffered much during his Confinment." The governor vouched for this "Man of Interest & Int[e]grity," who "has a Family, & do not think him Culpable in the matter laid to his Charge, or deserving the Treatment he has rec[eive]d." Trumbull actually sounded a little unsure: "At least I think he Ought to be heard." He wanted Washington to nominate Fellows for a prisoner exchange. Washington relayed that request to Joshua Loring, the British army's commissary general of prisoners.[2]

Colonel Stephen Moulton, a paroled captive, told Trumbull that "Capt. Fellows is under particular Circumstances, & treated with uncommon Severity, whereby his Life is in Danger." Trumbull complained that the British had not just treated Fellows with "Inhumanity" but also refused to bring him to trial. It is not clear why the rebels expected a trial, which was not usually granted for prisoners of war or saboteurs. Regardless, the governor denounced the British treatment of all rebel prisoners: he was "extremely Sorry to find our Freinds in Captivity meet with so much Severity, we will not retaliate in that way, but Shew to the World, that American humanity rises Superior to that of our Enemys." A groundswell of such complaints was building in statehouses, the press, and in Congress. The rebels claimed to be much more humane.[3]

Between January 20 and 23, Commissary Loring moved many of the officers imprisoned in the city to the healthier air of house arrest on Long Island. For Fellows, though, it was too late—disease, malnourishment, and harsh treatment had taken their toll. Fitch wrote, "By means of [his] long and uncomfortable Confinement, he contracted such a complication of Disorders, as to End his Days soon after he came out of Prison." Fellows died on February 16, after about five months in captivity. "He was said to have been a man of intellect, and of great decision and firmness of character," Tolland's town historian wrote in 1861. "His death was considered a great loss to the cause, and it was said that had he survived he would have been promoted to a very superior grade." His tombstone joined those of his wife and three small children.[4]

A writer named Theron Brown was born in 1832, about fifteen miles from Tolland. He became a Baptist minister, hymnist, poet, and editor of *Youth's Companion*. He compared the Great Fire of New York to the burning of Moscow in 1812 and argued not only that Americans had burned the city but that it was a "patriotic deed." He wrote that the "bitter and desperate" rebels had satisfied their "passion for military retaliation" after losing New York by practicing "a sort of self-immolation." Unlike most patriots in 1776, Brown argued that Americans' "hatred of the British" justified their attempt to destroy the city. Brown quoted Cicero: "In times of arms, the laws fall silent." He had no patience for the critics who characterized the incendiaries as "little better than the demons of the Paris Commune." He concluded, "Call the act rash, unwise, reckless, if you will; but we may be excused for our inability to see where the shame for it comes in."[5]

Abraham Patten

The British did not catch all the incendiaries on September 21, but they found one eight months later with a story to tell. Abraham Patten was born to a large Scots Irish Presbyterian family that moved him from Pennsylvania to the Catawba River in the Carolinas as a child—the same region where Andrew Jackson grew up. By the late 1750s, Patten was old enough to sign his name to a backcountry Dissenters' petition criticizing the established Anglican church. His father, James, was a storekeeper too mired in debt to pass on any landholdings to his children. Between 1763 and 1768, Abraham Patten worked as a wheelwright and owned about a hundred acres in Sadsbury Township, Pennsylvania. He married Martha Crawford in 1766, and by May 1769 he moved to Baltimore (a town "chiefly settled by Scotch-Irish") and subscribed to a pew at the Presbyterian Church. Over the next five years, he celebrated the baptisms of three newborn daughters. His laborers were miserable: Patten pursued a couple of runaway white servants; one of his men (indentured or enslaved), hired out to Charles Ridgely at his Northampton ironworks, fell ill, ran away, was caught and returned, and cut himself in the throat in May 1774. In January 1775, Patten sold a young Black man named Sam. With the war about to begin, the Scots Irish of Baltimore were "to a man violently bent on supporting . . . the cause of fanaticism and sedition," one Loyalist wrote. Patten's countrymen had developed a reputation for restless mobility, religious dissent, frontier violence, and an antagonistic attitude toward outside authority.[6]

Sometime that year, Patten began marching with the Continental Army. Although his name does not appear in surviving military records, post office notices place him in Cambridge, Massachusetts, in December 1775 and New York in July 1776. He may still have been there in September. Months later, German officers were calling him a "rebel captain" who "passed himself as a merchant." And, sure enough, a Philadelphia newspaper of January 5, 1777, noted an unclaimed letter for "Captain Abraham Patten." While Alexander Graydon (a Pennsylvania rebel) was imprisoned in New York City, he saw Patten "under the disguise of a zealous royalist." Patten may have served (or posed) as a sutler for Edward Hand's Pennsylvania rifle regiment, which had burned Brooklyn and pillaged Westchester during the 1776 campaign.[7]

For at least five months in early 1777, Patten worked in the "provision trade," allowing him to travel between British garrisons at New York City (where Patten "generally resided") and New Brunswick, New Jersey (where he "had lived . . . for some time as a spy"), and Continental Army encampments.[8]

In January, General William Heath reported from Westchester, New York, that "One Patten" had arrived in his camp with a pass signed by Washington's aide-de-camp to enter the city with any mounts he brought with him. Heath didn't know the man and wasn't sure about the signature, so he detained Patten until Washington could give further orders. Heath was nervous because an informant had just given him news "that a man was hang'd in [New] York for being a Spy. . . . & Two others were to be try'd the next day." The British garrison was a dangerous place for rebels caught behind enemy lines.[9]

Patten made it safely to Manhattan. In early April, he was "indiscreet enough to unbosom himself very fully" to Major Otho Holland Williams of Maryland, a prisoner of war who had been paroled to Long Island. Williams was visiting New York City in hopes of being exchanged, and Patten (who may have known him from Baltimore) "gave him much information as to what was passing there." One gets the impression of a man who was restless, ruthless, and reckless.[10]

The British had taken New Brunswick on December 1 and commenced their plunder and destruction. In May 1777, Washington faced them from Morristown, desperate to know where they intended to move next. "On the road," Washington met an informant who had left New York City on May 24. Washington wrote about the meeting on the twenty-seventh: "P——n S[u]tt[le]r to [Edward] H[an]ds Regt," based in the city, indicated "that a successful attack might be made upon the Troops in Brunswick." He also gave Washington details about the seventy British transports getting ready to sail for Philadelphia and told him that at least four British officers and noncommissioned officers were spying on the Continental Army in New Jersey. If the sutler/spy was Patten—which seems likely—then sometime during the next couple of weeks, he hastened to New Brunswick to provide covert assistance for a rebel assault on the British post.[11]

At the New Brunswick encampment, Patten worked to undermine the British occupation by persuading "some [British] Grenadiers, to Desert" to the rebels. According to Hessian sources, Patten made various attempts to get a grenadier from the 49th Regiment to turn his coat, until "finally he believed the grenadier to be his friend and confidant." The *New-York Gazette*, a Loyalist paper (fig. 12.1), went into more detail about the plot: Patten had offered fifty guineas to a British grenadier to carry four letters to generals Washington and Putnam. It would take a British private more than four years to earn that much. Patten was evidently well financed.[12]

According to the German officers, Patten claimed that New Brunswick "was so weakly occupied that it would not take much effort to capture it," which matches what Washington had written. Patten gave details about the position of the camp, pickets, and sentries. On the king's birthday, June 4, he would "set Fire to Brunswick in four Places at once, blow up the Magazine, and then set off a Rocket as a Signal for the Rebels to attack the Town." That signal never came.[13]

Patten gave the letter to his friend the grenadier, who "took the Cash," the newspaper reported. "The grenadier was so conscientious however," wrote Lieutenant Johann Henrich von Bardeleben, that he betrayed the plot and gave the letter either to Brigadier General Alexander Leslie or Lord Cornwallis, who promptly had Patten arrested on June 4.[14]

Patten evidently confessed upon capture; the British, who called him a "Rascal," accused him of spying for Washington and plotting sabotage. On the morning of June 6, the British army reported its orders:

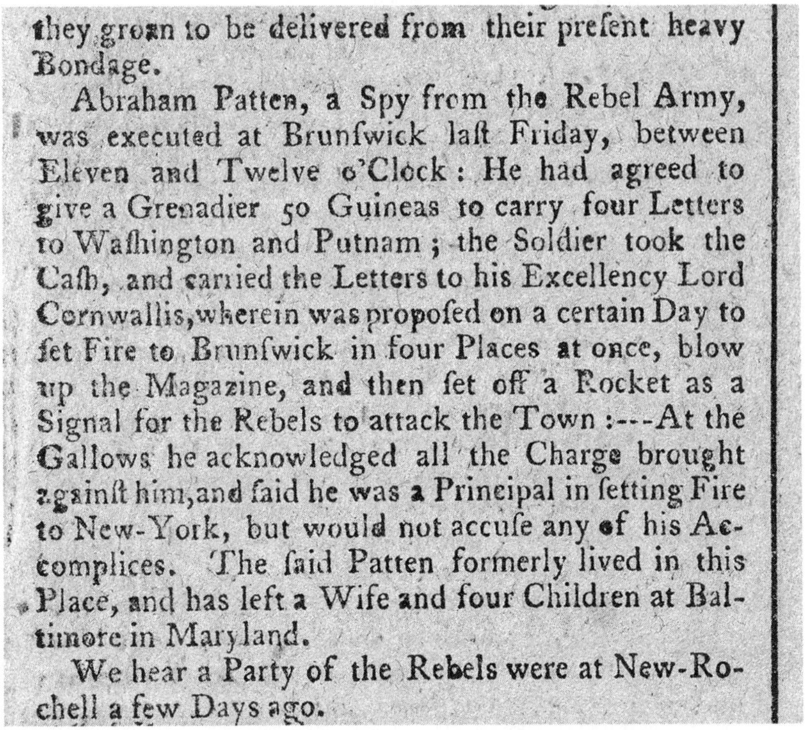

they groan to be delivered from their prefent heavy
Bondage.
　Abraham Patten, a Spy from the Rebel Army,
was executed at Brunfwick laſt Friday, between
Eleven and Twelve o'Clock : He had agreed to
give a Grenadier 50 Guineas to carry four Letters
to Wafhington and Putnam ; the Soldier took the
Caſh, and carried the Letters to his Excellency Lord
Cornwallis, wherein was propofed on a certain Day to
fet Fire to Brunfwick in four Places at once, blow
up the Magazine, and then fet off a Rocket as a
Signal for the Rebels to attack the Town :---At the
Gallows he acknowledged all the Charge brought
againſt him, and faid he was a Principal in fetting Fire
to New-York, but would not accufe any of his Accomplices.　The faid Patten formerly lived in this
Place, and has left a Wife and four Children at Baltimore in Maryland.
　We hear a Party of the Rebels were at New-Ro-
chell a few Days ago.

Fig. 12.1. The newspaper item describing the hanging of Abraham Patten.
New York Gazette and Weekly Mercury, June 9, 1777, p. 3, c. 1,
courtesy of the American Antiquarian Society.

"Abra.[m] Patton being by his own Confession a Spy for the Enemy . . . Will
this Day be Executed at 11 oClock." The men attached a rope to a stout
tree branch near camp.[15]

　"At the Gallows," the *Gazette* reported, "he acknowledged all the
Charge[s] brought against him, and said he was a Principal in setting
Fire to New-York, but would not accuse any of his Accomplices." This
was a stunning admission. Patten had been caught offering bribes, en-
couraging desertion, transmitting intelligence to the rebels, and plotting
fires in conjunction with rebel troop movements—it was unnecessary to
add the excess bit about New York. About to meet his death, Patten had
little reason to lie. He may have been moved of his own accord to give a
full accounting, unless angry soldiers coerced a false "confession" from

him. Legal and religious conventions of the day encouraged condemned men to unburden themselves as a way of redeeming their souls. Soldiers would grant honor to a patriot martyr who died a "good death" with stoicism. Perhaps Patten couldn't resist having one last laugh at the British; they had foiled his plot to detonate New Brunswick, but he had operated right under their noses for months, and they had never caught him for his greatest crime of all.[16]

Patten likely acted within a network of rebel saboteurs and spies. His British captors may have been fishing when they asked him to name his accomplices, or perhaps Patten himself dropped these hints. He faced his end with the assurance that he was not a lone wolf but part of something greater. He was "a Principal" actor, but not the only one.

"The enthusiasm of this spy was so great," Bardeleben said, "that as he came to the ladder and was about to climb it, he pulled the white hood over his eyes" himself. Patten declared, "I die for liberty, and do it gladly, because my cause is just." The British and Hessians were moved: "The spy supposedly died in the most noble manner and his death has been celebrated as a sacrifice for freedom." Such expressions of manly sensibility were common among officers; Lieutenant Colonel Alexander Hamilton and Major Benjamin Tallmadge repaid this admiration and sympathy when a British spy, Major John André, went to the gallows in 1780.[17]

Patten sounds a lot like Captain Nathan Hale of Coventry, Connecticut, which neighbored Amos Fellows's hometown. Hale also impressed his executioners with his stoicism and erudition. Just twenty-one years old, he met his fate the day after the Great Fire of New York City and supposedly said, "I only regret, that I have but one life to lose for my country." Hale's last words probably came from Joseph Addison's *Cato,* a popular eighteenth-century play about fighting tyranny in ancient Rome. "What pity is it," Cato had said, "That we can die but once to serve our country!"[18]

Patten could have read about Hale's hanging in any number of rebel newspapers in March 1777, which described the doomed captain's "sensible and spirited speech." According to this account, Hale said "that if he had ten thousand lives, he would lay them all down, if called to it, in defence of his injured bleeding country." American newspaper print-ers were encouraged to share "this tragical scene."[19]

Patten's valediction, "I die for liberty, and do it gladly, because my cause is just," echoes another line from Addison's play, in Cato's speech about his army's sacrifices:

> Do thou, great liberty, inspire our souls,
> And make our lives in thy possession happy,
> Or our deaths glorious in thy just defence.[20]

When the Loyalist *New-York Gazette* reported Patten's hanging, it left out his inspiring words—British public opinion makers had no de-sire to ennoble him. The paper only enumerated his confessed crimes, including the line about New York City. Perhaps the litany of offenses was invented by British officers and their sympathetic newspaper, but if so, their accusation stands alone and was not part of a larger effort of disinformation. We have no way to assess the truth of Patten's gallows confession with certainty.

Heath and Graydon confirm that Patten spied for the rebels. Wash-ington also noted Patten's role as a spy—and saboteur—for the Conti-nental cause. When Washington read the newspaper account of Patten's execution, he sent a eulogy to John Hancock, president of the Continen-tal Congress. Patten, Washington wrote, "conducted himself with great fidelity to our cause rendering Services and has fallen a sacrifice in pro-moting her Interest." Both men apparently knew of Patten's espionage activities, perhaps including his immolation of New York City. "His fam-ily well deserves the generous notice of Congress," Washington wrote; the *New-York Gazette* mentioned that Patten left behind "a Wife and four Children at Baltimore." He suggested "perhaps a public act of generosity, considering the character he was in, might not be so eligible, as a private donation." Since Congress could not publicly acknowledge Patten as their incendiary, rebel leaders could memorialize him only by slipping some money to Martha Patten under the table. Washington and Han-cock attempted to close the book on their complicity. After all, although Washington had privately praised the "honest Fellow" who had set the fire, he was still trying to avoid responsibility for a deed he knew not all Americans would endorse.[21]

Patten's confession and Washington's eulogy offer a compelling suggestion that Washington and Congress secretly endorsed the burning of New York. Patten seems not to have been an empty braggart at the gallows, and it would have been strange for the British to invent the accusation when they could already justify their sentence on other grounds. Instead, Washington's private endorsement of Patten's patriotic "Services" confirms something about his actions. Abraham Patten could have become a hero, a martyr, and a national symbol of bravery like Nathan Hale. Patten was not as young as Hale, however; he did not have collegiate connections, and he did not come from New England, a fount of nineteenth-century legacy building. Hale escaped the air of disrepute that surrounded espionage. Patten was quietly forgotten.[22]

Abraham Van Dyck

Both sides hotly disputed what happened to Abraham Van Dyck after his capture on September 16. He claimed he was under lock and key when the fire began, but the British argued that they had either first laid hold of Van Dyck during the fire or recaptured him then. (General Alexander McDougall said that Van Dyck hid until his capture "after the Fire.") Stephen Payne Adye and John Burns portrayed him as a skulking saboteur in their 1783 testimony. Adye recalled examining Van Dyck, "whose Person he had before known," in the Provost afterward. British officers asked around and discovered that he had threatened to burn New York "the Summer before the Town was taken" and later "denie[d] his having ever said any Thing on this Head."[23]

On February 6, 1778, Colonel Elias Boudinot, the American commissary general of prisoners, entered the city with British permission and met with Van Dyck. He learned that back in September 1776, Van Dyck had hidden in the Leary house and asked Mrs. Leary to find George Brewerton, the Loyalist militia colonel, so that Brewerton could take him into custody. This was a problem: as a military officer, Van Dyck should have given himself up immediately. Perhaps Van Dyck had broken parole and hidden himself again, as Richard Brown may also have done.

Van Dyck himself insisted that he was trying to surrender when the British found his hiding place.[24]

Van Dyck remained in prison for a year after Fellows's death. Writing about him and three other men from General Scott's brigade, the New York Committee of Safety suspected that their "Political Characters . . . must render them peculiarly Obnoxious to the Enemy."[25]

Reports surfaced that these prisoners were victims of "the greatest Cruelty." McDougall, Van Dyck's commanding officer, wrote that he "has Since remained confined, notwithstanding he hath repeatedly prayed for a trial, on that charge, but in Vain." Again, it is not clear why advocates for Fellows and Van Dyck expected a trial when the city was under martial law. Regardless, the British had a particular grudge against Van Dyck: "The Enemy I know are much exasperated against him, because the Granadier Company and other Corps, used to exercise in his Tenis Court, and inclosures." Van Dyck was a renowned rebel and a notorious bully. He had helped Marinus Willet disarm British soldiers in June 1775, and he had led the independent militia company that menaced Loyalists like Christopher Benson in 1776 and probably rode four of them on rails.[26]

Van Dyck had become an "unhappy man," McDougall wrote, who "complains, that he has been particularly neglected, while others who were taken after him, have been exchanged." Congress finally sent Boudinot to Manhattan in February 1778. He checked the written record of Van Dyck's imprisonment: "On my calling for the Provost Books it appeared that he had been made Prisoner & closely confined by the Provost 4 Days before the Fire happened."[27]

General James Robertson conceded the point: "It is agreed that he was secreted in a House & found four days before it & confined in the Provost." Yet Robertson insisted that Van Dyck had openly discussed his intention to burn the city, so he was "fully convinced" that the rebel captain "had planned and encouraged the burning of the Town, altho' he was taken up previously to it." The commandant insisted that there was "full evidence of his being concerned in burning the Town," since he was "found secreted in a house for that purpose." Van Dyck was therefore "confined on suspicion of aiding & abetting the setting fire to the town." Robertson refused to release Van Dyck without express approval from General Howe, "lest the remainder of the Town should be endangered." Van Dyck was still considered an active threat. When Boudinot left the city, these discussions were still at an impasse.[28]

Van Dyck was finally exchanged and released on May 8, 1778. His allies continued to argue that the British had treated an innocent man unjustly. Colonel Ethan Allen's polemical memoir of 1779 raised the case as an example of the "frivolous" accusations that the British had made against confined rebel officers: "Captain Vandyke bore with uncommon fortitude near twenty months confinement in this place." The hero of Fort Ticonderoga continued: "The allegation against him, as the cause of his confinement, was very extraordinary. He was accused of setting fire to the city of New York . . . when it was a known fact, that he had been in the provost a week before the fire broke out." The rebels argued that Van Dyck was no perpetrator of an atrocity but the victim of one—the harsh conditions of British imprisonment.[29]

In May 1780, Washington recommended Van Dyck to Congress's Board of Admiralty: "He was treated by the enemy with uncommon rigor during the whole time of a long captivity." He "was particularly obnoxious" to New York City Loyalists "on account of his fixed opposition to their measures from the commencement of the dispute," and those Loyalists' "influence" had led to this harsh treatment. When Benson confronted Washington in June 1776, Washington had disavowed any responsibility for Van Dyck's Grenadiers; now in 1780, the commander in chief sought a captaincy in the marines for Van Dyck, "from a knowledge of his character and his circumstances." Washington was convinced that "no man, considering his abilities, has made greater sacrifice for the cause." It was quite an endorsement for a man imprisoned for incendiarism, a characterization of the Great Fire that Washington had done everything to dispel. General Philip Schuyler concurred: "Everybody about headquarters speaks well, very well of him"; Schuyler was impressed that Van Dyck had "maintained his principles" even "under the severest tryals." Congress assigned Van Dyck to service as a marine lieutenant aboard the frigate *Saratoga*. This had been his original rank during the Seven Years' War, even after all that he had sacrificed, and he may have perceived it as a slight to his honor. Before the year was out, he had resigned his commission. He died, somehow, before the war ended.[30]

Van Dyck may not have helped burn New York City; the evidence is contradictory and offers no more than a suggestion that he was complicit. Boudinot checked the British records and reported that Van Dyck was closely confined *before* the fire broke out—for that matter, Tench Tilghman had insisted on September 25 that *all* rebels discovered in or near the city were under close British confinement. The rebels had every reason to deny Van Dyck's involvement, but if they were right, then the British were making a flimsy accusation: sometime between the Continental Army's evacuation from the city on September 15 and Van Dyck's imprisonment on September 16, he had helped to coordinate the city's destruction from his hiding place; or he did it later, from a prison cell. Van Dyck became a scapegoat for the burning of Broadway: he was a notorious Grenadier, and it was bad enough that he had had stoked the flames of rebellion.[31]

Boudinot may also have been mistaken about what the British records signified, in which case the following scenario is also possible: Van Dyck was captured on September 16 and then paroled. He had experience with clandestine rebel actions, so he linked up with other saboteurs and helped to perpetrate the deed, then hid himself a second time. He and Fellows were caught again before they could escape. Adye remembered the "Negro man" who said Van Dyck had been involved, and local Loyalists chimed in that the Grenadier captain was likely to have helped burn his own city. The British authorities believed these accusations had merit.

Whatever the accusers said, the allies of Fellows and Van Dyck maintained their innocence—in part to try to bring an end to their harsh imprisonment. Yet more than five years after freeing him, two British officers and a Loyalist civilian not only repeated their accusations against Van Dyck but told vivid accounts of his arrest *after* the fire started. These later accounts may well have been fabrications or mistaken memories, in which case it seems unlikely that Van Dyck personally lit a match to help burn New York City; but if Van Dyck was at large between his initial capture and the outbreak of the fire, perhaps the 1783 stories were true.

Innocent or guilty, Van Dyck endured almost twenty months imprisoned in the Provost, seething over his betrayal, and no doubt at great cost to his health. Fellows, a younger man, died after five months under similar conditions.

Between January 1777 and May 1780, General Washington wrote letters on behalf of three army captains whom the British specifically accused of burning New York: Amos Fellows, Abraham Patten, and Abraham Van Dyck. None of them lived to see the redcoats finally driven from New York City.

A War of Devastation and Restraint

I t was well before dawn on November 5, 1776, when soldiers returned to White Plains, New York. They set fire to the courthouse
where the Provincial Congress had met for most of the summer,
the tavern next door, and several houses. At one, the soldiers found
an old woman, a fourteen-year-old girl, and a cat, who had spent the
past few weeks hearing "the Thunder of Two great Armies, and the daily
whizzing of Bombs," echoing from Throgs Neck to Pell's Point and then
just "over their heads." The British had withdrawn to prepare their attack
on Fort Washington and the long-awaited expulsion of the rebels from
Manhattan. "It was cold. It was dark," and the old woman and the young
girl did not know which army had sent the officer who now crashed
through their door. They "begged for mercy!" but "in vain!" and so "their
trembling hands snatched a few clothes in haste, they were indecently
urged out." They watched as the soldiers burned their house to the ground.[1]

Scenes like this became common during the Revolutionary War,
and among white settlements, most of the torch-bearing soldiers and
officers were acting on the Crown's behalf. On this night, however, the
officer was Major Jonathan Williams Austin of the 16th Continental Regiment, the son of a Boston selectman. At Harvard, where he was William
Tudor's roommate, Austin got himself briefly expelled for trying to lead
a student rebellion. After graduation, he and Tudor worked as law clerks

under John Adams. About a month before his nineteenth birthday, Austin participated in the crowd action on March 5, 1770, that led to the Boston Massacre. At twenty-three, he was chairing the Chelmsford committee of correspondence; at twenty-four, he was major of a Massachusetts regiment. Adams tried several times to get his former pupil promoted, but Colonel Henry Knox replied that Austin's character and judgment were lacking. He may have had a drinking problem.[2]

Austin's men burst into another house and told Mrs. Adams (no relation to John) to pack her things as fast as possible. When she lingered in the bedroom, they threatened to "Blow her thro" and did not even give her time to dress her children. (Other soldiers said they helped remove some of her furniture, including the bed where her aged mother slept.) Austin announced he was acting under orders from General John Sullivan. Her sister grabbed Austin by the arm, saying, "You are an Officer & can prevent such treatments," but Austin was unmoved. When Adams asked why he couldn't spare her house, he answered, "Because you are all Damn'd Tories."[3]

The rebels could not pass this off as the action of civilians or militiamen; it happened within the Continental Army lines, and there was no way to deflect the monstrosity onto the British or bury it with rumors. Several Continental soldiers heard the cries of the women and children—Austin's unit had set a bad example for the whole army, and Washington called them "base and cowardly Wretches" the next day. He had enjoined the soldiers not to burn houses (without special permission) on November 2, and so the army characterized Austin's actions as contrary to orders and to American ideals. Whatever Austin might have accomplished strategically by burning White Plains, it was not worth the opprobrium from civilians at home and abroad.[4]

Even so, Colonel Jedediah Huntington spared a "happy thought" for burning houses in White Plains, because it "struck terrour into the Tories" and showed that the rebels were willing to sacrifice American property for military advantage. After General Alexander McDougall began holding a court-martial on November 8, "upon Charge of 'Burning the houses at White-Plains, contrary to General orders,'" the officers sentenced Austin to a mere reprimand. General Charles Lee, who had heard from Washington about "Public Justice" for Austin, ordered a new trial on November 12–13, on "a charge of wanton barbarous conduct un-becoming not only an Officer but a human Creature." At his second trial, Austin claimed he had overheard General Israel Putnam saying that "it would be best to burn all the houses" of White Plains. Austin had found several buildings already in ruins, so he decided to finish the job. Conti-nental officers judged him guilty "of behaving in a scandalous, infamous manner" and ordered him discharged from the service.[5]

New York's political leaders were furious with Austin. New York State was willing to make sacrifices for the common cause, they said, but they would not allow the senseless destruction of their towns, least of all by the men who were supposed to be defending them. The Committee of Safety at Fishkill complained to Congress and to Washington, asking for the Continental Army to be "seasonably restrained from such acts of barbarity," otherwise the United States could hardly claim to be "ad-vocates for the rights of mankind, against the tyranny and oppression of lawless power." They wanted to make a "severe example" of Austin and prosecute him for arson, a capital crime.[6]

But it was good to be the son of a Boston selectman. "Friends of Major Austin" leaned on General William Heath four months later to ask Washington to reinstate him. Washington considered it: Austin had been "an excellent Officer," his crime may have been the result of "an un-guarded hour" of inebriation, and perhaps he had been punished enough; but Washington wanted to know whether Austin had sobered up, which seems to have put the matter to rest. Even so, a year later, Samuel Adams and other Boston grandees invited Austin to give the eighth annual ora-tion commemorating the Boston Massacre.[7]

Remarkably, Austin spoke about the danger of soldiers: "We shud-der when the faithful page of history opens to our view the conduct of armies, flush'd with victories, sacking towns, burning villages, and per-petrating murders, with all the other dreadful concomitants," he said, calling for "vengeance" against British troops for their "crimes" in New Jersey and Esopus (now Kingston), New York. Austin was admitted to the bar in August and joined a privateering expedition a few months later. He was in his twenties when he died somewhere in the South, the cause of death unclear.[8]

The rebels skillfully managed their own destructive actions in the court of public opinion; they disavowed property destruction and irregular warfare when a few rebel soldiers went too far, yet still allowed the responsible parties to salvage their reputations. Rebel opinion makers repeatedly claimed that they were the true protectors of property owners' interests. Like Austin, they portrayed the British, conversely, as wanton destroyers. Complaints about British devastation remained a perennial source of political strength for the American rebellion. Nevertheless, the Great Fire of 1776 may well have marked a turning point for rebel attitudes about the destruction of towns—so long as their inhabitants were white settlers.[9]

At the end of November 1776, a writer in England, "MARCELLUS," mocked the hypocrisy of British and Loyalist complaints about the burning of New York. All might feel an "honest indignation against such Acts of Barbarity" as "disgraceful to Arms, and to any Cause." Yet if readers were tempted to criticize the "Wretches" who burned New York City, they should "Blush" with "Remorse" as they recalled the British burning of Charlestown, Massachusetts, and Portsmouth and Gosport in Virginia. Marcellus accepted the grim justice of Americans "destroying their own Towns," calling it "their Right to dispose of their own Property" and "deprive their Enemies of Shelter and the Means of Annoyance." He believed that the Great Fire called for Britons to have a little perspective and perhaps a sense of shame.[10]

Yet British critics of the Great Fire would not be deterred. The Reverend Myles Cooper, president of King's College in New York, gave a fast day sermon at Oxford in December 1776 decrying the "barbarian fury" of New York's "desperate incendiaries" who had set out to harm their neighbors. The writer "ALSOP" replied with sangfroid: "It is, Sir, ever the practice to destroy the country, to prevent the enemy from receiving any succour from it." He added (and there was some truth to this) that "the wisest and best men in America" had called for destroying all of America's seaport towns to prevent them from becoming staging points for the British army and navy. "On this principle," Alsop concluded, "New-York was set on fire." Like Marcellus, Alsop argued that it was hypocritical for Britons to pursue an aggressive war against the American colonists and then lament the burning of New York.[11]

"A.B." made a similar argument: "When General Howe talks so peevishly of the Burning of New-York . . . he throws aside all Memory of the Burning of Falmouth and other Towns, and of the Conduct of the Hessians." Besides, Congress had ordered New York's evacuation *"to prevent it's being burnt."* The writer added ambiguously (possibly referring to another deed), "Nothing is more common in War than the Resentment of the Peasantry." Even writers who thought the Great Fire was justifiable blamed depoliticized, lower-status actors, not rebel leaders.[12]

This debate had even more urgency amid the battlefields of America as the British and their enemies continued to launch destructive raids. "A civil war is a dreadful thing," wrote Lieutenant Colonel Enoch Markham of the 46th Regiment in December 1776, "what with the devastation of the rebels, and that of the English and Hessian troops, every part of the country, where the scene of action has been, looks deplorable. Furniture is broken to pieces; good houses deserted and almost destroyed, others burnt; cattle, horses, and poultry carried off; and the old plundered of their all."[13]

After Governor William Tryon and his men burned houses in Philipse Manor, New York, on November 18, 1777, General Samuel H. Parsons retaliated by burning the Loyalist Oliver DeLancey's estate, arguing that Tryon had committed an "injustice and savageness" that went beyond any military "necessity." The governor replied sarcastically, "The ruins from the conflagration of New-York, by the emissaries of your party, last year, remain a memorial of their tender regard for their fellow beings," now refugees. If given command, Tryon wrote, he would "burn every Committee Man's house within my reach," because he held these rebel leaders responsible for "the continued calamities of this Country." British hard-liners like Tryon believed that the Great Fire should inspire further aggression against the rebellion.[14]

Governor William Livingston of New Jersey, using a pseudonym, called Tryon *"Conflagrator General* of all America" and "Master *Combustion."* Tryon's "charging the firing of New-York upon the inhabitants, whose interest it was to save it, is such a complication of cruelty and falsehood, as is rather to be detested in silence than capable of being expressed in words." The rebels' campaign of disinformation was still in effect.[15]

Later that year, Great Britain's peace commission (led by the earl of Carlisle) bragged about having "thus far checked the extremes of war" because they had no desire to "desolate a country shortly to become again a source of mutual advantage." Thomas Paine, author of *Common Sense*, mocked their claims of benevolence. He warned that the British Isles "are far more exposed to incendiary desolation than America"; its cities, warehouses, ships, country seats, the East India House, and the Bank of England were all potential targets. Paine even confessed that he had volunteered to set fire to the British fleet near Philadelphia. "It has never been the custom of France and England, when at war," he wrote, "to make those havocs on each other, because the ease with which they could retaliate, rendered it as impolitic as if each had destroyed his own." That consideration, as well as "the humanity of America," had held the rebels back. "But think not . . . that our distance secures you, or our invention fails us. . . . If you *openly* profess yourselves savages, it is high time we should treat you as such, and if nothing but distress can recover you to reason, to punish will become an office of charity."[16]

These arguments were premised on the idea that the Continental cause was principled and just, that only their enemies behaved barbarically, and only the righteous motives of self-defense or last-ditch retaliation led rebels to adopt destructive tactics. Crown supporters, with their suspicions about the Great Fire of 1776, must have been staggered by the rebels' arguments.

George Washington learned valuable lessons in 1776. First, to keep order, he needed a professionalized army that would reliably obey its commanders and adhere to the rules of war. Second, to win strategically, he needed to avoid facing the British in coastal areas where the British navy kept him at a disadvantage and large population centers would suffer from his presence. Third, since his allies controlled the press, he could win the civil war by prevailing in the battle for public opinion. To convince the world that the rebellion was just, he would have to try to restrain the Continental Army from misbehavior and blame the British for any atrocities.

Washington had faced the terrible choice of defending, abandoning, or burning New York City. Now he adopted the Fabian strategy of retreating, keeping his army intact, and fighting on more favorable ground. The army under Washington never occupied another large city (although he defended Philadelphia amid its suburbs, and the southern army held out disastrously at Charleston). Washington fantasized about retaking New York but also knew that cities were undesirable places to station his forces; he encamped at Valley Forge, Morristown, and Newburgh, negating the British advantage on the high seas and managing relations with local farmers. He realized that hungry armies made enemies, and he largely stopped using the scorched-earth tactics he had used on Long Island, except in Indian homelands. He never again had to watch his men defiling town houses, declaring war on sex workers, and mingling with violent crowds. He never again had to pine for tar and brimstone while the British breathed down his neck. He had a harsher system of punishments when his men stepped out of line.[17]

After September 20, 1776, the new articles of war took effect, although Tudor still complained about the "Scoundrels getting Commissions" as officers, the "Rabble, called Militia," and "the Disorders of the Army, composed of Troops from nine different Colonies," which "keeps me perpetually employ'd" as judge advocate general. He was frustrated that the officers had too much "Timidity and Backwardness . . . to inflict capital Punishments," and it was too "difficult to get a Villain hang'd in the Camp." Disciplinary problems persisted, especially among the militia, but the new rules eventually forged an army that defeated the British. Holding the American coalition together and disciplining one's own citizen-soldiers were enduring challenges: toward the end of the war, the men mutinied a few times over, terrifying the congressional delegates in Philadelphia. State and Continental authorities had to make strenuous efforts to keep their coalition together.[18]

The British sought other large cities as naval bases, supply depots, and winter headquarters. They hoped that capital cities like Newport, Philadelphia, Savannah, and Charleston would become centers of Loyalist mobilization and the restoration of imperial government and commerce. They quickly found that securing these seaports was not enough to conquer whole provinces. They also failed to establish the cities as public opinion beachheads of their own. As Continental forces retreated upriver, British forces made themselves obnoxious through procurements, raids, and unsoldierly behavior—in 1777, Congress began gathering evidence of British atrocities, and the rebel press made the most of their enemies' misdeeds. "Had plunder & Devastation been restrained," wrote the Loyalist John Tabor Kempe, "the War in this part of the Continent [would have] ended with the last campaign." William Smith Jr. wrote two years later that "a Day scarcely happens that Multitudes are not offended." Although plenty of Americans might well have inclined toward neutrality or Loyalism, the British army drove many of them into the arms of the rebellion.[19]

The next five years saw wave after wave of British and Loyalist raiders destroying towns, including Danbury, Connecticut, and Kingston, New York, in 1777; Warren and Bristol, Rhode Island, in 1778; Fairfield and Norwalk, Connecticut, Bedford, New York, and Somerset Courthouse, New Jersey, in 1779; Springfield, New Jersey, in 1780; and Georgetown, South Carolina, and New London, Connecticut, in 1781 (fig. 13.1). Gilbert Saltonstall, who had fantasized in 1775 about the burning of New York, would bear witness to the destruction of New London on September 6, 1781. He called it "a Scene too distressing to dwell upon." British soldiers and their allies burned thousands of homes throughout the revolted colonies. Army officers disagreed about the wisdom of such actions. General James Robertson fretted that "burning houses . . . gives the people a notion that we despair of possessing" North America, which undermined confidence in the project of British pacification, but Captain Frederick Mackenzie urged his superiors to let more Americans know "the horrors of War" until "their resentment would turn upon Congress" and the state legislatures. As the war went on, the British did not so much adopt Mackenzie's way of thinking as succumb to frustration, a desire for revenge, and a growing fear that victory was impossible. Although some Americans simply abandoned their political commitments as devastation led to despair, others were galvanized by British outrages. Britain's halfhearted policy toward destruction was enough to discourage most Americans from reconciling.[20]

The leaders of the rebellion continued to stoke American resentment: Paine would later remind the British, "We can look round and see the remains of burnt and destroyed houses, once the fair fruit of hard industry, and now the striking monuments of British brutality." Not surprisingly, many members of Congress loudly clamored to fulfill Paine's revenge fantasies. While some cautioned against letting the war degen-

Fig. 13.1. An Opposition satire accuses the king and his ministers of driving families to beggary by continuing to prosecute the war; the satire also blames Washington. In the background, Norfolk (destroyed in 1776) and Esopus (burned in 1777) are aflame. "Mr. Trade & family or the state of ye nation," [London], 1779, Library of Congress, Prints and Photographs Division.

erate into a war of retaliation, others called for expeditions to burn towns in England and Scotland.[21]

Commodore John Paul Jones's "revenge raid" on Whitehaven in 1778 did not achieve much physical destruction, but he shocked English civilians, who had not seen a coastal invasion in over a hundred years. Writing to Franklin the following year, a Massachusetts delegate wondered, "Will no one under Commission from these United States retaliate on the Coasts of England for the Burning of our beautiful Fairfield?" He suggested giving the enemy "a striking Sample of the Species of War now carried on by Britain against America." Congress even suggested that destroying British towns might become "a common cause of all nations to punish a people who so daringly violate the rights of humanity" and "those laws which are held sacred among civilized nations."[22]

Congress then instructed Franklin and his colleagues in France to "employ Incendiaries to set fire to the Capital of the British Dominions, particularly the royal Palace, and to such other Towns in Great Britain as may be most expedient." Congress would issue a manifesto declaring that Americans "are determined at all times to meet their enemies in whatever kind of war they shall chuse to carry on, whether it be of civilized or of savage nations." Nothing came of this, but Franklin wrote that news of the burning of Fairfield had "demolish'd all my Moderation."[23]

In September 1781, a congressional committee complained that the British no longer respected "the benevolent rules by which civilized nations have tempered the severities and evils of war." The committee wished for "the demolition of cities and villages in the Kingdom of Great Britain so as fully to retaliate." Although they took pity on the "unoffending inhabitants" of British towns, they would nonetheless be "fully justified by the laws of self defence and sound policy," deeper than "any light and hasty suggestions of anger or revenge." They gave this idea up as unrealistic but still authorized officers to summarily execute incendiaries, either by throwing them into the flames or by other means, as the British had done five years earlier. Within a month, this prospect became irrelevant when the British surrendered at Yorktown. By February 1782, Parliament voted to end its offensive operations in North America.[24]

Washington and Congress never undertook these attacks, but loose allies and louche bandits wreaked devastation. John the Painter, a loner with tenuous connections to the rebels, set fires in Portsmouth and Bristol in England during the winter of 1776–77, doing almost £20,000 worth of damage to the Portsmouth rope house. In North America, bandits roamed the inlets and no-man's-lands where the armies never set foot, from the Long Island Sound to Georgia's southern border. James Willing's men burned plantations along the Mississippi River below Natchez in 1778. Rebels on the Pennsylvania frontier torched property as part of their ongoing land disputes with rival white settlers. Massachusetts privateers raided the Nova Scotia coast. State militia units launched destructive campaigns against other whites, particularly in the Carolinas.[25]

Angry crowds also launched scattered attacks on Loyalist civilians and price-gouging merchants. Mutinous soldiers were also suspected of aiming for private property. People committed many types of collective violence during the Revolutionary War, much of it auxiliary to the formal movement of well-organized armies, and much of it destructive. Although some of these groups aligned with the Continental Army's goals, they did so at a remove from congressional responsibility, with less obligation to show restraint.[26]

Rebel leaders did take direct oversight of the 1779 Sullivan-Clinton campaign against the Iroquois, who called George Washington "Conotocarious" or "Town Destroyer" (also "devourer of villages"). State militias also launched destructive campaigns against the Cherokee in 1776 (Hugh Gaine's newspaper published an item about Colonel Andrew Williamson's determination to "carry fire and sword" to the Cherokee on September 21, the same day as the Great Fire). As Native Americans retaliated, settlements burned in upstate New York, western Pennsylvania, the Ohio Country, and elsewhere. The same white Americans who complained about the uncivilized acts of burning white settlements believed that burning Indian towns was necessary for their displacement, so that whites' domain of civilization could extend. Although many Americans have been taught to remember the war as moderate, restrained, and civilized, the war was often destructive and riven with unrestrained violence.[27]

Justice Thomas Jones, a Loyalist, noted how the rebels and their allies in Parliament "made great complaints during the war against the royal army for burning houses, mills, and towns. It was called inhumanity, and contrary to the usage of civilized nations." Yet he insisted on putting these acts in context: he was aware of the destruction of towns, from Falmouth to Springfield, but "Who burnt a fourth part of the city of New York . . . ? The Americans." He noted the rebels' incendiarism in Norfolk, Manhattan, Long Island, White Plains, Hoboken, Weehawken, and Quebec. "Yet, these were the people who had the impudence to charge Great Britain with carrying on an inhuman war." The Great Fire of 1776 had "reduced" so many Loyalists "from affluence, to indigence, and some lost their all." Jones did not approve of Great Britain's senseless acts of plunder and destruction, either: "It occasioned rancor and inveteracy, and instead of conciliating, it widened the breach." Still, he insisted that "the burning of towns in times of war, in all civilized nations, is a usual practice," hardly worth the furious condemnations of the British war effort by the rebels and the Opposition in Parliament.[28]

Great Britain lost the war for a number of reasons: with hardly any

European allies, the kingdom was forced to fight several enemies in multiple theaters; the Crown suffered from problems of generalship, manpower, communication, and supply, and a waning of commitment at home. The British never convinced Americans that the rebellion was more destructive to peace and order than the policies of Parliament and the king. Had the Crown successfully turned public opinion against the Revolution, using the Great Fire as part of its argument, it might have secured more allies. For a variety of reasons, the British could not do that: they had already burned Charlestown and Falmouth, they helped destroy Norfolk, and their men had summarily executed people at New York. For every flagrant act the rebels committed, from White Plains to the Carolinas, they insisted that the British were even worse. Once the British lost the war, the rebel perception dominated its history—including the story of the Great Fire of 1776.

The Unresolved War

The fighting had ended, but questions about the Great Fire remained. General Guy Carleton, Knight of the Bath and commander in chief of His Majesty's forces on America's eastern seaboard, issued a warrant on October 18, 1783: "A very considerable part of this City having been destroyed by fire, in the month of September 1776," the general was "desirous for diverse important considerations, to ascertain whether the same was accidental, or the effect of design? and if of design, to whom generally or individually the same imputable?"[1]

By then, the civil war was all but over. Both sides had ceased offensive operations, and the two exhausted nations were rushing to close the book on the Revolutionary War. The Continental Army had mostly disbanded. Many of the city's Loyalists had gone into exile. The final draft of the Treaty of Paris would reach New York City in less than two weeks. What were these "diverse important considerations" about an event from seven years ago? The Great Fire of 1776 offers many mysteries, and the investigation of 1783 offers one more: why did Carleton bother to investigate it when he did? No evidence suggests that the British government ordered Carleton's investigation; he apparently acted on his own. When he issued the warrant, he had not read any significant dispatches from

London for two months. He does not mention the commission in his public correspondence, and he had his personal papers destroyed.[2]

In 1782, Parliament decided it was ready for peace; it sent Carleton back to North America for the first time in four years and handed him the worst possible assignment. Carleton was stiff, taciturn, and authoritarian, but widely admired for his honesty and integrity. Some members of Parliament worried that he might act too aggressively, but everyone professed confidence he would do his duty. The earl of Shelburne, home secretary under the new Rockingham ministry, instructed the general "to revive old affections and extinguish late jealousies" to entice Americans away from their French allies. Carleton reached New York City on May 5, 1782, under the mistaken impression that he would continue the war against recalcitrant rebels, reconcile the revolted colonies to Great Britain, and broker a peace treaty that would bring honor to the Crown. In reality, Parliament had no appetite to continue the war, the rebels wanted nothing less than independence, and Shelburne directed peace negotiations through emissaries in Paris. Carleton became embittered at both the rebels' "studied incivility" and the British government's desire for surrender. He would be neither peacemaker nor warrior.[3]

Parliament was ready to let the thirteen colonies go. In Paris, the rebel negotiators—Benjamin Franklin, John Adams, and John Jay—were fortunate that Shelburne was anxious to keep French power at bay by making significant concessions to the United States. Britain agreed to recognize American independence, grant the United States a western boundary at the Mississippi River, and allow access to the North Atlantic fisheries. Among other key additions, it was agreed that Americans would pay any debts to British creditors. When the news of the tentative treaty provisions arrived on July 31, 1782, Carleton tried to resign rather than serve as a "mere Inspector of Embarkations." His request was denied. He remained at his post and did his duty while occasionally acting independently of his changing superiors in London.[4]

The Great Fire's lasting consequences must have been evident to the commander in chief when he first reached New York City. "New York is no more the same City it was," wrote the Reverend John Milner in early 1777. "The Glory is departed—all gloom & despair—the rich are become poor & the last desperate." That same winter, a British officer wrote, "We begin now severely to want that part of the city which those unhappy destroyers of their country have consumed." When Nicholas Cresswell visited the city a few months later, he reflected, "When I see this once flourishing, opulent and happy City, one third part of it now in ruins, it brings a sadness and melancholy upon my mind." He was disgusted at the way the rebels had "formed a hellish design, burnt it down to the ground and then laid the blame upon our troops," evidence of the "strange madness and folly that reigns among them." Walking from Hull's tavern to the shore, Cresswell and a friend passed some of the burned houses and heard the cries of a woman in labor. They brought her to the house of a saddler in Broadway, who tried to turn her away but then relented and let them use his shop out back. An "old drunken woman" agreed to deliver the baby for two dollars, while the saddler's wife remained in bed, slinging curses at the new mother. Hungry, tired people draped ships' sails over the roofless husks of burned houses, a "scene of ruin and abomination." The neighborhood, vice ridden and dangerous, became known as "Canvas Town," a haven for "the lowest followers of the army," sailors ashore, and Black refugees who had escaped their rebel enslavers.[5]

The fire also left behind emotional ruins. The fate of Reverend Samuel Auchmuty, rector of Trinity Church, gives some idea. Auchmuty was Boston born and Harvard educated, but he was ordained as an Anglican minister and began ministering to Trinity Church in 1748. When he continued to pray for the king during the rebel occupation of New York, the rebels supposedly threatened to display him in his pulpit with "his Ears cut off, his Nose slit, [and] to be tarr'd, & feather'd." He escaped through the back door of Trinity Church to New Jersey. The rebels there compelled him to flee to the king's ships, and he only returned to Manhattan after the fire. He was "shocked on viewing the Ruins of so great a Part of the City . . . Especially those of Trinity Church, that ancient and once venerable Edifice! The Sight drew Floods of Tears from him." His parsonage house, furniture, linens, books, and legal papers were "all burnt by the Americans," except for some silver plate he found in the rubble. "The Shock proved too severe for him," his widow recalled. "From that time he decayed daily, till Death freed him from Misery" on March 4,

Fig. 14.1. Some inhabitants of occupied New York found the church ruins to be picturesque. [Francis, Lord Rawdon?], *An original sketch of the ruins of Trinity Church N. York, taken by an English officer in the Revolution,* ca. 1780, watercolor, Emmet Collection, Miriam and Ira D. Wallach Division of Art, Prints, and Photographs, New York Public Library.

1777. He was only fifty-six. His son testified that after his losses, valued at over £6,000, he "sunk under the weight of his misery, leaving a Widow and six Children."[6]

Others returned to New York City and did their best to resume life and work. The charred ruins of the "Burnt Church" became a fashionable promenade: ladies walked arm in arm among the gravestones with handsome soldiers and listened to hired musicians (fig. 14.1). British officers and wealthy Loyalists enjoyed theater, music, dances, sports, and celebrations. Meanwhile, thousands of prisoners suffered shocking rates of death in the Bridewell, the Provost, sugarhouses, and prison ships in Wallabout Bay. The revolutionary states, including New York, had aggressively dispossessed many Loyalists from their homes outside the city and expropriated their goods, distributing them (for sale or lease) to rebel refugees who had left the occupied city or to other interested buyers. These Loyalist refugees sought charity in the garrison: "Several good families, whom their army have ruined," a British officer wrote, "come daily shivering in for our protection." Harsh winters, disease, privation, price hikes, corruption, crime, misbehaving soldiers, and martial law all made life in wartime New York City a trial, but Black and white inhabitants nonetheless did their best to seek greater freedom, maintain family ties, and engage in new business ventures. Fires, too, plagued the occupied city, occasionally inviting fears that the rebels had sent incendiaries to finish the job.[7]

The Great Fire's destruction of so many homes had exacerbated the city's housing shortages and sent hundreds to the almshouse. The population of civilians steadily increased as the city's Loyalist fugitives returned home and refugees from elsewhere sought opportunities in the city. The printer John Kerr complained in March 1778 that he "was almost ruin'd by the fire" after three of his houses burned along with the furniture. For a year and a half, he had groups of officers and soldiers, and then an officer and his wife, billeted on him, and he was unable to pay rent. When the city was "burnt (as the universal opinion was, by the Rebels)," the leather dresser and breeches maker Cornelius Ryan lost three houses, "which has reduced him to very distressing circumstances." Ryan served with the British. After his wife Isabella was robbed of clothing and plate in Westchester, she moved back to the city and had to put up with three officers wrecking her furniture while billeted in her town house. Her husband had employed twenty journeymen and apprentices before the war; now she had to ask the vestry for rent relief.[8]

Carleton sympathized with the Loyalists he met in New York City, and his concern for them and their property probably weighed on his mind when he ordered the investigation of the Great Fire. By October 1783 the city was again a "chaos zone," where no one could be too sure about the future. The British, their Loyalist allies, and their rebel opponents contended bitterly with one another over property, and these disputes were crucial to the negotiations in Paris. The states had passed bills of attainder and acts of confiscation to seize property from the king's supporters. Many hard-line Americans argued that they were entitled to keep the proceeds from these sales as redress for property losses owing to British plunder, devastation, and seizure, including enslaved persons who had fled to British lines. Franklin, Jay, Adams, and many other hard-liners claimed that the Crown's wartime depredations—including the liberation of enslaved people—negated any obligation to compensate Loyalists for confiscated property. With "Canvas Town" and the surrounding ruins dominating the west side of Broadway, Carleton must have been repulsed at the false idea that the war's devastations were all the fault of his colleagues.[9]

The British negotiators in Paris (including Henry Strachey) tried to insist that Congress should compensate the Loyalists for confiscated property. Even the French and Spanish envoys raised the issue, as a way of delaying the peace. "I cannot conceive," Shelburne wrote, that it would be in "the interest of America to leave any root of animosity behind, much less to lodge it with posterity in the heart of the Treaty." The Americans repeatedly refused to entertain any such suggestion: "If the [Loyalist] Refugees have any claim it is on England to whom they have adhered and not on America whom they have plundered. They have been entirely the cause of the War and in fact merit nothing from either Party." The American delegation would reconsider only if the British were willing "to make retribution to our Citizens" for "the *unnecessary* Destruction of their private Property." At a "moment of conciliatory Overtures," they wrote, "it would not be proper to call certain Scenes into view, over which, a variety of Considerations should induce both Parties . . . to draw a veil." Franklin was indignant at the idea: the Loyalists had "done infinite Mischief to our Properties by wantonly burning and destroying Farmhouses, Villages, and Towns"; he mentioned Charlestown and Falmouth, Norfolk and New London, Fairfield and Esopus, with a glancing reference to devastations in the Wyoming Valley. Why should the states "restore their Properties who have destroy'd ours"? If the British demanded compensation, the states were prepared to "exhibit against it, an Account of all the Ravages they had Committed" and "recall to View Scenes of Barbarity that must inflame instead of conciliating." The Loyalists had little recourse except to petition the British government—and when they eventually did, many of them would mention property they lost in the Great Fire of 1776. In Paris, the negotiators' desire for peace outweighed the thorny issue of property destruction.[10]

The American negotiators in Paris agreed only to "earnestly recommend" to the thirteen states that they return seized Loyalist property and prevent future confiscations. This "recommendation" turned out to be toothless, and for a few years the states violated this part of the treaty with impunity. Everyone understood that the states, localities, and much of the populace were determined to ignore all treaty provisions concerning Loyalist property. In New York State alone, the rebels planned to seize at least "half a million" more pounds' worth of property after the British evacuated Staten Island, Long Island, and Manhattan.[11]

Leading Loyalists therefore begged the king not to finalize any treaty "until full and sufficient security be had for our future personal safety and restitution of our property," plus asylum for exiles. Members of Parliament sympathized with the Loyalists' plight; even as they approved the treaty, they expressed concern that all those civilians who had walked out on a limb to defend the Crown during the war were having the branch sawn off behind them. Unfortunately, it was not "possible to satisfy all reasonable claims which may be urged by the numerous sufferers from this unfortunate war." Parliament could only instruct Carleton to offer these sufferers his "tenderest and most honourable care."[12]

Some of New York City's Loyalists wanted to pursue new acts of aggression. Carleton threw cold water on their militant plans, but it was clear that a faction of Loyalists would never reconcile with the rebels who had done them so much harm. When Carleton first arrived in New York, he wrote to George Washington directly, calling for an end to the war of "Retaliation." Washington agreed in principle, but as British naval operations continued, he claimed he had no influence with states (like New Jersey) who proposed to execute Loyalists for treason. "Ever since the commencement of this unnatural war," Washington wrote, "my Conduct has [borne?] invariable testimony against those inhuman Excesses, which, in too many Instances, have marked its various progress." Carleton did extricate himself from a delicate situation that might have escalated badly when he promised to investigate the Loyalists' hanging of the rebel captain Joshua Huddy: those investigations came up empty, and both sides tacitly agreed to let the matter drop. It was an important preview of what would happen with the fire investigation.[13]

Washington's principal concern was the thousands of Black people who had escaped from American slavery and remained under Carleton's protection. During the negotiations that took place between the two generals at Tappan, New York, in early May 1783, Washington argued that individuals claimed as slaves should be returned, but Carleton categorically refused to break faith with the Crown's promises to people who had escaped from rebel enslavers to British lines. When the Loyalists demanded compensation for their lost property under the treaty, Washington and Congress had nothing to offer, yet when it came to the enslaved, Washington demanded more than a full accounting (which Carleton did provide); he asked for wrenching detainments of self-emancipated people to return them to bondage. Washington argued that balancing the ledger was not enough. In October 1783, a Loyalist observed, the rebels were "extremely out of Temper about their Negroes, & accuse Sir Guy Carleton of a Breach of Treaty, on that Head."[14]

Thousands of white Loyalists in New York City, meanwhile, despaired at the news from Paris and London. "You cannot easily [con]ceive of such a Scene of Confusion as this Place is, Assisted [as] they are by their Hopes & fears; when every Thing that [is] dear to them is at Stake," wrote Henry Addison, an Anglican minister from Maryland. Another Loyalist complained, "No faith can be placed in a Government which has abandoned its best friends, forfeited all pretensions to honor and honesty by consigning them to the mercy of their enemies, on the slender security of a cold recommendation." Without "something more to compel the States to an execution of the Provisional Articles," a third Loyalist wrote, the states would do nothing to restore the Loyalists' property or compensate them for rebel confiscations. Rebels who visited New York "laugh at the idea of compensation for our property" and had no fears that Britain would ever compel enforcement of this part of the treaty.[15]

Over the course of 1782–83, tens of thousands of American Loyalists chose exile in Canada and other parts of the British Empire. News of the formal peace treaty arrived in the spring of 1783, and Carleton proclaimed a "cessation of arms." Within days, more Loyalists abandoned the American countryside for New York City, desperate to settle their affairs and evacuate. Feeling betrayed and hopeless, "many have lost their senses, and are now in a state of perfect madness," according to a New York gentleman whose account was printed in a London newspaper.

Some had taken their own lives, and this writer was pessimistic about the fate of those headed to Nova Scotia: "I have already consigned two-thirds of them to the grave."[16]

The commander in chief took seriously his mandate to do what he could for the Loyalists; to encourage adherence to the treaty, Carleton even returned estates that the British had sequestered from rebels and opened the city to rebel civilians. He expressed hope that his beneficent leadership would attract more Americans to British government for the inevitable day when the United States collapsed, but he had little to show for his magnanimity. He asked state and national authorities to ease up on anti-Loyalist legislation, but they did nothing.[17]

By May 1, Robert R. Livingston (Congress's secretary for foreign affairs) complained that Carleton had not yet evacuated. If the British were delaying the evacuation to obtain leverage for the Loyalists, they might delay forever. Livingston knew the United States would never accede to the Loyalists' demands unless the British paid reparations for all the damage they had done.[18]

State governments not only refused to return Loyalist property but passed legislation allowing further property seizures. Writers made dire threats; "brutus" mocked New York City's Loyalists in August 1783, as their "delusive prospects of conquest, plunder, and revenge are now forever vanished." He encouraged them to depart, since they could expect only "irresistible vengeance . . . blood or your banishment from this land of liberty." The writer specifically targeted William Smith Jr. (a close adviser of Carleton's) and the Reverend Charles Inglis for "complaining about the injustice of our laws and severity of our measures against you." Their arguments, the writer said, would be "as unsuccessful" as their schemes of "persuading the British army to *burn our houses and cut our throats.*" Brutus saw no problem with appropriating Loyalist property to discharge American debts. He had no patience with the accusation that Americans were violating the provisional treaty, because the British were transporting "many thousand negroes, the property of citizens of these states," out of town. Brutus even referenced the fraught aftermath of September 15, 1776: "What was intended by marking our houses with G. Rex and an arrow, when the British army took possession of New-York in 1776?" The rebels had fled the city then, "animated with the hope, that, in due time, their cause would be vindicated, their cause revenged," and independence won.[19]

Rebel crowds followed up these threats with outright violence against Loyalists who ventured outside New York. Throughout the region, Loyalists reported harassment, robbery, and violence, including murders and summary executions. John Morin Scott, now New York's secretary of state under Governor George Clinton, warned, "It is most certain We are not at peace with Great Britain." Carleton complained to Clinton about such treatment: "Every person who attempted to go from hence, into any part of the country beyond our limits, was driven back," sometimes with "great violence," while the rebels who came into New York City splattered civilians with "Menaces & insults." New York was violating "that spirit which since the pacification ought to prevail," and it was Clinton's responsibility to restrain the "lower classes" from "acts of vindictive violence." The bloody brutality of 1776 had returned with a vengeance, and Clinton had little inclination to restrain it.[20]

Once again, many called for reconciliation. As Addison, a Loyalist, had hoped in April, "Nations have their Fits of Inebriation," but "having washed away the Blood, they will [become] Friends over a mugg." In July, he hoped that the more humane and reasonable faction would carry more weight than "Ignorance, villany, Fanaticism & religious Intolerance." But by October 29, he understood that the villains and fanatics had prevailed: "I detest them more & more every Day. . . . They have no Bowels; no Feeling," and "Equal to their cruelty is their folly too; in driving away, in Despair, 40,000 Persons with (at the lowest Computation) Half a million in their Pockets."[21]

William Stephens Smith, Washington's aide, appreciated what Addison meant: he regretted that Loyalists "will be drove from this Country who are not conscious of any other Crime than that of residing within the British Lines"; he worried that the evacuation would leave behind "a City destitute of Inhabitants" and invite resentful Loyalists to become "troublesome neighbours" in Canada. Alexander Hamilton, too, thought it was shortsighted to allow the "popular phrenzy" to drive the Loyalists away; Robert R. Livingston replied, "I seriou[s]ly lament with you the violent spirit of persecution which prevails here," which he thought would harm "the wealth commerce & future tranquility of the state." New York was destined to be an important economic engine, if only cooler heads could extinguish these petty concerns. From what Livingston could see, vengeance against Loyalists stemmed not from "patriotic motives" but from "a blind spirit of revenge & resentment" or "the most sordid interest": to acquire Loyalists' houses, to banish the Loyalists as commercial rivals and creditors, and to "reduce the price of Living by depopulating the town." For the time being, the American advocates for reintegration got very little traction; in the long run, however, their desire to restore peace allowed thousands of former Loyalists to remain in the United States.[22]

Many in Britain, too, wanted to see a renewed amity with the United States, which might keep the new nation away from the French (fig. 14.2). On July 22, 1783, a group of merchants called for the resumption of trade with the United States. Although Britain restricted American trade with the West Indies, other trading routes flourished. The British government had little appetite for stoking the embers of the American war. David Hartley, one of the British peace commissioners, suggested that "the Alliance of America" might effectively substitute for former colonial ties. If Britain could dispel any "suspicion of retaining secret thoughts of resentment," its commerce with America would give it an advantage over its European rivals. "We have sacrificed too much to passion already," Hartley wrote. "Let us be wiser now." There was no sense in fostering "regret for things which are past recovery," because such bitterness would only lead to "our inevitable ruin."[23]

General Carleton saw things differently. In October 1782, he still believed the ministry wanted to hold on to its American colonies; he was zealous for "more fighting" to recover them. He felt certain that the American republic was bound to collapse under its own weight. With the help of the navy, the empire could manipulate American anarchy for its own ends. Carleton looked for signs of unrest everywhere. Continental troops had mutinied. A faction of Vermonters might be threatening to split off and join the British Empire. Perhaps Britain could unite its remaining colonies under "One chief" who could provide "the model of a wise and mild government" nearby. It might even be possible to arrange "the return of the thirteen states" to the king's dominions once "they . . . feel the consequences of their own folly."[24]

Fig. 14.2. This satire shows America (represented by a Native American woman) and Britannia preparing to kiss and reconcile as other European powers strain to keep them apart. Thomas Colley, *The reconciliation between Britania and her daughter America*, [London], 1782, Library of Congress, Prints and Photographs Division.

Five days before he issued the warrant for the Great Fire commission, Carleton wrote, "Men of all parties consider another revolution as inevitable and at no great distance." Noting a dispute between Connecticut and New York, he reported that many Americans were alarmed about restrictions on trade with the British West Indies. He believed that the "fierce republicans" were "on the decline," while "Many others" were waxing nostalgic for monarchical government and the security of the British Empire.[25]

A week later, Carleton dined with Daniel Parker, an American official appointed to supervise property interests in New York. Parker reported that Carleton was awaiting news that he would be appointed Britain's ambassador to the United States. If Carleton really expected this, he was due for further disappointment, but it would be significant if Carleton believed, as late as October 1783, that his relationship with the United States would continue—and might even lead to his having a leadership role in New York once again.[26]

Nothing came of these fantasies, but they show that Carleton perceived the American situation differently from his superiors back in London. Even after his dreams of using the New York garrison had fizzled, he still saw opportunities for the British lion to press its advantage. While Franklin and Washington might complain about British depredations and enslaved property, Carleton wanted to show that Great Britain knew how to ensure peace and safety with honor. The states were confiscating Loyalist property, claiming it was their due, and Carleton may have been defiantly trying to balance the ledger. He probably knew that obtaining recompense from the rebels for the Great Fire was impossible, but perhaps the British government could use the investigation as another opportunity to show its munificence and gratitude toward the Loyalists. To him, such considerations would have been important.

Perhaps he thought of publicizing the findings of his investigation. He could have revived the charge that New Englanders had burned New York City, exposed the "fierce republicans" for what they were, watered the "root of animosity" among Americans, and argued that rejoining the British Empire was preferable to living among the continent's violent, anarchic factions. War or no war, Great Britain and the United States were destined for entanglement—as two countries with a shared language, as commercial rivals, as geopolitical adversaries, as North American neighbors, and as former partners with outstanding debts. Carleton did not think the relationship would be a peaceable one, but he could at least find some justice for the Loyalists and give Great Britain the moral leverage it needed to entice Americans back to the empire.

Carleton's deputy adjutant general and secretary, Major Frederick Mackenzie—a witness to the 1776 fire—delivered a warrant to three officers, asking them "diligently to pursue the necessary investigation." Carleton chose Brigadier General William Martin of the Royal Artillery, Major William John Darby of the Royal Fusiliers (or 7th Regiment), and Major George Beckwith of the 37th Regiment of Foot. Martin had supplied Carleton with important intelligence and advice over the past year.

Darby had captained a light infantry company in the 17th Regiment during the 1776 campaign and was captured at the Battle of Stony Point in 1779. Beckwith was Carleton's senior aide-de-camp and ran his secret service.[27]

The three commissioners were empowered to gather documentary evidence, swear witnesses, and compel assistance from anyone under Carleton's "command and protection." They appointed a secretary to keep minutes: Ward Chipman, a lawyer from Marblehead, Massachusetts, had served as deputy muster master general for the Loyalist provincial troops. Chipman had returned, eleven days before, from a journey through New England to visit family one last time before resettling in Nova Scotia and New Brunswick. He had heard that his mentor's house in Cambridge had been confiscated, which he was tempted to shrug off as "the common misfortune of the Loyalists"; but when he saw the house and recalled the "happy hours" he had spent there, he "reflected that he was now banished from his Country & rob'd of his property, his hopes of providing for his Children frustrated, & all the agreable prospects he had formed at an end—Pity, resentment, indignation, grief alternately operated & distress'd me." A few weeks later, Chipman returned to New York and began keeping records of the 1783 commission. As a result, unlike whatever trials or hearings General William Howe might have held in 1776, some written testimony survives: Carleton's warrant, the minutes of the board's first meeting, a partial schedule of interviews, and thirty-eight depositions.[28]

Realizing that many important witnesses had already departed for Canada, the commissioners began by writing to Benjamin Marston (another Marblehead Loyalist, who had fled to Nova Scotia in 1776) and justices of the peace in Shelburne and Port Roseway, asking them to examine other witnesses who had already migrated from New York. Having heard nothing ten days later, they sent the request again. They also requested information from the local Board of Police under Andrew Elliot; the board replied on October 24.[29]

After their initial meeting, the commissioners began interviewing witnesses on Monday, October 20. The commission met for six days, rested on Sunday, and met for the next five days; they usually interviewed between one and four witnesses beginning at 11 a.m., or occasionally at noon or 1 p.m. When news arrived on October 29 that the final peace treaty had been signed in Paris, the committee's work slowed, and they met only five times during the first two weeks of November. They interviewed Sergeant John Norton of the 43rd Regiment on November 12, the same day Carleton finally resolved on a date for evacuation; although the commissioners adjourned until 11 a.m. the following day, there is no evidence of further meetings.[30]

As they learned more about what they wanted to ask, by the fifth day (October 24), the commissioners hit upon the first four questions that they repeated to several witnesses:

1. Whether he at any time supposed the fire was accidental,
2. Whether he ever conceived the City of New York was set on fire by the King's Troops either designedly or otherwise,
3. Whether he knows any thing of the Pumps or fire Buckets or Engines being designedly destroyed or rendered useless the night of the fire or previous to it, and
4. Whether he knows of any Matches or combustibles being found in any house in the City at or near the time of the fire.[31]

The rest of the questions came up in subsequent days:

5. Had the witness seen incendiaries with combustibles?[32]
6. What was the fire's place of origin and progress?[33]
7. What direction was the wind blowing?[34]
8. Did the witness observe active interference with fire-fighting efforts?[35]
9. Had the witness heard prior rumors about rebel troops setting fire to the city?[36]
10. What did the witness know about the removal of fire buckets?[37]

11. What did the witness know about the removal of the city's bells?[38]

12. How far had the fire spread when Trinity Church caught fire?[39]

The commissioners wanted to know whether British troops had set the fire. No one answered yes to this question; even Comfort Sands, a rebel legislator, replied, "It must have been equally against their interest as of the Americans." The investigators kept asking anyway, apparently to eliminate it as an explanation for the fire.[40]

They also probed the theory that the fire was an accident by asking witnesses what they remembered about the wind, engines, pumps, buckets, and bells, and whether incendiary materials had been carelessly left in the city. The commissioners tried to fish out the rebels' designs by asking about rumors, sabotage, incendiaries caught in the act, combustibles they used, and interference with firefighters.

From the testimonies, the commissioners heard about a number of alleged incendiaries: Abraham Van Dyck and Wright White, the boat crews from New England, the man in the white cap, the five men and a woman behind St. Paul's Chapel, the men and women dragged from Cruger's Wharf with their matches, the Scotsman and the foreigner in the Provost, and others. They heard theories about how the fire started, learned about the incendiary materials squirreled away in various parts of the city, and heard dramatic tales about the fire's progress. They probed whether the New York Provincial Congress might have been behind it all, or the New Englanders, or a rebel army officer. They heard a cacophony of voices, a jumble that may add up to nothing, or they heard some of history's most detailed hints of a radical conspiracy to burn New York City.

The commissioners interviewed William Waddell, a wealthy merchant. When the uprising against Great Britain broke out, Waddell was serving as one of the city's aldermen. He was an ardent Loyalist who served as lieutenant colonel for one of the provincial regiments; at the end of the war, he left his native New York City for London. When the British occupied New York on September 15, 1776, Howe directed Waddell "to see the Pumps, fire-buckets & Engines repaired & put in order that they might be ready for use in case a fire should happen." On the night of the fire, he "exerted himself during the Night to stop its progress."[41]

Despite his political sympathies, Waddell called the fire an accident. He had an answer for every suggestion that the fire was intentional. Did the rebels sabotage the firefighting equipment before the fire? Waddell had examined the pumps, buckets, and engines before the fire, and they were "put in order." Were matches and combustibles discovered on Cruger's Wharf? Yes, but these "were prepared for the purpose of fitting out fire-Ships." Did the troops catch saboteurs with combustible materials? Yes, but "he supposes they had taken [them] from the stores from mere motives of curiosity, without any design of doing mischief with them." He had not heard about any interference with firefighting efforts, or the rebel rumors about setting the city on fire. How, then, had the fire started? "He heard the next day that it began in a small house at Whitehall where it was said some Sailors or Soldiers had carelessly left a fire." Waddell did concede that the handles of "Several fire Buckets . . . had been cut during the fire."[42]

By the time the commissioners came to their last question, about whether anyone had obstructed firefighting efforts, even Waddell seemed to doubt himself. He mentioned the baker, Samuel Charlotte, "a disaffected character" (meaning a rebel) who had hidden a fire ladder. The ladder would have required from six to eight men to lift, but Charlotte refused to name any accomplices. Waddell never found out what happened to Charlotte, and that was the end of his interview with Carleton's officers. Waddell may have believed the fire was an accident, but he still acknowledged the suspicious characters lurking at the fire, committing acts that looked a lot like sabotage.[43]

Furthermore, when he applied for a Loyalist claim a few months later in March 1784, Waddell wrote that he had done everything he could "for the preservation of the City from the Meditated Conflagration of the disaffected, Still remaining, which they had Almost Effected on the Great Fire." Despite his testimony before the army commission, he concluded along with his fellow New York Loyalists that the rebels had planned to burn New York City and almost succeeded. It is unclear why Waddell offered contradictory testimony, but his eventual conclusion makes the overall results of the commission look even more definitive.[44]

Out of thirty-eight surviving depositions, only six other witnesses suggested that the fire was an accident. The committee interviewed Comfort Sands and Isaac Stoutenburgh, two members of the New York Provincial Congress in 1776, asking whether their colleagues had ordered the fire. Both said no. Neither man was present in the city on the night of the fire, and these committed rebels had every reason to say the fire was an accident.[45]

James Wells said, "It appeared to me to be accidental," and he based some of his testimony on information from a woman who was later deemed unreliable. The firefighter Jeronymus Alstyne was uncertain whether the fire was deliberate or an accident. Curiously, in January 1777, General James Robertson announced, "There is Ground to believe that the Rebels, not satisfied with the Destruction of Part of the City, entertain Designs of burning the Rest." A few of the town's "principal Inhabitants" had asked him to form a watch to prevent further incendiarism, and Robertson appointed eighteen people, including both Wells and Alstyne, as ward superintendents. Back then, did they agree with Robertson that the fire was deliberate as they stood ready to arrest future fire starters? When the committee asked Wells in 1783 whether he intended to remain in town after the British evacuation, he said he did. Alstyne also stayed in New York City.[46]

William Shipman, a Loyalist who also believed that the fire began accidentally, returned to New York in 1792. The peruke maker Alexander Bridges said the fire was an accident; at the same time, he reported threats that vandals had made to his landlord in August 1776 and gave testimony about a man in custody carrying incendiary materials on the morning after the fire. It is not clear where he lived after his testimony. For the most part, the seven witnesses who called the fire an accident either gave mixed testimony or were outright rebels or were reconcilable Loyalists who seem to have adjusted their memories for the sake of pursuing their happiness in federal New York.[47]

On the other side of the debate was a formidable list of British officers and soldiers, garrison officials, clergymen, firefighters, and prominent Loyalist civilians. Twenty-one of them, when asked whether they thought the fire was accidental, answered "no," "I did not," and "I never did" or otherwise affirmed that the fire had been set deliberately—Captain

George Tripp said, for instance, "I always understood that the City was designedly set on fire by the Americans."[48]

Eight other deponents did not say as much outright but pointed to other evidence implying a deliberate fire: John L. C. Roome, John Alstyne, and William Elsworth had heard rumors; the merchant William Hervey found a powder train leading to a cartridge under a straw bed, and four men of the 43rd Regiment caught incendiaries in the act or found incendiary materials. The statements of these twenty-nine witnesses added up to an overwhelming majority vote that the fire had been set on purpose. (Two other witnesses gave less useful testimony, and the clerk crossed out all or part of their statements.) The board could not have been impressed with the theory that the conflagration was accidental, though they did give it a fair hearing. If they reached a conclusion, however, it is lost to history. The investigation seems to have petered out, with no indication of its findings being sent to the bureaucracy in London or publicized in newspapers. It was the last time any deliberative body would inquire into the Great Fire of 1776.[49]

Guy Carleton's commission, like William Howe's trials, had failed. The commissioners could not interview everyone they wanted, because too many had died or left town. The evidence they collected was based on seven years' recollection; the deponents' testimony was the product of fright, confusion, anger, the limits of personal perception, and the imperfections of memory. The commissioners must have concluded that the rebels had deliberately set the fire, but proving it was another matter. Even if the commissioners had been able to complete their work and offer a verdict, Carleton may have suspected that his superiors would have little interest.

The British were doing their best to settle the city's debts as the treaty and the evacuation brought the war to an end. The Great Fire would remain unresolved: it was too expensive to warrant compensation, too uncertain to offer resolution, and too inflammatory to bring about peace. In the end, Carleton's "important considerations" were not important enough, except to the Loyalists whose homes and estates had burned. To them, the rebels had a lot to answer for.[50]

For a few years, a spirit of violence and vengeance against the Loyalists stalked America, particularly New York; in March 1784, the memory of the king's men destroying American towns (as opposed to "fair and mitigated Hostilities") was so raw that the legislature refused to abide by provisions for Loyalists in the Treaty of Paris. These vengeful impulses did fade; frightened by the localist parties that had emerged during the Revolution, a more conservative group of financiers and nationalists intervened. They believed in the repayment of American debts, the re-integration of Loyalists to help capitalize the new nation, enduring trade relationships with Great Britain, and a centralization of power in a stronger federal government. Alexander Hamilton, John Jay, George Washington, and other nationalists built a new constitutional order out of their insistence that Americans should respect property rights. To redeem the confiscations and devastation that had helped define the war, they offered new opportunities for investment. Both factions hastened the disappearance of the Great Fire from people's consciousness. Forget-ting the Great Fire became essential to building an American nation that would be acceptable among the community of nations.[51]

Hard-line Loyalists, British veterans, and Carleton himself appar-ently hoped that an accusation of a deliberate fire might somehow serve as leverage, perhaps as an argument for compensating the Loyalists. He may have formed the commission with such schemes in mind. Reconcil-iationists on both sides had no interest, however; nor did ardent Ameri-can patriots, who were deeply invested in laying all the war's atrocities at the feet of the British. The peaceable faction of Parliament wanted the war to end and gave up on trying to pressure the Americans. British mer-chants wanted to resume trade with America, and cosmopolitan Ameri-cans like Alexander Hamilton wanted to include wealthy Loyalists in their dreams for American prosperity. Anglicans on both sides of the Atlantic acceded to the creation of a new Episcopal Church in the United States. Loyalists like Wells, Jeronymus Alstyne, and the tavern keeper David Grim (whose map and story of the Great Fire became highly influential) hoped to quietly reintegrate by sliding away from the gaze of the die-hard anti-Loyalists in New York State and elsewhere. For these groups to achieve their pragmatic aims, the Carleton commission had to come to nothing. The consolidating forces that built the United States had no room for whatever radical actors had set fire to New York City.

The new nation could only enjoy a peaceful transfer of sovereignty if the origins of the Great Fire remained ambiguous.[52]

The commission became a footnote to the British army's evacuation from New York. Americans started crafting their own version of what the Revolution ought to mean for future generations. In Great Britain, people were already forgetting about the loss of the American colonies. Carleton returned to North America as Baron Dorchester, enacting his visions of imperial governance from Quebec City, alongside William Smith Jr. as chief justice and Charles Inglis as British North America's first bishop. They were joined by thousands of Loyalist refugees who helped make up the backbone of British Canada.[53]

Applicants to the Loyalist claims commission had one last chance to report the ruinous effects of the Great Fire on their children's future. Some did receive recompense from the British government, though not as much as they hoped, and losses from the Great Fire were never, by themselves, a valid basis for a claim. Some misfortunes were chalked up to the exigencies of war. As for Americans, Congress discussed wartime damage claims on June 3, 1784: "According to the laws and usages of nations, a State is not obliged to make compensation for damages done to its citizens by an enemy, or wantonly and unauthorised by its own troops"; although "humanity requires" some poor relief, Congress referred such petitioners to the states. When a veteran mentioned his losses from the fire, he sounded hopeless that he would ever recover. In 1789, John Lasher, former colonel of the New York militia, wrote to Washington lamenting "the loss of three Houses of considerable value in the City of New York in the great Fire which hapned a few days after the evacuation of this City by our Army." These losses, combined with currency depreciation and military service, hurt Lasher's wealth when otherwise he might have "supported his Family with comfort & decency." Elizabeth Thompson, who kept house for Washington during the war, did receive a pension after describing the properties she lost during the Great Fire.[54]

New York's leaders had another task: to erase the ashy relics that the fire had left. At the behest of the mayor, a grand jury investigated "Canvas-town" in the summer of 1784 and found "numerous receptacles for the vicious and abandoned," which they endeavored to "suppress."

The next month, the sheriff demolished some of these houses as a "public nuisance," while the "Canvas-town heroines . . . tore their dishevel'd hair—and mutter'd curses, horrible to hear." Parades and rioters gathered at the "Burnt-Church" when they marched down Broadway. For decades the area was known for crime and vice, as city and state government worked to restore the infrastructure between Broadway and the Hudson River.[55]

People characterized the ruins as romantic or pitiable, to better highlight the phoenix-like success story that New York City became. William Alexander Duer was a grandson of Lord Stirling, a judge, and president of Columbia College. His earliest memory, at age three, was returning to the city after the British evacuation. "No visible attempts had been made since the fire to remove the ruins," he remembered in 1848, "and as the edifices destroyed were chiefly of brick, the skeletons of the remaining walls cast their grim shadows upon the pavement, imparting an unearthly aspect to the street. The semi-circular front of old Trinity still reared its ghastly head, and seemed to deepen while it hallowed the solitude of the surrounding graves." His gothic evocation of New York's ruins was comforting, since a grand new Trinity Church building had already risen at the head of Wall Street, and the city had grown to more than half a million people.[56]

Later generations reimagined the Great Fire as a disaster that wiped the slate clean and inspired new beginnings. They celebrated the destruction of the crooked colonial streets in favor of the nineteenth-century grid, which they saw as a sign of progress. In 1917, Henry Collins Brown (who founded the Museum of the City of New York) wrote about the "dumps" and "shanties" that "were erected temporarily in lower Broadway" after the Great Fire, which "gave the noble thoroughfare a decidedly poverty stricken appearance." He mocked the grocers, tinmen (including John Baltus Dash), saddlers, and other artisans who lived on lower Broadway in 1785 as "squatters," "nondescripts and hucksters," compared with illustrious families like Livingston, Lawrence, Varick, and Gracie, who replaced them by 1793. To Brown, the sooner the Great Fire was erased from the landscape, the better. New York was still a city that never learns its lessons.[57]

On November 2, 1783, Washington bid his troops farewell, trusting

that the "steady & decent tenor of behaviour" that "has generally distinguished . . . the army" would carry over into their lives as citizens. Three
of his senior generals wrote, "Most gladly would we cast a veil on every
act which sullies the reputation of our Country—never should the page
of history be stained with its dishonor—even from our memories should
the idea be erased." The officers were referring to Congress's failure to
provide for the veterans, but the desire to cast a veil over the war's frightful nature was powerful. Washington triumphantly rode into town on
November 22 and congratulated Ephraim Brasher and his committee
of returning rebel refugees. (Brasher had been third lieutenant of the
Grenadiers under Abraham Van Dyck.) These New Yorkers had bravely
persevered, Washington said, and Americans would remember them
"with admiration and applause to the latest Posterity." He gave his benediction: "May the tranquility of your City be perpetual," he wrote. "May
the Ruins soon be repaired, Commerce flourish, Science be fostered,
and all the civil and social virtues be cherished." New York was now an
American city, destined for cruelty and greatness, genius and folly.[58]

Forgetting the Fire

John Joseph Henry remembered staring at the Great Fire of 1776, "a most beautiful and luminous, but baleful sight" from the deck of a British frigate, where he was a prisoner of war. "The effect upon the eye was astonishingly grand," even "sublime." Henry was born in Lancaster, Pennsylvania; as a teenager, he enlisted against his father's will and joined the Continental Army expedition that tried to conquer Canada in late 1775. After being captured, months as a prisoner of war left him with scurvy that impaired his health for life. Aboard the *Pearl* in New York harbor, he saw the fire from four miles away.[1]

From that distance, the light looked like "the flame of a candle." Suddenly Henry saw "an original, distinct, and new formed fire" on Broadway, just a moment after it first appeared on Whitehall Slip. At first, like General Silliman, the prisoners of war aboard the *Pearl* "harboured suspicions" that the British had set the fire. But as the wind picked up and the fire spread—for hours—Henry and his comrades reconsidered. They saw boats stream away from the British fleet, sending sailors to help put out the fire, which "repelled the idea, that our enemies were the incendiaries." Some of the *Pearl*'s sailors came back aboard with tales of thieves and incendiaries being bayoneted or tossed into the fire.[2]

Considering the facts before him, Henry concluded that "the most low and vile of persons" had tried to destroy New York City. Although "for the honor of our country and its good name," American history books were already attributing the fire to "accidental circumstances," Henry refused to play along: "As the fact occurred within my own view, the eloquence of Cicero could not convince me that the firing was accidental."[3]

Writing many years later, Henry had become disillusioned by Americans' failure to properly venerate the nation's veterans, the excesses of the French Revolution, and the democratic impulses that swept Jeffersonian Republicans to victory in his home state. His embittered stance resembles that of another Pennsylvania veteran, Alexander Graydon. The British had captured Graydon at Fort Washington and let him wander the city on parole: because "nothing is more congenial to the soul in gloom than to wander among ruins," he took a stroll through Canvas Town and "meditated on the horrors of this guilty city." Although he recognized that American prisoners of war (particularly the enlisted men) suffered terribly, he was inclined to keep this in perspective. "War, indeed, in its essence is cruelty, especially civil war: its tendency is to make men ferocious and merciless," Graydon wrote. "Though the abuse of power is always detestable, yet it may not be improper to look at home" before calling the British "monsters of unheard of cruelty."[4]

Graydon and Henry both became members of Pennsylvania's establishment. The Jeffersonians drummed Graydon out of office in 1799. Henry remained a president judge (or chief justice) of the state's second district court until his enemies started demanding his removal in 1809, on account of the health problems that had plagued him since Quebec. Although the effort failed, Judge Henry died a broken man in 1811, the same year his account was published. Henry yearned to celebrate the righteousness of the American Revolution—he had seen too many men suffer and die to be anything but grateful for their service.[5]

Henry and Graydon lamented that the veterans had sacrificed their bodies for their country, only to see worthless, petty upstarts replace them in positions of public leadership. Henry was unwilling to let an illusory narrative of American greatness obscure the realities of the war against Great Britain. His education, his political discontent, his health troubles, and a lifetime of experience had pried open a place in his heart. He could think the unthinkable. He could bear witness. Incendiarism was wrong, mistreatment of prisoners was wrong, and summary killings were wrong, and wiser heads must face the hard facts: war brings destruction and suffering, and it takes an emptiness of soul to look away.[6]

After sharing the army's ordeal during the failed invasion of Canada, Henry told the tale of the Great Fire: the last thing he saw before the British released him. He concluded, "It may be well, that a nation, in the heat and turbulence of war, should endeavor to promote its interests, by propagating reports of its own innocency and prowess, and accusing its enemy of flagrant enormity and dastardliness." Henry knew how the rebels had spread tales of British atrocity during the war. "But when peace comes," he continued, "let us, in God's name, do justice, to them and ourselves. Baseness and villa[i]ny are the growth of all climes, and of all nations."[7]

Henry insisted that the fire was important. After all his horrible experiences on the Canadian expedition, he believed that his searing final image of the war—a city on fire—had meaning. An avid reader of history, he thought it was perilous to forget.

Henry was engaged in a conflict that continues to this day: How do we remember the American Revolution, and what stories should we tell about it? Why do some deeds of the Revolution seem unthinkable, and why do some parts of the Revolution not seem to fit the heroic narrative? What do we make of "disaffected" Americans who never joined the common cause, Black people who refused their chains, women with torches in their hands, schemes to disunite the Union, and the devastation of thousands of homes? Why do we not remember the Great Fire of 1776, when a group of rebels tried to burn New York City, successfully burned more than a fifth of it, and then covered up their crime to protect the story of the Revolution? The Great Fire shows how much is still misunderstood about the American Revolution. Forgetting the fire was essential to the creation of a national story.[8]

Since women were supposed to tend the home fires—not start house fires—their wartime involvement (except as victims) disappeared. Since whites attempted to exclude people of color from the boundaries of citizenship, the revolutionary service of Native Americans, Black people, and mixed-race people was excised from memory. Since American elites wanted an orderly society, they dismissed the suggestion that people's resentment of wealthy and established figures had spurred many to action. Since the United States was supposed to be humane, honorable, and just, a due respecter of property rights and an equal participant in the community of nations, it could not have committed atrocities or scurrilous acts. The British, too, had reasons to suppress the fire—their troops had killed several incendiaries on the spot, after all—and by 1783 it was clear that the Crown was abandoning its Loyalist allies and planning a new commercial relationship with the United States.

Wartime havoc or human intent, or both, caused the fire. It happened either by means of neglect, a nihilistic impulse to destroy, a radical imperative to disrupt, or a strategic initiative to slow the British offensive. To believe that the fire was a complete accident, all the following would have to be true:

Americans' previous threats to burn New York City were empty words.

American generals discussed burning New York City upon retreat, but at the urging of legislative assemblies, they decided against this plan, and nothing came of it.

Rank-and-file soldiers and civilian allies obeyed directives not to cause devastation without positive orders.

The fire overwhelmed the city's infrastructure at a moment of wartime disarray. The city had built with wood instead of stone, brick, and slate. It was too difficult to deploy water quickly. The rebels had removed the church bells, so the warning did not sound in time. Many of the city's firefighters were gone, and too few civilians remained to form bucket brigades. Firefighting equipment was misplaced or in disrepair.

The fire spread so swiftly, aided by the wind and flaming shingles, that witnesses mistakenly believed that it had more than one ignition point.

British soldiers were driven into such irrational frenzy by this accidental fire that they falsely accused several people of being incendiaries and killed them.

The British apprehended people and erroneously accused them of tampering with firefighting equipment and carrying combustible materials. Those people were doing nothing wrong.

Amos Fellows and Abraham Van Dyck were imprisoned before September 21, 1776, and the British falsely accused them of burning New York City.

British and Loyalist accusers were propagating a conspiracy theory born of their own prejudices, anger, and fear. They were also trying to cover for their incompetence, since they had not prevented the fire from spreading.

The British propagated a conspiracy theory in print, hoping to paint the rebels as wanton, indiscriminate destroyers of an important American city.

Any rebels who suggested that the Americans had started the fire were unreliable, because they were at a distance from the fire; their judgments were mistaken or based on hearsay.

Although rebel newspapers also propagated wild theories about the fire, this does not mean that they were deliberately trying to bury a secret truth.

The British invented Abraham Patten's confession. Washington urged Congress to arrange discreet support for Patten's family in recognition of his other espionage activities.

By 1783, supporters of the Crown were so convinced of their prior conclusions about the Great Fire that they still clung to a false idea about its origins.

Read a certain way, the evidence can support each of these statements. Together, they may well represent a safer interpretation. The "ac-

cident thesis" disregards a great deal of evidence offered by Crown supporters by assuming that animosity toward the rebels motivated their
observations. If the fire had no cause but the chaos of history, then chaos
might best explain the troubling, irrational parts of the story, such as the
summary executions and accusations that look hasty or outright false.
The "accident thesis," appropriately, draws no conclusions from missing
evidence, such as the records of the 1776 inquest that Howe kept in his
papers, any reference to the 1783 inquest in Carleton's personal papers,
the prison records lost at sea, or a "secret" order, if any, that Congress
might have sent to Washington. Lost documents can offer no evidence,
nor is it possible to conjure documents that may never have existed. Skep-
tics may well still deny that the fire was set intentionally, but perhaps no
evidence could satisfy such doubts.

A historical claim for a purposeful fire would be easier if a deliberative body had rendered a conclusive verdict, if an incendiary had left a
written firsthand confession, or if other direct evidence had emerged.
Incendiarism was not "proven" in a judicial hearing of any kind, and it
never will be. If the skeptic wants to insist that a deliberate fire cannot be
proven beyond reasonable doubt, well, that is true; but then it is also true
that an accidental fire also cannot meet that standard of proof. Given the
imperfect evidence, there might be room for doubt either way; yet historians have told hundreds of stories about the Revolution with much
more limited evidence.

Rebel commanders, including Washington, saw the strategic wisdom of destroying New York. Soldiers threatened to burn it at least as
early as May 1776 for a variety of reasons, including revenge against the
British. By the middle of August, rumors of this plan became particularly intense. Some New Yorkers, including the newly appointed fire
chief, buried their valuables as a precaution. Residents found combustible materials before, during, and after the event. Someone set a house
on fire on September 15 as the rebels evacuated, and soldiers found a
trail of gunpowder. Multiple witnesses reported that the fire broke out
in several places at once. Others caught suspects setting fires, carrying
combustibles, and tampering with equipment. At least one rebel spy *did*
confess, at least according to the Loyalist press.

The British held hearings in 1776 and 1783 without any public announcement of convictions, perhaps because such pronouncements would have had little political value for the British at those moments. Still, the extensive testimony before the Carleton commission and the Loyalist claims commission added further evidence. The problem is immediately apparent: most of this evidence comes from the British and their allies. Not all of it, however—some Americans, like Silliman or Henry, also agreed that fellow rebels must have set the fire. Plenty of Americans accepted this suggestion, both at the time and in some of the histories they wrote. In this book, I have endeavored to resolve the conflicting accounts of the Great Fire of New York, and I argue that the evidence is sufficient to prove that rebels deliberately set New York City on fire.

Did Washington order the burning of New York? For many Americans, such an act would be unthinkable. Even many Britons believed that burning New York would have been out of character for Washington. Most Americans have heard of Mason Weems's fictional story of the young boy too honest to lie about a cherry tree. Could Washington have made kindling of an entire city and never told? One might readily believe this of later American leaders, many of whom gave orders to burn or destroy—but many people think of Washington as different. Native Americans, of course, were under no such illusions.[9]

Setting aside notions of Washington's innate character, we must consider his stated deference to civilian authority, his directives about destructive warfare, and the obedience of his men.

Every biographer of Washington emphasizes his respect for Congress's authority, which he acknowledged when he accepted the post of commander in chief. The delegates did not, however, necessarily expect him to follow their orders to precision. Congress understood that it was a large legislative body whose members had different opinions, and they were usually far removed from the battlefield. As a matter of trust and pragmatism, Congress granted Washington leeway in his military decisions. They even clarified for Washington that the decisions of his war councils were not binding, and he was free to act as he saw fit.[10]

It may appear as if John Hancock unambiguously ordered Washington not to fire the town. Yet Washington may still have burned New York City without leaving a paper trail that would have damaged his reputation. He was ready to destroy Boston during the siege of 1776 for the sake of military advantage. He understood the political risks and strategic benefits of burning New York City. Whether or not Washington authorized the Great Fire beforehand, he certainly applauded it afterward in his private correspondence and personally vouched for three officers associated with the fire: Amos Fellows, Abraham Patten, and Abraham Van Dyck, just as he considered Jonathan Williams Austin's reinstatement.

Finally, it would be unrealistic to expect that Washington's authority over his men was absolute. In 1776, his army mainly included undisciplined, liberty-minded young men and boys. The militiamen (and many regular soldiers) felt more loyalty to their province than to a Continental institution; they often resented taking orders from commanders who hailed from other provinces and had different notions of discipline. In a vast, diverse army, some men grew defiant, and disobedience appears to have risen to a crescendo during the weeks leading up to the fire.

Before the fire, the rebel troops around New York had only known garrison duty, fortification, retreat, and defeat. The routs at Long Island and Kip's Bay dealt morale a severe blow, which the small engagement at Harlem Heights could only partially redeem. The rebels fastened on an idea they had discussed for months, which was to burn New York and deprive the British of the headquarters they coveted. Perhaps Washington gave some troops or secret agents permission (tacitly or explicitly) to burn New York City. His permission may have been designed to appease the more radical factions in his army. Or perhaps a group of soldiers and civilians slipped the bonds of elite control and did what they thought was best for American liberty, acting of their own volition. There is not always a puppeteer pulling the strings when street actions occur; and it may be too hasty to dismiss the fire as an inchoate, opportunistic crime with no underlying political or military strategy. People can think for themselves, act in accordance with their own ideologies, and make coherent political statements. The evidence suggests the possibility of coordination among the men and women who remained in town and the soldiers who skulked into the city by land or by sea. On the other hand, the incendiaries may have acted with more haste and spontaneity—a sudden, amorphous coalition taking matters into their own hands.[11]

The Great Fire emerges, in this picture, as a purposeful, political deed. Radicals wanted to attack wealthy Loyalists' property, destroy an Anglican church, stop the British army, disrupt the occupation, damage mighty warships, and kill the soldiers in garrison. Their motivations resound with the Dissenter's abhorrence for the Church of England, the New Englander's revulsion at New York City, the radical commoner's resentment of the elite, the soldier's impatience with his officers, the republican's hatred of New York's notorious Loyalists, and the zealous patriot's willingness to sacrifice the city in the face of outside invaders. The Great Fire, as a deliberate act, is still open to interpretation. We can call it a war crime, callous strategy, an act of social and political resistance, terrorism, or misguided folly.[12]

To the rebels, the Crown seduced people with trade, imperial ties, religious toleration, sexual freedom, and the laws of war. By contrast, the incendiaries stood for sect, republic, homeland, and new opportunities for freedom, or even for vengeance, frustration, and desperation. Some mixture of these ideals and feelings fused together among radical civilians and soldiers. Perhaps these motivations offer insight into the actions of spies like Patten, uniformed officers like Van Dyck and Fellows, soldiers like John Durkee's whaleboat men, and allied civilians like the "first Incendiary."

One of Britain's fatal mistakes was its persistent belief that thousands of Loyalists were waiting for the British army to arrive so that they could rise up and overthrow the small minority of rebellious Americans who had seized the levers of government. The fire should have taught the British, as early as 1776, that they were wrong to count on this. Even if a plurality of Americans had been willing to reconcile with the mother country, there was always a radical faction eager to push the British farther away. The rumors of an impending fire that became reality were an example of the radicals' unwillingness to reconcile. The New York Provincial Convention and the Continental Congress reluctantly acceded to Washington's retreat from New York City. On paper, they apparently encouraged Washington to leave the city intact, but the evidence suggests that either Washington or his men disobeyed them.[13]

The menacing of the city by the Royal Navy, its occupation by the rebels and subsequent occupation by the British army, had disrupted city life in countless ways. The fire certainly disrupted it further. A long night of firefighting delayed the British campaign only slightly, and in any case most of New York City survived; as Washington ruefully noted, "Enough of it remains to answer their purposes."

The Great Fire reveals an American rebellion that engaged in targeted destruction. Americans simultaneously condemned their enemies for doing much the same thing, which is why the central narrative of the American Revolution could never incorporate a story of Americans burning New York City. Rebel newspapers denied and minimized that story, drowning it in sizzling, blood-soaked stories of British summary executions. Historians, forced to choose between muddled evidence on the one side and strident denials on the other, used the seemingly straightforward evidence from Washington and Congress. Congress insisted to Washington that "no damage be done to the said city by his troops." That letter motivated many historians to dismiss the mass of rumors, eyewitnesses, incendiary materials, and even confessions. To them, the fire was nothing more than a footnote to the story of American origins.[14]

The British never convinced Americans of the justice of their rule, before or after the Declaration of Independence. They burned plenty of towns themselves, after all. A significant portion of their fellow Britons refused to believe that the rebels' aims were entirely wrong. Some of their own newspapers admired Washington and scorned American Loyalists. As a result, the Loyalists and British officers never convinced Britons or Americans that the rebels had burned New York—they could not even implant the idea that the fire was important. In the realms of public opinion, the fire was eclipsed by other elements of the campaign, other events of the war, and other branches of the empire. After the war, the British did what most losing sides do: they traded recriminations and even helped Americans to bury the memory. By then, the rebuilding of New York was someone else's responsibility. Thus the British felt no need to uphold their insistence that the rebels had burned New York. They abandoned the field, allowing the rebels to argue that the fire was a twist of fate.[15]

If the fire was deliberate, perhaps we might change our opinion of Franklin, who propagated the "accident thesis" for an international audience along with Robert Morris. We might change our perception of

Washington. His staff officers—Joseph Reed, Tench Tilghman, and William Tudor—claimed they knew nothing, as Henry Knox worked to insert more favorable stories in the newspaper. Many of the rebels who shaped the fire's story became leaders in the new republic.

A deliberate fire calls into question the importance of Nathan Hale, who was hanged for espionage the day after several other incendiaries were executed. He was remembered, but they were not. Abraham Patten, too, spoke noble words from *Cato* on the gallows. There are statues for Hale, but none for Patten.

The identification of incendiaries compels a reckoning with the idea that people from the margins—including women and people of color—played a central role in the drama of the Revolution. Americans eventually celebrated some women's contributions to the American Revolution, but mainstream American culture would not have celebrated female violence. Yet the "first Incendiary" may well have been the first American woman killed in action by the British army.[16]

Many rebels of color experienced fair treatment in the army, survived, claimed their autonomy, raised families, and received pensions from the United States government. Yet these surviving veterans had to fight for respect, land, and a livelihood in a society that increasingly discriminated against them on the basis of race and tried to render them invisible. Perhaps a Connecticut community mourned the soldier who helped to burn America's second-largest English city. Unfortunately, evidence about him and many other people of color who fought with the Continental Army is scarce, because the rebels mostly failed to acknowledge their service.[17]

New York City has never honestly reckoned with its baptism by fire. Washington Irving was born in April 1783, only a few blocks from Canvas Town. His family lived through the British occupation. He would later write that the history of New York is "worthy of being pondered over attentively, for it is by thus raking among the ashes of departed greatness, that the sparks of knowledge are to be found, and the lamp of wisdom illuminated." Irving and John Pintard (a founder of the New-York Historical Society) both denied that American rebels were responsible for the fire of 1776, a narrative that aligned with their shaping of colonial New York's history and their invention of Saint Nicholas as a patron saint for the city.[18]

Pintard seemed pleased that the Great Fire had made room for more growth, but thought it would have been better if the whole city had been razed, so that it could be rebuilt with the more orderly, rectangular grid plan. Like Graydon and Henry, Irving and Pintard were Federalists. But unlike the others, they were New Yorkers. To them, the city's renewal would be the key to its greatness, while its troubling revolutionary history offered little hope of guidance for the conservative future they envisioned. Along with most New York writers, they played down discomfiting stories like the burning of New York City and the devastating death toll of rebel soldiers aboard British prison ships. Instead they told stories that were better for civic harmony and the city's commercial growth.[19]

Irving, Pintard, and the earliest historians of New York City would not have identified with the extremist New Englanders, radical New Yorkers, or backcountry Scots Irishmen who were accused of setting the fire. Nor would they have aligned with an embittered Loyalist exile like Justice Thomas Jones, who criticized the atrocities perpetrated by both sides, and whose reminiscences were not published until 1879. Had New York's local writers been of a different cast of mind, they might have celebrated the fire as an act of patriotic self-sacrifice. Or, like John Joseph Henry, they might have grimly conceded that both sides had been guilty of wartime misconduct. They never told that story.

Many American historians have instead prioritized the celebration of liberty, equality, and unity. But the war itself mattered, because it tested these worthy ideals. The destruction and loss of property mattered: state legislatures, the Loyalist claims commission, and the Carleton commission all attempted to account for civilians' material suffering. People's lives, deaths, and wartime experiences also mattered, even when they did not fit the heroic tales of the Revolution that parents later told their children. The desire for reconciliation among Great Britain, many Loyalists, and the United States ended discussion of the harshest aspects of the war. People had an interest in cooperating to suppress a horrific and inglorious event.[20]

New York City is the product of its past destructions. Writers, artists, and filmmakers have imagined a hundred different catastrophes for it. Audiences thrill to these destructive fantasies, but an acknowledgment of New York's real past may better help prepare us for the disasters we face today, and in the future.[21]

Notes

Abbreviations

ADM	Admiralty
AFC	*Adams Family Correspondence,* ed. Lyman H. Butterfield (Cambridge, Mass.: Harvard University Press, 1963)
AO	Audit Office
BF	Benjamin Franklin
Bowater to Denbigh	John Bowater to Basil Feilding, Sixth Earl of Denbigh, Sept. 26, 1776, in *The Lost War: Letters from British Officers during the American Revolution,* ed. Marion Balderston and David Syrett (New York: Horizon Press, 1975)
CCHS	Connecticut Historical Society *Collections*
CCM	Minutes of a Commission to Investigate the Causes of the Fire in New York City, New York City Misc. MSS, NYHS
Cliffe to BC	Loftus Cliffe to Bartholomew Cliffe, Sept. 21–22, 1776, Loftus Cliffe Papers, WLCL
Cliffe to JC	Loftus Cliffe to Jack Cliffe, September 21, 1776, Loftus Cliffe Papers, WLCL
CO	Colonial Office
DAR	K. G. Davies, ed., *Documents of the American Revolution, 1770–1783 (Colonial Office Series)* (Dublin: Irish Academic Press, 1972–81)

DCHSNY · *Documents Relative to the Colonial History of the State of New York* [. . .], ed. E. B. O'Callaghan and Berthold Fernow (Albany, N.Y., 1853–87)

Duncan Journal · "Journals of Henry Duncan, Captain, Royal Navy, 1776–1782," ed. J. K. Laughton, in *Publications of the Navy Records Society,* vol. 20, *The Naval Miscellany,* vol. 1 (London, 1902)

Grant to Rigby · James Grant to Richard Rigby, Sept. 24, 1776, James Grant Papers, Army Career Series, GD 494, Box 29, Macpherson Grant of Ballindalloch Papers, National Records of Scotland, microfilm at David Library of the American Revolution

GW · George Washington

Hamond Account · Account of Andrew Snape Hamond's part in the American Revolution, 1775–77, 1783–85, Tracy W. McGregor Library of American History, Albert and Shirley Small Special Collections Library, University of Virginia

Hamond to Stanley · Andrew Snape Hamond to Hans Stanley, Sept. 24, 1776, in *Naval Documents of the American Revolution,* ed. William James Morgan (Washington, D.C.: Naval History Division, Department of the Navy, 1972), 6:974

Howe to Germain · William Howe to Lord George Germain, September 23, 1776, TNA CO 5/93, 559–60, LOC transcripts

Inglis to Hind · Charles Inglis to Richard Hind, Oct. 31, 1776, *DCHSNY* (Albany, N.Y., 1853), 3:643

JCC · *Journals of the Continental Congress, 1774–1789,* ed. Worthington C. Ford, Gaillard Hunt (Washington, D.C.: U.S. Government Printing Office, 1904–37)

JFBVHC · Journal of the First Brigade of the Von Heister Corps, 1776–77, English Translation, Letter H (from 1993 supplement), in Lion G. Miles and James L. Kochan, eds., Lidgerwood Collection of Hessian Transcripts on the American Revolution, Morristown National Historical Park

JPCNY · *Journals of the Provincial Congress, Provincial Convention, Committee of Safety and Council of Safety of the State of New-York, 1775–1777,* 2 vols. (Albany, N.Y., 1842)

LDC · *Letters of Delegates to Congress, 1774–1789,* ed. Paul H. Smith (Washington, D.C.: Library of Congress, 1977–2000)

Leslie to Leven · William Leslie to Earl of Leven and Melville, Sept. 25, 1776, Leven and Melville Muniments, G.D. 26/9/513, Scottish Record Office

LOC	Library of Congress
Mackenzie Diary	*Diary of Frederick Mackenzie: Giving a Daily Narrative of His Military Service as an Officer of the Regiment of Royal Welch Fusiliers during the Years 1775–1781 in Massachusetts Rhode Island and New York* (1930; New York: New York Times and Arno, 1968)
MCCNY	*Manual of the Corporation of the City of New York*
MHS	Massachusetts Historical Society
NMM	National Maritime Museum
NYGWM	*New-York Gazette, and Weekly Mercury*
NYHS	New-York Historical Society
NYJ	*New-York Journal*
PBF	*The Papers of Benjamin Franklin* (New Haven, Conn.: Yale University Press, 1959–2017)
Percy to Northumberland	Hugh, Earl Percy to the Duke of Northumberland, Sept. 23, 1776, Percy Papers, Alnwick Castle, Northumberland, microfilm, LOC
PGW:RS	*The Papers of George Washington, Revolutionary War Series* (Charlottesville: University Press of Virginia, 1985–2018)
PJA	*The Papers of John Adams* (Cambridge, Mass.: Harvard University Press, 1977–2008)
PMHB	*Pennsylvania Magazine of History and Biography*
PTJ	*The Papers of Thomas Jefferson*, ed. Julian P. Boyd (Princeton, N.J.: Princeton University Press, 1950)
Rawdon to Huntingdon	Lord Rawdon to Earl of Huntingdon, Sept. 23, 1776, Hastings Collection, Huntington Library
Serle Journal	Edward H. Tatum Jr., ed., *The American Journal of Ambrose Serle, Secretary to Lord Howe, 1776–1778* (San Marino, Calif.: Huntington Library, 1940)
Shewkirk to Seidel	Ewald G. Shewkirk to Nathanael Seidel, Dec. 2, 1776, Historical Society of Pennsylvania
Smith Memoirs	William H. W. Sabine, ed., *Historical Memoirs of William Smith, Historian of the Province of New York, Member of the Governor's Council and Last Chief Justice of that Province under the Crown, Chief Justice of Quebec* (1956–58; New York: New York Times and Arno, 1969)
Strachey to JS	Henry Strachey to Jane Strachey, Sept. 25, 1776, in Henry Strachey Papers, WLCL
T	Treasury
Thompson to Huntingdon	[John Thompson] to the Earl of Huntingdon, Sept. 25, 1776, Hastings Collection, Huntington Library

TNA   The National Archives of the United Kingdom
Tryon to Germain   William Tryon to Lord George Germain, Sept. 24, 1776,
                             DCHSNY, 8:686
WLCL   William L. Clements Library
WMQ   *William and Mary Quarterly*

Introduction

1. For examples asserting the innocence of the rebels (or Washington), see, among many others, William Gordon, *The History of the Rise, Progress, and Establishment, of the Independence of the United States of America* [. . .] (London, 1788), 2:330; David Ramsay, *The History of the American Revolution* (Philadelphia, 1789), 1:308; John Marshall, *Life of George Washington* [. . .] (Philadelphia, 1804), 2:475–76n; Mary L. Booth, *History of the City of New York from Its Earliest Settlement to the Present Time* (New York, 1859), 2:540–42; George Bancroft, *History of the United States from the Discovery of the American Continent* (Boston, 1866), 9:129. Other historians found insufficient evidence for a deliberate fire, e.g.: Philander D. Chase and Frank E. Grizzard Jr., eds., *PGW:RS* (1994), 6:370n1; Joseph S. Tiedemann, *Reluctant Revolutionaries: New York City and the Road to Independence, 1763–1776* (Ithaca, N.Y.: Cornell University Press, 1997), 254–56; Edwin G. Burrows and Mike Wallace, *Gotham: A History of New York City to 1898* (New York: Oxford University Press, 1999), 240–42; Barnet Schecter, *The Battle for New York: The City at the Heart of the American Revolution* (New York: Walker, 2002), 205–9; David McCullough, *1776* (New York: Simon and Schuster, 2005), 221–23. Some historians considered the possibility: William L. Stone, *History of New York City from the Discovery to the Present Day* (New York, 1872), 250–53; Theophilus F. Rodenbough, "New-York during the Revolution, 1775–1783," in *The Memorial History of the City of New-York from Its First Settlement to the Year 1892*, ed. James Grant Wilson (New York, 1892), 2:524–27; John R. Alden, *A History of the American Revolution* (New York: Knopf, 1969), 269–71; Philip Ranlet, *The New York Loyalists* (Knoxville: University of Tennessee Press, 1986), 73–76; David Hackett Fischer, *Washington's Crossing* (New York: Oxford University Press, 2004), 107; John Ferling, *Almost a Miracle: The American Victory in the War of Independence* (New York: Oxford University Press, 2007), 142.

2. McCullough, *1776*, 247; on the Revolution as a civil war, see, among others, David Armitage, *Civil Wars: A History in Ideas* (New York: Knopf, 2017), chap. 4.

3. Kathleen Donegan, *Seasons of Misery: Catastrophe and Colonial Settlement in Early America* (Philadelphia: University of Pennsylvania Press, 2014), 12 ("chaos zone"); Danielle S. Allen, *Our Declaration: A Reading of the Declaration of Independence in Defense of Equality* (New York: Liveright, Norton, 2014), 98, 103, 235, 266, 272–73.

4. Janice Potter, *The Liberty We Seek: Loyalist Ideology in Colonial New York and Massachusetts* (Cambridge, Mass.: Harvard University Press, 1983), 5–7, 16–25, 20 ("envy"), 34–38, 136–39, 150–52; Gordon S. Wood, "Conspiracy and the Paranoid Style: Causality and Deceit in the Eighteenth Century," *WMQ* 39, no. 3 (1982): 401–41.

ONE   A Small City Still Standing

1. Henry Knox to Lucy Knox, Jan. 5, 1776, Henry Knox Papers, Gilder Lehrman Collection.

2. Edwin G. Burrows and Mike Wallace, *Gotham: A History of New York City to 1898* (New York: Oxford University Press, 1999), xii–xiv, xxii–xxiv; Max Page, *The Creative Destruction of Manhattan, 1900–1940* (Chicago: University of Chicago Press, 1999).

3. Burrows and Wallace, *Gotham,* 24; Benjamin L. Carp, *Rebels Rising: Cities and the American Revolution* (New York: Oxford University Press, 2007), 225; Joseph S. Tiedemann, *Reluctant Revolutionaries: New York City and the Road to Independence, 1763–1776* (Ithaca, N.Y.: Cornell University Press, 1997), 13.

4. Joyce D. Goodfriend, *Who Should Rule at Home? Confronting the Elite in British New York City* (Ithaca, N.Y.: Cornell University Press, 2017), chap. 2, pp. 220–21, 237; Richard W. Pointer, *Protestant Pluralism and the New York Experience: A Study of Eighteenth-Century Religious Diversity* (Bloomington: Indiana University Press, 1988), esp. chaps. 3–4; George U. Wenner, *The Lutherans of New York: Their Story and Their Problems* (New York: Petersfield, 1918), 1–14.

5. *Book of Common Prayer* (quote); Inglis to Hind; *NYGWM* (New York), Oct. 7, 1776; Patricia U. Bonomi, "New York: The Royal Colony," *New York History* 82, no. 1 (2001): 20–21.

6. Edward H. Hart, *Almost a Hero: Andrew Elliot, The King's Moneyman in New York, 1764-1776* [. . .] (Unionville, N.Y.: Royal Fireworks, 2005), 263–64.

7. David T. Valentine, "History of Broadway," *MCCNY* (1865), 509–72; Martha J. Lamb, *History of the City of New York: Its Origin, Rise and Progress* (New York, 1877), 1:654–56, 732, 757; Esther Singleton, *Social New York under the Georges, 1714-1776* (New York: D. Appleton, 1902), 18–19; Hans Huth, ed., "Letters from a Hessian Mercenary," *PMHB* 62 (1938): 495; *Narrative of the American Voyages and Travels of Captain William Owen* [. . .], ed. Victor Hugo Paltsits (New York: New York Public Library, 1942), 33; *Serle Journal,* 107.

8. Serena R. Zabin, *Dangerous Economies: Status and Commerce in Imperial New York* (Philadelphia: University of Pennsylvania Press, 2009); Nan A. Rothschild, *New York City Neighborhoods: The 18th Century* (1990; Clinton Corners, N.Y.: Percheron, 2008), 128–30.

9. Anne-Claire Faucquez, "'A Bloody Conspiracy': Race, Power and Religion in New York's 1712 Slave Insurrection," in *Fear and the Shaping of Early American Societies,* ed. Lauric Henneton and L. H. Roper (Leiden: Brill, 2016), 204–25; Kenneth Scott, "The Slave Insurrection in New York in 1712," *New-York Historical Society Quarterly* 45 (1961): 43–74; Thelma Wills Foote, "'Some Hard Usage': The New York City Slave Revolt of 1712," *New York Folklore* 18 (1993): 147–59; Burrows and Wallace, *Gotham,* 38–39, 68, 72–73, 83, 97, 100, 148.

10. Burrows and Wallace, *Gotham,* 159–66; Peter Charles Hoffer, *The Great New York Conspiracy of 1741: Slavery, Crime, and Colonial Law* (Lawrence: University Press of

Kansas, 2003); Jill Lepore, *New York Burning: Liberty, Slavery, and Conspiracy in Eighteenth-Century Manhattan* (New York: Knopf, 2005); *New-York Mercury,* Mar. 24, 1760, Aug. 17, 1761, June 10, 1765; *New-York Gazette,* Mar. 3, 1762, June 2, 1766; *NYJ,* July 25, 1771, June 25, 1772, Nov. 24, 1774; *NYGWM,* Sept. 6, 1773.

11. Dixon Ryan Fox, *Yankees and Yorkers* (New York: New York University Press, 1940); [Anne MacVickar] Grant, *Memoirs of an American Lady* [. . .] (New York, 1846), 241, 255, 256; Pauline Maier, *The Old Revolutionaries: Political Lives in the Age of Samuel Adams* (New York: Knopf, 1980), 58, 70, 79–89, 275–76; Philip Ranlet, *The New York Loyalists* (Knoxville: University of Tennessee Press, 1986); Jerrilyn Greene Marston, *King and Congress: The Transfer of Political Legitimacy, 1774–1776* (Princeton, N.J.: Princeton University Press, 1987), 236–50.

12. Marc Egnal, *A Mighty Empire: The Origins of the American Revolution* (1988; Ithaca, N.Y.: Cornell University Press, 2010); Eliga H. Gould, *The Persistence of Empire: British Political Culture in the Age of the American Revolution* (Chapel Hill: University of North Carolina Press, 2000), chap. 4; P. J. Marshall, *The Making and Unmaking of Empires: Britain, India, and America, c. 1750–1783* (Oxford: Oxford University Press, 2005); Andrew D. M. Beaumont, *Colonial America and the Earl of Halifax, 1748–1761* (New York: Oxford University Press, 2014); Justin du Rivage, *Revolution against Empire: Taxes, Politics, and the Origins of American Independence* (New Haven, Conn.: Yale University Press, 2017).

13. Bernard Bailyn, *The Ideological Origins of the American Revolution,* enlarged edition (1967; Cambridge, Mass.: Harvard University Press, 1992); Andrew Jackson O'Shaughnessy, *An Empire Divided: The American Revolution and the British Caribbean* (Philadelphia: University of Pennsylvania Press, 2000).

14. *NYGWM,* Aug. 1, Nov. 7, 1768; *New York Packet,* Feb. 20, 1787; Carp, *Rebels Rising,* chap. 2; Vaughn Scribner, *Inn Civility: Urban Taverns and Early American Civil Society* (New York: New York University Press, 2019); Jesse Lemisch, *Jack Tar vs. John Bull: The Role of New York's Seamen in Precipitating the Revolution* (New York: Garland, 1997); Pauline Maier, *From Resistance to Revolution: Colonial Radicals and the Development of American Opposition to Britain, 1765–1776* (New York: Knopf, 1972), 78–79, 83, 90–91, 97, 99, 302–7; Tiedemann, *Reluctant Revolutionaries,* 93–94; D. T. Valentine, "List of Retailers of Spirituous Liquors in the City of New York, April 24, 1776," *MCCNY* (1857), 556–62.

15. Patricia U. Bonomi, *A Factious People: Politics and Society in Colonial New York* (New York: Columbia University Press, 1971); Cynthia Anne Kierner, *Traders and Gentlefolk: The Livingstons of Colonial New York, 1675–1790* (Ithaca, N.Y.: Cornell University Press, 1992), chaps. 5–6; Tiedemann, *Reluctant Revolutionaries;* Christopher F. Minty, "Mobilization and Voluntarism: The Political Origins of Loyalism in New York, c. 1768–1778" (PhD diss., University of Stirling, 2014).

16. [William Livingston], "The American Whig, No. XLV," *New-York Gazette, or Weekly Post-Boy,* Jan. 16, 1769; Charity Clarke to Joseph Jekyll, [Mar.?] 31, 1769, Moore Family Papers, Columbia Manuscripts, 1572–1986, Columbia University Archives; Nancy L. Rhoden, *Revolutionary Anglicanism: The Colonial Church of England Clergy during the*

American Revolution (New York: New York University Press, 1999), pp. 14–15, 17, chaps. 3–4; Joseph S. Tiedemann, "Presbyterianism and the American Revolution in the Middle Colonies," *Church History* 74, no. 2 (2005): 306, 312; James B. Bell, *A War of Religion: Dissenters, Anglicans, and the American Revolution* (New York: Palgrave Macmillan, 2008), 107–9, 113, 117–18, 120; Thomas N. Ingersoll, *The Loyalist Problem in Revolutionary New England* (Cambridge: Cambridge University Press, 2016), chaps. 1–2, pp. 5–6, 131, 151–52, 160.

17. "A Linen Draper," in *The Commercial Conduct of the Province of New-York Considered* (New York, 1767), 11 ("proof," "Coaches"); Simon Middleton, *From Privileges to Rights: Work and Politics in Colonial New York City* (Philadelphia: University of Pennsylvania Press, 2006), 227–28; Edward Countryman, *A People in Revolution: The American Revolution and Political Society in New York, 1760–1790* (New York: Norton, 1981), pp. 5–13, 55–67, chap. 3, pp. 143–45; Gary B. Nash, *The Urban Crucible: Social Change, Political Consciousness, and the Origins of the American Revolution* (Cambridge, Mass.: Harvard University Press, 1979), esp. 338, 362–74.

18. Steven J. Stewart, "Skimmington in the Middle and New England Colonies," in *Riot and Revelry in Early America*, ed. William Pencak, Matthew Dennis, and Simon P. Newman (University Park: Pennsylvania State University Press, 2002), 41–86.

19. Bonomi, "Royal Colony," 5, 9, 20, 22; Peter Charles Hoffer, *Sensory Worlds in Early America* (Baltimore, Md.: Johns Hopkins University Press, 2003), 214–15, 224.

20. Tiedemann, *Reluctant Revolutionaries,* introduction, chap. 3.

21. Thomas Gage to Lord Shelburne, Apr. 3, 1767, *The Correspondence of General Thomas Gage with the Secretaries of State, 1763–1775*, ed. Clarence Edwin Carter (New Haven, Conn.: Yale University Press, 1931), 1:124–28; quoted in Rohit T. Aggarwala, "'I Want a Packet to Arrive': Making New York City the Headquarters of British America, 1696–1783," *New York History* 98, no. 1 (2017): 31; *NYJ,* June 10, 1773; John Gilbert McCurdy, "From Fort George to the Fields: The Public Space and Military Geography of New York City," *Journal of Urban History* 44, no. 4 (2018): 625–42; Wendy Bellion, *Iconoclasm in New York: Revolution to Reenactment* (University Park: Pennsylvania State University Press, 2019), chap. 1; Countryman, *People in Revolution,* 37–45; Tiedemann, *Reluctant Revolutionaries,* 45–46, 77, 84–85, 90, 95, 130, 160, 164–65, 179, 192, 246.

22. *New-York Mercury,* June 10, 1765; *NYJ,* Mar. 15, 1770; William Pencak, "The Social Structure of Revolutionary Boston: Evidence from the Great Fire of 1760," *Journal of Interdisciplinary History* 10, no. 2 (1979): 267–78; Matthew Mulcahy, "The 'Great Fire' of 1740 and the Politics of Disaster Relief in Colonial Charleston," *South Carolina Historical Magazine* 99, no. 2 (1998): 135–57.

23. Herbert L. Osgood et al., eds., *Minutes of the Common Council of the City of New York, 1675–1776* (New York, 1905), 4:436–40; Benjamin L. Carp, "Fire of Liberty: Firefighters, Urban Voluntary Culture, and the Revolutionary Movement," *WMQ* 58, no. 4 (2001): 781–818.

24. *Smith Memoirs,* 1:212 ("prohibiting," "Condescensions," "Votes"); *NYJ,* Apr. 30, 1768; [E. B. O'Callaghan, ed.], "Names of the Principal Male Inhabitants of New-York,

Anno 1774," *MCCNY* (1850), 427–42, 427, noted, "The citizens paid dearly" on Sept. 21, 1776.

25. *NYGWM,* June 17, 1776 ("Oligarchy"); *London Chronicle,* Aug. 10–12, 1775 ("authority"); Staughton Lynd, "The Mechanics in New York Politics, 1774–1788," *Labor History* 5, no. 3 (1964): 225–46; Bailyn, *Ideological Origins;* Countryman, *People in Revolution;* Tiedemann, *Reluctant Revolutionaries,* 189–96, 200–204, 246–51; Gary B. Nash, *The Unknown American Revolution: The Unruly Birth of Democracy and the Struggle to Create America* (New York: Viking, 2005).

26. Diary entry, Aug. 22, 1774, in *Diary and Autobiography of John Adams,* ed. L. H. Butterfield (Cambridge, Mass.: Harvard University Press, 1961), 2:106; for this and the following paragraphs, see John A. Neuenschwander, *The Middle Colonies and the Coming of the American Revolution* (Port Washington, N.Y.: Kennikat, 1973); Ranlet, *New York Loyalists,* chaps. 3–4; Tiedemann, *Reluctant Revolutionaries,* chap. 10; Marston, *King and Congress,* 182–86; Ingersoll, *Loyalist Problem;* Robert M. Calhoon, "The Loyalist Perception," and Timothy M. Barnes and Robert M. Calhoon, "Loyalist Discourse and the Moderation of the American Revolution," in *The Loyalist Perception and Other Essays,* by Robert M. Calhoon, Timothy M. Barnes, and Robert S. Davis, rev. ed. (1989; Columbia: University of South Carolina Press, 2010), 3–14, 160–203; Minty, "Mobilization."

27. Diary entry, Aug. 22, 1774, in *Diary of John Adams,* 2:106 ("levelling"), 107; [Thomas Bradbury Chandler], *A Friendly Address to All Reasonable Americans* [. . .] (New York, 1774), 21 ("zealots"), 23 ("yoke"); [Ambrose Serle], *Americans against Liberty* [. . .] (London, 1775), 8, 28, 29 ("inflammatory," "Factious"), 54, 59.

28. Ruma Chopra, *Unnatural Rebellion: Loyalists in New York City during the Revolution* (Charlottesville: University of Virginia Press, 2011), 33; Alfred F. Young, *The Democratic Republicans of New York: The Origins, 1763–1797* (Chapel Hill: University of North Carolina Press, 1967), 10–16; Kierner, *Traders and Gentlefolk,* chap. 6; Countryman, *People in Revolution,* chaps. 4–7.

29. Countryman, *People in Revolution,* pt. 3; Tiedemann, *Reluctant Revolutionaries,* 4–9; Daniel J. Hulsebosch, *Constituting Empire: New York and the Transformation of Constitutionalism in the Atlantic World, 1664–1830* (Chapel Hill: University of North Carolina Press, 2005), chap. 6ff.; Howard Pashman, *Building a Revolutionary State: The Legal Transformation of New York, 1776–1783* (Chicago: University of Chicago Press, 2018).

30. Tiedemann, *Reluctant Revolutionaries,* 221–25.

31. Petition of William Cunningham, Mar. 17, 1784, TNA AO 13/64, f. 183; *Pennsylvania Journal* (Philadelphia), Apr. 26, 1775 ("calamities," "Fly"); Thomas Jefferson Wertenbaker, *Father Knickerbocker Rebels: New York City during the Revolution* (New York: Charles Scribner's Sons, 1948), 47, 54–55; Tiedemann, *Reluctant Revolutionaries,* 217–19, 229–30.

32. "Colonel Marinus Willett's Narrative," in Mercantile Library Association of New York City, *New York City during the American Revolution* [. . .] (New York, 1861), 53–65, 65 ("Whig"); General Orders, Aug. 21, 1776, *PGW:RS,* ed. Philander D. Chase and

Frank E. Grizzard Jr. (1994), 6:96, 97n4; Tiedemann, *Reluctant Revolutionaries*, 231-32; William Dunlap, *History of New Netherlands, Province of New York, and State of New York* [. . .] (New York, 1840), 2:clxxxvi; Alan C. Aimone and Eric I. Manders, "A Note on New York City's Independent Companies, 1775-1776," *New York History* 63, no. 1 (1982): 59-73; *NYJ*, July 20, 1775; T. W. Egly Jr., *History of the First New York Regiment, 1775-1783* (Hampton, N.H.: Peter E. Randall, 1981), 1-5; "The Burghers of New Amsterdam and the Freemen of New York, 1675-1866," NYHS *Collections* 18 (1885): 183.

33. Bruce Bliven Jr., *Under the Guns: New York, 1775-1776* (New York: Harper and Row, 1972), chap. 1; Tiedemann, *Reluctant Revolutionaries*, 3-4, 230-32, 239-40.

34. Samuel Graves to James Wallace, Nov. 5, 1775, in *Naval Documents of the American Revolution*, ed. William Bell Clark (Washington, D.C.: U.S. Government Printing Office, 1966), 2:894 ("assuredly"); William Tryon to Earl of Dartmouth, Sept. 5, 1775, *DCHSNY* (1857), 8:632; Bliven, *Under the Guns*, 26-29, 31-39; Paul David Nelson, *William Tryon and the Course of Empire: A Life in British Imperial Service* (Chapel Hill: University of North Carolina Press, 1990), 133.

35. George Vandeput to Samuel Graves, Dec. 18, 1775, TNA ADM 1/484, pt. 2, LOC transcripts, 55 ("expect"); Gilbert Saltonstall to Nathan Hale, Nov. 27, 1775, in *Documentary Life of Nathan Hale* [. . .], by George Dudley Seymour (New Haven, Conn.: Tuttle, Morehouse, and Taylor, 1941), 51 ("Foundation," "Virtue"); Jedediah Huntington to Jonathan Trumbull, Jan. 14, 1776, MHS *Collections*, 5th ser., 9 (1885): 509 ("moth").

36. Isaac Sears to Roger Sherman et al., Nov. 28, 1775, Sol Feinstone Collection no. 1254, David Library of the American Revolution (quotes); Bliven, *Under the Guns*, 62-71; Tiedemann, *Reluctant Revolutionaries*, chap. 10.

TWO Destroying Towns in a Civil War

1. Isaac Foster to Mary Foster, June 2, 1776, Isaac Foster Papers, Misc. MSS Collection, LOC ("barbarity"); Richard Frothingham Jr., *History of the Siege of Boston* [. . .], 2nd ed. (Boston, 1851), 143-45, 201-4, 203n1; Nathaniel Philbrick, *Bunker Hill: A City, a Siege, a Revolution* (London: Doubleday, 2013), 217-20.

2. Abigail Adams to John Adams, June 18, 25, 1775, *AFC*, 1:223 ("Spirits"), 230; Charles Royster, *A Revolutionary People at War: The Continental Army and American Character, 1775-1783* (Chapel Hill: University of North Carolina Press, 1979), chap. 1.

3. John Adams to Abigail Adams, July 7, 1775, *AFC*, 1:241 (quotes); *JCC* (1905), 2:152, 165, 216; John Dickinson to Arthur Lee, Apr. 29, 1775, in *Life of Arthur Lee* [. . .], ed. Richard Henry Lee (Boston, 1829), 2:311; John Langdon to Matthew Thornton, July 3, 1775, *LDC* (1977), 1:574; BF to Jonathan Shipley, July 7, 1775, *PBF*, ed. William B. Willcox (1982), 22:93-98.

4. *Serle Journal*, 25; Piers Mackesy, *The War for America, 1775-1783* (1964; Lincoln: University of Nebraska Press, 1993), 32-40, 70-72; Ira D. Gruber, *The Howe Brothers and the American Revolution* (New York: Atheneum, 1972), chap. 1; Stephen Conway, "To Subdue America: British Army Officers and the Conduct of the Revolutionary War," *WMQ* 43, no. 3 (1986): 381-407; Julie Flavell, "British Perceptions of New England and

the Decision for a Coercive Colonial Policy, 1774–1775," in *Britain and America Go to War: The Impact of War and Warfare in Anglo-America, 1754–1815,* ed. Julie Flavell and Stephen Conway (Gainesville: University Press of Florida, 2005), 95–115.

5. "Reflections on the Means Necessary to Reduce the Americans," Mar. 1775, Liverpool Papers, Add. MSS 38374, British Library, f. 111 ("harass"); Andrew Jackson O'Shaughnessy, *The Men Who Lost America: British Leadership, the American Revolution, and the Fate of the Empire* (New Haven, Conn.: Yale University Press, 2013), 53–61; Conway, "To Subdue America."

6. Eliga H. Gould, *The Persistence of Empire: British Political Culture in the Age of the American Revolution* (Chapel Hill: University of North Carolina Press, 2000), 150n3; Stephen Conway, "From Fellow-Nationals to Foreigners: British Perceptions of the Americans, circa 1739–1783," *WMQ* 59, no. 1 (2002): 65–100; Troy Bickham, *Making Headlines: The American Revolution Seen through the British Press* (DeKalb: Northern Illinois University Press, 2009), 65–67, 74–75, 77–80, 111–12, 207–9, 241.

7. John Grenier, *The First Way of War: American War Making on the Frontier, 1607–1814* (Cambridge: Cambridge University Press, 2005), 89–93; Wayne E. Lee, *Barbarians and Brothers: Anglo-American Warfare, 1500–1865* (New York: Oxford University Press, 2011); T. Cole Jones, *Captives of Liberty: Prisoners of War and the Politics of Vengeance in the American Revolution* (Philadelphia: University of Pennsylvania Press, 2020), chap. 1.

8. Lee, *Barbarians and Brothers;* Stephen Porter, *Destruction in the English Civil Wars* (Gloucestershire: Alan Sutton, 1994), chap. 2; James Q. Whitman, *The Verdict of Battle: The Law of Victory and the Making of Modern War* (Cambridge, Mass.: Harvard University Press, 2012), chap. 5.

9. Wayne E. Lee, *Crowds and Soldiers in Revolutionary North Carolina: The Culture of Violence in Riot and War* (Gainesville: University Press of Florida, 2001), 112; Grenier, *First Way of War,* 5, 87, 89, 91–92; Gruber, *Howe Brothers,* 92, 113, 145–46, 194–95, 242–44, 350; Stephen Conway, "'The Great Mischief Complain'd of': Reflections on the Misconduct of British Soldiers in the Revolutionary War," *WMQ* 47, no. 3 (1990): 387–90.

10. Samuel Graves to Thomas Gage, Sept. 1, Gage to Graves, Sept. 4, 1775, in *Naval Documents of the American Revolution,* ed. William Bell Clark (Washington: U.S. Government Printing Office, 1964, 1966), 1:1281, 2:7–8; William Glanville Evelyn to [William] Evelyn, Oct. 7, 1775, in *Memoir and Letters of Captain W. Glanville Evelyn [. . .],* ed. G. D. Scull (Oxford, 1879), 71 ("stacks"); Conway, "To Subdue America."

11. BF to [Joseph Priestly], July 5, BF to David Hartley, Sept. 12, 1775, *PBF,* 22:91 ("begun"), 91–92 ("outrage"), 196 ("legitimate," "barbarous").

12. *A Discourse on the Times* (Norwich, Conn., 1776), 2–3, 10 ("seaports"), 11; GW to John Hancock, Oct. 24, John Sullivan to GW, Oct. 29, 1775, *PGW:RS,* ed. Philander D. Chase (1987), 2:227 ("Outrage"), 252–54; Form Letter Requesting Information on British Depredations, Oct. 19, Committee Report on Petition from Nova Scotia, Nov. 9, John Adams to James Warren, Oct. 19, Adams to Joseph Ward, Nov. 14, 1775, *PJA,* ed. Robert J. Taylor (1979), 3:140–41, 143–45, 213 ("Posterity," "Retribution"), 297 ("conduct"); Joseph Reed to Esther Reed, Oct. 24, 1775, quoted in Esther Reed to Charles Pettit, Nov. 1, 1775,

Joseph Reed Papers, NYHS; *Connecticut Journal* (New Haven), Sept. 25, 1776; Donald A. Yerxa, "The Burning of Falmouth, 1775: A Case Study in British Imperial Pacification," *Maine Historical Society Quarterly* 14, no. 3 (1975): 119–60; Kevin Phillips, *1775: A Good Year for Revolution* (New York: Viking, 2012), chap. 14.

13. *Dunlap's Maryland Gazette* (Baltimore), May 16, 1775.

14. Edmund Burke, *A Philosophical Enquiry into the Origin of Our Ideas of the Sublime and Beautiful* (London, 1759), 73–74 ("terror"), 77 ("conflagration"); Royster, *Revolutionary People*, 111–18.

15. BF to Shipley, July 7, 1775, *PBF*, 22:95 ("Luxuries"); *The Literary Diary of Ezra Stiles* [. . .], ed. Franklin Bowditch Dexter (New York: Charles Scribner's Sons, 1901), 1:624; Abigail Adams to John Adams, Oct. 25, 1775, *AFC*, 1:313; *Discourse*, 4–5; T. H. Breen, *The Marketplace of Revolution: How Consumer Politics Shaped American Independence* (New York: Oxford University Press, 2004).

16. Benjamin H. Irvin, *Clothed in the Robes of Sovereignty: The Continental Congress and the People out of Doors* (New York: Oxford University Press, 2011), 153–63; David S. Shields and Fredrika J. Teute, "The Meschianza: Sum of All Fêtes," *Journal of the Early Republic* 35, no. 2 (2015): 185–214; Serena R. Zabin, *The Boston Massacre: A Family History* (Boston: Houghton Mifflin Harcourt, 2020); Donald F. Johnson, *Occupied America: British Military Rule and the Experience of Revolution* (Philadelphia: University of Pennsylvania Press, 2020), esp. chap. 2.

17. Thomas Jefferson to Francis Eppes, July 4, 1775, *PTJ*, 1:185 ("intent," "distress").

18. GW, Address to Continental Congress, [June 16, 1775], *PGW:RS* (1985), 1:1 ("service"); Don Higginbotham, *George Washington and the American Military Tradition* (Athens: University of Georgia Press, 1985), 62–64, 67, 86–95; Jerrilyn Greene Marston, *King and Congress: The Transfer of Political Legitimacy, 1774–1776* (Princeton, N.J.: Princeton University Press, 1987), 145–48, 384n46; Edward G. Lengel, *General George Washington: A Military Life* (New York: Random House, 2005), 95, 110; John Ferling, *Almost a Miracle: The American Victory in the War of Independence* (New York: Oxford University Press, 2007), 39–44, 48, 69–70, 75–80, 99–101; Lindsay M. Chervinsky, *The Cabinet: George Washington and the Creation of an American Institution* (Cambridge, Mass.: Harvard University Press, 2020), chap. 1.

19. Journal of Dr. Jeremy Belknap, Oct. 1775, MHS *Proceedings* 4 (1858–60): 82–83, 83 (quotes); Council of War, Sept. 11, 1775, *PGW:RS*, 1:450–51; Joseph Reed to Thomas Bradford, Sept. 14, 1775, Joseph Reed Papers, NYHS; diary entry, Sept. 23, 1775, in *Diary and Autobiography of John Adams*, ed. L. H. Butterfield (Cambridge, Mass.: Harvard University Press, 1961), 2:178.

20. Minutes of the Conference between a Committee of Congress, Washington, and Representatives of the New England Colonies, Oct. 24, 1775, *PBF*, 22:240; Thomas Lynch to Ralph Izard, Nov. 19, 1775, *LDC*, 2:362.

21. John Dickinson's Notes for a Speech in Congress, [Dec. 21–22, 1775], *LDC*, 2:502 ("Price"), 503; Richard Smith, diary, Dec. 22, 1775, *LDC*, 2:513; *JCC*, 3:444–45; Hancock to GW, Dec. 22, 1775, *PGW:RS*, 2:590; Lengel, *General George Washington*, 115–16.

22. Thomas Jefferson to John Page, Oct. 31, Page to Jefferson, Nov. 11, 1775, *PTJ*,

1:251, 258–59 ("Scoundrels," "Sigh"); Robert Howe to Edmund Pendleton, Dec. 14, 1775, in *Revolutionary Virginia: The Road to Independence,* ed. Robert L. Scribner and Brent Tarter (Charlottesville: University Press of Virginia, 1979), 5:141, also pp. 12, 16, 160, 171–72, 182, 217–18, 319; William Bell Clark, ed., *Naval Documents of the American Revolution* (Washington, D.C.: U.S. Government Printing Office, 1968), 3:617–19, 621–22.

23. *Revolutionary Virginia,* 5:16–19, 24n89, 308, 319, vol. 6 (1981), 86n13; *Naval Documents,* 3:563–65, 737–38; *Lloyd's Evening Post* (London), Apr. 15–17, 1776.

24. John Dalrymple to Earl of Dumfries, Jan. 14, 1776, CO 5/40, f. 125v ("Inhumanity," "upon our own"); *Virginia Gazette* (Williamsburg) (Pinkney), Jan. 6, 1776 ("design"); Hancock to GW, Jan. [16], 1776, *PGW:RS* (1988), 3:43 ("barbarity"); Hamond Account, Feb. 15, 1776; Holger Hoock, *Scars of Independence: America's Violent Birth* (New York: Crown, 2017), 92–101.

25. GW to Joseph Reed, Jan. 31, 1776, *PGW:RS,* 3:228.

26. Robert Morris to Robert Herries, Feb. 15, 1776, *LDC* (1978), 3:258 ("destructive," "wanton"), 259; BF to Anthony Todd, Mar. 29, 1776, *PBF,* 22:392–93 ("Plundering").

27. Samuel Adams to Samuel Cooper, Apr. 30, 1776, John Dickinson, notes for a speech in Congress, [July 1, 1776], *LDC,* 3:602 ("kindled"), 4:355 ("Destroying").

28. For Canada, see Guy Carleton to William Tryon, May 17, 1776, TNA CO 5/1107; Mark R. Anderson, *The Battle for the Fourteenth Colony: America's War of Liberation in Canada, 1774–1776* (Lebanon, N.H.: University Press of New England, 2013), 112, 186, 263, 279, 283, 300, 311, 322, 329–30; on southern campaigns, see John Graham, Lewis Johnston, and John Stuart to Sir James Wright, Mar. 2, 1776, Clinton Papers, WLCL, 14:20; Patrick Tonyn to David Taitt, Apr. 20, 1776, *DAR,* 12:108–9; *NYGWM* (Newark, N.J.), Sept. 21, Nov. 2, 1776; William Henry Drayton to Francis Salvador, July 24, 1776, Andrew Williamson to Drayton, Aug. 22, 1776, in *A Documentary History of the American Revolution,* ed. Robert W. Gibbes, vol. 2 (New York, 1857), 29–30, 32; Sylvia R. Frey, *Water from the Rock: Black Resistance in a Revolutionary Age* (Princeton, N.J.: Princeton University Press, 1991), 82–83; Edward J. Cashin, *The King's Ranger: Thomas Brown and the American Revolution on the Southern Frontier* (Athens: University of Georgia Press, 1989), 52–54; Lee, *Crowds and Soldiers,* 158–62; on the Caribbean, see Andrew Jackson O'Shaughnessy, *An Empire Divided: The American Revolution and the British Caribbean* (Philadelphia: University of Pennsylvania Press, 2000), 151–53; on Portsmouth and Bristol, see Jessica Warner, *John the Painter: Terrorist of the American Revolution* (New York: Thunder's Mouth, 2004), chaps. 4–8; see also Harry M. Ward, *Between the Lines: Banditti of the American Revolution* (Westport, Conn.: Praeger, 2002), 19, 170; Hoock, *Scars of Independence,* chap. 3; Jones, *Captives of Liberty,* 109–18.

29. Council of War, Jan. 16, GW to Hancock, Jan. 24, Council of War, Feb. 16, GW to Hancock, Feb. 18–21, GW to Jonathan Trumbull Sr., Feb. 19, 1776, *PGW:RS,* 3:103–4, 179 ("ardently"), 320–24, 335–37, 345–47; Joseph Ward to John Adams, Feb. 14, 1776, *PJA,* 4:24 ("Pirates"); Ward to Elizabeth Partridge, Jan. 6, 1776, Misc. MSS, American Philosophical Society ("build"); Lengel, *General George Washington,* 118–21.

30. Boston Selectmen to GW, Mar. 8, 1776, *PGW:RS,* 3:434 (all quotes); Josiah Quincy to James Bowdoin, Mar. 13, 1776, Bowdoin-Temple Papers, MHS *Collections,* 6th

ser., vol. 9 (1897): 397; Paul Allen, [John Neal, and Tobias Watkins], *A History of the American Revolution* [. . .] (Baltimore, 1822), 1:324–25.

31. GW to Hancock, Mar. [9], 1776, *PGW:RS*, 3:424, 425 ("Answer"), 427n18; Harry Miller Lydenberg, ed., *Archibald Robertson, Lieutenant-General Royal Engineers: His Diaries and Sketches in America, 1762–1780* (New York: New York Public Library, 1930), 76–77; *Lloyd's Evening Post,* May 13–15, 1776.

32. "Order Books of Lieut.-Col. Stephen Kemble, [. . .] 1775–1778," NYHS *Collections* 16 (1883): 315–18, 317 ("utmost"), 322–25, 322 ("caught"), 325 ("Irregularities").

33. General Orders, Mar. 10, GW to Hancock, Mar. 13, 1776, *PGW:RS*, 3:446n1 ("Cannonade"), 447n1, 462 ("uncertainty").

34. John Bowater to Basil Feilding, 6th Earl of Denbigh, Mar. 25, 1776, William Feilding to Denbigh, Apr. 28, 1776, in *The Lost War: Letters from British Officers during the American Revolution,* ed. Marion Balderston and David Syrett (New York: Horizon, 1975), 71–72 ("seat"), 76–77 ("Certainly," "laid," "sorry"); Lydenberg, *Archibald Robertson,* 79–80.

35. GW to Hancock, Mar. 19, 1776, Address from the Boston Selectmen [Mar. 28?, 1776], *PGW:RS*, 3:489, 490, 572 ("elegant"); Charles W. Akers, ed., "'A Place for My People Israel': Samuel Cooper's Sermon of 7 April 1776," *New England Historical and Genealogical Register* 132 (1978): 137 ("Marks," "Disgrace"); *NYJ,* Nov. 23, 1775; *Boston Gazette,* Dec. 25, 1775; G. B. Warden, *Boston, 1689–1776* (Boston: Little, Brown, 1970), 325; Jacqueline Barbara Carr, *After the Siege: A Social History of Boston, 1775–1800* (Boston: Northeastern University Press, 2005), 38–40.

36. GW to Hancock, Feb. 18, 1776, *PGW:RS*, 3:336.

THREE The Armies Approach New York

1. John Hancock to GW, Oct. 5, 1775, John Adams to GW, Jan. 6, 1776, *PGW:RS*, ed. Philander D. Chase (1987, 1988), 2:108–10, 3:36–38 (quotes); George C. Daughan, *Revolution on the Hudson: New York City and the Hudson River Valley in the American War of Independence* (New York: Norton, 2016); Rohit T. Aggarwala, "'I Want a Packet to Arrive': Making New York City the Headquarters of British America, 1696–1783," *New York History* (2017): 7–9, 35–39.

2. *Smith Memoirs,* 1:260; William Tryon to Lord George Germain, Apr. 6, 1776, *DCHSNY* (1857), 8:673–74; John Shy, "American Strategy: Charles Lee and the Radical Alternative," in *A People Numerous and Armed: Reflections on the Military Struggle for American Independence,* rev. ed. (1976; Ann Arbor: University of Michigan Press, 1990), 133–62; Phillip Papas, *Renegade Revolutionary: The Life of General Charles Lee* (New York: New York University Press, 2014).

3. Charles Lee to Richard Henry Lee, Dec. 12, 1775, "The Lee Papers," NYHS *Collections* 4 (1871): 229 ("strongly"); Nathanael Greene to Samuel Ward Sr., Jan. 4, [1776], in *The Papers of General Nathanael Greene,* ed. Richard K. Showman (Chapel Hill: University of North Carolina Press, 1976), 1:177–78; Charles Lee to GW, Jan. 5, GW to Joseph Reed, [Mar. 3], 1776, *PGW:RS*, 3:30, 371 ("Capitol," "irremediable").

4. *JPCNY,* 1:258–59; *Smith Memoirs,* 1:258–59. For this and subsequent paragraphs,

see Thomas Jefferson Wertenbaker, *Father Knickerbocker Rebels: New York City during the Revolution* (New York: Charles Scribner's Sons, 1948), chap. 3; Bruce Bliven Jr., *Under the Guns: New York, 1775–1776* (New York: Harper and Row, 1972), chap. 2.

5. N.Y. Committee of Safety to Charles Lee, Jan. 21, Lee to Peter V. B. Livingston, Jan. 23, James Duane, William Floyd, and Henry Wisner to N.Y. Committee of Safety, Jan. 27, 1776, *JPCNY*, 1:259 ("cheerfully," "judgment," "metropolis"), 266 ("funeral," "holds"), 274–75, 277–79; *JCC*, 4:92–94; Oliver Wolcott to Samuel Lyman, Feb. 3, 1776, *LDC* (1978), 3:191.

6. Sir Henry Clinton, memorandum, interview with William Tryon, Feb. 1776, Clinton Papers, WLCL, 14:11 ("reconcile," "wantonly"); Andrew Allen to Sarah Allen, Feb. 5, 1776, *LDC*, 3:196; *Smith Memoirs*, 1:263–64; Barnet Schecter, *The Battle for New York: The City at the Heart of the American Revolution* (New York: Walker, 2002), 71–74.

7. John Adams to Abigail Adams, Feb. 11, 1776, *AFC*, 1:345 ("Tory"); Charles Lee to GW, Feb. 14, 1776, *PGW:RS*, 3:310 ("cannonade"); Tryon to Germain, Apr. 6, 1776, *DCHSNY*, 8:674.

8. Lee to GW, Feb. 14, 1776, *PGW:RS*, 3:310 ("laugh"); Lee to Hyde Parker, n.d., Lee, "Report on the Defence of New York, March 1776," "Lee Papers," 341 ("wanton," "pile"), 355–57.

9. John Eustace to Lee, Mar. 21, 1776, "Lee Papers," 366 ("Tory Town"); *Smith Memoirs*, 1:265; John A. Neuenschwander, *The Middle Colonies and the Coming of the American Revolution* (Port Washington, N.Y.: Kennikat, 1973), chap. 7.

10. "THE SENTINEL," *To the inhabitants of New-York* (Jan. 27, 1776) ("scoff," "dastards," "suffering"); GW to John Augustine Washington, Mar. 31, GW to N.Y. Committee of Safety, Apr. 17, N.Y. Committee of Safety to GW, Apr. 18, 1776, *PGW:RS*, 3:568 ("declare"), vol. 4 (1991), 77–79, 81–82; *JPCNY*, 1:411–13; *NYJ*, May 2, 1776.

11. BF to Anthony Todd, Mar. 29, 1776, *PBF*, ed. William B. Willcox (1982), 22:394 ("Spirit," "Merchants"); *Pennsylvania Evening Post* (Philadelphia), Apr. 4, 1776 ("refugees"); Tryon to Germain, Apr. 6, 18, 1776, *DCHSNY*, 8:675, 677; William Heath to John Hancock, Apr. 3, 1776, *American Archives* [. . .], ed. Peter Force, 4th ser. (Washington, D.C., 1843), 5:776, also pp. 218–20; Tryon to David Matthews, Apr. 19, 1776, in *Naval Documents of the American Revolution*, ed. William Bell Clark (Washington, D.C.: U.S. Government Printing Office, 1969), 4:165; General Orders, Apr. 29, 1776, *PGW:RS*, 4:163, 163–64n2; *NYGWM*, May 6, 1776; John Varick Jr. to Richard Varick, May 14, 1776, in Mercantile Library Association of New York City, *New York City during the American Revolution* [. . .] (New York, 1861), 92; Judith L. Van Buskirk, *Generous Enemies: Patriots and Loyalists in Revolutionary New York* (Philadelphia: University of Pennsylvania Press, 2002), 14–16.

12. John Milner to Myles Cooper, Jan. 6, 1776, John Wetherhead to Myles Cooper, Apr. 25, 1776, Fettercairn Papers, National Library of Scotland, f. 80v ("rival"), f. 87 ("miracle"); Frederick Rhinelander to Peter Van Schaack, Feb. 23, 1776, in Force, *American Archives* (1843), 4:1480 ("evacuated"); John Jones to Thomas Allen, Feb. 21, 1776, Allen Family Collection, American Antiquarian Society; Otto Lohrenz, "Anglican Parson, Alleged Sodomite, and Loyalist Perjurer: John Milner of Colonial and Revolutionary New York and Virginia," *Social Science Journal* 36, no. 3 (1999): 533–40.

13. Frederick Rhinelander to Peter Van Schaack, Feb. 23, 1776, *American Archives,* 4:1480 ("Troops," "quarter"); *London Evening Post,* June 4–6, 1776 ("dirtiest"); Memorial of Bernard Michael Houseal, Oct. 5, 1785, AO 13/65, ff. 578–79, 580 ("Tory," "counsel"); Charles Inglis to Richard Hind, Oct. 31, 1776, *DCHSNY* (Albany, N.Y., 1853), 3:641 ("traitor"); William Tudor to Delia Jarvis, Apr. 16, 1776 ("Subtlety"), William Tudor to John Tudor, June 23, 1776 ("butcher"), Tudor Family Papers, MHS.

14. Nathan Hale to Abigail Hale, Apr. 12, 1776, Allyn Kellogg Ford Collection of Historical Manuscripts, Minnesota Historical Society, microfilm, David Library of the American Revolution ("wickedest"); *Journal of Lieutenant Isaac Bangs, April 1 to July 29, 1776,* ed. Edward Bangs (1890; New York: Arno, 1968), 29–30, 59–60; *Journal of Solomon Nash: A Soldier of the Revolution, 1776–1777,* ed. Charles L. Bushnell (New York, 1861), 13; Loammi Baldwin to Mary Baldwin, Apr. 19, June 12, 1776, Loammi Baldwin papers, Houghton Library, Harvard University (hereafter Baldwin Papers); John Noyes to Mary Noyes, May 12, 1776, Gilder Lehrman Collection; Danske Dandridge, *Historic Shepherdstown* (Charlottesville, Va.: Michie, 1910), 140; William Tudor to Delia Jarvis, May 10, 1776, Tudor Family Papers, MHS; General Orders, Apr. 27, 1776, *PGW:RS,* 4:140–41; Philip C. Mead, "Melancholy Landscapes: Writing Warfare in the American Revolution" (PhD diss., Harvard University, 2012), chap. 2.

15. *Serle Journal,* 30 ("Fury"); Orders to Israel Putnam, May 21, GW to Hancock, June 10, 1776, *PGW:RS,* 4:357–58, 488; *JPCNY,* 1:450, 453, 456–57, 459; Howard Pashman, *Building a Revolutionary State: The Legal Transformation of New York, 1776–1783* (Chicago: University of Chicago Press, 2018), 36–42.

16. *JPCNY,* 1:476–78; John Varick Jr. to Richard Varick, June 10, 1776, *New York City during the American Revolution,* 95–96.

17. Christopher Benson deposition, June 16, 1776, Frederick Mackenzie Papers, WLCL ("tumultuous," "pelting," "Grenadiers"); William Waddell to Henry Clinton, Oct. 18, 1780, copy in TNA AO 13/10, ff. 249 ("Ill treated"), 250; Memorial of Lorenda Holmes, AO 13/65, f. 529v ("Mobb," "Swords," "stripp," "exposing"); William Waddell memorial, Oct. 15, 1787, AO 12/24, f. 185v; Estimate of Effects the Property of W'm Waddell, AO 13/56, f. 489; "Diary of Rev. Mr. Shewkirk [. . .]," in *The Campaign of 1776 around New York and Brooklyn,* by Henry P. Johnston (1878; New York: Da Capo, 1971), 108 (2nd pagination).

18. George Rapelje, *A Narrative of Excursions, Voyages, and Travels* [. . .] (New York, 1834), 13 ("mangled"); Henry Brevort, John Hardenbrook, and Abel Hardenbrook Jr. to William Tryon, Mar. 1778, Clinton Papers, 32:40, WLCL ("Terror"); *JPCNY,* 1:491 ("real regard," "detestation"); Peter Elting to Richard Varick, June 13, 1776, Richard Varick Papers, NYHS; "Diary of Ensign Caleb Clap, of Colonel Baldwin's Regiment [. . .], March 29 until October 23, 1776," *Historical Magazine, and Notes and Queries concerning the Antiquities, History, and Biography of America* 3, no. 3 (1874): 135; *Journal of Isaac Bangs,* 43–44; *Morning Post* (London), Oct. 4, 1776; Thomas Jones, *History of New York during the Revolutionary War* [. . .], ed. Edward Floyd De Lancey (1879; New York: Arno, 1968), 1:101–3, 596–98.

19. Elting to Varick, June 13, 1776, Richard Varick Papers, NYHS ("Toory"); Ben-

son Deposition, June 16, 1776, Mackenzie Papers, WLCL ("begged," "Complaints," "trouble," "Provincials"); on the Grenadiers, see *Gaine's Universal Register, or American and British Kalendar, for the Year 1776* (New York, 1776), 160–61; *Calendar of Historical Manuscripts Relating to the War of the Revolution* [. . .] (Albany, N.Y., 1868), 223–24, 260, 288, 340, 370–72; *American Archives* (1840), 3:149–50, 1627–29, 4th ser. (1846), 6:1152–53, 1173–74, 1179, 1366; Alan C. Aimone and Eric I. Manders, "A Note on New York City's Independent Companies, 1775–1776," *New York History* 63, no. 1 (1982): 59, 71.

20. Edward Hand to GW, June 20, Second Brigade to GW, June 29, 1776, *PGW:RS* (1993), 5:58 ("bombardment"), 5:153; Loammi Baldwin to Mary Baldwin, June 22, 1776, Baldwin papers ("Hellish," "blow"); J[ames?] Townsend to his father, June 22, 1776, American Historical Manuscript Collection, NYHS ("nine"); Ebenezer Huntington to Jabez Huntington, June 23, 1776, "Letters of Ebenezer Huntington, 1774–1781," *American Historical Review* 5 (1900): 711 ("Diabolical"); Memorial of Lorenda Holmes, AO 13/65, f. 529v.

21. Loammi Baldwin to Mary Baldwin, June 24, July 4–5 [5–6], 1776, Baldwin papers; John Cotton to Samuel Bartlett, July 6, 1776, Misc. Coll., WLCL; "Diary of Clap," 135–37; *JPCNY*, 1:497, 500; *London Chronicle*, Oct. 24–26, 1776; Bliven, *Under the Guns*, 290–91, 300–316; *New York City during the American Revolution*, 66–81; *Journal of Isaac Bangs*, 48, 50, 54–55.

22. Loammi Baldwin to Mary Baldwin, July 4–5 [5–6], 1776, Baldwin papers ("Inhabitants"); *JPCNY*, 1:512, 518; GW to Hancock, July 4–5, 1776, *PGW:RS*, 5:199–203; Schecter, *Battle*, chap. 6; Phillip Papas, *That Ever Loyal Island: Staten Island and the American Revolution* (New York: New York University Press, 2007), chap. 4; Rick Atkinson, *The British Are Coming: The War for America, Lexington to Princeton, 1775–1777* (New York: Henry Holt, 2019), 316–21.

23. GW to Hancock, July 22, 1776, *PGW:RS*, 5:424; Ira D. Gruber, *The Howe Brothers and the American Revolution* (New York: Atheneum, 1972), chap. 2, p. 101; Andrew Jackson O'Shaughnessy, *The Men Who Lost America: British Leadership, the American Revolution, and the Fate of the Empire* (New Haven, Conn.: Yale University Press, 2013), chap. 3.

24. William Howe, *The Narrative of Lieut. Gen. Sir William Howe, in a Committee of the House of Commons, on the 29th of April 1779* [. . .], 2nd ed. (London, 1780), 9 ("afford," "means," "devastation"); Gruber, *Howe Brothers*; David Smith, *William Howe and the American War of Independence* (London: Bloomsbury, 2015), 144–45; Kevin Phillips, *1775: A Good Year for Revolution* (New York: Viking, 2012), 355.

25. *Serle Journal*, 34 ("hearty"); Henry Strachey to Jane Strachey, Sept. 3, 1776, Henry Strachey Papers, WLCL ("lamentable"); William Howe to Lord George Germain, Apr. 26, 1776, in Historical Manuscripts Commission, *Report on the Manuscripts of Mrs. Stopford-Sackville* (Hereford: His Majesty's Stationery Office, 1910), 2:30; *London Gazette*, Aug. 6–10, 1776; Piers Mackesy, *The War for America, 1775–1783* (1964; Lincoln: University of Nebraska Press, 1993), 82–85, 91; Gruber, *Howe Brothers*, chaps. 3–4; O'Shaughnessy, *Men Who Lost America*, 59–60, 93, 98–105; Smith, *Howe*, chap. 2.

26. John Varick Jr. to Richard Varick, Apr. 1, 1776, in *New York City during the American Revolution*, 89–91; Edward G. Lengel, *General George Washington: A Military*

Life (New York: Random House, 2005), 131; John Ferling, *Almost a Miracle: The American Victory in the War of Independence* (New York: Oxford University Press, 2007), 130; Smith, *Howe*, 63–65, 86.

27. General Orders, July 2, GW to William Livingston, July 6, N.Y. inhabitants to GW, July 9–14, GW to Secret Committee of N.Y. Convention, July 13, 15, GW to NYC Committee of Safety, July 19, 1776, *PGW:RS*, 5:180 ("pillaged"), 223, 224 ("Kindness"), 252, 298–99, 327–28, 388–89; N.Y. inhabitants to GW, July 9–14, 1776, Petitions, GW Papers, ser. 4, General Correspondence, LOC; Schecter, *Battle*, chaps. 4–6; Robert G. Parkinson, *The Common Cause: Creating Race and Nation in the American Revolution* (Chapel Hill: University of North Carolina Press, 2016), chap. 3.

28. *Serle Journal*, 67–69; William Heath to GW, Aug. 24, 1776, *PGW:RS*, ed. Philander D. Chase and Frank E. Grizzard Jr. (1994), 6:119 ("Unrighteousness"); Letter K: Journal of the Grenadier Battalion von Minnegrode, 1776–84, Lidgerwood Collection of Hessian Transcripts on the American Revolution, Morristown National Historic Park, ed. Lion G. Miles and James L. Kochan, microfilm, 10–11.

29. Rapelje, *Narrative*, 14 ("heart"); Brevort et al. to Tryon, Mar. 1778, Clinton Papers, 32:40, WLCL.

FOUR   The Rankled Rank and File

1. Enoch Hawksworth to William Knox, Sept. 16, 1776, TNA CO 5/154, f. 182 ("unanimously report"); see also *London Chronicle*, Aug. 20–22, 1776; Francis Hutcheson to Frederick Haldimand, July 10, 1776, Haldimand Papers, Add. MS 21680, British Library, f. 123.

2. *Serle Journal*, 127 ("Newspapers"); Gregory Evans Dowd, *Groundless: Rumors, Legends, and Hoaxes on the Early American Frontier* (Baltimore, Md.: Johns Hopkins University Press, 2015), 6.

3. Charles Royster, *A Revolutionary People at War: The Continental Army and American Character, 1775–1783* (Chapel Hill: University of North Carolina Press, 1979), chap. 1, pp. 102–7; Ricardo A. Herrera, *For Liberty and the Republic: The American Citizen as Soldier, 1775–1861* (New York: New York University Press, 2015), esp. chaps. 1–3; Gregory T. Knouff, *The Soldiers' Revolution: Pennsylvanians in Arms and the Forging of Early American Identity* (University Park: Pennsylvania State University Press, 2004), xiii–xiv, 1–7, 35–54, 74–85, 98, 271, 273–78; Stephen Conway, "Moral Economy, Contract, and Negotiated Authority in American, British, and German Militaries, ca. 1740–1783," *Journal of Modern History* 88, no. 1 (2016): 34–59.

4. [Alexander Graydon], *Memoirs of a Life, Chiefly Passed in Pennsylvania* [. . .] (Harrisburg, Pa., 1811), 130 ("motley," "irregularity"), 139 ("contemptible"); *Serle Journal*, 88 ("strangest"); *Memoir of Lieut. Col. Tench Tilghman* [. . .] (Albany, N.Y., 1876), 97–98; Charles Patrick Neimeyer, *America Goes to War: A Social History of the Continental Army* (New York: New York University Press, 1996), chaps. 1–4.

5. General Orders, Jan. 1, GW to John Hancock, Feb. 9, 1776, *PGW:RS*, ed. Philander D. Chase (1988), 3:1 ("Mob," "Subordination," "formidable"), 275 ("Recruits");

Royster, *Revolutionary People at War,* chap. 2; Holly A. Mayer, "Soldierly Subordination: The Issue of Deference in the Continental Army," in *The Military and Society,* ed. Peter Karsten, vol. 2, *The Training and Socializing of Military Personnel* (New York: Garland, 1998), 293–307.

6. Allen Bowman, *The Morale of the American Revolutionary Army* (Port Washington, N.Y.: Kennikat, 1943); Royster, *Revolutionary People at War,* chaps. 2, 5; James D. Scudieri, "The Continentals: A Comparative Analysis of a Late Eighteenth-Century Standing Army, 1775–83" (PhD diss., City University of New York, 1993); Mayer, "Soldierly Subordination," 301–2, 305; Wayne Bodle, *The Valley Forge Winter: Civilians and Soldiers in War* (University Park: Pennsylvania State University Press, 2002), chaps. 9–11; David Hackett Fischer, *Washington's Crossing* (New York: Oxford University Press, 2004), 84–88; Wayne E. Lee, *Barbarians and Brothers: Anglo-American Warfare, 1500–1865* (New York: Oxford University Press, 2011), chap. 7; Seanegan P. Sculley, *Contest for Liberty: Military Leadership in the Continental Army, 1775–1783* (Yardley, Pa.: Westholme, 2019), chap. 5.

7. Richard L. Bushman, *From Puritan to Yankee: Character and the Social Order in Connecticut, 1690–1765* (New York: Norton, 1967), 288 ("defensive independence"); Fred Anderson, *A People's Army: Massachusetts Soldiers and Society in the Seven Years' War* (New York: Norton, 1984), chap. 7; Anderson, "The Hinge of the Revolution: George Washington Confronts a People's Army, July 3, 1775," *Massachusetts Historical Review* 1 (1999): 20–48; Jerrilyn Greene Marston, *King and Congress: The Transfer of Political Legitimacy, 1774–1776* (Princeton, N.J.: Princeton University Press, 1987), 132–45, 149–69; Royster, *Revolutionary People at War,* 13–24, 27–29, 108, 119, 152–77; Barry Levy, *Town Born: The Political Economy of New England from Its Founding to the Revolution* (Philadelphia: University of Pennsylvania Press, 2009).

8. Jonathan Trumbull Sr. to GW, Dec. 7, 1775, *PGW* (1987), 2:511 ("pulse"); William Tudor, "Remarks on the Rules & Articles for the Government of the Continental Troops," Memorials Addressed to Congress, item 41, M247, Papers of the Continental Congress, National Archives and Records Administration, 1:4 ("Relinquishment"); Tudor to John Adams, Sept. 23, 1776, *PJA,* ed. Robert J. Taylor (1983), 5:36 ("Tyranny"); Anderson, *People's Army,* 167; Don Higginbotham, *George Washington and the American Military Tradition* (Athens: University of Georgia Press, 1985), 52–53, 60; Mayer, "Soldierly Subordination," 298–99; Herrera, *For Liberty,* 34, 56–59, 88, 111.

9. Anderson, *People's Army,* chaps. 3, 6; Neimeyer, *America Goes to War,* chaps. 6–7; Herrera, *For Liberty,* chap. 3; Knouff, *Soldiers' Revolution,* 97–104; James Kirby Martin, "A 'Most Undisciplined, Profligate Crew': Protest and Defiance in the Continental Ranks, 1776–1783," in *Arms and Independence: The Military Character of the American Revolution,* ed. Ronald Hoffman and Peter J. Albert (Charlottesville: University Press of Virginia, 1984), 119–40; Ilya Berkovich, *Motivation in War: The Experience of Common Soldiers in Old-Regime Europe* (Cambridge: Cambridge University Press, 2017).

10. Joseph Reed to Esther De Berdt Reed, Oct. 11, 1776, in *Life and Correspondence of Joseph Reed,* ed. William B. Reed (Philadelphia, 1847), 1:243 ("levelling spirit"); John Adams to Joseph Hawley, Nov. 25, 1775, *PJA* (1979), 3:316 ("accustomed"); GW to Hancock, Sept. 25, 1776, *PGW:RS,* ed. Philander D. Chase and Frank E. Grizzard Jr.

(1994), 6:393–401; Alfred F. Young, *The Democratic Republicans of New York: The Origins, 1763–1797* (Chapel Hill: University of North Carolina Press, 1967), 17n51.

11. Graydon, *Memoirs*, 130, 131 ("degrading"), 138 ("clown"), 156–57; "Some Extracts from the Papers of General Persifor Frazer," *PMHB* 31, no. 2 (1907): 133–37, 134 ("shocking"); Bushman, *Puritan to Yankee*, 286 ("testy"); Jonathan Gregory Rossie, *The Politics of Command in the American Revolution* (Syracuse, N.Y.: Syracuse University Press, 1975), pp. 27–28, 37–38, 98–101, chaps. 4–5.

12. GW to Hancock, Feb. 9, 1776, *PGW:RS*, 3:275 (quotes); for this and the next paragraph, see Christine Daniels and Michael V. Kennedy, eds., *Over the Threshold: Intimate Violence in Early America* (London: Routledge, 1999); Caroline Cox, *A Proper Sense of Honor: Service and Sacrifice in George Washington's Army* (Chapel Hill: University of North Carolina Press, 2004), chap. 3; Levy, *Town Born*, chap. 2, pp. 2–4, 169–70, 176–79, 182, 205; Lee, *Barbarians and Brothers*, 205; John J. Navin, "Intimidation, Violence, and Race in British America," *Historian* 77, no. 3 (2015): 464–97; Holger Hoock, *Scars of Independence: America's Violent Birth* (New York: Crown, 2017), chap. 4; Kelly A. Ryan, *Everyday Crimes: Social Violence and Civil Rights in Early America* (New York: New York University Press, 2019).

13. Fischer, *Washington's Crossing*, 12–30; Michael A. McDonnell, *The Politics of War: Race, Class, and Conflict in Revolutionary Virginia* (Chapel Hill: University of North Carolina Press, 2007), 93–116, 181–83; Cox, *Proper Sense of Honor*, 79–81, 83–85, 91–93, 96–99; Mayer, "Soldierly Subordination"; Knouff, *Soldiers' Revolution*, 92–97; Sculley, *Contest for Liberty*, 67–82.

14. William Tudor to John Adams, July 7, 1776, *PJA* (1979), 4:367 ("corrupt," "Severity"); Joseph Reed to [John Hancock], July 25, 1776, *American Archives* [. . .], ed. Peter Force, 5th ser. (Washington, D.C., 1848), 1:576 ("contemptible," "rum"); Cox, *Proper Sense of Honor*, 83, 93–96, 98–100.

15. Tudor to Adams, Sept. 6, 1776, *PJA* (1983), 5:13 ("Ravages," "mutinous," "Highwaymen"), 15 ("Virtue," "Punishment").

16. Autobiography entry, Aug. 19, 1776, in *Diary and Autobiography of John Adams*, ed. L. H. Butterfield (Cambridge, Mass.: Harvard University Press, 1961), 3:409–10.

17. *Chester Chronicle* (London), Mar. 21, 1776 ("inhabitants"); *Morning Chronicle* (London), Mar. 21, 1776; *The Diary and Letters of His Excellency Thomas Hutchinson* [. . .], comp. Peter Orlando Hutchinson (Boston, 1886), 2:24; *Daily Advertiser* (London), May 4, 1776; *Middlesex Journal* (London), Aug. 22–24, 1776 ("Congress"); *London Chronicle*, Aug. 22–24, 1776; *St. James's Chronicle* (London), Aug. 22–24, 1776.

18. Ambrose Serle to Earl of Dartmouth, July 25, 1776, in *Facsimiles of Manuscripts in European Archives Relating to America, 1773–1783*, vol. 24, ed. B. F. Stevens (London, 1895), no. 2040 ("Connecticut People," "Rival," "deprived"); *Serle Journal*, 34 ("mad multitude"), 36 ("Eastern," "declare"), 93, 160.

19. *Serle Journal*, 47 ("Savages"), 48.

20. Philip Schuyler to GW, July 12–13, General Orders, Aug. 1, 5, 1776, *PGW:RS*, ed. Philander D. Chase (1993), 5:286, 534 ("irritate," "injure"), 563 ("strangers," "public"); *JCC*, 5:591; Joseph Reed to [John Hancock], July 25, 1776, *American Archives*, 1:576;

David C. Hendrickson, *Peace Pact: The Lost World of the American Founding* (Lawrence: University Press of Kansas, 2003), esp. chap. 16; John C. Dann, *The Revolution Remembered: Eyewitness Accounts of the War for Independence* (Chicago: University of Chicago Press, 1980), 408–9; George Athan Billias, *General John Glover and His Marblehead Mariners* (New York: Henry Holt, 1960), 68–69; Rossie, *Politics of Command,* pp. 7, 10, 12, 15, 26–27, 32, 38, 42, 59–60, 82, 84–85, 98–103, chap. 5.

    21. *Morning Post* (London), Oct. 4, 1776 ("desert," "putrid"); *General Evening Post* (London), Oct. 3–5, 1776; *Serle Journal,* 60 ("Rags"), 64; GW to Jonathan Trumbull Sr., Aug. 7, Hugh Mercer to GW, Aug. 9, N.Y. Convention to GW, Aug. 9, Mercer to GW, Aug. 10, 11, Sept. 17, 1776, *PGW:RS,* 5:616, 651, 652–54, 660 ("humour"), 666–67, 6:327–28; *Public Advertiser* (London), Oct. 15, 1776 ("Dispute"); Solomon Drowne Jr. to Solomon Drowne Sr., Aug. 9, [1776], in Mercantile Library Association of New York City, *New York City during the American Revolution* [. . .] (New York, 1861), 105; Clement Biddle to John Shaw, Aug. 11, Aug. [?], 1776, John Shaw correspondence, Special Collections, Rutgers University Libraries; *Memoirs of Major-General William Heath,* ed. William Abbatt (New York: William Abbatt, 1901), 44; Philip Vickers Fithian, *Journal, 1775–1776,* ed. Robert Greenhalgh Albion and Leonidas Dodson (Princeton, N.J.: Princeton University Press, 1934), 2:196–97; Tench Tilghman to James Tilghman, Aug. 18, 1776, in *Memoir of Tilghman,* 133.

    22. Hutcheson to Haldimand, Aug. 8, 1776, Haldimand Papers, ff. 133v ("thought," "preservation"), 135v ("determined"); John Bowater to Basil Feilding, 6th Earl of Denbigh, Aug. 15, 1776, in *The Lost War: Letters from British Officers during the American Revolution,* ed. Marion Balderston and David Syrett (New York: Horizon, 1975), 96 ("intend"); *London Evening Post,* Oct. 5–8, 1776 ("fine"); *Public Advertiser,* Oct. 15, 1776 ("Combustibles"); *Kentish Gazette* (Canterbury), Oct. 2 ("fourth"), 5, 1776; *London Chronicle,* Oct. 15–17, 1776 ("not to burn," "certainly"); *Hampshire Chronicle* (Winchester), Oct. 7, 1776 ("Lord Howe"); *North British Intelligencer,* Oct. 2, 23, 1776, 22, 118; *Morning Post,* Oct. 4, 1776; Joseph Howell Jr. to Joseph Howell Sr., Aug. 14, 1776, in *A Salute to Courage: The American Revolution as Seen through Wartime Writings of Officers of the Continental Army and Navy,* ed. Dennis P. Ryan (New York: Columbia University Press, 1979), 36.

    23. *JPCNY,* 1:567–68, 568 *("whole"),* 588, 595–96, 634; *North British Intelligencer,* Oct. 23, 1776, 118 ("committee"); Benjamin Trumbull to Martha Trumbull, Aug. 13, 1776, Trumbull Family Correspondence, John Trumbull Papers, NYHS ("destroy," "Ways"); GW to N.Y. Convention, Aug. 11, GW to Hancock, Aug. 12, 1776, *PGW:RS,* 5:668, 678; *CCM,* 44, 56–57.

    24. Evacuation broadside, Aug. 17, GW to N.Y. Convention, Aug. 17, 1776, *PGW:RS,* 6:45 ("Bombardment"), 45–46 ("Women"), 46 ("Safety"), 54–55; [Ewald Shewkirk], "Occupation of New York City by the British, 1776: Extracts from the Diary of the Moravian Congregation," ed. A. A. Reinke, *PMHB* 1, no. 2 (1877): 251 ("fright"); *JPCNY,* 1:578.

    25. Silas Deane to Charles W. F. Dumas, Oct. 6, 1776, in *The Diplomatic Correspondence of the American Revolution,* ed. Jared Spark[s] (Boston, 1830), 9:292; Jessica Warner, *John the Painter: Terrorist of the American Revolution* (New York: Thunder's Mouth, 2004).

26. William Douglas to [Hannah Douglas], Aug. 23, 1776, "Revolutionary War Letters of Colonel William Douglas," *New-York Historical Society Quarterly Bulletin* 13, no. 2 (1929): 81.

27. Philip Vickers Fithian to Elizabeth Beatty Fithian, Aug. 26, 1776, in *Philip Vickers Fithian of Greenwich, New Jersey* [. . .] *Letters to His Wife*, ed. Frank D. Andrews (Vineland, N.J., 1932), 34 ("fluttered"); *Serle Journal*, 71, 74 ("covered"), 75, 79 ("Ignoble"); letter of [Johann von] Hinrichs, Sept. 18, 1776, *Briefwechsel meist historischen und politischen Inhalts*, ed. August Ludwig von Schlözer, 3 (1778): 105 ("beautiful"); William L. Stone, trans., *Letters of Brunswick and Hessian Officers during the American Revolution* (Albany, N.Y.: Joel Munsell's Sons, 1891), 195–96; James Chambers to Kitty Chambers, Sept. 3, 1776, in Ryan, *Salute to Courage*, 37–39; Hutcheson to Haldimand, Aug. 26, 1776, Haldimand Papers, f. 147v.

28. Orders to Israel Putnam, Aug. 25, 1776, *PGW:RS*, 6:126–27.

29. [Shewkirk], "Occupation of New York City," 148 ("damp," "sickly"); Barnet Schecter, *The Battle for New York: The City at the Heart of the American Revolution* (New York: Penguin, 2002), chaps. 7–10, esp. pp. 128–29, 140, 148, 153 (casualty figures); John J. Gallagher, *The Battle of Brooklyn, 1776* (New York: Sarpedon, 1995), 75, 80, 89, 91, 95, 131–32; Henry P. Johnston, *The Campaign of 1776 around New York and Brooklyn* (1878; New York: Da Capo, 1971), 146–47, 188n2; Tench Tilghman to James Tilghman, Sept. 3, 1776, in *Memoir of Tilghman*, 135.

30. John Morin Scott to GW, Aug. 31, William Heath to GW, Sept. 3, GW to Hancock, Sept. 6, 1776, *PGW:RS*, 6:190, 207–8, 231–33; *Smith Memoirs*, 2:5; however, see Isaac Sherman to Loammi Baldwin, Sept. 1, 1776, Loammi Baldwin papers, Houghton Library, Harvard University; William Shippen to Edward Shippen, [Sept.] 2, 1776, Shippen Papers, Historical Society of Pennsylvania, 12:46.

31. CCM, 43 (quote). Most historians rely on the excerpts in I. N. Phelps Stokes, ed., *The Iconography of Manhattan Island, 1498–1909* (New York: Robert H. Dodd, 1926), 5:1168–69, and Catherine S. Crary, ed., *The Price of Loyalty: Tory Writings from the Revolutionary Era* (New York: McGraw-Hill, 1973), 168–71. Oscar Theodore Barck Jr., *New York City during the War for Independence with Special Reference to the Period of British Occupation* (New York: Columbia University Press, 1931), 79–82, apparently consulted the manuscripts but shared no details and argued, "The investigation proved nothing"; see also Thomas Jefferson Wertenbaker, *Father Knickerbocker Rebels: New York City during the Revolution* (New York: Charles Scribner's Sons, 1948), 99–102.

32. [Joseph Plumb Martin], *A Narrative of Some of the Adventures, Dangers and Sufferings of a Revolutionary Soldier* [. . .] (Hallowell, Maine, 1830), 16–17.

33. *Lloyd's Evening Post* (London), Oct. 11–14, 1776 ("swimmingly," "ashes," "Magistrates," "orders," "quarter"); for codes of war relating to sieges, see Lee, *Barbarians and Brothers*, 47–50, 75–79, 84–91, 184–92.

34. *Serle Journal*, 84 ("Hand"), 88; R[ichard] G[renville] to [James Grenville], Aug. 31, 1776, Hastings Family Papers, Huntington Library ("dissatisfaction"); Henry Strachey to C[hristopher] D'Oyly, Sept. 3, 1776, Strachey Papers, WLCL; *General Evening Post*, Oct. 10–12, 1776.

35. James Murray to Elizabeth Smyth, Aug. 31, 1776, in *Letters from America, 1773 to 1780: Being the Letters of a Scots Officer, Sir James Murray* [. . .], ed. Eric Robson (New York: Barnes and Noble, 1950), 36 ("quarrelled," "insisted"); Charles Stuart to Lord Bute, Sept. 3, 1776, in *A Prime Minister and His Son* [. . .], ed. E. Stuart Wortley (London: John Murray, 1925), 85 ("fray"); *General Evening Post,* Oct. 10–12, 12–15 ("assured," "fury"), 1776; *Lloyd's Evening Post,* Oct. 14–16, 1776; *London Evening-Post,* Oct. 19–22, 1776.

36. Barnabas Binney to Nicholas Brown, [Sept. 4?], 1776, Brown Papers, John Carter Brown Library ("Harmony," "puffed"); GW to Hancock, Sept. 2, 1776, *PGW:RS,* 6:199 ("dispirited," "filled," "dismayed").

37. GW to Heath, Aug. 30, 1776, GW to Hancock, Sept. 2, 1776, *PGW:RS,* 6:165, 199 ("discipline," "disregard," "Infected," "obliged"), 200 ("exerted"); *Order Book Kept by Peter Kennan, July 7–September 4, 1776,* with an introduction by M. E. Kennan (Princeton, N.J.: Princeton University Press, 1931), 95 ("contemptible").

38. Sculley, *Contest for Liberty,* 151; Bowman, *Morale;* Neimeyer, *America Goes to War,* chap. 7; Martin, "Protest and Defiance."

39. General Orders, Sept. 3, 6, 1776, *PGW:RS,* 6:204–5 ("instances," "utterly"), 229 ("remembered").

40. Lewis Morris Jr. to Lewis Morris Sr., Sept. 6, 1776, NYHS *Collections* 8 (1875): 442 ("fever," "nuisance," "plunder," "unwarrantable"); Daniel Hitchcock to John Adams, Sept. 9, 1776, *PJA,* 5:21 ("farthing," "overcome"); Adams to Hitchcock, Oct. 1, 1776, autobiography entry, Oct. 1, 1776, in *Diary and Autobiography of John Adams,* 3:442 ("despondency"); GW to Hancock, Sept. 4, Jonathan Trumbull Sr. to GW, Sept. 5, 1776, *PGW:RS,* 6:215, 226.

41. *Serle Journal,* 91 ("Animosity"); Hutcheson to Haldimand, Sept. 5, 1776, Haldimand Papers, ff. 148–49 ("Confusion," "opposition"); Strachey to D'Oyly, Sept. 3, 1776, Strachey Papers, WLCL ("Fight," "trouble"); *General Evening Post,* Oct. 10–12, 1776.

42. William Douglas to [Hannah Douglas], Sept. 7, 11, 1776, "Revolutionary War Letters of Colonel William Douglas," *New-York Historical Society Quarterly Bulletin* 13, no. 3 (1929): 119 ("Fateauge"), 120 ("sell amarica"), 121; Joy Day Buel and Richard Buel Jr., *The Way of Duty: A Woman and Her Family in Revolutionary America* (New York: Norton, 1984), 118–20.

43. *Smith Memoirs,* 2:6–7 ("forbid"); CCM, 11 ("apprehensive"), 17–18, 25 ("Goal"), 26, 36 ("people," "burnt," "punish"), 64.

44. GW to Hancock, Sept. 8, 1776, *PGW:RS,* 6:248–54; Troy Bickham, *Making Headlines: The American Revolution Seen through the British Press* (DeKalb: Northern Illinois University Press, 2009), 88–94, 101–3.

FIVE   General Washington's Bad Options

1. Joseph Reed to Charles Pettit, Aug. 4, 1776, in *Life and Correspondence of Joseph Reed,* ed. William B. Reed (Philadelphia, 1847), 1:213 ("retiring," "propriety"); GW to Lund Washington, Oct. 6, 1776, *PGW:RS,* ed. Philander D. Chase and Frank E. Griz-

zard Jr. (1994), 6:494 ("dictates," "errors," "Barracks," "impossible"); coincidentally, see John Jay to Robert Morris, Oct. 6, 1776, NYHS *Collections* 11 (1878): 402.

2. *JPCNY*, 1:524 ("cheerfully," "abandon," "expedient"); William H. W. Sabine, *Murder, 1776 and Washington's Policy of Silence* (New York: Theo. Gaus' Sons, 1973), chaps. 3–5.

3. Abraham Yates Jr. to GW, Aug. 22, 1776, *PGW:RS*, 6:108 ("Prevailing").

4. Yates to GW, Aug. 22, 1776, *PGW:RS*, 6:108.

5. GW to N.Y. Convention, Aug. 23, 1776, *PGW:RS*, 6:114–15.

6. Paul K. Longmore, *The Invention of George Washington* (Charlottesville: University Press of Virginia, 1999).

7. John Ferling, *Almost a Miracle: The American Victory in the War of Independence* (New York: Oxford University Press, 2007), 142.

8. Philip Vickers Fithian, *Journal, 1775–1776*, ed. Robert Greenhalgh Albion and Leonidas Dodson (Princeton, N.J.: Princeton University Press, 1934), 2:221 ("Anxiety," "hourly"); Nathanael Greene to [Jacob Greene?], Aug. 30, 1776, in *The Papers of General Nathanael Greene*, ed. Richard K. Showman (Chapel Hill: University of North Carolina Press, 1976), 1:291 ("ashes"); Andrew Hunter war diary, Aug. 30, 1776, Princeton University Library.

9. Fithian, *Journal*, 2:222 ("Ruin"), 224 ("Whispers," "believe"); Jonathan Birge to Priscilla Birge, Sept. 1, 1776, Jonathan Birge Letters, Society of Cincinnati Library ("supposed"); Ludwigh Russell to unknown, Sept. 1, 1776, "A Centennial Letter," *New York Tribune*, Mar. 4, 1876, 4 ("Ranks"); William Shippen to Edward Shippen, [Sept.] 2, 1776, Shippen Papers, Historical Society of Pennsylvania, 12:46 ("deserted"); Benjamin Bogardus to Evert Bogardus, Sept. 4, 1776, NYHS ("Likely," "Seaport," "Expected").

10. *JPCNY*, 1:606 ("enemies"); GW to Yates, Sept. 1, Yates to GW, Sept. 4, 1776, *PGW:RS*, 6:197–98, 220–21; Graham Russell Hodges, *Root and Branch: African Americans in New York and East Jersey, 1613–1863* (Chapel Hill: University of North Carolina Press, 1999), 136–37, 140–42, 144–45; Thelma Wills Foote, *Black and White Manhattan: The History of Racial Formation in Colonial New York City* (New York: Oxford University Press, 2004), chap. 7; Phillip Papas, *That Ever Loyal Island: Staten Island and the American Revolution* (New York: New York University Press, 2007), 72–74, 77.

11. Philip Vickers Fithian to Elizabeth Beatty Fithian, Sept. 3, 1776, in *Philip Vickers Fithian of Greenwich, New Jersey [. . .] Letters to His Wife*, ed. Frank D. Andrews (Vineland, N.J., 1932), 39 ("Persecution"); GW to John Hancock, Sept. 2, 1776, *PGW:RS*, 6:199–201 (all other quotes).

12. GW to Hancock, Sept. 2, 1776, *PGW:RS*, 6:200–201. The attorney John Adolphus argues that this letter "shewed that he entertained a predilection" for burning the city. Adolphus suspected that GW was "privy" to a clandestine conspiracy. Congress may have resolved against destruction, but either (a) Continental operatives set the fire "in consequence of private instructions, incompatible with their public orders," (b) individuals acted "from their own judgment," or (c) vandals set the fire out of "mere malice." John Adolphus, *The History of England from the Accession of King George the Third, to the*

Conclusion of Peace in the Year 1783 (London, 1802), 2:427 ("predilection," "private," "judgment," "malice"), 427n ("privy").

13. Eliga H. Gould, *Among the Powers of the Earth: The American Revolution and the Making of a New World Empire* (Cambridge, Mass.: Harvard University Press, 2012), 115; David Armitage, *The Declaration of Independence: A Global History* (Cambridge, Mass.: Harvard University Press, 2007).

14. Rufus Putnam to GW, Sept. 3, 1776, *PGW:RS*, 6:210, 211 ("Ravaged").

15. John Haslet to Caesar Rodney, Aug. 31, Sept. 4, 1776, in *Delaware Archives: Revolutionary War in Three Volumes* (1919; New York: AMS, 1974), 3:1390, 1391 (all quotes).

16. *JCC*, 5:733 ("especial," "recover"); Hancock to GW, Sept. 3, 1776, *PGW:RS*, 6:207. The Italian historian Carlo Botta was impressed that Congress "humanely" urged preservation. Charles [Carlo] Botta, *History of the War of the Independence of the United States of America,* trans. George Alexander Otis, 6th ed. (1809; 1834; New Haven, Conn., 1837), 1:380–83, 380 ("humanely").

17. General Orders, Apr. 16, 1776, *PGW:RS*, ed. Philander D. Chase (1991), 4:74 ("Citizens"). An early history surmised that Washington would not have burned New York unless "that was the only method of saving the country," and blamed a "frolicking" group of British sailors; it also argued that Washington's correspondence with Congress "could not itself be sufficient to destroy the presumption that it was done by Americans." It was now "too late" to solve the mystery, "but this will be conceded by all: that if it had been destroyed by Congress, it would not have been avowed at the time, and probably never afterwards." Paul Allen, [John Neal, and Tobias Watkins], *A History of the American Revolution* [. . .] (Baltimore, 1822), 1:474 ("method"), 475, 507 ("frolicking," "presumption," "too late"), 507–8 ("conceded").

18. GW to Hancock, Sept. 4, 1776, *PGW:RS*, 6:215, 216 ("resources").

19. Nathanael Greene to GW, Sept. 5, 1776, *PGW:RS*, 6:222–24.

20. GW to Hancock, Sept. 6, GW to Heath, Sept. 6, GW to Lund Washington, Oct. 6, 1776, *PGW:RS*, 6:231 ("Perceiving"), 231–32 ("baffle"), 233–34, 494 ("forbid," "repent"). In GW's correspondence with Congress, he deferred to civilian authority, and his stated demurral satisfied most readers. *Journals of Congress containing the Proceedings from January 1, 1776, to January 1, 1777* (York, Pa., 1778), 2:341; *Official Letters to the Honorable American Congress,* [. . .] *by His Excellency, George Washington* [. . .] (London, 1795), 1:248 ("no damage"), 255; Jared Sparks, ed., *The Writings of George Washington* (Boston, 1834), 4:76, 76n, 86, 100n.

21. Hugh Mercer to GW, Sept. 7, GW to Hancock, Sept. 8, 1776, *PGW:RS*, 6:243–44, 248–54 (all quotes). After the fire, Washington and Lee complained about Congress's management; GW to Lund Washington, Sept. 30, 1776, *PGW:RS*, 6:440–42; Charles Lee to Horatio Gates, Oct. 14, 1776, "Lee Papers," vol. 4, NYHS *Collections* 7 (1874): 371; Clements R. Markham, *A Naval Career during the Old War: Being a Narrative of the Life of Admiral John Markham* [. . .] (London, 1883), 35.

22. Yates to GW, Sept. 5, GW to Yates, Sept. 8, Hancock to GW, Sept. 10, 1776, *PGW:RS*, 6:228, 261, 273 ("wish"); *JPCNY*, 1:610; *JCC*, 5:749; [Alexander Graydon], *Memoirs of a Life, Chiefly Passed in Pennsylvania* [. . .] (Harrisburg, Pa., 1811), 149–50.

23. *Mackenzie Diary*, 1:41 ("decisive"), 42 ("attacked," "consequence").

24. Tench Tilghman to James Tilghman, Aug. 15, Sept. 9, 1776, in *Memoir of Lieut. Col. Tench Tilghman* [. . .] (Albany, N.Y., 1876), 131 ("Family"), 136 (all other quotations).

25. "Henry Strachey's Notes on Lord Howe's Meeting with a Committee of Congress," Sept. 11, Josiah Barlett to William Whipple, Sept. [14?], 1776, *LDC* (1979), 5:140 ("Towns"), 162 ("ravaging"); Hamond Account, Sept. 3, 1776 ("object," "bloodshed"); Ira D. Gruber, *The Howe Brothers and the American Revolution* (New York: Atheneum, 1972), 116–22.

26. William Douglas to [Hannah Douglas], Sept. 11, 1776, "Revolutionary War Letters of Colonel William Douglas," *New-York Historical Society Quarterly Bulletin* 13, no. 3 (1929): 121 ("Cost"); Nathanael Greene et al. to GW, Sept. 11, GW to Hancock, Sept. 11, Council of War, Sept. 12, 1776, *PGW:RS*, 6:279–80, 280–81, 288–89.

27. Douglas Southall Freeman, *George Washington: A Biography* (New York: Charles Scribner's Sons, 1951), 4:188n80 ("fool"); George Clinton to GW, Sept. 12, Heath to GW, Sept. 13, 1776, *PGW:RS*, 6:290–92, 290 ("furnishes"), 302–4, 303 (all other quotes).

28. *Fithian Journal*, 2:231.

29. GW to Hancock, Sept. 14, 1776, *PGW:RS*, 6:308.

30. CCM, 65 ("intended"); Abstract of Captain Thomas W. Foster's Company, Jan. 1776, Henry Knox Papers, Gilder Lehrman Collection; Francis B. Heitman, *Historical Register of Officers of the Continental Army during the War of the Revolution* [. . .], rev. ed. (Washington, D.C.: Rare Book Shop, 1914), 234.

31. William Tudor to John Tudor, Sept. 14, 1776, Tudor Family Papers, MHS.

32. Bruce Bliven Jr., *Battle for Manhattan* (New York: Henry Holt, 1955), 18; William Henry Shelton, *The Jumel Mansion: Being a Full History of the House on Harlem Heights* [. . .] (Boston: Houghton Mifflin, 1916).

SIX The Loss of New York City

1. Philip Vickers Fithian, *Journal, 1775–1776*, ed. Robert Greenhalgh Albion and Leonidas Dodson (Princeton, N.J.: Princeton University Press, 1934), 2:233; *Serle Journal*, 104–5; Henry P. Johnston, *The Campaign of 1776 around New York and Brooklyn* (1878; New York: Da Capo, 1971), 230–31; Bruce Bliven Jr., *Battle for Manhattan* (New York: Henry Holt, 1955), 26–28; Barnet Schecter, *The Battle for New York: The City at the Heart of the American Revolution* (New York: Penguin, 2002), 179–82.

2. [Ewald Shewkirk], "Occupation of New York City by the British, 1776: Extracts from the Diary of the Moravian Congregation," *PMHB* 1, no. 3 (1877): 251 ("cannonading," "ceased," "stillness," "only"); Shewkirk to Seidel, 2 ("Bricks"); Charles E. Corwin, "Incidents of Reformed Church Life in New York City during the Revolutionary War," *Journal of the Presbyterian Historical Society* 9, no. 8 (1918): 356.

3. Bliven, *Battle for Manhattan*, 14–22, 25–27; Schecter, *Battle*, 179.

4. Rawdon to Huntingdon ("fervency"); Benjamin Trumbull to Martha Trum-

bull, Sept. 17, 1776, Trumbull Family Correspondence, John Trumbull Papers, NYHS ("Entrenchments"); *Mackenzie Diary,* 1:46; Johnston, *Campaign of 1776,* 231–33; Schechter, *Battle for New York,* 182–83.

5. *Serle Journal,* 104 ("So terrible"); Shewkirk to Seidel, 2 ("Slaughter"); Benjamin Trumbull to Martha Trumbull, Sept. 17, 1776, John Trumbull Papers, NYHS; *Journal of Rear-Admiral Bartholomew James, 1752–1828,* ed. John Knox Laughton with James Young F. Sulivan, *Publications of the Navy Records Society,* vol. 6 (1896), 31; *Mackenzie Diary,* 1:46–49; Jonathan Birge to [Priscilla Birge], Sept. 24, 1776, Society of the Cincinnati Library; Ira D. Gruber, *The Howe Brothers and the American Revolution* (New York: Atheneum, 1972), 122–24.

6. William Hooper to Samuel Johnston, Sept. 26, 1776, in *The Colonial Records of North Carolina,* ed. William L. Saunders (Raleigh, N.C., 1886), 10:817 ("saw"); Nicholas Fish to John McKesson, Sept. 19, 1776, "The Military Occupation of New York, by the British, September, 1776," *The Historical Magazine, and Notes and Queries, concerning the Antiquities, History and Biography of America,* 2nd ser., 3, no. 1 (1868): 34 ("infuse," "dastardly," "infected"); *Fithian Journal,* 2:233 ("Shame," "timorous"); Henry Knox to William Knox, Sept. 23, 1776 ("rabble," "raggamuffins," "ignorant"), Henry Jackson to Henry Knox, Sept. 26, 1776, Henry Knox Papers, Gilder Lehrman Collection; Nathanael Greene to Nicholas Cooke, Sept. 17, 1776, in *The Papers of General Nathanael Greene,* ed. Richard K. Showman (Chapel Hill: University of North Carolina Press, 1976), 1:300 ("disorderly"); GW to Nicholas Cooke, Sept. 17, 1776, *PGW:RS,* ed. Philander D. Chase and Frank E. Grizzard Jr. (1994), 6:321–26, 324 ("disgraceful").

7. Thompson to Huntingdon ("cellar," "presence"); *Ordinary Courage: The Revolutionary War Adventures of Joseph Plumb Martin,* ed. James Kirby Martin, 4th ed. (Malden, Mass.: Wiley-Blackwell, 2013), 23, 25 ("demons"), 27 ("confused," "rid").

8. Benjamin Trumbull, "Journal of the Campaign at New York, 1776–7," *Orderly Books and Journals Kept by Connecticut Men while Taking Part in the American Revolution, 1775–1778, CCHS* 7 (1899): 195; *Literary Diary of Ezra Stiles* [. . .], ed. Franklin Bowditch Dexter (New York: Charles Scribner's Sons, 1901), 2:59.

9. Andrew Hunter, war diary, Sept. 15, 1776, Princeton University Library ("applauded"); William Smallwood to Maryland Convention, Oct. 12–13, 1776, *American Archives* [. . .], ed. Peter Force, 5th ser. (Washington, D.C., 1851), 2:1013 ("transactions," "wretches"); Tench Tilghman to [James Tilghman], Sept. 16, 1776, in *Memoir of Lieut-Col. Tench Tilghman* [. . .] (Albany, N.Y., 1876), 137.

10. Samuel Holden Parsons to John Adams, Sept. [19?], 1776, *PJA,* ed. Robert J. Taylor (1983), 5:29 ("blasting," "daily," "Measure"), 30 ("Misconduct"); entry, Oct. 1, 1776, in *Diary and Autobiography of John Adams,* ed. L. H. Butterfield (Cambridge, Mass.: Harvard University Press, 1961), 3:447 ("disrespectfully").

11. William Heath to GW, Sept. 19, 1776, *PGW:RS,* 6:342–43, 342 ("Duty," "Volunteers"); Patrick Anderson to Council, Sept. 22, 1776, *Pennsylvania Archives,* ed. Samuel Hazard (Philadelphia, 1853), 1st ser., 5:27–28; "Pennsylvania Rifle Regiment, Col. Samuel Miles," *Pennsylvania Archives,* ed. Thomas Lynch Montgomery (Harrisburg, Pa., 1906), 5th ser., 2:253–55, 254 ("used well"); John Richardson to John Crozier, Sept. 24, 1776,

"Letters of Lieutenant John Richardson, 1776," *PMHB* 16, no. 2 (1892): 205; *JCC*, 5:831–32; for New Jersey, *Connecticut Courant* (Hartford), Oct. 7, 1776; Peter DuBois to Cadwallader Colden Jr., Sept. 16[–18], 1776, John McKesson Papers, NYHS; GW to John Glover, Sept. 17, Hugh Mercer to GW, Sept. 17, Glover to GW, Sept. 18, 1776, *PGW:RS*, 6:326–30.

12. William Douglas to [Hannah Douglas], Sept. 26, 1776, "Revolutionary War Letters of Colonel William Douglas," *New-York Historical Society Quarterly Bulletin* 13, no. 4 (1930): 157 ("unjust," "Stigmatise," "Dangerous"); [Gold Selleck] S[illiman] to [Mary] S[illiman], Oct. 6, 1776, Finch Family Papers, photocopies, University of Southern California Special Collections ("rancour," "killed"); Joshua Shepherd, "George Washington Convenes a Firing Squad," *Journal of the American Revolution*, Feb. 9, 2016, https://all thingsliberty.com/2016/02/george-washington-convenes-a-firing-squad/.

13. *Mackenzie Diary*, 1:49–50; GW to Philip Schuyler, Sept. 20, 1776, *PGW:RS*, 6:357; Bliven, *Battle for Manhattan*, 57–59; Gruber, *Howe Brothers*, 122–24; Schecter, *Battle*, 189; John Ferling, *Almost a Miracle: The American Victory in the War of Independence* (New York: Oxford University Press, 2007), 140–42; David Smith, *William Howe and the American War of Independence* (London: Bloomsbury, 2015), 84–85, 104, 106–7, 153.

14. David Humphreys, *An Essay on the Life of the Honorable Major-General Israel Putnam* (Hartford, Conn., 1788), 132 ("foam"); Johnston, *Campaign of 1776*, 237–39; Matthew L. Davis, *Memoirs of Aaron Burr* [. . .] (New York, 1837), 1:100–106, 104 ("dogs"); George Clinton to New York Committee of Correspondence, Sept. 18, 1776, in *A Salute to Courage: The American Revolution as Seen through Wartime Writings of Officers of the Continental Army and Navy*, ed. Dennis P. Ryan (New York: Columbia University Press, 1979), 44 ("Choice").

15. CCM, 64, 65 ("care," "certainly"); Henry P. Johnston, *The Battle of Harlem Heights, September 16, 1776* [. . .] (New York, 1897), 186–88, 188 ("disguise").

16. *Fithian Journal*, 2:234 ("sinful"), 235; Humphreys, *Life of Putnam*, 133, 136–37 ("hearts," "warmth"); Martin, *Ordinary Courage*, 25–26; Jonathan Birge to [Priscilla Birge], Sept. 24, 1776, Society of the Cincinnati Library; Stiles, *Literary Diary*, 2:59–60; "Letters of Douglas," 157.

17. Bowater to Denbigh, 101 ("precipitation," "nothing"); *Serle Journal*, 109 ("handsome," "Regret," "Resolution"); *Mackenzie Diary*, 1:50, 51, 66–67; *Morning Post* (London), Dec. 9, 1776.

18. Grant to Rigby ("Panic"); Peter Tappen to George Clinton, Sept. 23, 1776, in *Public Papers of George Clinton, First Governor of New York* [. . .], ed. Hugh Hastings (New York, 1899), 1:358 ("allarmed"); *Newport (R.I.) Mercury*, Oct. 21, 1776 ("rats").

19. Shewkirk, "Diary," 251–52; *Mackenzie Diary*, 1:50, 51 ("inhabitants," "Stores"); Francis Hutcheson to Frederick Haldimand, Sept. 24, 1776, Haldimand Papers, Add. MS 21680, British Library, ff. 153–54.

20. Duncan Journal, 128 ("blessing"); *Serle Journal*, 104 ("Bedlamites," "Joy"); *Mackenzie Diary*, 1:49 ("escape"); Shewkirk, "Diary," 252; *St. James's Chronicle* (London), Nov. 7–9, 1776.

21. Alexander McDougall to GW, Feb. 17, 1778, *PGW:RS*, ed. Edward G. Lengel (2003), 13:572 (quotes); CCM, 68; Warren B. Stout, "Ancestral Line of the Somerset Van

Dykes," *Somerset County Historical Quarterly* 4, no. 4 (1915): 264; William B. Aitken, *Distinguished Families in America Descended from Wilhelmus Beekman and Jan Thomasse Van Dyke* (New York: G. P. Putnam's Sons, 1912), 226.

22. *Serle Journal*, 104–5 ("pulled down," "trampling," "Defence"); *Hampshire Chronicle* (Winchester), Nov. 18, 1776 ("wife"); Shewkirk, "Diary," 252 ("Usurpers"); entry, Sept. 15, journal written in Goldsmith's *Almanac* for 1776, Guy Johnson Papers, Beinecke Rare Book and Manuscript Library, Yale University, https://collections.library.yale.edu/catalog /16344299.

23. CCM, 62–63.

24. *Serle Journal*, 105 ("lie close"); *Harrison's Derby Journal*, Nov. 1, 1776 ("fever"); Bruce E. Burgoyne, ed., *Enemy Views: The American Revolutionary War as Recorded by the Hessian Participants* (Bowie, Md.: Heritage, 1996), 78 ("terribly," "geese").

25. Joseph Reed to Esther De Berdt Reed, Sept. 17, 1776, Joseph Reed Papers, NYHS ("insulting," "Bugle," "Sensation"); *Memoirs of the Life of John Adlum in the Revolutionary War*, ed. Howard H. Peckham (1939; Chicago: Caxton Club, 1968), 22 ("raising").

26. Burr to [Rhoda] Edwards, Sept. 26, 1776, in *Memoirs of Aaron Burr*, 107 ("false"); [Stephen Brown], *Connecticut Gazette* (New London), Sept. 27, 1776 ("Dozen," "split"); reprints: *Boston Gazette, and Country Journal* (Watertown, Mass.), Oct. 7, 1776; *Massachusetts Spy* (Worcester), Oct. 9, 1776; *Essex Journal* (Newburyport, Mass.), Oct. 11, 1776; Johnston, *Harlem Heights*, 155; Fish to McKesson, "Military Occupation," 34 ("shot"); *Journal of Bartholomew James*, 31 ("sever"); Humphreys, *Life of Putnam*, 140 ("thirst"); Gustavus Brown Wallace to Michael Wallace, Sept. 15, 1776, in Ryan, *Salute to Courage*, 43.

27. *Serle Journal*, 77, 86–87, 108 ("Complaints," "plunder"); Cliffe to BC ("Cellar"); "Journals of Lieut.-Col. Stephen Kemble," NYHS *Collections* 16 (1883): 91; *Independent Chronicle* (Boston), Oct. 3, 1776; Jos[eph] Royal[l] Loring to Archibald McNeal, Oct. 6, 1776, *Niles' Weekly Register* (Baltimore), May 7, 1836, 184.

28. Catharena Clopper, "Circumstances, on Deposition of the Conduct of Scotch & Hessian Troops on Sep:'t 16th and 18th, 1776 [. . .]," Nicholas Jones Papers, American Historical Manuscript Collection, NYHS; David Stewart, *Sketches of the Character, Manners, and Present State of the Highlanders of Scotland* [. . .] (Edinburgh, 1822), 2:90; Memorial of Brigadier General Oliver DeLancey to Henry Clinton, July 11, 1778, TNA AO 13/3, ff. 287–90; Memorial of William Waddell, Feb. 1, 1790, AO 13/10, ff. 246–47.

29. Benjamin Rush to Julia Rush, [Sept. 18–25?, 1776], William Williams to Jonathan Trumbull Sr., *LDC* (1979), 5:198 ("Affairs," "melancholy"), 199 ("ripen," "purged"), 208 ("directed"), 209 ("Soul," "kindle"); *Connecticut Courant* (Hartford), Oct. 14, 1776; Mary Silliman to Gold Selleck Silliman, Sept. 19, 1776, quoted in Joy Day Buel and Richard Buel Jr., *The Way of Duty: A Woman and Her Family in Revolutionary America* (New York: Norton, 1984), 121 ("dirty," "boast").

30. GW to John Hancock, Sept. 16, General Orders, Sept. 18–22, 1776, *PGW:RS*, 6:313–17, 328 ("Plunder," "whipped"), 340 ("restrain"), 341, 348 ("instantly"), 359–60, 364 ("Complaints"), 365–67; Humphreys, *Life of Putnam*, 142.

31. Tench Tilghman to [James Tilghman], Sept. 19, 1776, in *Memoir of Tilghman*, 139 ("plundering"); Andrew Hunter, war diary, Sept. 18, 1776, Princeton University Library ("Scoundrel," "Excrement"); John Eccleston to Joseph Richardson, Sept. 18, 1776, Eccleston Letters (photocopies), Special Collections, Rutgers University Libraries; [Gold Selleck] S[illiman] to [Mary] S[illiman], Sept. 29, Oct. 3, 6, 1776, Finch Family Papers, photocopies, University of Southern California Special Collections; John Sullivan to Meshech Weare, Feb. 13, 1777, *Letters and Papers of Major-General John Sullivan*, ed. Otis G. Hammond, *Collections of the New Hampshire Historical Society* 13 (1930): 319–20.

32. GW to Hancock, Sept. 25, 1776, *PGW:RS*, 6:393–401, 396 ("dragged," "timid," "accustomed," "proper"), 399 ("infamous," "horrid").

33. *JCC* (1906), 5:798 ("plunder"), 799 ("officers," "maliciously," "commander"), 806; Jerrilyn Greene Marston, *King and Congress: The Transfer of Political Legitimacy, 1774–1776* (Princeton, N.J.: Princeton University Press, 1987), 155–58; Charles Patrick Neimeyer, *America Goes to War: A Social History of the Continental Army* (New York: New York University Press, 1996), 139–46; Caroline Cox, *A Proper Sense of Honor: Service and Sacrifice in George Washington's Army* (Chapel Hill: University of North Carolina Press, 2004), chap. 3; Harry M. Ward, *George Washington's Enforcers: Policing the Continental Army* (Carbondale: Southern Illinois University Press, 2006), esp. chaps. 3, 14, 16; Wayne E. Lee, *Barbarians and Brothers: Anglo-American Warfare, 1500–1865* (New York: Oxford University Press, 2011), 198–202; Stephen Brumwell, *George Washington: Gentleman Warrior* (New York: Quercus, 2012), 250–53; Holger Hoock, *Scars of Independence: America's Violent Birth* (New York: Crown, 2017), 143.

34. *Mackenzie Diary*, 1:51 ("loyal," "empty"); *St. James's Chronicle*, Nov. 7–9, 1776 ("desolate"); *Morning Chronicle* (London), Nov. 26, 1776 ("true description"); Shewkirk to Seidel, 3 ("looked suspicious"); *Pennsylvania Journal* (Philadelphia), Nov. 20, 1776; *Ipswich Journal*, Nov. 9, 1776; *St. James's Chronicle*, Nov. 2–5, 1776; Esmond Wright, "The New York Loyalists: A Cross-Section of Colonial Society," in *The Loyalist Americans: A Focus on Greater New York*, ed. Robert A. East and Jacob Judd (Tarrytown, N.Y.: Sleepy Hollow Restorations, 1975), 82.

35. Abraham B. Bancker to [Evert Bancker], Sept. 17, 1776, Bancker Papers, NYHS ("Encouraged"); CCM, 15–16, 15 ("Negro man"), 59; Michael J. O'Brien, "The Story of Old Leary Street, or Cortland Street: The Leary Family in Early New York History," *Journal of the American Irish Historical Society* 15, no. 1 (1916): 112–17; Graham Russell Hodges, "Black Revolt in New York City and the Neutral Zone, 1775–1783," in *Slavery, Freedom and Culture among Early American Workers* (1998; New York: Routledge, 2015), 65–86; Bernard L. Herman, *Town House: Architecture and Material Life in the Early American City, 1780–1830* (Chapel Hill: University of North Carolina Press, 2005), 119–23, 142–50, 154; Judith L. Van Buskirk, *Generous Enemies: Patriots and Loyalists in Revolutionary New York* (Philadelphia: University of Pennsylvania Press, 2002), 138; Jill Lepore, *New York Burning: Liberty, Slavery, and Conspiracy in Eighteenth-Century Manhattan* (New York: Knopf, 2005), 148–60.

36. *Serle Journal*, 106 ("Concourse," "madmen," "Tyranny," "Release"); Shewkirk, "Diary," 252; Shewkirk to Seidel, 2 ("Joy"), 3.

37. *Leeds Intelligencer,* Nov. 12, 1776 (quotes); *St. James's Chronicle,* Nov. 14–16, 1776.

38. *Serle Journal,* 106–7 ("handsome"); *Mackenzie Diary,* 1:51 ("unable"); Deborah Lubken, "Joyful Ringing, Solemn Tolling: Methods and Meanings of Early American Tower Bells," *WMQ* 69, no. 4 (2012): 823–42; Philip J. Deloria, *Playing Indian* (New Haven, Conn.: Yale University Press, 1998); David Waldstreicher, "Reading the Runaways: Self-Fashioning, Print Culture, and Confidence in Slavery in the Eighteenth Century Mid-Atlantic," *WMQ* 56, no. 2 (1999): 243–72; Dror Wahrman, *The Making of the Modern Self: Identity and Culture in Eighteenth-Century England* (New Haven, Conn.: Yale University Press, 2004), esp. chap. 6; Alfred F. Young, *Masquerade: The Life and Times of Deborah Sampson, Continental Soldier* (New York: Knopf, 2004), 6–9, 83–84, 111–12, 160, 318–19; Thomas Agostini, "'Deserted His Majesty's Service': Military Runaways, the British-American Press, and the Problem of Desertion during the Seven Years' War," *Journal of Social History* 40, no. 4 (2007): 957–85; Serena R. Zabin, *Dangerous Economies: Status and Commerce in Imperial New York* (Philadelphia: University of Pennsylvania Press, 2009), chap. 1; Kate Haulman, *The Politics of Fashion in Eighteenth-Century America* (Chapel Hill: University of North Carolina Press, 2011), esp. pp. 14–31; Steven C. Bullock, *Tea Sets and Tyranny: The Politics of Politeness in Early America* (Philadelphia: University of Pennsylvania Press, 2016), chap. 5; Jennifer Van Horn, *The Power of Objects in Eighteenth-Century British America* (Chapel Hill: University of North Carolina Press, 2017), chap. 4.

39. David L. Sterling, ed., "American Prisoners of War in New York: A Report by Elias Boudinot," *WMQ* 13, no. 3 (1956): 388 ("secreted"); Joshua Loring, "Return of Prisoners Taken on the Island of New-York 15th and 16 of Sept.r 1776," enclosed in GW to John Hancock, Sept. 25, 1776, Letters from GW, 2:260, Papers of the Continental Congress, National Archives and Records Administration; N.Y. Committee of Safety to GW, Feb. 13, 1777, *PGW:RS,* ed. Frank E. Grizzard Jr. (1998), 8:326–27.

40. *Serle Journal,* 109 ("loyal"); DuBois to Colden Jr., Sept. 16[–18], 1776, McKesson Papers, NYHS ("Yorkers"); Memorial of John Wetherhead, Oct. 3, 1783, TNA AO 12/22, p. 70, f. 35v ("unpardonable," "promiscuous").

41. "Journals of Kemble," 89; Milton M. Klein and Ronald W. Howard, "General James Robertson and Civil Government in Revolutionary New York," in *The Twilight of British Rule in Revolutionary America: The New York Letter Book of General James Robertson, 1780–1783* (Cooperstown, N.Y.: New York State Historical Association, 1983), 1–69; Memorial of William Waddell, Feb. 1, 1790, TNA AO 13/10, f. 254r–v; Memorial of Cornelius Ryan, 1786, TNA AO, 13/26, f. 433 ("make a return").

42. *Serle Journal,* 109 ("Doors"), 110 ("Dwellings"); Shewkirk, "Diary," 252 ("personal resentment"); Shewkirk to Seidel, 3 ("rubb'd off").

43. Shewkirk, "Diary," 252; Edwin G. Burrows, *Forgotten Patriots: The Untold Story of American Prisoners during the Revolutionary War* (New York: Basic, 2008), 15–26, 50, 92, 105–6.

44. CCM, 18 ("observing," "Wharf"), 21 ("effects"), 23 ("walking," "discovered"), 59 ("quantities").

45. CCM, 9 ("charge"), 11 ("dug"); "Firemen of New York," in *Calendar of Historical Manuscripts Relating to the War of the Revolution* (Albany, N.Y., 1868), 1:315–16; *American Archives* (1848), 1:257; Memorial of William Waddell, Feb. 1, 1790, TNA AO 13/10, f. 254r–v.

46. Shewkirk, "Diary," 252 ("secure"); *St. James's Chronicle,* Nov. 7–9, 1776 ("flattered"); CCM, 21; Shewkirk to Seidel, 3.

47. *NYGWM* (New York), Sept. 30, 1776; *Mackenzie Diary,* 1:59.

48. *Mackenzie Diary,* 1:58; "Journals of Kemble," 89.

49. CCM, 37 ("Sailors"), 58, 73, 78–79; for Shipman, *New-York Gazette,* Sept. 24, 1764; for Ann Lynch (later McDonnell), E. B. O'Callaghan, ed., *Names of Persons for Whom Marriage Licenses Were Issued* [. . .], *Previous to 1784* (Albany, N.Y., 1860), 241.

SEVEN　The Great Fire

1. *Conflagration. A Poem* (New York, 1780), [3].

2. CCM, 72–78, 73 ("barrel"); TNA AO 12/20, ff. 53–56, 57v.

3. *Conflagration,* [5].

4. CCM, 4–5, 7.

5. *Conflagration,* [4].

6. For *Orpheus* logs, TNA ADM 51/650, pt. 5, f. 5, 52/1893; NMM ADM L/O/45; for outlying timing, CCM, 60–61; Benjamin Trumbull, "Journal of the Campaign at New York, 1776–7," *Orderly Books and Journals Kept by Connecticut Men while Taking Part in the American Revolution, 1775–1778,* CCHS 7 (1899): 197; Percy to Northumberland; TNA ADM 51/776, pt. 5. For between midnight and 1 a.m., see Henry Stirke, "A British Officer's Revolutionary War Journal, 1776–1778," ed. S. Sydney Bradford, *Maryland Historical Magazine* 56, no. 2 (1961): 159, and other contemporary sources in this chapter. For modern investigation practice, see Justin A. Geiman and James M. Lord, "Systematic Analysis of Witness Statements for Fire Investigation," *Fire Technology* 48 (2012): 219–31.

7. TNA ADM 52/1725 ("Rays"), 51/331, f. 59 ("body"); *Mackenzie Diary,* 1:59 ("Column"); CCM, 1, 29–30, 35, 44, Inglis insert; TNA ADM 51/4104, pt. 10, 51/168, f. 288, 51/493, 51/600, 51/720, pt. 5, 52/1965, f. 16v, 51/931, pt. 5, f. 193, 51/972; but see also ADM 52/2029, pt 1.

8. CCM, 37, 58, 74; "David Grim's Account," D. T. Valentine, "The Great Fires in New York City in 1776 and 1778," *MCCNY* (1866), 766 ("bad"). John Joseph Henry, *An Accurate and Interesting Account of the Hardships and Sufferings of That Band of Heroes Who Traversed the Wilderness in the Campaign against Quebec in 1775* (Lancaster, Pa., 1812), 184, believed he had stayed at this tavern, calling it the "Fighting Cocks." The Loyalist merchant Edward Laight thought the fire started at "a small Blacksmith's shop"; CCM, 23. The collector of customs, Andrew Elliot, said it was at "some Wooden Buildings adjoining the Custom House"; Andrew Elliot to the Lords Commissioners of His Majesty's Treasury, Nov. 30, 1776, TNA T 1/520, f. 170. Another observer mentioned "Jacob Remsen's Storehouse"; *St. James's Chronicle* (London), Nov. 14–16, 1776. Stephen Kemble

pointed to "that block of Houses fronting Mr. Watt's, and near the Exchange, in a House facing the Water"; "Journals of Lieut.-Col. Stephen Kemble," NYHS *Collections* 16 (1883): 89. Charles Inglis ran down Broadway and stopped at the corner of Stone Street, and from there he learned that the fire had begun "on the South East side of the Slip at White Hall"; CCM, Inglis insert. See also TNA ADM 51/375, pt. 9, f. 11; Shewkirk to Seidel, 3; *Mackenzie Diary*, 1:58; *St. James's Chronicle*, Nov. 7–9, 1776; CCM, 81; entry, Sept. 21, journal written in Goldsmith's *Almanac* for 1776, Guy Johnson Papers, Beinecke Rare Book and Manuscript Library, Yale University, https://collections.library.yale.edu/catalog /16344299.

9. [Thomas James?], *Kentish Gazette* (Canterbury), Nov. 9, 1776 ("two places"); CCM, 18, 49 ("five"), 60, 61 ("two or three," "independent"); *Mackenzie Diary*, 1:58 ("three"), 60 ("wilfully"); Trumbull, "Journal," 197; Duncan Journal, 130; Strachey to JS; *Serle Journal*, 110–11; Thomas Moffat, diary, Sept. 22, 1776, Peter Force Collection, LOC; George Clinton to Peter Tappen, Sept. [22], 1776, in Mercantile Library Association of New York City, *New York City during the American Revolution* [. . .] (New York, 1861), 116; Hamond Account, Sept. 22, 1776; Hamond to Stanley; TNA ADM 51/67, f. 122, 51/987, pt. 3, 52/1583, pt. 3; Percy to Northumberland; Leslie to Leven; William Erskine to Sir John Halkett, [Sept. 21 or 22, 1776], Halkett Papers, National Library of Scotland, f. 68v; William Glanville Evelyn to [Margaret] Evelyn, Sept. 25, 1776, in *Memoir and Letters of Captain W. Glanville Evelyn* [. . .], ed. G. D. Scull (Oxford, 1879), 89; Rawdon to Huntingdon; [Friedrich] von der Malsburg to Wilhelm von Ditfurth, Oct. 4, 1776, Letter Z: Military Reports and Accounts of the Hessian Corps in America, 1776–1782, Lidgerwood Collection of Hessian Transcripts on the American Revolution, Morristown National Historic Park, ed. Lion G. Miles and James L. Kochan, microfilm, 18; Jos[eph] Royal[l] Loring to Archibald McNeal, Oct. 6, 1776, *Niles' Weekly Register* (Baltimore), May 7, 1836; *Saunders's News-Letter* (Dublin), Nov. 4–6, 1776; and several other newspaper and officers' accounts cited in this chapter.

10. Bruce E. Burgoyne, trans., *The Diary of Lieutenant von Bardeleben and Other von Donop Regiment Documents* (Bowie, Md.: Heritage, 1998), 65 ("everywhere"); Loammi Baldwin to Mary Baldwin, Sept. 23, 1776, Loammi Baldwin papers, Houghton Library, Harvard University; *London Packet*, Nov. 18–20, 1776 [twenty]; JFBVHC, 113 [fifty]; *Connecticut Gazette* (New London), Sept. 27, 1776.

11. Tryon to Germain.

12. *Conflagration*, [5].

13. Bernard A. Uhlendorf, trans., *Revolution in America: Confidential Letters and Journals, 1776–1784, of Adjutant General Major Baurmeister of the Hessian Forces* (New Brunswick, N.J.: Rutgers University Press, 1957), 51 ("carelessness," "inadequacy"); *St. James's Chronicle*, Nov. 7–9, 1776; *Mackenzie Diary*, 1:59; David Garrioch, "Why Didn't Paris Burn in the Seventeenth and Eighteenth Centuries?" *French Historical Studies* 42, no. 1 (2019): 35–65, esp. pp. 41–42; Garrioch, "Fires and Firefighting in 18th and Early 19th-Century Paris," *French History and Civilization: Papers from the George Rudé Seminar* 7 (2017): 1–13.

14. Tryon to Germain ("ringing"); Inglis to Hind ("speedily"); CCM, 37, 41, 47,

78 ("firemen," "People," "strangers"); [Ewald Shewkirk], "Occupation of New York City by the British, 1776: Extracts from the Diary of the Moravian Congregation," ed. A. A. Reinke, *PMHB* 1, no. 2 (1877): 254; *Mackenzie Diary*, 1:59; "Bamford's Diary: The Revolutionary Diary of a British Officer," *Maryland Historical Magazine* 28 (1933): 11, 12; *Minutes of the Common Council of the City of New York, 1675–1776* (New York: Dodd, Mead, 1905), 8:137; Carl Bridenbaugh, *Cities in Revolt: Urban Life in America, 1743–1776* (New York: Knopf, 1955), 108–9, 297–98.

15. CCM, 9, 23 ("vain," "other parts"), 30 ("exerted"), 39, 41 ("reached"); Account of William Waddell, enclosed with Memorial dated Feb. 1, 1790, TNA AO 13/10, ff. 254–55.

16. CCM, 8, 11–12, 19 ("many"), 24, 59 ("most," "Cisterns"); *St. James's Chronicle,* Nov. 7–9, 1776.

17. *Mackenzie Diary,* 1:59 ("Scarcity"); CCM, 8, 39 ("Key"), 40 ("purposely"); JFBVHC, 111; [Shewkirk], "Occupation," 254. Hamond Account, Sept. 22, 1776, described the town as being "exceedingly well supplied with Engines & Buckets."

18. *Conflagration,* [5].

19. CCM, 40 ("violence"), 46 ("moderate," "increased"); *Diary of Bardeleben,* 65 ("set fire," "strong wind"); *Mackenzie Diary,* 1:58 ("irresistible"); Francis Hutcheson to Frederick Haldimand, Sept. 24, 1776, Haldimand Papers, Add. MS 21680, British Library, f. 153. Accounts varied as to the dryness of the weather: Inglis to Hind said it was "very dry," and William Carter, *A Genuine Detail of the Several Engagements, Positions, and Movements of the Royal and American Armies* [. . .] (London, 1784), 41, mentioned the "dry weather and a brisk wind"; see also *St. James's Chronicle,* Nov. 7–9, 1776. But according to "Bamford's Diary," 9, "It blew fresh all n[ight]t w[i]t[h] some rain"; and JFBVHC, 111, reported that "the night was very rainy."

20. *Conflagration,* [5].

21. *Mackenzie Diary,* 1:59–60 ("flakes"); TNA ADM 52/1921, pt. 4, 52/1866, pt. 8; Cliffe to JC; NMM ADM L/P/266; Inglis to Hind; Strachey to JS; Hamond Account, Sept. 22, 1776; Carlos Sanchez Tarifa, Pedro Perez del Notario, Francisco Garcia Moreno, and Antonio Rodriguez Villa, "Transport and Combustion of Firebrands," Final Report of Grants FG-SP-114, FG-SP-146, vol. 2, U.S. Department of Agriculture, Forest Service, and Instituto Nacional de Tecnica Aeroespacial (1967); Eunmo Koo, Patrick J. Pagni, David R. Weise, and John P. Woycheese, "Firebrands and Spotting Ignition in Large-Scale Fires," *International Journal of Wildland Fire* 19 (2010): 818–43; Samuel L. Manzello, Sayaka Suzuki, Michael J. Gollner, and A. Carlos Fernandez-Pello, "Role of Firebrand Combustion in Large Outdoor Fire Spread," *Progress in Energy and Combustion Science* 76 (2020), https://doi.org/10.1016/j.pecs.2019.100801.

22. CCM, Nooth insert ("rapidity"), 7 ("setting"), 8, 23–24, 35–36 ("Sparks"), 37–38, 40, 45, 60–61, 63 ("accident," "flakes," "designedly"); "David Grim's Account," 766 ("amazing"); *St. James's Chronicle,* Nov. 14–16, 1776; Lot of Mr. Edward Laight in Water Street . . . , Sept. 24, 1780, South Side Water Street . . . (1787?), Bancker Plans, Manuscripts and Archives Division, New York Public Library Digital Collections, https://digitalcollections.nypl.org/items/870a5f20-7571-0135-a995-0089e10679d4, https://digitalcollections

.nypl.org/items/64f59de0-59e8-0135-30ab-43ae1ac6d840; John Austin Stevens Jr., *Colonial New York: Sketches Biographical and Historical, 1768–1784* (New York, 1867), 159–60.

23. Thompson to Huntingdon ("gale," "Villainy"); Johannes Reuber, *Diary of a Hessian Grenadier of Colonel Rall's Regiment,* trans. Bruce E. Burgoyne (s.l., [2006?]), 20 ("extinguished"); *A List of the General and Staff Officers* [. . .] (Philadelphia, 1778), 35.

24. CCM, Inglis insert (all quotations); *Mackenzie Diary,* 1:57, 59.

25. CCM, Inglis insert.

26. CCM, Inglis insert ("persuaded," "speedy"), 9; Inglis to Hind; "David Grim's Account," 767.

27. [James] Robertson to Treasury, TNA CO 5/116, f. 177 (all quotes); Robertson to John Robinson, Aug. 4, 1780, *DCHSNY* (1857), 8:798–99; "Journals of Kemble," 89; Howe to Germain; Grant to Rigby.

28. Hamond Account, Sept. 22, 1776 ("long time," "fury"); NMM ADM L/E/11 "Saveing the Town"); TNA ADM 52/1921, pt. 4 ("out of danger"), 52/1965 ("extinguishing the Fire"); *Mackenzie Diary,* 1:59 ("proper"); NMM ADM L/P/266, L/T/182; TNA ADM 51/67, f. 122, 51/293, pt. 1, f. 29, 51/493, 51/720, pt. 5, 51/776, pt. 5, 51/972, pt. 8, 51/987, pt. 3, 52/1953, 52/2029; Duncan Journal, 130; Henry, *Account,* 185, CCM, 61.

29. TNA ADM 52/1921, pt. 4 ("Violence"); *Mackenzie Diary,* 1:57–58, 59 ("Brigade of Guards"), 60 ("No assistance"); Howe to Germain; Grant to Rigby; *Letters of Baurmeister,* 51; TNA ADM 51/776, pt. 5, 52/1953, pt. 3; NMM ADM L/P/266; Henry, *Account,* 185; Thomas Glyn, "Journal of American Campaign, 1776–77," Princeton University Library, f. 13v.

30. Hamond Account, Sept. 22, 1776 ("astonishment," "rouzed," "heartily"); *Mackenzie Diary,* 1:58, 60 ("active"); *Diary of Bardeleben,* 66 ("ashes"); Tryon to Germain; Account of William Waddell, enclosed with Memorial dated Feb. 1, 1790, TNA AO 13/10, f. 254r–v; Glyn, "Journal," f. 13v; Strachey to JS; Inglis to Hind; Thomas Lewis O'Beirne, *A Sermon Preached at St. Paul's, New York, September 22, 1776* (New York, 1776), 17; *St. James's Chronicle,* Nov. 7–9, 1776; *Newcastle Courant,* Nov. 16, 1776.

31. *Conflagration,* [6].

32. *Mackenzie Diary,* 1:60.

33. [Shewkirk], "Occupation," 253 ("struck," "much frightened"); Shewkirk to Seidel, 4 ("hardly walk," "some Comfort"), 5–6.

34. *Conflagration,* [6–7].

35. Inglis to Hind ("vigorous"); [Shewkirk], "Occupation," 253 ("industry of all," "street," "southeast"); *St. James's Chronicle,* Nov. 7–9 ("inconceivable"), 9–12, 1776; *Mackenzie Diary,* 1:59; Hans Huth, ed., "Letters from a Hessian Mercenary," *PMHB* 62 (1938): 494; "Journal of Lieutenant Rueffer of Melsungen, 1 March 1776 to 28 December 1777," trans. Bruce E. Burgoyne, in *The Hesse-Cassel Mirbach Regiment in the American Revolution* (Bowie, Md.: Heritage, 1998), 57; William Glanville Evelyn to [Frances] Boscawen, Sept. 24, 1776, in *Letters of Evelyn,* 86; William Haslewood, "Journal of a British Officer during the American Revolution," ed. Louise Phelps Kellogg, *Mississippi Valley Historical Review* 7, no. 1 (1920): 55; Carter, *Genuine Detail,* 41; "David Grim's Account," 766–67.

36. *Connecticut Courant* (Hartford), Oct. 7, 1776 ("spread"); *Serle Journal*, 111 ("extended"); Percy to Northumberland ("threaten"). Todd Braisted believes this chaplain was Andrew Lee of Norwich; see Andrew Lee, no. S13748, Pension and Bounty Land Application Files, M-804, U.S. National Archives and Records Administration. Other sources, e.g., William James Morgan, ed., *Naval Documents of the American Revolution* (Washington, D.C.: U.S. Government Printing Office, 1972), 6:862, identify the author as Benjamin Boardman.

37. *Mackenzie Diary*, 1:60–61.

38. [Alexander Graydon], *Memoirs of a Life, Chiefly Passed in Pennsylvania* [. . .] (Harrisburg, Pa., 1811), 156 ("heavens"); TNA ADM 51/168, pt. 6, f. 288 ("Guns"); *Connecticut Journal* (New Haven), Sept. 25, 1776; Henry, *Account*, 185; Cliffe to JC; JFBVHC, 111; Johannes Reuber, *Diary of a Hessian Grenadier of Colonel Rall's Regiment*, trans. Bruce E. Burgoyne (s.l., [2006?]), 20.

39. *Conflagration*, [6].

40. "The Journal of Ensign/Lt. Wilhelm Johann Ernst Freyenhagen, Part 1, 1776," trans. Henry J. Retzer, annotated by Donald M. Londahl-Smidt, *The Hessians: Journal of the Johannes Schwalm Historical Association* 13 (2010): 6 ("Some people," "refused"); *St. James's Chronicle*, Nov. 9–12, 1776 ("Chain"); *London Packet*, Nov. 18–20, 1776 ("straps"); CCM, 23 ("wresting"), 30, 40, 48–49, 79; JFBVHC, 113 ("arsonists," "stones"); Cliffe to JC ("audacity," italics added).

41. *Conflagration*, [6].

42. *Conflagration*, [5].

43. CCM, 64–67, 66 ("very short"); James Cutbush, *A System of Pyrotechny: Comprehending the Theory and Practice* [. . .] (Philadelphia, 1825), 246–49, 479–80.

44. CCM, 1–2. Sergeant Norton entered a Chatham Row house with its roof on fire and found combustible matches in the garret; CCM, 86.

45. *Conflagration*, [7].

46. *Diary of Bardeleben*, 66 ("fortunate"); Thompson to Huntingdon ("cinders," "fierce," "effects").

47. *Letters of Baurmeister*, 51–52 ("sailors," "rewarded"); Shewkirk to Seidel, 4; *Mackenzie Diary*, 1:59.

48. *Conflagration*, [8].

49. Shewkirk to Seidel, 4 ("pleased"); *Connecticut Courant* (Hartford), Oct. 7, 1776 ("vipers"); Tryon to Germain ("sudden change"); Bowater to Denbigh, 101 ("utmost"); [Shewkirk], "Occupation," 253; CCM, 68; Thomas Moffat, diary, Sept. 22, 1776, Peter Force Collection, LOC; Valentine, "Great Fires," 769; Grant to Rigby; Cliffe to BC.

50. *Mackenzie Diary*, 1:58 ("preventing," "danger"); Shewkirk to Seidel, 3 ("raged"); [Shewkirk], "Occupation," 253; "Bamford's Diary," 9; Strachey to JS; TNA ADM 51/137, pt. 3, 51/600, 51/805, pt. 1, f. 27, 52/1921, pt. 4, 52/1640, 52/1965, f. 16v; Hamond Account, Sept. 22, 1776; Valentine, "Great Fires," 769; *Diary of Bardeleben*, 66; TNA ADM 51/637, 52/1909, pt. 6, 52/1893; NMM ADM L/O/45; TNA ADM 51/776, pt. 5, 52/1909, pt. 4, 52/1953, pt. 3, 52/1882.

51. *Diary of Bardeleben*, 66 ("confusion"); Valentine, "Great Fires," 769 ("extin-

guished"); JFBVHC, 111 ("quenched"); Duncan Journal, 130; [Thomas James?], *Kentish Gazette,* Nov. 9, 1776.

52. *Conflagration,* [5, 8].

53. *Letters of Baurmeister,* 52 ("desolation"); Carter, *Genuine Detail,* 41 ("rubbish"); *St. James's Chronicle,* Nov. 7–9, 1776 ("Distresses," "Beggary"); Grant to Rigby; Tryon to Germain; Cliffe to BC; *Morning Chronicle* (London), Nov. 26, 1776; *Newcastle Chronicle,* Nov. 30, 1776.

54. Strachey to JS.

EIGHT Firebrands

1. *Conflagration. A Poem* (New York, 1780), [6].

2. *Mackenzie Diary,* 1:59 ("caught"); CCM, Inglis insert ("repeatedly"), 22, 50 ("cutting the handles"); Inglis to Hind; Bruce E. Burgoyne, trans., *The Diary of Lieutenant von Bardeleben and Other von Donop Regiment Documents* (Bowie, Md.: Heritage, 1998), 66; Thompson to Huntingdon; TNA ADM 51/331, f. 59; Thomas Moffat, diary, Sept. 22, 1776, Peter Force Collection, LOC.

3. CCM, 84–85 ("cried"); Strachey to JS ("kneading"); *St. James's Chronicle* (London), Nov. 9–12, 1776 ("first," "availed"); *Mackenzie Diary,* 1:57; Benjamin L. Carp, "'The First Incendiary': A Female Firebrand and the New York City Fire of 1776," in *Women Waging War in the American Revolution,* ed. Holly Mayer (Charlottesville: University of Virginia Press, 2022), 23–37.

4. *The Parliamentary Register; or, History of the Proceedings and Debates of the House of Commons* [. . .], 14th Parliament, 3rd Session (London, 1777), 60 ("miserable"); Dror Wahrman, *The Making of the Modern Self: Identity and Culture in Eighteenth-Century England* (New Haven, Conn.: Yale University Press, 2004), 223; Linda Grant De Pauw, "Women in Combat: The Revolutionary War Experience," *Armed Forces and Society* 7, no. 2 (1981): 209–26; Linda K. Kerber, "'History Can Do It No Justice': Women and the Reinterpretation of the American Revolution," in *Toward an Intellectual History of Women* (Chapel Hill: University of North Carolina Press, 1997), 63–99.

5. Holly A. Mayer, *Belonging to the Army: Camp Followers and Community during the American Revolution* (Columbia: University of South Carolina Press, 1996); John A. Lynn II, *Women, Armies, and Warfare in Early Modern Europe* (Cambridge: Cambridge University Press, 2008), 202–8.

6. Tryon to Germain ("hellish design"); *Diary of Bardeleben,* 66 ("suspicious," "thrown"); Howe to Germain; Percy to Northumberland; Duncan Journal, 130; *Mackenzie Diary,* 1:59; Bowater to Denbigh, 101; Serle Journal, 111; Rawdon to Huntingdon; CCM, 25; Jos[eph] Royal[l] Loring to Archibald McNeal, Oct. 6, 1776, *Niles' Weekly Register* (Baltimore), May 7, 1836; *St. James's Chronicle,* Nov. 2–5, 9–12, 1776; *Morning Post* (London), Nov. 4, 1776; *Oxford Journal,* Nov. 16, 1776; *Newcastle Chronicle,* Nov. 30, 1776; *Scots Magazine* 38 (Nov. 1776): 15.

7. Emer de Vattel, *The Law of Nations, or, Principles of the Law of Nature* [. . .], ed. Béla Kapossy and Richard Whitmore (Indianapolis: Liberty Fund, 2008), bk. 1, chap.

19, §233:228 ("incendiaries"), bk. 3, chap. 8, §145:549 ("maxim," "women"), bk. 3, chap. 15, §226:613, https://oll.libertyfund.org/titles/2246; D. T. Valentine, "The Great Fires in New York City in 1776 and 1778," *MCCNY* (1866), 769 ("enraged"); *Journal of Rear-Admiral Bartholomew James, 1752–1828,* ed. John Knox Laughton with James Young F. Sulivan, *Publications of the Navy Records Society,* vol. 6 (1896), 34 ("consequence"); Francis Hutcheson to Frederick Haldimand, Sept. 24, 1776, Haldimand Papers, Add. MS 21680, British Library, ff. 152–53; *St. James's Chronicle,* Nov. 14–16, 1776.

8. *Serle Journal,* 111 ("enraged"); Strachey to JS ("difficulty"); *NYGWM* (New York), Sept. 30, 1776 ("rescued"); Hamond Account, Sept. 22, 1776; CCM, 1–2, 46.

9. TNA ADM 52/1725 ("Marines"); CCM, 75 ("some Sailors"); Cliffe to BC ("fury," "Deserts").

10. CCM, 10 ("resentment"), 48 ("rescued"), 49, 78, 79–80 ("push'd," "escaped"), 83–84 ("bundle," "short," "Briton").

11. *St. James's Chronicle,* Nov. 7–9, 1776 ("Fellow"); Charles Inglis to Myles Cooper, Mar. 27, 1777, Fettercairn Papers, National Library of Scotland ("Matthew," "General," "Gaol"), transcribed by Peter William Walker; see also Benjamin Moore to Myles Cooper, June 28, 1775, Fettercairn Papers, National Library of Scotland.

12. "Samuel Handleigh," *St. James's Chronicle,* Nov. 14–16, 1776.

13. *Diary of Bardeleben,* 66.

14. JFBVHC, 112; Bernard A. Uhlendorf, trans., *Revolution in America: Confidential Letters and Journals, 1776–1784, of Adjutant General Major Baurmeister of the Hessian Forces* (New Brunswick, N.J.: Rutgers University Press, 1957), 51.

15. CCM, Inglis insert.

16. Rawdon to Huntingdon ("Scoundrels"); *Saunders's News-Letter* (Dublin), Nov. 4–6, 15–18, 1776 ("cockade"); Tryon to Germain ("privy," "concealed"); *Newcastle Courant,* Nov. 16, 1776.

17. Brown had been appointed "First Lieutenant of the Second Company of [Pennsylvania] Riflemen" under Captain Robert Cluggage and Colonel William Thomson. This commission, dated June 25, 1775, had been superseded: a newspaper listed "Capt. Richard Brown" of the Pennsylvania Rifle Regiment's 1st Battalion; *Edinburgh Advertiser,* Nov. 26–29, 1776 ("detected," "First Lieutenant"); *General Evening Post* (London), Dec. 3–5, 1776; *Pennsylvania Gazette* (Philadelphia), Sept. 11, 1776 ("Capt. Richard Brown"); Samuel Miles to Joseph Reed, Sept. 1, 1776, Samuel Miles Papers, American Philosophical Society; "Diary of Captain John Nice, of the Pennsylvania Line," *PMHB* 16, no. 4 (1893): 407; Thomas Lynch Montgomery, ed., *Pennsylvania Archives* (Harrisburg, Pa.: Harrisburg, 1906), 5th ser., 2:297–310, 450; *Pennsylvania Packet* (Philadelphia), Mar. 18, 1776, indicates that he was from Bedford County; the Pennsylvania Assembly voted on his commission on March 8.

18. *St. James's Chronicle,* Nov. 9–12, 1776 ("sacrificed"); Samuel Curwen to George Russell, Dec. 20, 1776, in *Journal and Letters of the Late Samuel Curwen,* [. . .] *1775–1784,* ed. George Atkinson Ward (New York, 1842), 92; Richard C. Wiggin, *Embattled Farmers: Campaigns and Profiles of Revolutionary Soldiers from Lincoln, Massachusetts, 1775–1783* (Lincoln, Mass.: Lincoln Historical Society, 2013), 399n2, 403–6; Donald L. Hafner, *Wil-*

liam Smith, Captain: Life and Death of a Soldier of the American Revolution (Lincoln, Mass.: Lincoln Historical Society, 2017), 86–87; Abigail Adams to John Adams, Sept. 29, 1776, *AFC*, 2:135.

19. CCM, 15 ("Negro man," "Street," "show," "secreted"), 16 ("saw this Man").

20. CCM, 59 ("particularly remember").

21. Alexander McDougall to GW, Feb. 17, 1778, *PGW:RS*, ed. Edward G. Lengel (2003), 13:572 ("betrayed"); CCM, 15–16.

22. Leslie M. Harris, *In the Shadow of Slavery: African Americans in New York City, 1626–1863* (Chicago: University of Chicago Press, 2003), chaps. 1–2, p. 45; John Wood Sweet, *Bodies Politic: Negotiating Race in the American North, 1730–1830* (Baltimore, Md.: Johns Hopkins University Press, 2003), chap. 2, esp. pp. 69–73, 77, 97–101; Jill Lepore, *New York Burning: Liberty, Slavery, and Conspiracy in Eighteenth-Century Manhattan* (New York: Knopf, 2005), 97–98.

23. Benjamin Quarles, *The Negro in the American Revolution* (1961; Chapel Hill: University of North Carolina Press, 1996); Sylvia R. Frey, *Water from the Rock: Black Resistance in a Revolutionary Age* (Princeton, N.J.: Princeton University Press, 1991); Alan Taylor, *The Internal Enemy: Slavery and War in Virginia, 1772–1832* (New York: Norton, 2013), chap. 1.

24. CCM, 81 ("observe," "Soldiers," italics added, "torch"), 83; W. H. W. Sabine, ed., *The New-York Diary of Lieutenant Jabez Fitch* (1954; New York: Arno, 1971), 157; "City Hall" may have meant the Provost: Burrows, *Forgotten Patriots*, 277n15.

25. Joel N. Eno, "Connecticut Cemetery Inscriptions," *New England Historical and Genealogical Register* 72, no. 285 (1918): 69; Loren P. Waldo, *The Early History of Tolland* [. . .] (Hartford, Conn., 1861), 75; Connecticut Archives, Militia, 2nd ser., 1747–88, 10:1869a, 11:1979b, 2200b; Henry P. Johnston, ed., "The Record of Connecticut Men [. . .], 1775–1783," in *Record of Service of Connecticut Men* [. . .] (Hartford, Conn., 1889), 23.

26. Joshua Loring to William Heath, Feb. [probably March] 1, 1777, William Heath Papers, MHS (microfilm ed.), item 243 ("lurk't," "blazed," "ferry," "convinced," "One of those"); *NYGWM* (New York), Sept. 30, 1776 ("New-England Man"); *Saunders's News-Letter* (Dublin), Nov. 15–18, 1776 ("reward"); Shewkirk to Seidel, 4–5; *St. James's Chronicle*, Nov. 7–9, 1776; *The Literary Diary of Ezra Stiles* [. . .], ed. Franklin Bowditch Dexter (New York: Charles Scribner's Sons, 1901), 2:66.

27. CCM, 24–25 (quotes); John Varick Jr. to Richard Varick, May 14, 1776, in Mercantile Library Association of New York City, *New York City during the American Revolution* [. . .] (New York, 1861), 92; *JPCNY*, 1:507–8; TNA AO 13/116, ff. 603–4, 612–13; Johnston, *Record of Service*, 106; Oscar Jewell Harvey, *A History of Wilkes-Barré* [. . .] (Wilkes-Barré, Pa.: Raeder, 1909), 1:480–87; Harry M. Ward, *Between the Lines: Banditti of the American Revolution* (Westport, Conn.: Praeger, 2002), chap. 3.

28. Gilbert Saltonstall to Nathan Hale, Dec. 18, 1775, in *Documentary Life of Nathan Hale* [. . .], by George Dudley Seymour (New Haven, Conn.: Tuttle, Morehouse, and Taylor, 1941), 63 ("Genius"); John Durkee to Martha Durkee, Aug. 4, 1775, Durkee and Tauzin Families, 1760–1817, photostats from Faith Trumbull Chapter of the Daughters of the American Revolution (Norwich, Conn.), Connecticut State Library ("Indians");

Harold E. Selesky, *War and Society in Colonial Connecticut* (New Haven, Conn.: Yale University Press, 1990), 63, 84, 91, 159, 167, 172–75, 200, 201, 211n, 214–15; Amos A. Browning, "A Forgotten Son of Liberty," *Records and Papers of the New London County Historical Society* 3, no. 2 (1912): 257–79; Robert J. Taylor, ed., *The Susquehannah Company Papers* (1930; Ithaca, N.Y.: Cornell University Press, 1962, 1968), 4:92–93, 141–43, 200–204, 320–22, 320, 5:22; Hubertis M. Cummings, *Scots Breed and Susquehanna* (Pittsburgh: University of Pittsburgh Press, 1964), 146–50; Oscar Zeichner, *Connecticut's Years of Controversy, 1750–1776* (1949; New York: Archon Books, 1970), 50–54, 72–73, 222–23, 349n11; Robert Owen Decker, *The New London Merchants: The Rise and Decline of a Connecticut Port* (New York: Garland, 1986), chaps. 1–2; David O. White, *Connecticut's Black Soldiers, 1775–1783* (Chester, Conn.: Pequot, 1973), 29–35, 39–43; George Quintal Jr., *Patriots of Color: A Peculiar Beauty and Merit, African Americans and Native Americans at Battle Road and Bunker Hill* (Boston: Boston National Historical Park, 2004); "Rolls of Connecticut Men in the French and Indian War, 1755–1762," vols. 1–2, *CCHS* 9 (1903): 180–82, 10 (1905): 65–66, 163–64, 216, 229, 241–43, 301–3; "Lists and Returns of Connecticut Men in the Revolution, 1775–1783," *CCHS* 12 (1909): 196; Johnston, *Record of Service,* 53–54; Barbara W. Brown and James M. Rose, *Black Roots in Southeastern Connecticut, 1650–1900* (Detroit: Gale Research Company, 1980), 332, 337, 379–80, 450.

29. Peter Linebaugh and Marcus Rediker, *The Many-Headed Hydra: Sailors, Slaves, Commoners, and the Hidden History of the Revolutionary Atlantic* (Boston: Beacon, 2000), chaps. 6–7 ("motley crew"); Johnston, *Record of Service,* 106; Charles J. Hoadly, ed., *Public Records of the Colony of Connecticut, 1772–1775* (Hartford, Conn., 1887), 14:483–91; Russel Lawrence Barsh, "'Colored' Seamen in the New England Whaling Industry: An Afro-Indian Consortium," in *Confounding the Color Line: The Indian-Black Experience in North America,* ed. James F. Brooks (Lincoln: University of Nebraska Press, 2002), 76–107; Jason Mancini, "'In Contempt and Oblivion': Censuses, Ethnogeography, and Hidden Indian Histories in Eighteenth-Century Southern New England," *Ethnohistory* 62, no. 1 (2015): 82 ("crossroads"), 83; Mancini, "Beyond Reservation: Indian Survivance in Southern New England and Eastern Long Island, 1713–1861" (PhD diss., University of Connecticut, 2009), esp. chap. 5.

30. White, *Connecticut's Black Soldiers,* 17–19, 27; John Saillant, *Black Puritan, Black Republican: The Life and Thought of Lemuel Haynes, 1753–1833* (New York: Oxford University Press, 2003), 15, 47–48; David J. Naumec, "Connecticut Indians in the War of Independence," *Connecticut History* 47, no. 2 (2008): 181–218; Robert G. Parkinson, *The Common Cause: Creating Race and Nation in the American Revolution* (Chapel Hill: University of North Carolina Press, 2016), 173–76, 265, 336–37, 455–56, 527; Judith L. Van Buskirk, *Standing in Their Own Light: African American Patriots in the American Revolution* (Norman: University of Oklahoma Press, 2017), 66–69; Lepore, *New York Burning,* 129–60.

31. Naumec, "Connecticut Indians"; Brian D. Carroll, "From Warrior to Soldier: New England Indians in the Colonial Military, 1675–1763" (PhD diss., University of Connecticut, 2009); Linford D. Fisher, *The Indian Great Awakening: Religion and the Shaping of Native Cultures in Early America* (New York: Oxford University Press, 2012),

chap. 7; on ambiguous ethnic labels, Joanne Pope Melish, *Disowning Slavery: Gradual Emancipation and "Race" in New England, 1780–1860* (Ithaca, N.Y.: Cornell University Press, 1998), 35–40; Daniel R. Mandell, *Tribe, Race, History: Native Americans in Southern New England, 1780–1880* (Baltimore, Md.: Johns Hopkins University Press, 2008), chap. 2; Mancini, "Contempt and Oblivion"; Mancini, "Beyond Reservation," esp. chaps. 2–3, esp. p. 30; A. B. Wilkinson, *Blurring the Lines of Race and Freedom: Mulattoes and Mixed Bloods in English Colonial America* (Chapel Hill: University of North Carolina Press, 2020), 93–105, 223–45.

32. C[harles] Stedman, *The History of the Origin, Progress, and Termination of the American War* (London, 1794), 1:209 ("cheers," "grand"); *Connecticut Courant* (Hartford), Oct. 7, 1776.

33. TNA ADM 51/987, pt. 3 ("Occasioned"); "The Journal of Ensign/Lt. Wilhelm Johann Ernst Freyenhagen, Part 1, 1776," trans. Henry J. Retzer, annotated by Donald M. Londahl-Smidt, *The Hessians: Journal of the Johannes Schwalm Historical Association* 13 (2010): 6 ("boat"); *Letters of Baurmeister*, 51.

34. *The Journal of Nicholas Cresswell, 1774–1777* (New York: Dial, 1924), 159.

35. Receipts, 1776, Joshua Huntington Papers, American Antiquarian Society; Johnston, *Record of Service*, 25–26, 53–55; Seth C. Cary, *John Cary: The Plymouth Pilgrim* (Boston, 1911), 98.

36. Possible identities include the following:

a. Charles Scadoab (also Charles Charles), Mashantucket Pequot from Groton. One man with this name was a sachem whose son (also Charles) fought in the Seven Years' War. The younger Charles Scadoab (born ca. 1734) may also have been the Charles Charles who served in the 10th Continental Regiment, reported missing on Sept. 22, 1776; Johnston, *Record of Service*, 100; *CCHS*, 9:192; John Avery, *History of the Town of Ledyard, 1650–1900* (Norwich, Conn.: Noyes and Davis, 1901), 281; Naumec, "Connecticut Indians," 212n63; Brown and Rose, *Black Roots*, 73; see also "Petition of Pequots at Groton for New Trial," Mar. 29, 1759, "Memorial of John Wood and Summons for Charles Scadoab et al.," Apr. 28, 1760, "Vote of Pequot Indians at Groton with Regard to Appointment of Overseers," Oct. 24, 1760, "Memorial of Daniel Quocheats and Others," May 10, 1773, "Appointment of Edward Mott as Pequot Overseer," May 1774, *The Native Northeast Portal*, ed. Paul Grant-Costa and Tobias Glaza (2019), http://nativenortheast portal.com/; Notes on Pequot Indians, Miscellanies (MVP no. 200), Ezra Stiles Papers, Beinecke Library, Yale University, p. [386]; Mancini, "Beyond Reservation," 23n6.

b. Fontain (Fortune) Quamono, "Negro," enlisted in "Capt. Huntington's Co. in Norwich," reported deceased, Sept. 16, in the retreat from New York; Johnston, *Record of Service*, 405; Brown and Rose, *Black Roots*, 331; Estate of Quoming, Lebanon, 1781, no. 3109, Windham Probate District records, microfilm, Connecticut State Library.

c. Robert Ashbo (Norwich, Mohegan, 10th Continental) reported as killed, Sept. 16; Johnston, *Record of Service*, 100; Naumec, "Connecticut Indians," 193.

The dates when they were listed as killed or missing may be incorrect. Additionally, soldiers who belonged to different regiments might have turned up at Paulus Hook after the chaos of the September 15 retreat; for an example of a Connecticut soldier who was separated from his regiment on September 15 and reached New Jersey, see Petition of Eleazer Scripture, May 18, 1778, Connecticut Archives, Revolutionary War Series I, 10:393–96.

It may not be possible to positively identify the mixed-race man. Durkee (if not Roome) probably knew enough not to identify a Pequot with two Pequot parents as "Mulatto." On the systematic usage of "mulatto" to disempower Indians, see Mancini, "Contempt and Oblivion," 84–85. I am grateful to David Naumec (Mashantucket Pequot Museum and Research Center) for sharing his data, and to Jason R. Mancini (Connecticut Humanities) and Paul Grant-Costa (Native Northeast Research Collaborative) for additional insights and references.

37. Nathanael Greene to GW, Sept. 23, 1776, *PGW:RS,* ed. Philander D. Chase and Frank E. Grizzard Jr. (1994), 6:376–77.

38. William Carter, *A Genuine Detail of the Several Engagements, Positions, and Movements of the Royal and American Armies* [. . .] (London, 1784), 41 ("feeble"); *Letters of Baurmeister,* 51 ("murderous"); *Mackenzie Diary,* 1:59; *NYGWM* (New York), Sept. 30, 1776; "James Drewitt," *St. James's Chronicle,* Nov. 16–19, 1776; JFBVHC, 113; *Diary of Bardeleben,* 66; *London Packet,* Nov. 18–20, 1776. Wright White married Mary Barker in 1765; *New York Marriages previous to 1784* (1860; Baltimore, Md.: Genealogical, 1984), 457.

39. *NYGWM* (New York), Sept. 30, 1776 ("provoked"); *Diary of Bardeleben,* 66 ("ceremony"); "Drewitt," *St. James's Chronicle,* Nov. 16–19, 1776; *London Packet,* Nov. 18–20, 1776; *Serle Journal,* 111; "David Grim's Account," Valentine, "Great Fires," 767; "Journal of Lieutenant Rueffer of Melsungen, 1 March 1776 to 28 December 1777," trans. Bruce E. Burgoyne, in *The Hesse-Cassel Mirbach Regiment in the American Revolution* (Bowie, Md.: Heritage, 1998), 57; Cliffe to BC; Carter, *Genuine Detail,* 41; Hans Huth, ed., "Letters from a Hessian Mercenary," *PMHB* 62 (1938): 494; Jos[eph] Royal[l] Loring to Archibald McNeal, Oct. 6, 1776, *Niles' Weekly Register* (Baltimore), May 7, 1836.

40. *Letters of Baurmeister,* 51 ("fanatical"); *Pennsylvania Journal* (Philadelphia), Nov. 20, 1776 ("shipwright," "inhumanity"); Shewkirk to Seidel, 5 ("against," "account," "drunk"); "David Grim's Account," 767; CCM, 19; "Officers of Different Beats in New York," in *Calendar of Historical Manuscripts Relating to the War of the Revolution* (Albany, N.Y., 1868), 1:267.

41. CCM, 5–6 ("bundles"), 18–19 ("several," "Stores," "dragged," "women").

42. Duncan Journal, 130 ("brimstoned," "tow"); Howe to Germain ("ingenuity"); Strachey to JS ("Bundles"); *Serle Journal,* 111 ("caught"); Hamond to Stanley; CCM, 71.

43. Harry Miller Lydenberg, ed., *Archibald Robertson, Lieutenant-General Royal Engineers: His Diaries and Sketches in America, 1762–1780* (New York: New York Public Library, 1930), 99 ("Rebels," "Brimstone"); [Thomas James?], *Kentish Gazette* (Canterbury), Nov. 9, 1776 ("villains," "port-fires"); Leslie to Leven ("Torches"); Grant to Rigby ("Skulking"); CCM, 10, 27, 46; *Mackenzie Diary,* 1:59; Hamond Account, Sept. 22, 1776; Shewkirk to Seidel, 5; *St. James's Chronicle,* Nov. 7–9, 14–16, 1776; *Morning Chronicle* (London), Nov. 26, 1776.

44. Cliffe to BC ("Powder"); CCM, 75 ("Sailors," "shabbily").

45. CCM, Inglis insert ("Bundles"), 59, 86; *Mackenzie Diary*, 1:59; "Bamford's Diary: The Revolutionary Diary of a British Officer," *Maryland Historical Magazine* 28 (1933): 9; TNA WO 116/8; *St. James's Chronicle*, Nov. 9–12, 1776; *Caledonian Mercury* (Edinburgh), Nov. 13, 1776.

46. CCM, 31 ("curiosity"), 33 ("bundle," "barrel"), 39 ("rafts"), 50; *JCC*, 4:406–7; Kingsbury Sanford, no. S14398, Pension and Bounty Land Application Files, M-804, U.S. National Archives and Records Administration; Stephen Hempstead Sr., "The Olden Time," *National Republican and Daily Mercantile Advertiser* (Cincinnati), July 2, 1831; *Diary of Samuel Richards: Captain of Connecticut Line, War of the Revolution, 1775–1781* (Philadelphia: Leeds and Biddle, 1909), 32; H. P. Smith, *History of Essex County* [. . .] (Syracuse, N.Y., 1885), 253.

47. Shewkirk to Seidel, 5 ("forbidden"); CCM, 22, 32–33 ("Cartridge," "Hauser"), 34, 40–41 ("Hallett's"), 50, 74; "Journals of Kemble," 90 ("stairways," "doubted"); for Hallet, "Wall, William, Dutch, John, Duke, Queen, Beekman, [. . .]," pp. 38–39, Bancker Plans, Manuscripts and Archives Division, New York Public Library Digital Collections, https://digitalcollections.nypl.org/items/dc75f440-8c41-0135-0c73-255a255e2612; for Hauser or Houser, see [E. B. O'Callaghan, ed.], "Names of the Principal Male Inhabitants of New-York, Anno 1774," D. T. Valentine, *MCCNY* (1850), 439.

48. CCM, 6–7 ("Walnut"), Nooth insert ("concealed," "violence").

49. *Journal of Bartholomew James*, 34.

50. Judith L. Van Buskirk, *Generous Enemies: Patriots and Loyalists in Revolutionary New York* (Philadelphia: University of Pennsylvania Press, 2002), 51; Bernard L. Herman, *Town House: Architecture and Material Life in the Early American City, 1780–1830* (Chapel Hill: University of North Carolina Press, 2005), 154, 223, 264; Shane White, *Somewhat More Independent: The End of Slavery in New York City, 1770–1810* (Athens: University of Georgia Press, 1991), 65, 100, 133, 145–46, 155; on local knowledge, Lepore, *New York Burning*, chap. 3; Barbara Clark Smith, *The Freedoms We Lost: Consent and Resistance in Revolutionary America* (New York: New Press, 2010), 15–17, 24, 27–33, 90–91.

NINE   Surveying the Wreckage

1. "The Journal of Ensign/Lt. Wilhelm Johann Ernst Freyenhagen, Part 1, 1776," trans. Henry J. Retzer, annotated by Donald M. Londahl-Smidt, *The Hessians: Journal of the Johannes Schwalm Historical Association* 13 (2010): 6 ("quench"); John C. Travis, ed., "The Memoirs of Stephen Allen, 1767–1852 [. . .]," typescript, NYHS, 15–16 ("enveloped," "dense," "handkerchiefs"); Bruce E. Burgoyne, trans., *The Diary of Lieutenant von Bardeleben and Other von Donop Regiment Documents* (Bowie, Md.: Heritage, 1998), 67; Wendy E. Harris, "Place and Memory on the City Streets: The Revolutionary War Childhood of New York's Artisan-Mayor, Stephen Allen," in *Tales of Gotham, Historical Archaeology, Ethnohistory and Microhistory of New York City*, ed. Meta F. Janowitz and Diane Dallal (New York: Springer, 2013), 285–312.

2. Thompson to Huntingdon.

3. Cliffe to BC (quotes); [Thomas James?], *Kentish Gazette* (Canterbury), Nov. 9,

1776; William Henry Shelton, *The Jumel Mansion: Being a Full History of the House on Harlem Heights* [. . .] (Boston: Houghton Mifflin, 1916), 55–66; Shelton, "What Was the Mission of Nathan Hale?" *Journal of American History* 9, no. 2 (1915): 269–89; Morton Pennypacker, *General Washington's Spies: On Long Island and New York* (Garden City, N.Y.: Country Life, 1939), 27–28; George Dudley Seymour, *Documentary Life of Nathan Hale* [. . .] (New Haven, Conn.: Tuttle, Morehouse, and Taylor, 1941), 292; Virginia De-John Anderson, *The Martyr and the Traitor: Nathan Hale, Moses Dunbar, and the American Revolution* (New York: Oxford University Press, 2017), 143, 146, 148–49.

    4. CCM, 9 ("experience," "verily"), 40 ("Americans," "barns"); Shewkirk to Seidel, 3, 4–5 ("hellish"); [Ewald Shewkirk], "Occupation of New York City by the British, 1776: Extracts from the Diary of the Moravian Congregation," ed. A. A. Reinke, *PMHB* 1, no. 2 (1877): 254.

    5. *Mackenzie Diary*, 1:59 ("doubt," "Villains"), 60 ("nest," "occupied"); Leslie to Leven ("concerted," "infamous"); Howe to Germain; Tryon to Germain; William Carter, *A Genuine Detail of the Several Engagements, Positions, and Movements of the Royal and American Armies* [. . .] (London, 1784), 41; Harry Miller Lydenberg, ed., *Archibald Robertson, Lieutenant-General Royal Engineers: His Diaries and Sketches in America, 1762–1780* (New York: New York Public Library, 1930), 99; "Journals of Lieut.-Col. Stephen Kemble," NYHS *Collections* 16 (1883): 90; "Bamford's Diary," *Maryland Historical Magazine* 28 (1933): 10; Bowater to Denbigh, 101; Cliffe to JC; JFBVHC, 111; Bernard A. Uhlendorf, trans., *Revolution in America: Confidential Letters and Journals, 1776–1784, of Adjutant General Major Baurmeister of the Hessian Forces* (New Brunswick, N.J.: Rutgers University Press, 1957), 51; Johannes Reuber, *Diary of a Hessian Grenadier of Colonel Rall's Regiment*, trans. Bruce E. Burgoyne (s.l., [2006?]), 20; *St. James's Chronicle* (London), Nov. 7–9, 1776; *Caledonian Mercury* (Edinburgh), Nov. 13, 1776; D. T. Valentine, "The Great Fires in New York City in 1776 and 1778," *MCCNY* (1866), 769.

    6. Duncan Journal, 130 ("evident," "maliciously," "proof"); Hamond Account, Sept. 22, 1776; *Journal of Rear-Admiral Bartholomew James, 1752–1828*, ed. John Knox Laughton with James Young F. Sulivan, *Publications of the Navy Records Society*, vol. 6 (1896), 34; TNA ADM 51/331, f. 59, 51/650, pt. 5, f. 5, 51/694, f. 14, 51/931, pt. 5, f. 193, 52/1725, 52/1893, 52/1909, pt. 4, pt. 6; NMM: ADM L/A/195, L/O/45; Hamond to Stanley; Jos[eph] Royal[l] Loring to Archibald McNeal, Oct. 6, 1776, *Niles' Weekly Register* (Baltimore), May 7, 1836.

    7. Thomas Lewis O'Beirne, *A Sermon Preached at St. Paul's, New York, September 22, 1776* (New York, 1776), 16 ("escaped," "congratulating," "Midnight"), 16–17 ("Guardians").

    8. *St. James's Chronicle*, Nov. 2–5, 1776 ("great ones," "Wretches," "labouring"); CCM, 75 ("lower Class"); [Thomas James?], *Kentish Gazette*, Nov. 9, 1776 ("superb"); Percy to Northumberland ("best Part"); Leslie to Leven ("most elegant"); *Mackenzie Diary*, 1:60; Thompson to Huntingdon; *Diary of Bardeleben*, 65; *Robertson Diaries*, 99; Bowater to Denbigh, 101; Cliffe to JC; *Letters of Baurmeister*, 51; *The Journal of Nicholas Cresswell, 1774–1777* (New York: Dial, 1924), 244; *Conflagration. A Poem* (New York, 1780), [6]. For other discrete newspaper accounts, see *Morning Post* (London), Nov. 4,

1776; *St. James's Chronicle*, Nov. 7–9, 14–16, 16–19, 1776; *Newcastle Courant*, Nov. 16, 1776; *Saunders's News-Letter* (Dublin), Nov. 15–18, 1776; *London Packet*, Nov. 18–20, 1776; *Morning Chronicle* (London), Nov. 26, 1776.

9. Samuel Clossy to Myles Cooper, Nov. 30 ("sight," "800"), John Milner to Myles Cooper, Dec. 12, 1776 ("awful," "reproaching," "impious"), Fettercairn Papers, National Library of Scotland, transcribed by Christopher Minty; James Grant Wilson, ed., *The Memorial History of the City of New-York* [. . .] (New York, 1893), vol. 4, pt. 2, p. 636.

10. *London Packet*, Nov. 18–20, 1776; *Mackenzie Diary*, 1:58–59; Inglis to Hind; *St. James's Chronicle*, Nov. 7–9, 9–12, 14–16, 1776; Duncan Journal, 130; NMM ADM L/O/45; TNA ADM 52/1909, pt. 6; Isaac Gallup to [Benadam Gallup], Oct. 6, 1776, Connecticut State Library; Loring to McNeal, Oct. 6, 1776, *Niles' Weekly Register*, May 7, 1836; Cliffe to BC; [Shewkirk], "Occupation," 254; Tryon to Germain; Howe to Germain; Grant to Rigby; *NYGWM* (Newark, N.J.), Sept. 28, 1776; "Bamford's Diary," 9–11. Using Claude J. Sauthier, "Plan of the City of New-York [. . .]," Oct. 1776, Archives of the Duke of Northumberland at Alnwick Castle, D2M: IV.8, and other data, the geographer William Keegan and I calculated the burned area as being 12.44 percent of the urbanized part of Manhattan (including wharfage, open spaces, some fortifications, and streets), or 22.73 percent of the city's blocks, although the denominator is disputable. In assessing contemporary estimates, it is not clear how witnesses estimated the number of buildings or the degree of damage. See also Richard Howe, "Notes on the Great Fires of 1776 and 1778," *Gotham Center for New York City History*, blog, Dec. 31, 2014, https://www.gothamcenter.org/blog /notes-on-the-great-fires-of-1776-and-1778.

11. Cliffe to BC; Andrew Elliot to the Lords Commissioners of His Majesty's Treasury, Nov. 30, 1776, TNA T 1/520, f. 170; *Hampshire Chronicle* (Winchester), Nov. 18, 1776: the fire raged "only in the suburbs."

12. Samuel Auchmuty to Society for the Propagation of the Gospel in Foreign Parts, Nov. 20, 1776, "Old New York and Trinity Church," 274 ("unable"); JFBVHC, 113; Inglis to Hind; [Charles Inglis] to Myles Cooper, Oct. 28, 1776, Fettercairn Papers, National Library of Scotland, transcribed by Christopher Minty; *St. James's Chronicle*, Nov. 14–16, 1776; *NYGWM*, Mar. 10, 1777. For the £9 to 40 Reichsthaler ratio, see Matthias Böhne and Olaf Simons, "The Marteau Early 18th-Century Currency Converter," 2004, http://www.pierre-marteau.com/currency/converter/bra-eng.html.

13. Thomas Moffat, diary, Sept. 22, 1776, Peter Force Collection, LOC ("Miracle"); *St. James's Chronicle*, Nov. 14–16, 1776 ("Sufferers"); *NYGWM* (Newark), Sept. 28, 1776; Francis Hutcheson to Frederick Haldimand, Sept. 24, 1776, Haldimand Papers, Add. MS 21680, British Library, ff. 153–54; Tryon to Germain; John Sloss Hobart to N.Y. Convention, Sept. 25, 1776, *JPCNY*, 2:222.

14. O'Beirne, *Sermon*, 17 ("Comfort," "turned"); Grant to Rigby ("quantity," "Quality"); Hans Huth, ed., "Letters from a Hessian Mercenary," *PMHB* 62 (1938): 495 ("handsome," "distinction"); Henry Stirke, "A British Officer's Revolutionary War Journal, 1776–1778," ed. S. Sydney Bradford, *Maryland Historical Magazine* 56, no. 2 (1961): 159; for home values, Memorial of [James] Robertson to Treasury, TNA CO 5/116, f. 177; Robertson to John Robinson, Aug. 4, 1780, *DCHSNY* (1857), 8:798–99; Samuel Auchmuty to

Society for the Propagation of the Gospel, Nov. 20, 1776, "Old New York and Trinity Church," NYHS *Collections* 3 (1870): 274; Memorial of John Oakes Hardy, Feb. 14, 1788, TNA AO 13/113, ff. 218–19; Oscar Theodore Barck Jr., *New York City during the War for Independence with Special Reference to the Period of British Occupation* (New York: Columbia University Press, 1931), 80.

15. Tryon to Germain ("afflicting"); John Tabor Kempe to Myles Cooper, Mar. 24, 1777, Fettercairn Papers, National Library of Scotland, f. 119 ("Debtors"); Memorial of Bernard Michael Houseal, Oct. 5, 1785, AO 13/65, ff. 580 ("kindled"), 581; Estimate of Losses Sustained by Cornelius Ryan, [Feb. 26?], 1789, TNA AO 13/26, f. 443; Shewkirk to Seidel, 4; [Shewkirk], "Occupation," 253–54; Clinton Papers, WLCL, 31:44; Nan A. Rothschild, *New York City Neighborhoods: The 18th Century* (1990; Clinton Corners, N.Y.: Percheron, 2008), 129–30.

16. Valentine, "Great Fires," 769 ("distressing," "unhappy"); *St. James's Chronicle*, Nov. 7–9, 1776 ("confessedly," "interrupted," "Agitation"); Lord George Germain to William Howe, Nov. 6, 1776, TNA CO 5/243, f. 87; William Erskine to Sir John Halkett, [Sept. 21 or 22, 1776], Halkett Papers, National Library of Scotland, f. 68v; Edward H. Hart, *Almost a Hero: Andrew Elliot, the King's Moneyman in New York, 1764–1776* [. . .] (Unionville, N.Y.: Royal Fireworks, 2005), 264.

17. Hutcheson to Haldimand, Sept. 24, 1776, ff. 153–54 ("Chiefly"); Petition of Thomas Petit, Mar. 25, 1777, in *Calendar of Historical Manuscripts Relating to the War of the Revolution* (Albany, N.Y., 1868), 1:680, 681 ("unfortunate").

18. "Bamford's Diary," 11 ("deserted Place"); *Diary of Bardeleben*, 67 ("nothing unoccupied"); *Morning Post*, Nov. 5, 1776 ("valuable," "barracks"); Shewkirk to Seidel, 10 ("spacious"); *Pennsylvania Journal* (Philadelphia), Nov. 20, 1776; Barck, *New York City*, 48, 74–91, 96–97; Edwin G. Burrows, *Forgotten Patriots: The Untold Story of American Prisoners during the Revolutionary War* (New York: Basic, 2008), 16–18, 50, 277n15.

19. *Serle Journal*, 111 ("deferred").

20. *Letters of Baurmeister*, 51 ("atrocious," "justifiable"); Cliffe to BC ("destroy," "timely"); *Saunders's News-Letter* (Dublin), Nov. 15–18, 1776 ("troops"); Hamond Account, Sept. 22, 1776 ("Houses to be filled"); Hamond to Stanley, 6:974 ("opportunity").

21. Tryon to Germain ("directed"); Inglis to Hind ("intended"); Ambrose Serle to Earl of Dartmouth, Nov. 8, 1776, in *Facsimiles of Manuscripts in European Archives Relating to America, 1773–1783*, vol. 24, ed. B. F. Stevens (London, 1895), no. 2045 ("religious"); *Serle Journal*, 115 ("Presbyterian"); *St. James's Chronicle*, Nov. 7–9 ("Malice"), 14–16, 1776; *Morning Post*, Nov. 11, 1776 ("prevent"); Jonathan Boucher to [John] James, "Letters of Jonathan Boucher," *Maryland Historical Magazine* 9, no. 3 (1914): 235, 236 ("single"); Thompson to Huntingdon.

22. *Serle Journal*, 111 ("Plot"); Grant to Rigby ("Yorkers"); *St. James's Chronicle*, Nov. 2–5 ("Saints"), 9–12 ("Captain"), 14–16, 1776 ("Fanaticks," "Republican"); *NYGWM* (New York), Oct. 7, 1776 ("Incendiaries"); Valentine, "Great Fires," 769 ("miscreants").

23. "Bamford's Diary," 12–13; compare *NYGWM* (New York), Oct. 7, 1776.

24. Grant to Rigby ("Zeal"); William Erskine to Sir John Halkett, [Sept. 21 or 22, 1776], Halkett Papers, National Library of Scotland, f. 68v.

25. *Newcastle Courant,* Nov. 16, 1776 ("infamous"); *NYGWM* (New York), Oct. 7, 1776 ("Malice").

26. *NYGWM* (New York), Sept. 30, 1776 ("Miscreants").

TEN   The Commandant's Conundrum

1. John C. Travis, ed., "The Memoirs of Stephen Allen, 1767–1852 [. . .]," typescript, NYHS, 16–17.

2. Howe to Germain; printed in *St. James's Chronicle* (London), Nov. 2–5, 1776; *NYGWM,* Feb. 24, 1777; *Independent Chronicle* (Boston), Mar. 13, 1777; *Connecticut Gazette* (New London), Mar. 21, 1777.

3. Inglis to Hind ("enemies"); Hamond to Stanley ("openness"); Hamond Account, Sept. 22, 1776.

4. Thomas Lewis O'Beirne, *A Sermon Preached at St. Paul's, New York, September 22, 1776* (New York, 1776), 17 ("treacherous"), 18–19, 20 ("Reciprocation").

5. CCM, 26–27 ("concealed," "yet"); Strachey to JS ("attempts," "defeated"); Howe to Germain; *St. James's Chronicle,* Nov. 7–9, 1776.

6. Lord George Germain to William Howe, Nov. 6, 1776, TNA CO 5/243, ff. 86–87, 87 ("Attempt," "Inquiry"); *Morning Post* (London), Nov. 4, 1776; *Ipswich Journal,* Nov. 9, 1776; Ira D. Gruber, *The Howe Brothers and the American Revolution* (New York: Atheneum, 1972), 166–68.

7. *The Parliamentary Register; or, History of the Proceedings and Debates of the House of Commons* [. . .], 14th Parliament, 3rd Session (London, 1777), 60.

8. James Robertson, *Proclamation* (Sept. 23, 1776), Revolutionary Broadsides, NYHS ("Proof," "hellish," "Householder," "Citizens"); Tryon to Germain ("measure"); *Mackenzie Diary,* 1:68 ("remainder"); Shewkirk to Seidel, 5.

9. Hans Huth, ed., "Letters from a Hessian Mercenary," *PMHB* 62 (1938): 494, 495 ("complicity"); Grant to Rigby ("confined"); Shewkirk to Seidel, 5 ("aiding"); Charles Stedman, *The History of the Origin, Progress, and Termination of the American War* (London, 1794), 1:209 ("old women"); *Pennsylvania Journal* (Philadelphia), Nov. 20, 1776 ("many hundreds"); "Journal of Lieutenant Rueffer of Melsungen, 1 March 1776 to 28 December 1777," trans. Bruce E. Burgoyne, in *The Hesse-Cassel Mirbach Regiment in the American Revolution* (Bowie, Md.: Heritage, 1998), 57; Bruce E. Burgoyne, trans., *The Diary of Lieutenant von Bardeleben and Other von Donop Regiment Documents* (Bowie, Md.: Heritage, 1998), 66; Bernard A. Uhlendorf, trans., *Revolution in America: Confidential Letters and Journals, 1776–1784, of Adjutant General Major Baurmeister of the Hessian Forces* (New Brunswick, N.J.: Rutgers University Press, 1957), 51; JFBVHC, 113; Rawdon to Huntingdon; Cliffe to BC; [Ewald Shewkirk], "Occupation of New York City by the British, 1776: Extracts from the Diary of the Moravian Congregation," ed. A. A. Reinke, *PMHB* 1, no. 2 (1877): 254; Tryon to Germain; Bowater to Denbigh, 101; Duncan Journal, 130; NMM ADM L/O/45; TNA ADM 51/805, pt. 1, f. 27, 52/1970, pt. 3; *Pennsylvania Packet* (Philadelphia), Oct. 8, 1776; *Caledonian Mercury* (Edinburgh), Nov. 13, 1776; "James Drewitt," *St. James's Chronicle,* Nov. 16–19, 1776; *Morning Chronicle* (London), Nov. 26, 1776; *Newcastle Chronicle,* Nov. 30, 1776; *Scots Magazine* 38 (Nov. 1776): 15; CCM, 49.

10. CCM, 12.

11. *Newcastle Chronicle,* Nov. 30, 1776 ("exemplary"); Thomas Andrew Green, *Verdict According to Conscience: Perspectives on the English Criminal Trial Jury, 1200–1800* (Chicago: University of Chicago Press, 1985).

12. CCM, 13 ("forty"); "David Grim's Account," D. T. Valentine, "The Great Fires in New York City in 1776 and 1778," *MCCNY* (1866), 767 ("satisfactory"); *Morning Chronicle,* Nov. 26, 1776; Edwin G. Burrows, *Forgotten Patriots: The Untold Story of American Prisoners during the Revolutionary War* (New York: Basic, 2008), 18–25.

13. CCM, 44–47, 47 ("released," "Character"); Shewkirk to Seidel, 5 ("Conrad," "Suspicion").

14. CCM, 31–32 (quotes).

15. CCM, 12, 49 ("descriptions," "Seamen"), 50; Strachey to JS ("Contrivers"); John Peebles, "Orderly Book, 4th Battalion Grenadiers," GD 21/492/2, Papers of the Cuninghame Family of Thorntoun, 1776–1782, National Archives of Scotland, transcribed by Paul Pace, *RevWar '75,* Feb. 2012, p. 37 ("Persons"), http://www.revwar75.com/library/pace/4th-Brit-Gren-Bn-OB-1776.pdf; Huth, "Hessian Mercenary," 494; Bowater to Denbigh, 101; W. H. W. Sabine, ed., *The New-York Diary of Lieutenant Jabez Fitch* (1954; New York: Arno, 1971), 50, 144; on Cunningham, see Burrows, *Forgotten Patriots,* 22–23, 94, 97, 120, 122–23.

16. CCM, 12–13 ("present," "paraded"); Hamond Account, Sept. 22, 1776 ("changing"); John H. Langbein, "The English Criminal Trial Jury on the Eve of the French Revolution," in *The Trial Jury in England, France, Germany, 1700–1900,* ed. Antonio Padoa Schioppa (Berlin: Duncker and Humblot, 1987), 30.

17. Rawdon to Huntingdon ("left," "purpose"); CCM, 50 ("denied," "removing"); Jill Lepore, *New York Burning: Liberty, Slavery, and Conspiracy in Eighteenth-Century Manhattan* (New York: Knopf, 2005), 84; compare with Jason T. Sharples, *The World That Fear Made: Slave Revolts and Conspiracy Scares in Early America* (Philadelphia: University of Pennsylvania Press, 2020), chap. 3.

18. Barbara Clark Smith, *The Freedoms We Lost: Consent and Resistance in Revolutionary America* (New York: New Press, 2010), 18–34, 88–95, 119–27; Benjamin L. Carp, *Defiance of the Patriots: The Boston Tea Party and the Making of America* (New Haven, Conn.: Yale University Press, 2010), 144–46, 218–19.

19. CCM, 3, 12–17, 49–51; Peebles, "Orderly Book," 37–38, 41–44; Orderly Book, 1776, Eyre Coote Papers, WLCL; William P. Tatum III, "'To Annoy Rebels, or Other Enemies in Arms against Us': The Limits of Legitimate Violence against Civilians during the American Revolution," in *Justifying Revolution: Law, Virtue, and Violence in the American War of Independence,* ed. Glenn A. Moots and Phillip Hamilton (Norman: University of Oklahoma Press, 2018), 190–209; Ruma Chopra, *Unnatural Rebellion: Loyalists in New York City during the Revolution* (Charlottesville: University of Virginia Press, 2011), 60–64.

20. CCM, 16–17 ("recollection," "probable," "scrutiny"); Stephen Payne Adye, *A Treatise on Courts Martial* [. . .] (New York, 1769), 132 ("wretches," "crimes"); Stephen Conway, "'The Great Mischief Complain'd of': Reflections on the Misconduct of British Soldiers in the Revolutionary War," *WMQ* 47, no. 3 (1990): 374.

21. CCM, 13–14; note, Jos[eph] Royal[l] Loring to Archibald McNeal, Oct. 6,

1776, *Niles' Weekly Register* (Baltimore), May 7, 1836, wrote, "The rest were carried to prison, where they will be hung or burnt, I believe, in a day or two."

22. CCM, 51 ("dismiss'd"); TNA PRO 30/55/21/37, no. 2555.

23. *Historical Anecdotes, Civil and Military: In a Series of Letters, Written from America, in the Years 1777 and 1778* [. . .] (London, 1779), 71 ("Example"); William Bayard to Myles Cooper, Jan. 17, 1778, Fettercairn Papers, National Library of Scotland, f. 161v ("Greatest," "Paradding"); Thomas Jones, *History of New York during the Revolutionary War* [. . .], ed. Edward Floyd De Lancey (1879; New York: Arno, 1968), 1:120 ("affidavits"); *Pennsylvania Journal* (Philadelphia), Nov. 20, 1776; dozens of historians have relied on David Grim's account, beginning with John F. Watson, "Appendix: Containing Olden Time Researches and Reminiscences of New York City," *Annals of Philadelphia* [. . .] (Philadelphia, 1830), 47, 56–58 [second pagination].

24. CCM, 16.

25. CCM, 14; Sylvia R. Frey, *The British Soldier in America: A Social History of Military Life in the Revolutionary Period* (Austin: University of Texas Press, 1981), 84–85; William P. Tatum III, "'For the Good of the King's Service': The British Legal-Military State, 1715–1781" (PhD diss., Brown University, 2016), chap. 2.

26. *Mackenzie Diary,* 1:112 ("perfectly easy"); Burrows, *Forgotten Patriots,* 9–10, 16, 19, 23, 26–31, 37–41, 49, 61, 66–67, 80, 95, 99; Sylvia R. Frey, "Courts and Cats: British Military Justice in the Eighteenth Century," *Military Affairs* 43, no. 1 (1979): 5–11; Wayne E. Lee, *Crowds and Soldiers in Revolutionary North Carolina: The Culture of Violence in Riot and War* (Gainesville: University Press of Florida, 2001), 108–9, 112–13, 185–99.

27. Affidavits of Robert Troup, Jan. 17, 1777, and Adolph Myer, Feb. 5, 1777, *JPCNY,* 2:411 ("privates," "hard usage"), 412 ("promiscuously"); *Diary of Fitch,* 119–20, 150 ("miserable confinement"); "Diary of Captain John Nice, of the Pennsylvania Line," *PMHB* 16, no. 4 (1893): 399, 404–5.

28. "Memoirs of Stephen Allen," 17 ("putrefaction"); *NYGWM,* Jan. 6, 1777.

29. Gruber, *Howe Brothers,* 371.

30. Strachey to JS (quotes); *Letters of Baurmeister,* 51.

31. *Newcastle Chronicle,* Nov. 30, 1776 ("barbarity"); *Gazetteer and the New Daily Advertiser* (London), Nov. 16, 1776 ("rash").

32. *NYGWM* (New York), Sept. 30 ("Sacrifice," "Blessings"), Oct. 21, 1776 ("Humanity," "Regard").

33. *NYGWM* (New York), Oct. 7, Nov. 4, Dec. 2, 1776 ("free Pardon," "speedy Remission"), Jan. 6, 1777; *Independent Chronicle* (Boston), Oct. 24, 1776; *Serle Journal,* 151, 154–55; Gruber, *Howe Brothers,* chap. 4, pp. 144–47, 150–53, 354–56, 359–65; Chopra, *Unnatural Rebellion,* 51–58, 64–68, 237nn 25, 34; Andrew Jackson O'Shaughnessy, *The Men Who Lost America: British Leadership, the American Revolution, and the Fate of Empire* (New Haven, Conn.: Yale University Press, 2013), 97–100, 114–18.

34. *Pennsylvania Journal* (Philadelphia), Nov. 20, 1776.

ELEVEN The Story of the Fire Takes Shape

1. Isaac Q. Leake, *Memoir of the Life and Times of General John Lamb* [. . .] (1850; New York: Da Capo, 1971), 146.

2. *Smith Memoirs,* 2:7 ("exulted"); Peter Tappen to George Clinton, Sept. 23, 1776, in *Public Papers of George Clinton, First Governor of New York* [. . .], ed. Hugh Hastings (New York, 1899), 1:358 ("joyfull"); Thomas Hartley to Horatio Gates, Oct. 10, 1776, *American Archives* [. . .], ed. Peter Force, 5th ser. (Washington, D.C., 1851), 2:981 ("intelligence").

3. Samuel Patterson to George Read, Sept. 22, 1776, in *Life and Correspondence of George Read* [. . .], by William Thompson Read (Philadelphia, 1870), 195, 196 ("without doubt," "absurd"); Gold Selleck Silliman to Mary Silliman, Sept. 22, 1776, in *History of New York during the Revolutionary War* [. . .], by Thomas Jones, ed. Edward Floyd de Lancey (New York, 1879), 1:614–15, 615 ("regulars"); Peter Tappen to George Clinton, Sept. 23, 1776, in *Papers of George Clinton,* 1:358; Isaac Nicoll to N.Y. Provincial Convention, Sept. 21, 1776, John McKesson Papers, NYHS; Robert Greenhalgh Albion and Leonidas Dodson, eds., *Philip Vickers Fithian: Journal, 1775–1776* (Princeton, N.J.: Princeton University Press, 1934), 2:237; *The New-York Diary of Lieutenant Jabez Fitch,* ed. W. H. W. Sabine (1954; New York: Arno, 1971), 47.

4. Benjamin Trumbull, "Journal of the Campaign at New York, 1776–7," *CCHS* 7 (1899): 197 ("various"); George Clinton to Peter Tappen, Sept. [22], 1776, in Mercantile Library Association of New York City, *New York City during the American Revolution* [. . .] (New York, 1861), 116 ("sundry"); *Fithian Journal,* 2:240 ("zealous"); Loammi Baldwin to Mary Baldwin, Sept. 23, 1776, Loammi Baldwin papers, Houghton Library, Harvard University ("Pollicy").

5. Benjamin Bogardus to Evert Bogardus, Sept. 28, 1776, NYHS ("1/3"); "Diary of Lieutenant Francis Nichols, of Colonel William Thompson's Battalion of Pennsylvania Riflemen, January to September, 1776," ed. Thomas H. Montgomery, *PMHB* 20, no. 4 (1896): 512 ("supposed"); *Diary of Fitch,* 144 ("Futile"); CCM, 14 ("credibility"), 15 ("ridiculous," "notoriety"). This is fourth-hand hearsay, but "general notoriety" seems warranted. *Smith Memoirs,* 2:37, 38 ("pleased," "Resentment").

6. Robert Ogden to Francis Barber, Oct. 6, 1776, American Historical Manuscript Collection, NYHS ("decide"); Trumbull, "Journal," 197 ("Persons," "Death"); Gold Selleck Silliman to Mary Silliman, Sept. 25, 1776, in Jones, *History of New York,* 1:615 ("executed").

7. John Lansing Jr. to Richard Varick, Sept. 27, 1776, Richard Varick Papers, NYHS.

8. William Howe to GW, Sept. 21, GW to Howe, Sept. 23, 1776, *PGW:RS,* ed. Philander D. Chase and Frank E. Grizzard Jr. (1994), 6:361 ("Treatment"), 362 ("Ball," "unwarrantable"), 377–79; William B. Reed, ed., *Life and Correspondence of Joseph Reed* (Philadelphia, 1847), 1:239n; *Continental Journal* (Boston), Oct. 3, 1776; Harold L. Peterson, *Arms and Armor in Colonial America, 1526–1783* (1956; Mineola, N.Y.: Dover Publications, 2000), 227–29, 228 ("mutilated"); William L. Calver, "Consider the Revolution-

ary Bullet," *New-York Historical Society Quarterly Bulletin* 11, no. 4 (1928): 120–27; Bill Ahearn and Robert Nittolo, *British Military Long Arms in Colonial America* (Pittsburgh: Dorrance, 2018), 329; George Dudley Seymour, *Documentary Life of Nathan Hale* [. . .] (New Haven, Conn.: Tuttle, Morehouse, and Taylor, 1941), 307–10, 452–53, 530–33.

9. Harold E. Selesky, "Colonial America," in *The Laws of War: Constraints on Warfare in the Western World,* ed. Michael Howard et al. (New Haven, Conn.: Yale University Press, 1994), 59–85; Wayne E. Lee, *Barbarians and Brothers: Anglo-American Warfare, 1500–1865* (New York: Oxford University Press, 2011), chaps. 7–8; Holger Hoock, *Scars of Independence: America's Violent Birth* (New York: Crown, 2017), esp. chaps. 4–5, p. 398; Craig Bruce Smith, *American Honor: The Creation of the Nation's Ideals during the Revolutionary Era* (Chapel Hill: University of North Carolina Press, 2018), chaps. 4–5; T. Cole Jones, *Captives of Liberty: Prisoners of War and the Politics of Vengeance in the American Revolution* (Philadelphia: University of Pennsylvania Press, 2020), 14–36, 47–57.

10. Philip G. Davidson, *Propaganda and the American Revolution, 1763–1783* (Chapel Hill: University of North Carolina Press, 1941); Carl Berger, *Broadsides and Bayonets: The Propaganda War of the American Revolution* (Philadelphia: University of Pennsylvania Press, 1961); James E. Bradley, "The British Public and the American Revolution: Ideology, Interest and Opinion," in *Britain and the American Revolution,* ed. H. T. Dickinson (Harlow: Longman, 1998), 124–54; Eliga H. Gould, *The Persistence of Empire: British Political Culture in the Age of the American Revolution* (Chapel Hill: University of North Carolina Press, 2000), chap. 5; Gould, *Among the Powers of the Earth: The American Revolution and the Making of a New World Empire* (Cambridge, Mass.: Harvard University Press, 2012); Troy O. Bickham, *Making Headlines: The American Revolution as Seen through the British Press* (DeKalb: Northern Illinois University Press, 2009); Gregory Evans Dowd, *Groundless: Rumors, Legends, and Hoaxes on the Early American Frontier* (Baltimore, Md.: Johns Hopkins University Press, 2015); and works cited hereafter.

11. Joseph Reed to Charles Pettit, Aug. 4, 1776, Joseph Reed to Esther De Berdt Reed, [Sept. 22, 1776], in *Life of Joseph Reed,* 1:213, 238–39 (quotes); *JCC,* 5:733, 749.

12. Tench Tilghman to James Tilghman, Sept. 9, 25, 1776, in *Memoir of Lieut. Col. Tench Tilghman* [. . .] (1876; New York: Arno, 1971), 136 ("observant"), 140 ("designedly," "prisoners").

13. GW to Howe, Sept. 23, 1776, *PGW:RS,* 6:378–79 (quotes); Jones, *Captives of Liberty,* 97–102. William Henry Shelton, "What Was the Mission of Nathan Hale?" *Journal of American History* 9, no. 2 (1915): 279, argues that the "dignity" of the two generals "forbade all mention" of the Great Fire and Hale's execution; Jared Sparks, ed., *The Writings of George Washington* (Boston, 1834), 4:76, 76n, 86, 100n, made much of the fact that Howe did not blame Washington in his official report; Benson J. Lossing, *Life of Washington: A Biography Personal, Military, and Political* (New York, 1860), 2:300–301, claimed that Howe believed the fire was an accident.

14. GW to John Hancock, Sept. 22, 1776, *PGW:RS,* 6:369–70, 369 (quotes).

15. GW to Jonathan Trumbull Sr., Sept. 23, 1776, *PGW:RS*, 6:382.

16. Russ Castronovo, *Propaganda 1776: Secrets, Leaks, and Revolutionary Communications in Early America* (New York: Oxford University Press, 2014), esp. intro. and chap. 4.

17. Tench Tilghman to James Tilghman, Sept. 25, 1776, in *Memoir of Tilghman*, 140. William Henry Shelton, *The Jumel Mansion: Being a Full History of the House on Harlem Heights* [. . .] (Boston: Houghton Mifflin, 1916), 51, 66, believed Tilghman was admitting that someone (perhaps Nathan Hale) had committed deliberate incendiarism.

18. Percy to Northumberland (quote); TNA ADM 51/776, pt. 5.

19. John Richardson to John Crozier, Sept. 24, 1776, "Letters of Lieutenant John Richardson, 1776," *PMHB* 16, no. 2 (1892): 205–6.

20. Noah Hobart, *Ministers of the Gospel Considered as Fellow Labourers* [. . .] (Boston, 1747), 20–26, 26 ("Irreligion"); John Sloss Hobart to N.Y. Convention, Sept. 25, 1776, *JPCNY*, 2:222 ("sincerity"), 222–23 ("conjecture"); James B. Bell, *A War of Religion: Dissenters, Anglicans, and the American Revolution* (Basingstoke: Palgrave Macmillan, 2008), chap. 5, esp. pp. 59–61.

21. *JPCNY*, 1:567–68, 596, 634; CCM, 44, 56–57; William H. W. Sabine, *Murder, 1776, and Washington's Policy of Silence* (New York: Theo. Gaus' Sons, 1973), 64, 68–69, 89–96, 115. Howe's report to Germain, noting incendiaries' role in starting the fire, was not reprinted in the United States until *NYGWM*, Feb. 24, 1777; *Independent Chronicle*, Mar. 13, 1777; *Connecticut Gazette*, Mar. 21, 1777.

22. Jedediah Huntington to [Jabez Huntington], Sept. 28, 1776, Sol Feinstone Collection no. 594, David Library of the American Revolution ("Barbarities"); Loammi Baldwin to Mary Baldwin, Sept. 28, 1776, Baldwin papers ("Ignorant").

23. William Hooper to Samuel Johnston, Sept. 26, 1776, in *The Colonial Records of North Carolina*, ed. William L. Saunders (Raleigh, N.C., 1886), 10:819 ("accident," "Rumour," "probability"); Philip Livingston, William Floyd, and Lewis Morris to N.Y. Committee of Safety, Sept. 24, 1776, William Hooper to Robert R. Livingston, Sept. 25, 1776, *LDC* (1979), 5:234 ("purpose"), 238 ("Calamity," "mad").

24. *Newcastle Courant*, Nov. 16, 1776 ("execution," "swear"); William Hooper and John Penn to N.C. Council of Safety, Sept. 19–26, 1776, in *Colonial Records of North Carolina*, 10:811 ("alarmed," "wicked").

25. Peter Tappen to George Clinton, Sept. 23, 1776, in *Papers of George Clinton*, 1:358 ("glorious"); Castronovo, *Propaganda 1776*, 12.

26. Robert Boucher Nicholls to Duke of Northumberland, Sept. 25, 1776, Percy Papers, Alnwick Castle, Northumberland, microfilm LOC.

27. Thomas Lewis O'Beirne, *A Sermon Preached at St. Paul's, New York, September 22, 1776* (New York, 1776), 16–17 ("Tyranny"); Grant to Rigby ("Yorkers," "forgive," "hatred"); *Caledonian Mercury* (Edinburgh), Nov. 13, 1776 ("rancour"); *NYGWM* (New York), Oct. 14, 1776; *St. James's Chronicle* (London), Nov. 9–12, 1776; *Morning Post* (London), Jan. 8, 1777.

28. Hamond Account, Sept. 22, 1776 ("pains," "nobody"); Thomas Moffat, diary, Sept. 22, 1776, Peter Force Collection, LOC ("wretches," "orders"); Cliffe to BC ("answer"); Bowater to Denbigh, 101; Tryon to Germain.

29. William Glanville Evelyn to Frances Boscawen, Sept. 24, 1776, in *Memoir and Letters of Captain W. Glanville Evelyn* [. . .], ed. G. D. Scull (Oxford, 1879), 85–86.

30. Ambrose Serle to Earl of Dartmouth, Nov. 26, 1776, in *Facsimiles of Manuscripts in European Archives Relating to America, 1773–1783*, vol. 24, ed. B. F. Stevens (London, 1895), no. 2046 ("astonished," "Congress"); Richard D. Brown, *Knowledge Is Power: The Diffusion of Information in Early America, 1700–1865* (New York: Oxford University Press, 1989); Joseph S. Tiedemann, *Reluctant Revolutionaries: New York City and the Road to Independence, 1763–1776* (Ithaca, N.Y.: Cornell University Press, 1997), 93–94; Judith L. Van Buskirk, *Generous Enemies: Patriots and Loyalists in Revolutionary New York* (Philadelphia: University of Pennsylvania Press, 2002); Carol Sue Humphrey, *The American Revolution and the Press: The Promise of Independence* (Chicago: Northwestern University Press, 2013), conclusion; Robert G. Parkinson, *The Common Cause: Creating Race and Nation in the American Revolution* (Chapel Hill: University of North Carolina Press, 2016), chap. 1; Jordan E. Taylor, "The Page of Revolutions: Information Politics and Atlantic Networks in Revolutionary North America, 1765–1800" (PhD diss., Indiana University, 2019), intro., pt. 1; Joseph M. Adelman, *Revolutionary Networks: The Business and Politics of Printing the News, 1763–1789* (Baltimore, Md.: Johns Hopkins University Press, 2019), chaps. 3, 5.

31. *NYGWM* (Newark, N.J.), Sept. 21, 1776.

32. *Pennsylvania Journal* (Philadelphia), Sept. 25, 1776 ("missing," "consumed," "Broadway"); *Pennsylvania Gazette* (Philadelphia), Sept. 25, 1776 ("consumed"); see also *Pennsylvania Packet* (Philadelphia), Sept. 24, 1776; *Providence (R.I.) Gazette*, Sept. 28, 1776; *Newport (R.I.) Mercury*, Sept. 30, 1776; *Dunlap's Maryland Gazette* (Baltimore), Oct. 1, 1776; *Maryland Journal* (Baltimore), Oct. 2, 1776; *Norwich (Conn.) Packet*, Oct. 7, 1776; *Virginia Gazette* (Williamsburg) (Purdie), Oct. 11, 1775.

33. *NYGWM* (Newark, N.J.), Sept. 28, 1776; reprints: *Pennsylvania Packet*, Oct. 1, 1776; *Pennsylvania Evening Post* (Philadelphia), Oct. 1, 1776; *Pennsylvania Journal*, Oct. 2, 1776; *Pennsylvania Gazette*, Oct. 2, 1776; *Connecticut Courant* (Hartford), Oct. 7, 1776; *Connecticut Journal* (New Haven), Oct. 9, 1776; *Maryland Gazette* (Annapolis), Oct. 10, 1776; *Connecticut Gazette* (New London), Oct. 11, 1776; *Virginia Gazette* (Williamsburg) (Dixon and Hunter), Oct. 11, 1776; *Virginia Gazette* (Purdie), Oct. 11, 1776; *Norwich Packet*, Oct. 14, 1776. Some papers did not reprint this account because other fire stories overtook them.

34. *Serle Journal*, 113–18, 113 ("undertake"); Serle to Dartmouth, Nov. 8, 26, 1776, in *Facsimiles*, vol. 24, nos. 2045, 2046; Parkinson, *Common Cause*, 316–22; Ruma Chopra, "Printer Hugh Gaine Crosses and Re-crosses the Hudson," *New York History* 90, no. 4 (2009): 271–85.

35. For this and the three following paragraphs, *NYGWM* (New York), Sept. 30, 1776; reprint: *Scots Magazine* 38 (Nov. 1776): 15. *Smith Memoirs*, 2:53, believed that rebel printers deliberately suppressed this account: see *Pennsylvania Ledger* (Philadelphia),

Nov. 9, 1776; *Maryland Gazette,* Nov. 14, 1776; *Essex Journal* (Newburyport, Mass.), Dec. 19, 1776; *Continental Journal,* Dec. 26, 1776; *Boston Gazette, and Country Journal,* Dec. 30, 1776; *Freeman's Journal* (Portsmouth, N.H.), Jan. 7, 1777.

36. *NYGWM* (New York), Oct. 7, 1776. See *Connecticut Journal,* Oct. 16, 1776, indicating receipt of the occupation-press *New-York Gazette* via Long Island; *Norwich Packet,* Oct. 21, 1776; *Continental Journal,* Oct. 24, 1776; *Independent Chronicle,* Oct. 24, 1776; *Essex Journal,* Oct. 25, 1776; *Pennsylvania Evening Post,* Oct. 26, 1776; *Freeman's Journal,* Oct. 29, 1776; *Massachusetts Spy* (Worcester), Oct. 30, 1776; *NYGWM* (Newark, N.J.), Nov. 2, 1776; *Virginia Gazette* (Dixon and Hunter), Nov. 8, 1776.

37. *Connecticut Journal,* Sept. 25, 1776 ("various"); reprints: *Connecticut Courant,* Sept. 30, 1776; *Massachusetts Spy,* Oct. 2, 1776; *Connecticut Gazette,* Sept. 27, 1776 ("*twelve*"); reprints: *Boston Gazette, or Country Journal* (Watertown, Mass.), Oct. 7, 1776; *Independent Chronicle,* Oct. 10, 1776.

38. *Connecticut Courant,* Oct. 7, 1776 ("prejudicial"); reprints: *Massachusetts Spy,* Oct. 16, 1776; *Connecticut Gazette,* Oct. 18, 1776 (also "Readers"); *Continental Journal,* Nov. 7, 1776; *Pennsylvania Evening Post,* Nov. 19, 1776; *Connecticut Gazette* item reprints: *Providence Gazette,* Oct. 19, 1776; *Connecticut Courant,* Oct. 21, 1776; *Continental Journal,* Oct. 24, 1776; *Essex Journal,* Nov. 1, 1776; *The Literary Diary of Ezra Stiles* [. . .], ed. Franklin Bowditch Dexter (New York: Charles Scribner's Sons, 1901), 2:95 ("Mixture"); "Civis," *To William Smith, Charles Inglis,* [. . .] [New York, 1783], 4 ("scurrilous").

39. Henry Jackson to Henry Knox, Oct. 2, 1776, Henry Knox Papers, Gilder Lehrman Collection ("desire"); *Independent Chronicle,* Oct. 3, 1776 ("purposely," "inhuman," "throats," "plundering," "mutiny").

40. Jackson to Knox, Oct. 2, 1776, Henry Knox Papers; reprints: *Providence Gazette,* Oct. 5, 1776; *Newport Mercury,* Oct. 7, 1776; *Norwich Packet,* Oct. 7, 1776; *Connecticut Journal,* Oct. 9, 1776; *Connecticut Gazette,* Oct. 11, 1776.

41. *Continental Journal,* Oct. 3, 1776 ("suspected," "barbarity"); reprints: *Essex Journal,* Oct. 4, 1776; *Freeman's Journal,* Oct. 5, 1776; *Providence Gazette,* Oct. 5, 1776; *Boston Gazette, and Country Journal,* Oct. 7, 1776; *Newport Mercury,* Oct. 7, 1776; *Massachusetts Spy,* Oct. 9, 1776; *Connecticut Journal,* Oct. 9, 1776; *Connecticut Gazette,* Oct. 11, 1776; *Essex Journal,* Nov. 8, 1776 ("savage," "mouths"); Parkinson, *Common Cause,* 295, 295n44, locates the original item in *Newport Mercury,* Oct. 28, 1776; see also *Connecticut Gazette,* Sept. 27, 1776; *Independent Chronicle,* Oct. 3, 1776; *Newport Mercury,* Oct. 7, 1776; *Virginia Gazette* (Purdie), Oct. 11, 1776; *NYGWM* (Newark, N.J.), Oct. 26, 1776.

42. *NYGWM* (New York), Nov. 11, 1776 ("Absurdities"); John Varick Jr. to Richard Varick, Oct. 31, 1776, Richard Varick Papers, NYHS ("various").

43. Committee of Secret Correspondence to Silas Deane, Oct. 1, 1776, *PBF,* ed. William B. Willcox (1982), 22:640–41.

44. Committee to Deane, *PBF,* 22:641–42.

45. GW to Lund Washington, Oct. 6, 1776, *PGW:RS,* 6:494. Charles Lee allegedly expressed similar laments on Dec. 14, 1776; Clements R. Markham, *A Naval Career during the Old War: Being a Narrative of the Life of Admiral John Markham* [. . .] (London, 1883), 35.

46. GW to Lund Washington, Oct. 6, 1776, *PGW:RS*, 6:495 ("speaking"). John C. Fitzpatrick, ed., *The Writings of George Washington* [. . .] (Washington, D.C.: U.S. Government Printing Office, 1940), 37:531-33, first introduced scholars to this letter. Since then, historians have not been able to resist this ironic line, which affirms GW's deference to Congress and winkingly suggests his approval of incendiarism. Douglas Southall Freeman, *George Washington: A Biography* (New York: Charles Scribner's Sons, 1951), 4:205; James Thomas Flexner, *George Washington in the American Revolution, 1775-1783* (Boston: Little, Brown, 1967, 1968), 131; John R. Alden, *George Washington: A Biography* (Baton Rouge: Louisiana State University Press, 1984), 134; Barnet Schecter, *The Battle for New York: The City at the Heart of the American Revolution* (New York: Penguin, 2002), 208.

47. *Smith Memoirs*, 2:38 (quotes); *St. James's Chronicle*, Nov. 26-28, 1776; *London Evening-Post*, Jan. 25-28, 1777.

48. John Varick Jr. to Richard Varick, Oct. 31, 1776, Richard Varick Papers, NYHS ("Imprudent"); Serle to Dartmouth, Nov. 26, 1776, in *Facsimiles*, vol. 24, no. 2046 ("Despondency"); Stiles, *Literary Diary*, 2:72, 94 ("uphold," "Shudder"); John Adams to Abigail Adams, Sept. 22-Oct. 1, 1776, *AFC*, 2:132; Committee of Secret Correspondence to William Bingham, Sept. 21[-Oct. 1], 1776, *PBF*, 22:615; *Maryland Gazette*, Nov. 21, 1776.

49. *Pennsylvania Journal*, Nov. 20, 1776; reprints: *Independent Chronicle*, Dec. 26, 1776; *Norwich Packet*, Jan. 13, 1777.

50. *Smith Memoirs*, 2:37-38, 166 ("Scheme"), 171.

51. Thomas Jefferson to John Adams, May 16, 1777, *PTJ* (1950), 2:19.

TWELVE   The Fates of Three Captains

1. *The New-York Diary of Lieutenant Jabez Fitch*, ed. W. H. W. Sabine (1954; New York: Arno, 1971), 157 ("Prisoner," "pretence"); Jonathan Trumbull Sr. to GW, Jan. 12, 1777, *PGW:RS*, ed. Frank E. Grizzard Jr. (1998), 8:53-54.

2. Trumbull to GW, Jan. 12, GW to Jonathan Loring, Jan. 20, GW to Trumbull, Jan. 24, 1777, *PGW:RS*, 8:53-54 (quotes), 118, 151.

3. Trumbull to GW, Jan. 12, 14, 1777, *PGW:RS*, 8:54 ("particular," "Sorry"), 71 ("Inhumanity"); Edwin G. Burrows, *Forgotten Patriots: The Untold Story of American Prisoners during the Revolutionary War* (New York: Basic, 2008), esp. pp. 55-77, 269n2, 280n36; Holger Hoock, *Scars of Independence: America's Violent Birth* (New York: Crown, 2017), chaps. 6-7; T. Cole Jones, *Captives of Liberty: Prisoners of War and the Politics of Vengeance in the American Revolution* (Philadelphia: University of Pennsylvania Press, 2020), chaps. 3-4.

4. *Diary of Fitch*, 103-6, 156, 157 ("Disorders"); Loren P. Waldo, *The Early History of Tolland* [. . .] (Hartford, Conn., 1861), 75 ("intellect," "loss"); Burrows, *Forgotten Patriots*, 67.

5. Theron Brown, "Who Burned New York?" *Independent* (New York) 28, no. 144 (July 20, 1876): 5-6, 6 (quotes); Alexander Mikaberidze, *The Burning of Moscow: Napoleon's Trial by Fire, 1812* (Barnsley: Pen and Sword, 2014), chap. 8.

6. *Rivington's New-York Gazetteer,* Feb. 9, 1775 ("chiefly," "fanaticism"); David V. Agricola, *Patton Lineages Originating in Pennsylvania Prior to the American Revolution: A Patton Compendium* [. . .], 3rd ed. (2003), 34.1–2, 34.5–7; *Pennsylvania Archives,* 2nd ser., vol. 9 (1880): 84, 98; *Pennsylvania Archives,* 3rd ser., vol. 11 (1897): 80, 381, 413; Robert Lewis & Son v. Abraham Patton, May 1765, Case no. 29, Court of Common Pleas Narratives, Chester County Archives; Carol Bryant, *Abstracts of Chester County, Pennsylvania, Land Records* (Westminster, Md.: Family Line, 1998), 5:256; Deed Book O, 14:227, Chester County Archives; Provincial Tax of 1764–68, P-7a:20, P-8:284, P-9:221, P-10:371, P-11b:73, Chester County Archives; *NYGWM,* June 9, 1777; "First Presbyterian Church Membership," *Maryland Historical Magazine* 35, no. 3 (1940): 260; Henry C. Peden Jr., *Presbyterian Records of Baltimore City, Maryland, 1765–1840* (Westminster, Md.: Family Line, 1995), 45–46; Joseph Lee Boyle, ed., *"Drinks Hard, and Swears Much": White Maryland Runaways, 1770–1774* (Baltimore, Md.: Genealogical, 2010), 94, 98, 119, 127–28, 273–74, 292–93; R. Kent Lancaster, "Almost Chattel: The Lives of Indentured Servants at Hampton-Northampton, Baltimore County," *Maryland Historical Magazine* 94, no. 3 (1999): 347–49, 361n18; Frederick County (Md.) Court, Land Records, BD-1, p. 12. A Hessian document calls him "a native of Pennsylvania"; Letter K: Journal of the Grenadier Battalion von Minnegrode, 1776–84, Lidgerwood Collection of Hessian Transcripts on the American Revolution, Morristown National Historic Park, ed. Lion G. Miles and James L. Kochan, microfilm, 60 (hereafter Minnegrode Journal); Peter N. Moore, *World of Toil and Strife: Community Transformation in Backcountry South Carolina, 1750–1805* (Columbia: University of South Carolina Press, 2007), 24, 49–50, 56–58; Kenneth E. Lewis, *The Carolina Backcountry Venture: Tradition, Capital, and Circumstance in the Development of Camden and the Wateree Valley, 1740–1810* (Columbia: University of South Carolina Press, 2017), 127–28.

7. *New England Chronicle* (Cambridge, Mass.), Dec. 21, 1775; *NYGWM,* July 15, 1776; Bruce E. Burgoyne, ed., *Enemy Views: The American Revolutionary War as Recorded by the Hessian Participants* (Bowie, Md.: Heritage, 1996), 141 ("rebel captain," "merchant"); *Pennsylvania Evening Post,* Jan. 16, 1777 ("Patton"); [Alexander Graydon], *Memoirs of a Life, Chiefly Passed in Pennsylvania* [. . .] (Harrisburg, Pa., 1811), 257 ("zealous"); GW to Nathanael Greene, May 27, 1777, *PGW:RS,* ed. Philander D. Chase (1999), 9:539n4.

8. Minnegrode Journal, 60 ("provision"); Graydon, *Memoirs,* 257 ("resided"); Burgoyne, *Enemy Views,* 141 ("spy").

9. William Heath to GW, Jan. 24, 1777, *PGW:RS,* 8:147 (quotes); Judith L. Van Buskirk, *Generous Enemies: Patriots and Loyalists in Revolutionary New York* (Philadelphia: University of Pennsylvania Press, 2002).

10. Graydon, *Memoirs,* 257 ("indiscreet," "information"); *Diary of Fitch,* 160; Burrows, *Forgotten Patriots,* 96–97; John A. Nagy, *George Washington's Secret Spy War: The Making of America's First Spymaster* (New York: St. Martin's, 2016), 98–100.

11. GW to Greene, May 27, 1777, *PGW:RS,* 9:539 (quotes), 539n4; JFBVHC, 227; Douglas Southall Freeman, *George Washington: A Biography* (New York: Charles Scribner's Sons, 1951), 4:638–39.

12. Orderly book of the British Troops under General Howe, Jan. 27, 1776–May 1,

1778, WLCL ("Desert"); Burgoyne, *Enemy Views*, 141, 142 ("confidant"); *NYGWM*, June 9, 1777; Thomas J. McGuire, *The Philadelphia Campaign: Brandywine and the Fall of Philadelphia* (Mechanicsburg, Pa.: Stackpole, 2006), 1:35–36. Minnegrode Journal, 60, stated the value as "£50 American money."

13. Burgoyne, *Enemy Views*, 141–42 ("weakly"); *NYGWM*, June 9, 1777 ("Signal").

14. *NYGWM*, June 9, 1777 ("Cash"); Burgoyne, *Enemy Views*, 142 ("conscientious").

15. *John Peebles' American War: The Diary of a Scottish Grenadier, 1776–1782*, ed. Ira D. Gruber (Mechanicsburg, Pa.: Stackpole, 1998), 114, 115 ("Rascal"); Howe Orderly Book, WLCL ("Confession"); Burgoyne, *Enemy Views*, 141; Holly A. Mayer, *Belonging to the Army: Camp Followers and Community during the American Revolution* (Columbia: University of South Carolina Press, 1996), 37–39, 244–45, 248–49.

16. *NYGWM*, June 9, 1777 ("Gallows," "Accomplices"); on gallows confessions and defiance, self-incrimination, coercion, and military executions, see Benjamin L. Carp, "The Night the Yankees Burned Broadway: The New York City Fire of 1776," *Early American Studies* 4, no. 2 (2006): 487–88n34.

17. Burgoyne, *Enemy Views*, 141 ("enthusiasm," "hood"), 142 ("gladly," "noble"); Andy Trees, "Benedict Arnold, John André, and His Three Yeoman Captors: A Sentimental Journey or American Virtue Defined," *Early American Literature* 35, no. 3 (2000): 246–78; Van Buskirk, *Generous Enemies*, 92–105; Sarah Knott, *Sensibility and the American Revolution* (Chapel Hill: University of North Carolina Press, 2009), chap. 4.

18. George Dudley Seymour, *Documentary Life of Nathan Hale* [. . .] (New Haven, Conn.: Tuttle, Morehouse, and Taylor, 1941), 310 ("regret"); Joseph Addison, *Cato: A Tragedy, and Selected Essays*, ed. Christine Dunn Henderson and Mark E. Yellin (Indianapolis: Liberty Fund, 2004), 84 (act IV, scene iv) ("pity"); F. K. Donnelly, "A Possible Source for Nathan Hale's Dying Words," *WMQ* 42, no. 3 (1985): 394–96; Virginia DeJohn Anderson, *The Martyr and the Traitor: Nathan Hale, Moses Dunbar, and the American Revolution* (New York: Oxford University Press, 2017), 148.

19. *Pennsylvania Evening Post* (Philadelphia), Mar. 25, 1777 (all quotes); *Essex Journal* (Newburyport, Mass.), Feb. 13, 1777; *Norwich (Conn.) Packet*, Mar. 3–10, 1777; *Connecticut Gazette* (New London), Mar. 14, 1777; Seymour, *Documentary Life*, 303.

20. Addison, *Cato*, 68 (act III, scene v); Frederic M. Litto, "Addison's Cato in the Colonies," *WMQ* 23, no. 3 (1966): 446; Mark Evans Bryan, "'Slideing into Monarchical Extravagance': *Cato* at Valley Forge and the Testimony of William Bradford Jr.," *WMQ* 67, no. 1 (2010): 137; Jason Shaffer, *Performing Patriotism: National Identity in the Colonial and Revolutionary American Theater* (Philadelphia: University of Pennsylvania Press, 2007), chap. 2.

21. GW to John Hancock, June [14], 1777, *PGW:RS*, ed. Frank E. Grizzard Jr. (2000), 10:27 ("conducted," "family," "perhaps"), 29n8; *NYGWM*, June 9, 1777 ("Baltimore").

22. Seymour, *Documentary Life*, 319; Robert E. Cray Jr., "The Revolutionary Spy as Hero: Nathan Hale in the Public Memory, 1776–1846," *Connecticut History* 38, no. 2 (1999): 85–104; Mary Beth Baker, "Nathan Hale: Icon of Innocence," *Connecticut History* 45, no. 1 (2006): 1–30; Anderson, *Martyr and Traitor*, 197–206.

23. Alexander McDougall to GW, Feb. 17, 1778, *PGW:RS*, ed. Edward G. Lengel

(2003), 13:572 ("after"); CCM, 16 ("known"); David L. Sterling, ed., "American Prisoners of War in New York: A Report by Elias Boudinot," *WMQ* 13, no. 3 (1956): 388 ("Summer," "this Head"); Helen Jordan, ed., "Colonel Elias Boudinot in New York City, February, 1778," *PMHB* 24, no. 4 (1900): 456.

24. Sterling, "American Prisoners," 388; Jordan, "Boudinot in New York," 456; Burrows, *Forgotten Patriots*, 84–85, 117–32.

25. N.Y. Committee of Safety to GW, Feb. 13, 1777, *PGW:RS*, 8:326, 327 ("Obnoxious"); note by Robert Hanson Harrison, copy of broadsheet, *In CONGRESS, December 19, 1777* (Jan. 21, 1778), Letters from GW, vol. 5, M247, Papers of the Continental Congress, roll 168, National Archives and Records Administration, item 152, p. 471.

26. Elias Boudinot to GW, June 26, 1777, McDougall to GW, Feb. 17, 1778, *PGW:RS*, 10:128–29, 129 ("Cruelty"), 13:572 ("confined," "exasperated").

27. McDougall to GW, Feb. 17, 1778, *PGW:RS*, 13:572 ("unhappy," "complains"); *The Life, Public Services, Addresses and Letters of Elias Boudinot* [. . .], ed. J. J. Boudinot (Boston, 1896), 1:94 ("Books").

28. Jordan, "Boudinot in New York," 456 ("he was secreted," "suspicion"), 461 ("full evidence"), 462 ("convinced," "planned and encouraged," "found secreted," "remainder"); Sterling, "American Prisoners," 388.

29. Ethan Allen, *A Narrative of Colonel Ethan Allen's Captivity* [. . .] (Philadelphia, 1779), 37 (all quotes); "A List of Prisoners of War, and State Prisoners Confin'd in the Provost Goal, New York, 5th. November 1777," [John Fell], Memorandom in the Provost Goal, New York, New York Society Library.

30. GW to Board of Admiralty, May 29, 1780, in *The Writings of Washington* [. . .], ed. John C. Fitzpatrick (Washington, D.C.: U.S. Government Printing Office, 1937), 18:443–44 ("rigor," "influence," "obnoxious," "fixed," "circumstances," "sacrifice"), 444n82; Philip Schuyler to James Duane, June 5, 1780, "The Duane Letters (Continued)," *Publications of the Southern History Association* 8, no. 5 (1904): 383 ("well," "principles," "tryals"); JCC (1910), 17:650–51, 661; Britt Zerbe, "'That most useful body of men': The Operational Doctrine and Identity of the British Marine Corps, 1755–1802" (PhD diss., Exeter, 2010), 89–93. References to "Mrs. Van Dyke's" tavern imply that she was a widow by 1783; *PGW:RS*, ed. Philander D. Chase and Frank E. Grizzard Jr. (1994), 6:97n4; *At a general meeting of the Committee of Mechanicks, at Mrs. Van Dyke's, the 27th December, 1783* (New York, 1783), http://dlib.nyu.edu/maassimages/amrev/jpg/n001235s.jpg; *New-York Packet*, May 5, 1785; *Daily Advertiser* (New York), Oct. 26, 1786; *New-York Packet*, Feb. 20, 1787; *Columbian* (New York), Aug. 4, 1813.

31. Philip Ranlet, *The New York Loyalists* (Knoxville: University of Tennessee Press, 1986), 219n53; Burrows, *Forgotten Patriots*, 81–82, 118–24, 175–79, 269n2.

THIRTEEN A War of Devastation and Restraint

1. Israel Keith to Cyrus Keith, Nov. 15, 1776, Israel Keith Papers, New York State Library (quotes); Miles Oakley petition, Nov. 9, 1776, *PGW:RS*, ed. Philander D. Chase (1997), 7:127–28; *Sibley's Harvard Graduates*, ed. Clifford K. Shipton (Boston: MHS, 1975),

17:120; Sung Bok Kim, "The Limits of Politicization in the American Revolution: The Experience of Westchester County, New York," *Journal of American History* 80, no. 3 (1993): 877–80.

2. *Sibley's Harvard Graduates,* 17:116–20.

3. Continental Army General Court-Martial, Nov. 12, 1776, Proceedings at Phillipsburg, N.Y., GW Papers, ser. 4, General Correspondence, LOC.

4. General Orders, Nov. 2, 6, 1776, *PGW:RS,* 7:78, 91 ("Wretches"), 92.

5. Jedediah Huntington to Jonathan Trumbull Sr., Nov. 7, 1776, *American Archives* [. . .], ed. Peter Force, 5th ser. (Washington, D.C., 1853), 3:559 ("happy," "struck"); General Orders, Nov. 8, GW to Charles Lee, Nov. 12, Lee to GW, Nov. 12, 1776, *PGW:RS,* 7:112 ("Charge"), 113, 150 ("Justice"), 151 ("barbarous"), 151–52; *JCC,* 5:804 ("behaving"); Continental Army General Court-Martial, Nov. 12, 1776, Proceedings at Phillipsburg, N.Y., GW Papers, ser. 4, LOC ("best"). Ironically, the next day, the Connecticut chaplain Benjamin Trumbull complained that the British were burning barns and "striping the Inhabitants entirely of Support and clothing . . . without Regard to whig or Tory"; Benjamin Trumbull, "Journal of the Campaign at New York, 1776–7," *CCHS* 7 (1899): 209, 210 ("clothing").

6. *JPCNY,* 1:723–24, 724 ("severe," "barbarity," "advocates"), 729.

7. William Heath to GW, Mar. 16, GW to Heath, Mar. 30, 1777, *PGW:RS,* ed. Frank E. Grizzard Jr. (1998), 8:587 ("Friends"), ed. Philander D. Chase (1999), 9:23 ("Officer," "hour"); *Sibley's Harvard Graduates,* 17:121–22; *Massachusetts Soldiers and Sailors of the Revolutionary War* (Boston, 1896), 1:358. Mercy Otis Warren, *History of the Rise, Progress and Termination of the American Revolution,* ed. Lester H. Cohen (1805; Indianapolis: Liberty Classics, 1988), 1:177–79, cast doubt on accusations that an "American commander" had set fire to White Plains.

8. Jonathan Williams Austin, *An oration, delivered March 5th, 1778, at the request of the inhabitants of the town of Boston* [. . .] (Boston, 1778), 11 ("shudder"), 12 ("crimes," "vengeance"); James Spear Loring, *The Hundred Boston Orators Appointed by the Municipal Authorities* [. . .] (Boston, 1853), 134; *Sibley's Harvard Graduates,* 17:121–22.

9. Pauline Maier, *From Resistance to Revolution: Colonial Radicals and the Development of American Opposition to Britain, 1765–1776* (1972; New York: Vintage, 1974); Don Higginbotham, "Reflections on the War of Independence, Modern Guerrilla Warfare, and the War in Vietnam," in *Arms and Independence: The Military Character of the American Revolution,* ed. Ronald Hoffman and Peter J. Albert (Charlottesville: University Press of Virginia, 1984), 5–8.

10. *St. James's Chronicle* (London), Nov. 26–28, 1776.

11. Myles Cooper, *A Sermon Preached before the University of Oxford, on Friday, December 13, 1776* [. . .] (Oxford, 1777), 19 ("barbarian"), 20 ("desperate"); *London Evening-Post,* Jan. 25–28, 1777 ("practice," "wisest," "principle").

12. *Public Advertiser* (London), Mar. 6, 1777.

13. Clements R. Markham, *A Naval Career during the Old War: Being a Narrative of the Life of Admiral John Markham* [. . .] (London, 1883), 35.

14. *Connecticut Courant* (Hartford), Dec. 23, 1777 (reprint of *New-York Packet* [Fishkill], Dec. 18, 1777).

15. *New-Jersey Gazette* (Trenton), Mar. 18, 1778; Milton M. Klein, *The American Whig: William Livingston of New York*, rev. ed. (New York: Garland, 1993), 559; James J. Gigantino II, *William Livingston's American Revolution* (Philadelphia: University of Pennsylvania Press, 2018), 133–36; Michel-Rolph Trouillot, *Silencing the Past: Power and the Production of History* (Boston: Beacon Press, 1995), 26, 72, 83, 96–97, 102–7, 147–48.

16. [Thomas Paine], "The CRISIS. No. VI," *Pennsylvania Packet* (Philadelphia), Oct. 22, 1778; see also Leonard J. Sadosky, *Revolutionary Negotiations: Indians, Empires, and Diplomats in the Founding of America* (Charlottesville: University of Virginia Press, 2009), 90–91.

17. Barnet Schecter, *The Battle for New York: The City at the Heart of the American Revolution* (New York: Penguin, 2002), chaps. 21–24; John Ferling, *Almost a Miracle: The American Victory in the War of Independence* (New York: Oxford University Press, 2007), 290–94, 347, 444–47, 504–7, 523–25, 571; Ferling, *Winning Independence: The Decisive Years of the Revolutionary War, 1778–1781* (New York: Bloomsbury, 2021), 81, 97–98, 106, 120–22, 138–39, 156–57, 165–68, 176, 185, 233–39, 288, 391–99, 458–72, 551.

18. William Tudor to John Adams, Oct. 3, 1776, *PJA*, ed. Robert J. Taylor (1983), 5:44 ("Scoundrels," "Rabble"), 45 ("Disorders," "perpetually," "Timidity," "Villain"); Seanegan P. Sculley, *Contest for Liberty: Military Leadership in the Continental Army, 1775–1783* (Yardley, Pa.: Westholme, 2019), p. 51, chaps. 3, 5; see also citations in chap. 4, earlier.

19. John Tabor Kempe to Myles Cooper, Mar. 24, 1777, Fettercairn Papers, National Library of Scotland, f. 119v ("plunder"); *Smith Memoirs*, 3:172–73 ("scarcely"); John Shy, "The Military Conflict Considered as a Revolutionary War," in *A People Numerous and Armed: Reflections on the Military Struggle for American Independence*, rev. ed. (Ann Arbor: University of Michigan Press, 1990), 213–44; Milton M. Klein, "Why Did the British Fail to Win the Hearts and Minds of New Yorkers?" *New York History* 64, no. 4 (1983): 357–75; Joseph S. Tiedemann, "Patriots by Default: Queens County, New York, and the British Army, 1776–1783," *WMQ* 43, no. 1 (1986): 35–63; Stephen Conway, "'The Great Mischief Complain'd of': Reflections on the Misconduct of British Soldiers in the Revolutionary War," *WMQ* 47, no. 3 (1990): 370–90; Holger Hoock, *Scars of Independence: America's Violent Birth* (New York: Crown, 2017), esp. chaps. 5, 8; Benjamin L. Carp, "'Disreputable among Civilized Nations': Destroying Homes during the Revolutionary War," in *Justifying Revolution: Law, Virtue, and Violence in the American War of Independence*, ed. Glenn A. Moots and Phillip Hamilton (Norman: University of Oklahoma Press, 2018), 168–89.

20. Gilbert Saltonstall to Silas Deane, Aug. 16, 1783, Deane Papers, *CCHS* (1930): 23:189 ("distressing"); James Robertson to Jeffrey Amherst, Oct. 27, 1777, quoted in Stephen Conway, "To Subdue America: British Army Officers and the Conduct of the Revolutionary War," *WMQ* 43, no. 3 (1986): 390 ("burning houses"), 397–98, 400; *Mackenzie Diary*, 1:298–99 ("horrors," "resentment"); Conway "Great Mischief"; Shy, "Military Conflict"; Kim, "Limits of Politicization."

21. [Thomas Paine], "To the Earl of Shelburne," Oct. 29, 1782, *Pennsylvania Gazette* (Philadelphia), Oct. 30, 1782 ("brutality"); Committee for Foreign Affairs to Commissioners at Paris, Oct. 31, 1777, *LDC* (1981), 8:215–16.

22. Committee for Foreign Affairs to BF, July 16, Marine Committee to BF [post July 19, 1779], *LDC* (1986), 13:228 ("retaliate," "striking"), 261–64; *JCC* (1909), 14:851–53, 915–16 ("daringly," "sacred"); Gardner W. Allen, *A Naval History of the American Revolution* (New York: Russell and Russell, 1962), 1:95–100, 139, 230, 266, 273, 292–95, 337–38, 342–48, 362, 595–96; Stephen Webbe, "Revenge Raid on Whitehaven," *MHQ: The Quarterly Journal of Military History* 12, no. 3 (2000): 20–27.

23. *JCC*, 14:915–16 ("Incendiaries," "determined"); BF, instructions to John Paul Jones, [Apr. 28], BF to James Lovell, Oct. 17, 1779, *PBF*, ed. Barbara B. Oberg (1992, 1993), 29:387, 30:547–48 ("demolish'd").

24. *JCC* (1912), 21:977–78 ("justified"), 1017 ("hasty"), 1018 ("demolition"), 1029 ("benevolent"), 1030 ("unoffending"); Arthur Middleton's draft resolves, [Sept.? 1781], *LDC* (1991), 18:89–91.

25. Jessica Warner, *John the Painter: Terrorist of the American Revolution* (New York: Thunder's Mouth, 2004), 141; Harry M. Ward, *Between the Lines: Banditti of the American Revolution* (Westport, Conn.: Praeger, 2002), chaps. 1, 3, 14; J. Leitch Wright Jr., *Florida in the American Revolution* (Gainesville: University Press of Florida, 1975), 46–53; Kathleen DuVal, *Independence Lost: Lives on the Edge of the American Revolution* (New York: Random House, 2015), 92–95, 102–11, 122–24, 128–29; Gregory T. Knouff, *The Soldiers' Revolution: Pennsylvanians in Arms and the Forging of Early American Identity* (University Park: Pennsylvania State University Press, 2004), 216–18; John D. Faibisy, "Privateering and Piracy: The Effects of New England Raiding upon Nova Scotia during the American Revolution, 1775–1783" (PhD diss., University of Massachusetts, 1972); Mark V. Kwasny, *Washington's Partisan War, 1775–1783* (Kent, Ohio: Kent State University Press, 1996); Wayne E. Lee, *Crowds and Soldiers in Revolutionary North Carolina: The Culture of Violence in Riot and War* (Gainesville: University Press of Florida, 2001); William E. H. Lecky, *A History of England in the Eighteenth Century* (London, 1882), 4:479ff.; Hoock, *Scars of Independence*.

26. Barbara Clark Smith, *The Freedoms We Lost: Consent and Resistance in Revolutionary America* (New York: New Press, 2010), chap. 4; Elias Boudinot to Benjamin Rush, July 25, 1783, *LDC* (1993), 20:451; Charles Tilly, *The Politics of Collective Violence* (Cambridge: Cambridge University Press, 2003), pp. 14–15, 110, 226–29, chap. 8.

27. "Conotocarious," *The Digital Encyclopedia of George Washington*, ed. James P. Ambuske, Mount Vernon Ladies' Association, 2012–, http://www.mountvernon.org/digital-encyclopedia/article/conotocarious; *NYGWM* (Newark), Sept. 21, 1776 ("carry"); Lee, *Crowds and Soldiers*, 158–63; Barbara Alice Mann, *George Washington's War on Native America* (Westport, Conn.: Praeger, 2005); John Grenier, *The First Way of War: American War Making on the Frontier, 1607–1814* (Cambridge: Cambridge University Press, 2005), chap. 5; Wayne E. Lee, *Barbarians and Brothers: Anglo-American Warfare, 1500–1865* (New York: Oxford University Press, 2011), chap. 8; Colin G. Calloway, *The Indian World of George Washington: The First President, the First Americans, and the Birth of the Nation* (New York: Oxford University Press, 2018), chap. 11.

28. Thomas Jones, *The History of New York during the Revolutionary War* [. . .],

ed. Edward Floyd De Lancey (New York, 1879), 1:121 ("indigence"), 314–15, 315 ("rancor"); 2:307 ("great complaints," "fourth part"), 308 ("impudence," "usual practice"), 309–14.

FOURTEEN The Unresolved War

1. CCM, General Guy Carleton's Warrant.

2. Eldon Lewis Jones, "Sir Guy Carleton and the Close of the American War of Independence, 1782–83" (PhD diss., Duke University, 1968), 43, 251–52; Paul H. Smith, "Sir Guy Carleton, Peace Negotiations, and the Evacuation of New York," *Canadian Historical Review* 50, no. 3 (1969): 245; Paul David Nelson, *General Sir Guy Carleton, Lord Dorchester: Soldier-Statesman of Early British Canada* (Madison, N.J.: Fairleigh Dickinson University Press, 2000), 173.

3. [Earl of Shelburne] to Guy Carleton, Apr. 4, [1782], *DAR*, 21:54 ("revive"); Guy Carleton to Earl Cornwallis, Oct. 27, 1782, in *Correspondence of Charles, First Marquis Cornwallis*, ed. Charles Ross (London, 1859), 141 ("incivility"); *Smith Memoirs*, 3:541–42; Jones, "Sir Guy Carleton," chap. 1, pp. 43–44; Smith, "Carleton"; Nelson, *Carleton*, 12–13, 139–42, 145, 147–48; P. J. Marshall, *Remaking the British Atlantic: The United States and the British Empire after American Independence* (Oxford: Oxford University Press, 2012), 24–26; Don Glickstein, *After Yorktown: The Final Struggle for American Independence* (Yardley, Pa.: Westholme, 2015), 343–44.

4. Guy Carleton to Henry Seymour Conway, Aug. 16, 1782, William Petty, 1st Marquis of Landsdowne, 2nd Earl of Shelburne Papers, 1665–1885, WLCL, 68:253 ("Inspector"); Guy Carleton to Shelburne, Aug. 14, 1782, *DAR*, 21:111; Smith, "Carleton," 261; Nelson, *Carleton*, 148–50; Glickstein, *After Yorktown*, 352; Richard B. Morris, *The Peacemakers: The Great Powers and American Independence* (New York: Harper and Row, 1965); Andrew Stockley, *Britain and France at the Birth of America: The European Powers and the Peace Negotiations of 1782–1783* (Exeter: University of Exeter Press, 2001).

5. John Milner to Myles Cooper, Feb. 3, 1777, Fettercairn Papers, National Library of Scotland, f. 118 ("same," "Glory"); *Letter from an Officer at New-York to a Friend in London* (London, 1777), 2 ("severely"); *The Journal of Nicholas Cresswell, 1774–1777* (New York: Dial, 1924), 234–36, 235 ("drunken"), 243–44 ("flourishing"), 244 ("hellish," "folly"); William Dunlap, *A History of the American Theatre* (New York, 1832), 42 ("lowest"), 43 ("abomination"), 44.

6. *NYGWM*, Mar. 10, 1777 ("shocked"); Mary Auchmuty, Petition for Temporary Support, Mar. 24, 1781, Memorial of Robert Auchmuty, read Nov. 23, 1782, Memorial of Robert [Nicholls] Auchmuty, Nov. 21, 1777, TNA AO 13/113A, ff. 83–95, 84 ("Ears," "severe," "decayed"), 92 ("all burnt"), 94 ("sunk"); Memorial of Robert Nicholls Auchmuty on behalf of Mary Auchmuty, Mar. 30, Apr. 12, 1787, AO 12/24, pp. 112–17; Samuel Auchmuty to Society for the Propagation of the Gospel, Nov. 20, 1776, "Old New York and Trinity Church," NYHS *Collections* 3 (1870): 274.

7. *Royal Gazette* (New York), Aug. 2, 1783 ("Burnt"); *Letter from an Officer*, 2

("several," "shivering"); Oscar Theodore Barck Jr., *New York City during the War for Independence with Special Reference to the Period of British Occupation* (New York: Columbia University Press, 1931), chaps. 3–5, 9; Thomas Jefferson Wertenbaker, *Father Knickerbocker Rebels: New York City during the Revolution* (New York: Charles Scribner's Sons, 1948); Judith L. Van Buskirk, *Generous Enemies: Patriots and Loyalists in Revolutionary New York* (Philadelphia: University of Pennsylvania Press, 2002), 23–37; Barnet Schecter, *The Battle for New York: The City at the Heart of the American Revolution* (New York: Penguin, 2002), chaps. 19, 21, 24; Ruma Chopra, *Unnatural Rebellion: Loyalists in New York City during the Revolution* (Charlottesville: University of Virginia Press, 2011); Howard Pashman, *Building a Revolutionary State: The Legal Transformation of New York, 1776–1783* (Chicago: University of Chicago Press, 2018); Christopher Sparshott, "Loyalist Refugee Camp: A Reinterpretation of Occupied New York, 1776–83," in *The Consequences of Loyalism: Essays in Honor of Robert M. Calhoon,* ed. Rebecca Brannon and Joseph S. Moore (Columbia: University of South Carolina Press, 2019), 61–74; Matthew P. Dziennik, "New York's Refugees and Political Authority in Revolutionary America," *WMQ* 77, no. 1 (2020): 65–96; Donald F. Johnson, *Occupied America: British Military Rule and the Experience of Revolution* (Philadelphia: University of Pennsylvania Press, 2020).

8. Clinton Papers, WLCL, 31:44 ("ruin'd"); Memorial of Cornelius Ryan, 1786, TNA AO, 13/26, f. 433 ("universal," "reduced"), Estimate of Losses Sustained by Cornelius Ryan, [Feb. 26?], 1789, f. 443; E. B. O'Callaghan, ed., *Names of Persons for Whom Marriage Licenses Were Issued* [. . .], *Previous to 1784* (Albany, N.Y., 1860), 53; John Stanford, "History of the Poor in the City of New York, 1699–1816," *MCCNY* (1862): 659.

9. Morris, *Peacemakers,* 364–66, 369–73, 375, 377–80; Benjamin Quarles, *The Negro in the American Revolution* (1961; Chapel Hill: University of North Carolina Press, 1996), chap. 9; Maya Jasanoff, *Liberty's Exiles: American Loyalists in the Revolutionary World* (New York: Knopf, 2011), 77–81; Pashman, *Building a Revolutionary State,* chap. 4; *Laws of the Legislature of the State of New York in Force against the Loyalists* [. . .] (London, 1786), 9–41, 87–98, 105–11, 117–21.

10. Shelburne to Richard Oswald, Nov. 21, 1782, in *Life of William Earl of Shelburne* [. . .], by Lord Fitzmaurice, rev. ed. (London: Macmillan, 1912), 2:204 ("cannot conceive," "root"); "Matthew Ridley's Diary during the Peace Negotiations of 1782," ed. Herbert E. Klingelhofer, *WMQ* 20, no. 1 (1963): 127–28 ("Refugees"); American Peace Commissioners to Oswald, Nov. 7, 1782, *PJA,* ed. Gregg L. Lint (2008), 14:41 ("retribution," "Destruction," "Overtures," "veil"); BF to Oswald, Nov. 26, 1782, *PBF,* ed. Ellen R. Cohn (2006), 38:351 ("Mischief," "Ravages," "recall"), 356 ("restore"); Roberta Tansman Jacobs, "The Treaty and the Tories: The Ideological Reaction to the Return of the Loyalists, 1783–1787" (PhD diss., Cornell University, 1974), chap. 2; Aaron N. Coleman, "Loyalists in War, Americans in Peace: The Reintegration of the Loyalists, 1775–1800" (PhD diss., University of Kentucky, 2008), chap. 3; Marshall, *Remaking the British Atlantic,* 37–40, 42–47, 49–51, 54.

11. "State of Loyalist Property in North America" [July 1783], *DAR,* 21:200 ("million"), 201; Harry Yoshpe, *The Disposition of Loyalist Estates in the Southern District of the State of New York* (New York: Columbia University Press, 1939); Aaron N. Coleman,

"Debating the Nature of State Sovereignty: Nationalists, State Sovereigntists, and the Treaty of Paris (1783)," *Journal of the Historical Society* 12, no. 3 (2012): 309–40.

12. Petition of Loyalists and Refugees at New York to the King, Aug. 10, 1782, *DAR*, 21:99 ("security"); Shelburne to Carleton, Apr. 4, June 5, 1782, *DAR*, 21:53 ("tenderest"), 83 ("satisfy").

13. Guy Carleton to GW, May 7 ("Retaliation"), GW to Carleton, May 10, 1782 ("commencement," "Conduct"), GW Papers, ser. 4, General Correspondence, LOC; *Smith Memoirs*, 3:506–11; Nelson, *Carleton*, 145–47, 152–55; Chopra, *Unnatural Rebellion*, 197–222; Holger Hoock, *Scars of Independence: America's Violent Birth* (New York: Crown, 2017), chap. 11.

14. Henry Addison to Jonathan Boucher, Oct. 29, 1783, Henry Addison Papers, WLCL ("Temper"); Guy Carleton to GW, May 12, 1783, in *The Writings of George Washington* [. . .], ed. Jared Sparks (Boston, 1835), 8:543–45; *Smith Memoirs*, 3:584–88; Graham Russell Hodges, ed., *The Black Loyalist Directory: African Americans in Exile after the American Revolution* (New York: Garland, 1995); Van Buskirk, *Generous Enemies*, 175–76; Christopher Leslie Brown, *Moral Capital: Foundations of British Abolitionism* (Chapel Hill: University of North Carolina Press, 2006), 298–300, 311–12; Jasanoff, *Liberty's Exiles*, 88–91; Chopra, *Unnatural Rebellion*, 207–8, 213–15; William M. Fowler Jr., *American Crisis: George Washington and the Dangerous Two Years after Yorktown, 1781–1783* (New York: Walker, 2011), 198–202.

15. Henry Addison to Jonathan Boucher, Apr. 14, 1783, Henry Addison Papers, WLCL ("Confusion"); *London Chronicle*, May 17–20 ("cold"), June 7–10, 1783 ("compel," "laugh").

16. Guy Carleton to Robert R. Livingston, Apr. 6, 1783, in *The Revolutionary Diplomatic Correspondence of the United States*, ed. Francis Wharton (Washington, D.C., 1889), 6:362 ("cessation"); *London Chronicle*, June 7–10, 1783 ("senses," "grave"); Jasanoff, *Liberty's Exiles*, chaps. 2–3, pp. 351–58; Brett Palfreyman, "Peace Process: The Reintegration of the Loyalists in Post-Revolutionary America" (PhD diss., Binghamton University, 2014), 42–43.

17. *Smith Memoirs*, 3:508, 570–71, 575–76, 582–83; Carleton to Livingston, Apr. 6, 1783, Livingston to Carleton, Apr. 11, 1783, Livingston to GW, Apr. 12, 1783, in *Revolutionary Diplomatic Correspondence*, 6:362, 367–68; 369; *JCC* (1922), 24:370–71; Jones, "Carleton," 227–31, 233–39; Nelson, *Carleton*, 149, 169–72.

18. Robert R. Livingston to Marquis de Lafayette, May 1, 1783, in *Lafayette in the Age of the American Revolution: Selected Letters and Papers, 1776–1790*, ed. Stanley J. Idzerda and Robert Rhodes Crout (Ithaca, N.Y.: Cornell University Press, 1983), 5:128.

19. "BRUTUS," *To All Adherents to the British Government* [. . .] (New York, Aug. 15, 1783) (all quotes); "Civis," *To William Smith, Charles Inglis* [. . .] [New York, July 10, 1783], 3, 8; Carleton to Elias Boudinot, Aug. 17, 1783, *DAR*, 21:208–9; *Royal Gazette* (New York), Sept. 13, 1783; *Laws against the Loyalists*, 41–87, 99–104, 111–16, 122–30.

20. John Morin Scott to George Clinton, Apr. 19, Carleton to Clinton, June 18, 1783, in *Public Papers of George Clinton* [. . .], ed. Hugh Hastings (Albany, N.Y.: Oliver A. Quayle, 1904), 8:148 ("not at peace"), 207–10, 207 ("driven," "Menaces"), 209 ("great vio-

lence"); Carleton to Clinton, July 25, 1783, *DAR*, 21:197 ("spirit," "lower classes"), 198 ("vindictive"); Carleton to Lord North, June 6, 17, 21, Aug. 29, 1783, *DAR*, 19:405, 409, 411, 21:214; *Smith Memoirs*, 3:591–93; Johann Ewald, *Diary of the American War: A Hessian Journal*, ed. Joseph P. Tustin (New Haven, Conn.: Yale University Press, 1979), 350; Thomas Jones, *History of New York during the Revolutionary War* [. . .], ed. Edward Floyd De Lancey, vol. 2 (New York, 1879), chap. 12; Wertenbaker, *Father Knickerbocker*, 251–53, 259–60; Van Buskirk, *Generous Enemies*, chap. 6; Chopra, *Unnatural Rebellion*, 212–13, 215–16.

21. Henry Addison to Jonathan Boucher, Apr. 28, 1783 ("Inebriation," "Blood"), July 12, 1783 ("Ignorance"), Oct. 29, 1783 ("detest," "cruelty"), Henry Addison Papers, WLCL.

22. William Stephens Smith to GW, Aug. 26, 1783, in Mercantile Library Association of New York City, *New York City during the American Revolution* [. . .] (New York, 1861), 144 ("drove"), 145 ("destitute," "neighbours"); Alexander Hamilton to Robert R. Livingston, [Aug. 13, 1783], Livingston to Hamilton, Aug. 30, 1783, John Jay to Hamilton, Sept. 28, 1783, in *The Papers of Alexander Hamilton*, ed. Harold C. Syrett (New York: Columbia University Press, 1962), 3:431 ("phrenzy"), 434–35 ("lament," "tranquility," "motives," "blind spirit," "sordid," "depopulating"), 459–60; Jacobs, "Treaty and Tories"; Daniel J. Hulsebosch, *Constituting Empire: New York and the Transformation of Constitutionalism in the Atlantic World, 1664–1830* (Chapel Hill: University of North Carolina Press, 2005), 192–202; Palfreyman, "Peace Process," 63–77; Christopher J. Sparshott, "The Popular Politics of Loyalism during the American Revolution, 1774–1790" (PhD diss., Northwestern University, 2007), chap. 5.

23. David Hartley to Charles James Fox, Nov. 6, 1783, David Hartley Papers, WLCL, 1:56 ("Alliance," "suspicion"), 57 ("passion," "wiser"), 58 ("regret," "ruin"); "Observations on British Trade with the U.S.A. by Committee of American Merchants," July 22, 1783, *DAR*, 21:189–96; Van Buskirk, *Generous Enemies*, 176; Marshall, *Remaking the British Atlantic*, chaps. 5, 13.

24. *Smith Memoirs*, 3:505, 507, 553 ("more fighting"), 554, 584; Carleton to Lord North, July 11, 1783, Observations by Carleton (enclosure, [July 11, 1783]), *DAR*, 21:186–87, 187 ("chief," "return," "folly"), 188 ("model"); Frederick Haldimand to Carleton, July 28, 1782, Information from New Hampshire, Jan. 8, 1783, enclosed in Carleton to Thomas Townshend, Jan. 18, 1783, "Petition of Loyalists and Refugees at New York to the King," Aug. 10, 1782, *DAR*, 19:327, 366, 21:98–100; Carleton to Lord Shelburne, Dec. 16, 1782, *The Correspondence of King George the Third* [. . .], ed. Sir John Fortescue (London: Macmillan, 1928), 6:189–90; Nelson, *Carleton*, 150–51.

25. Carleton to Lord North, Oct. 13, 1783, *DAR*, 21:221 ("all parties"), 222 ("fierce," "decline," "Many others").

26. Daniel Parker to GW, Oct. 20, 1783, GW Papers, ser. 4, General Correspondence, LOC.

27. CCM, Warrant; William Martin to Carleton, July 26, 1782, Carleton to Martin et al., Oct. 18, 1783, in *Report on American Manuscripts in the Royal Institution of Great Britain* (Hereford: His Majesty's Stationery Office, 1907), 3:37, 4:416; Jonathan Spain,

"Beckwith, Sir George (1752/3–1823)," *Oxford Dictionary of National Biography* (Oxford: Oxford University Press, 2004), online ed., Jan. 2008, http://www.oxforddnb.com/view /article/1911; Carleton to GW, Nov. 12, 1783, GW Papers, ser. 4, General Correspondence, LOC; L. F. S. Upton, *The Loyal Whig: William Smith of New York and Quebec* (Toronto: University of Toronto Press, 1969), 201; Frank T. Reuter, "'Petty Spy' or Effective Diplomat: The Role of George Beckwith," *Journal of the Early Republic* 10, no. 4 (1990): 471–92; GW to William John Darby, Dec. 21, 1779, *PGW:RS*, ed. William M. Ferraro (2015), 23:666–68.

28. CCM, Warrant, "Board of Enquiry" ("command"); Joseph B. Berry, ed., "Ward Chipman Diary: A Loyalist's Return to New England in 1783," *Essex Institute Historical Collections* 87, no. 3 (1951): 228 ("misfortune," "happy hours"), 229 ("banished"); *Sibley's Harvard Graduates,* ed. Clifford K. Shipton (Boston: MHS, 1975), 17:369–79; Phillip Buckner, "Chipman, Ward (1754–1824)," *Dictionary of Canadian Biography,* vol. 6 (University of Toronto / Université Laval, 2003–), http://www.biographi.ca/en/bio/chipman _ward_1754_1824_6E.html; Hoock, *Scars of Independence,* 362, 365–72. Chipman filed the minutes among his personal papers. In 1890, Joseph W. Lawrence, founding president of the New Brunswick Historical Society, donated the minutes to the NYHS; *Magazine of American History* 23 (1890): 509.

29. CCM, "Board of Enquiry," 27, 41; the commission may have received copies of depositions by Andrew Elliot, Lambert Moore, John Moore, James Moran, and [David] Matthews, relative to the fire of Sept. 1776, Oct. 18, 1783, enclosed in Elliot to R. B. Sheridan, Nov. 10, 1783, Andrew Elliot Papers, New York State Library.

30. *Royal Gazette* (New York), Nov. 1, 1783; Carleton to Clinton, Nov. 12, 1783, in *Papers of George Clinton,* 8:278–79.

31. CCM, 22. Items 1–4 of the list are direct quotations from the manuscript. The remaining items, 5–12, are paraphrased.

32. CCM, 31, 42, 46, 48, 50.

33. CCM, 31, 41, 42, 58.

34. CCM, 31, 36, 39, 41, 42, 44, 46, 58.

35. CCM, 48.

36. CCM, 25, 36, 43.

37. CCM, 37.

38. CCM, 41, 44, 47.

39. CCM, 47.

40. CCM, 29.

41. CCM, 29 ("Pumps," "exerted"); John W. Jordan, ed., *Colonial and Revolutionary Families of Pennsylvania: Genealogical and Personal Memoirs* (New York and Chicago: Lewis, 1911), 2:805.

42. CCM, 29 ("order"), 30 ("fitting," "Buckets"), 31 ("curiosity," "carelessly").

43. CCM, 31–32.

44. Memorial of William Waddell, Mar. 24, 1784, AO 13/56, f. 468v.

45. CCM, 28–29, 52–56.

46. CCM, 39–41, 72–80, 73 ("accidental"); *NYGWM,* Jan. 13, 1777 ("Designs,"

"principal"); *New-York Directory, and Register* [. . .] (New York, 1790), 6; *Daily Advertiser* (New York), Nov. 14, 1791.

47. CCM, 37–39, 41–43; *New-York Mercury,* Apr. 14, 1776; *NYGWM,* Nov. 4, 1776; William Duncan, *New-York Directory, and Register* [. . .] (New York, 1792), 121; Duncan, *New-York Directory, and Register* [. . .] (New York, 1794), 168; *Longworth's American Almanac* [. . .] (New York, 1802), 314; O'Callaghan, *Marriage Licenses,* 45; Neil MacKinnon, *This Unfriendly Soil: The Loyalist Experience in Nova Scotia, 1783–1791* (Kingston, Ont.: McGill-Queen's University Press, 1986), 177; Reinhart Koselleck, *Futures Past: On the Semantics of Historical Time* (Cambridge, Mass.: MIT Press, 1985), 275.

48. CCM, Nooth deposition, 1–2, 8, 11, 16, 19, 22, 24, 27, 33, 35, 43, 46, 48, 50, 58, 62 ("designedly"), 67, 70, 79.

49. CCM, 24–26, 32–35, 56–58, 70, 78–86.

50. Memoranda, Andrew Elliot Papers, New York State Library; *Royal Gazette* (New York), Oct. 15, 1783.

51. Jones, *History of New York,* 2:492–97, 494 ("mitigated"); Jacobs, "Treaty and Tories"; Coleman, "Loyalists in War," esp. chaps. 4–6; Barbara Clark Smith, *The Freedoms We Lost: Consent and Resistance in Revolutionary America* (New York: New Press, 2010), chap. 5; Eliga H. Gould, *Among the Powers of the Earth: The American Revolution and the Making of a New World Empire* (Cambridge, Mass.: Harvard University Press, 2012), chap. 4; Palfreyman, "Peace Process"; Tom Cutterham, *Gentlemen Revolutionaries: Power and Justice in the New American Republic* (Princeton, N.J.: Princeton University Press, 2017), chap. 3.

52. Chopra, *Unnatural Rebellion,* 101–7, 165–74, 194–95; Philander D. Chase, "Grim, David," *American National Biography,* Feb. 1, 2000, https://doi.org/10.1093/anb /9780198606697.article.0100355; "David Grim's Account," D. T. Valentine, "The Great Fires in New York City in 1776 and 1778," *MCCNY* (1866), 766–67.

53. Marshall, *Remaking the British Atlantic,* 16–17, 21; Ruma Chopra, "Postwar Loyalist Hopes: To Be 'Parts and Not Dependencies of the Empire,'" in *The Consequences of Loyalism: Essays in Honor of Robert M. Calhoon,* ed. Rebecca Brannon and Joseph S. Moore (Columbia: University of South Carolina Press, 2019), 228–43; Alan Taylor, *The Civil War of 1812: American Citizens, British Subjects, Irish Rebels, and Indian Allies* (New York: Knopf, 2010), esp. chap. 1.

54. JCC (1906, 1928), 5:812, 27:543 ("usages," "humanity"); John Lasher to GW, May 2, 1789, in *The Papers of George Washington, Presidential Series,* ed. Dorothy Twohig (Charlottesville: University Press of Virginia, 1987), 2:190, 191 ("loss," "supported"); John Dallas, "Elizabeth Thompson," *The Digital Encyclopedia of George Washington,* ed. James P. Ambuske, Mount Vernon Ladies' Association, 2012–, https://www.mountvernon.org /library/digitalhistory/digital-encyclopedia/article/elizabeth-thompson/; Craig B. Hollander, "'The Citizen Complains': Federal Compensation for Property Lost in the War of 1812," *Law and History Review* 38, no. 4 (2020): 659–98.

55. *New York Packet,* Aug. 19, 1784 ("Canvas-town," "receptacles," "suppress"), Sept. 4, 1787 ("Burnt-Church"); *Pennsylvania Packet* (Philadelphia), Sept. 24, Oct. 4, 1784 ("nuisance," "heroines"); I. N. Phelps Stokes, ed., *The Iconography of Manhattan Island,*

1498–1909 (New York: Robert H. Dodd, 1926), 5:1204, 1343; *Freeman's Journal* (Philadelphia), Sept. 13, 1786; *NYJ*, Sept. 21, 1786, Sept. 6, 1787; *Pennsylvania Mercury* (Philadelphia), Apr. 19, 1788; *Daily Advertiser* (New York), Oct. 14, 1791; *Columbian Gazetteer* (New York), Oct. 17, 1793; Laurie Todd, "Hints to Married Men and Bachelors," *Massachusetts Ploughman* (Boston), May 24, 1851, p. 4; *Laws of the State of New York* [. . .] (Albany, N.Y., 1886), 7th session (1784), chap. 56, pp. 1:704–5, 9th session (1786), chap. 50, pp. 2:294–95, 10th session (1787), chap. 75, p. 501; *Minutes of the Common Council of the City of New York, 1784–1831* (New York: City of New York, 1917), 1:36, 45–47, 109, 126–27, 142, 199, 207, 241–42, 296–97, 313, 333, 510, 540, 548, 556, 561–62, 564.

    56. William Alexander Duer, *New-York as It Was, during the Latter Part of the Last Century* [. . .] (New York, 1849), 8.

    57. Henry Collins Brown, *Glimpses of Old New-York* (New York: Lent and Graff, 1917), 130 ("shanties," "erected," "squatters," "noble"), 131 ("nondescripts," "dumps"); Jedidiah Morse, comp., "NEW-YORK City," in *The American Gazetteer* [. . .] (Boston, 1797); John F. Watson, "Appendix: Containing Olden Time Researches and Reminiscences of New York City," in *Annals of Philadelphia* [. . .] (Philadelphia, 1830), 17; "Obsolete Names of Localities on Manhattan Island," *MCCNY* (1856), 470; Barck, *New York City*, 229; Rebecca Solnit, *A Paradise Built in Hell: The Extraordinary Communities That Arise in Disasters* (New York: Viking, 2009), 173.

    58. "General Washington's farewell Orders, issued to the Armies [. . .]," Nov. 2, 1783, GW Papers, ser. 3, Varick transcripts, subser. 3B, Letterbook 16, LOC, p. 341 ("steady," "distinguished"); Continental Army officers' address to GW, Nov. 15, 1783, enclosure in Alexander McDougall, Henry Knox, and Timothy Pickering to GW, Nov. 15, 1783, GW Papers, ser. 4, General Correspondence ("sullies"); GW to Ephraim Brasher et al., Nov. 27, 1783, GW Papers, ser. 3, Varick transcripts, subser. 3C, Letterbook 5, LOC, p. 77 ("admiration," "tranquility"), pp. 77–78 ("Ruins"); *American Archives* [. . .], ed. Peter Force, 4th ser. (Washington, D.C., 1853), 3:708.

Conclusion

    1. John Joseph Henry, *An Accurate and Interesting Account of the Hardships and Sufferings of That Band of Heroes Who Traversed the Wilderness in the Campaign against Quebec* (Lancaster, Pa., 1812), 184 ("baleful," "effect"), 185 ("sublime"); Scott Paul Gordon, "The Trials of John Joseph Henry: The Politics of 'Revolutionary Services' in Jeffersonian America," *Pennsylvania History: A Journal of Mid-Atlantic Studies* 85, no. 3 (2018): 333–61.

    2. Henry, *Account*, 184 ("candle," "original," "harboured"), 185 ("repelled").

    3. Henry, *Account*, 185 ("vile"), 186 ("honor," "circumstances," "Cicero").

    4. [Alexander Graydon], *Memoirs of a Life, Chiefly Passed in Pennsylvania* [. . .] (Harrisburg, Pa., 1811), 212 ("gloom"), 213 ("meditated"), 213–15, 251 ("merciless"), 251–52 ("abuse"), 252 ("monsters"); Stephen Carl Arch, "Writing a Federalist Self: Alexander Graydon's Memoirs of a Life," *WMQ* 52, no. 3 (1995): 422–24; William Hunting Howell, "'Starving Memory': Antinarrating the American Revolution," in *Remembering the Rev-*

olution: Memory, History, and Nation Making from Independence to the Civil War, ed. Michael A. McDonnell, Clare Corbould, Frances M. Clarke, and W. Fitzhugh Brundage (Amherst: University of Massachusetts Press, 2013), 93–109.

5. Gordon, "Trials."

6. Gordon, "Trials."

7. Henry, *Account,* 186.

8. Michel-Rolph Trouillot, *Silencing the Past: Power and the Production of History* (Boston: Beacon, 1995); Sarah J. Purcell, *Sealed with Blood: War, Sacrifice, and Memory in Revolutionary America* (Philadelphia: University of Pennsylvania Press, 2002); David Waldstreicher, *Runaway America: Benjamin Franklin, Slavery, and the American Revolution* (New York: Hill and Wang, 2004), xiv; Michael A. McDonnell, "War and Nationhood: Founding Myths and Historical Realities," in McDonnell et al., *Remembering the Revolution,* 19–40; Donald F. Johnson, "Forgiving and Forgetting in Postrevolutionary America," in *Experiencing Empire: Power, People, and Revolution in Early America,* ed. Patrick Griffin (Charlottesville: University of Virginia Press, 2017), 171–88.

9. On assumptions about "character," see Annette Gordon-Reed, *Thomas Jefferson and Sally Hemings: An American Controversy* (Charlottesville: University Press of Virginia, 1997), esp. chap. 4; see also Marcus Cunliffe, *George Washington: Man and Monument* (Boston: Little, Brown, 1958), 14; Bernhard Knollenberg, *Washington and the Revolution: A Reappraisal: Gates, Conway, and the Continental Congress* (New York: Macmillan, 1940).

10. Edward G. Lengel, *General George Washington: A Military Life* (New York: Random House, 2005), 87–95, 176–77, 189, 214–15; *JCC* (1907), 7:196–97.

11. Pauline Maier, *The Old Revolutionaries: Political Lives in the Age of Samuel Adams* (New York: Knopf, 1980), 11; Alfred F. Young, "How Radical Was the American Revolution?" in *Liberty Tree: Ordinary People and the American Revolution* (New York: New York University Press, 2006), 215–61.

12. For analogous models, see Eric Hobsbawm, *Bandits* (New York: Delacorte, 1969); James C. Scott, *Weapons of the Weak: Everyday Forms of Peasant Resistance* (New Haven, Conn.: Yale University Press, 1985); Penny Roberts, "Arson, Conspiracy and Rumour in Early Modern Europe," *Continuity and Change* 12, no. 1 (1997): 9–29; Hugh D. Hudson Jr., "A Rhetorical War of Fire: The Middle Volga Arson Panic of 1839 as Contested Legitimacy in Prereform Russia," *Canadian Slavonic Papers / Revue Canadienne des Slavistes* 43, no. 1 (2001): 29–48; Philip M. Taylor, *Munitions of the Mind: A History of Propaganda from the Ancient World to the Present Era,* 3rd ed. (1990; 1995; Manchester: Manchester University Press, 2003), 1, 4, 8, 9; John Merriman, *The Dynamite Club: How a Bombing in Fin-de-Siècle Paris Ignited the Age of Modern Terror* (Boston: Houghton Mifflin Harcourt, 2009), 62–63, 207; Johannes Dillinger, "Organized Arson as a Political Crime: The Construction of a 'Terrorist' Menace in the Early Modern Period," *Crime, History and Societies* 10, no. 2 (2006): 101–21.

13. Andrew Jackson O'Shaughnessy, *The Men Who Lost America: British Leadership, the American Revolution, and the Fate of Empire* (New Haven, Conn.: Yale University Press, 2013).

14. On banalization, see Trouillot, *Silencing the Past*, 96; also Michael A. Mc-
Donnell, "War Stories: Remembering and Forgetting the American Revolution," in *The
American Revolution Reborn*, ed. Patrick Spero and Michael Zuckerman (Philadelphia:
University of Pennsylvania Press, 2016), 9–28.

15. Troy Bickham, *Making Headlines: The American Revolution Seen through the
British Press* (DeKalb: Northern Illinois University Press, 2009), pp. 97, 179–81, chap. 7;
The Annual Register [. . .] *for the Year 1776* (London: J. Dodsley, 1777), 180; James Murray, *An Impartial History of the Present War in America* [. . .] (London, [1778]), 2:173–74;
John Andrews, *History of the War with America,* [. . .] (London, 1785), 2:242; Robert
Beatson, *Naval and Military Memoirs of Great Britain, 1727–1783* (London, 1804), 4:166–
67; Lord Mahon, *History of England from the Peace of Utrecht* (London, 1851), 6:170–72,
175; William Massey, *A History of England during the Reign of George the Third* (London,
1858), 2:291; William E. H. Lecky, *A History of England in the Eighteenth Century* (London, 1882), 3:434, 4:3–5, 8; [Charles] Cooper King, *George Washington* (London, 1894),
115–16, 119; George Otto Trevelyan, *The American Revolution* (London: Longmans, Green,
1903), vol. 1, pt. 2, pp. 293–97, 309–11.

16. Peter C. Messer, "Writing Women into History: Defining Gender and Citizenship in Post-Revolutionary America," *Studies in Eighteenth-Century Culture* 28 (1999):
350; Teresa Ann Murphy, *Citizenship and the Origins of Women's History in the United
States* (Philadelphia: University of Pennsylvania Press, 2013).

17. Joanne Pope Melish, *Disowning Slavery: Gradual Emancipation and "Race" in
New England, 1780–1860* (Ithaca, N.Y.: Cornell University Press, 1998); John Wood Sweet,
Bodies Politic: Negotiating Race in the American North, 1730–1830 (Baltimore, Md.: Johns
Hopkins University Press, 2003), chap. 5; Jason Mancini, "'In Contempt and Oblivion':
Censuses, Ethnogeography, and Hidden Indian Histories in Eighteenth-Century South-
ern New England," *Ethnohistory* 62, no. 1 (2015): 61–94; John Samuel Harpham, "'Tumult
and Silence' in the Study of the American Slave Revolts," *Slavery and Abolition* 36, no. 2
(2015): 257–74; Robert G. Parkinson, *The Common Cause: Creating Race and Nation in
the American Revolution* (Chapel Hill: University of North Carolina Press, 2016), chap. 9;
Judith L. Van Buskirk, *Standing in Their Own Light: African American Patriots in the
American Revolution* (Norman: University of Oklahoma Press, 2017).

18. Diedrich Knickerbocker [Washington Irving], *A History of New York, from the
Beginning of the World to the End of the Dutch Dynasty,* 2 vols., 3rd ed. (Philadelphia,
1819), 2:259 ("raking"); Washington Irving, *Life of George Washington* (New York, 1855),
2:361–62; Martha J. Lamb, *History of the City of New York: Its Origin, Rise and Progress*
(New York, 1880), 2:135–36; Andrew Burstein, *The Original Knickerbocker: The Life of
Washington Irving* (New York: Basic Books, 2007); Elizabeth Bradley, *Knickerbocker: The
Myth behind New York* (New Brunswick, N.J.: Rutgers University Press, 2009).

19. Reminiscences of the Early Life of John Pintard, 1841, John Pintard Papers,
NYHS, 81; [John Pintard], *New-York Advertiser,* Aug. 25–28, 1826; John Pintard to Eliza
Noel Pintard Davidson, Aug. 23, 1826, *Letters from John Pintard to His Daughter, Eliza Noel
Pintard Davidson, 1816–1833,* NYHS *Collections* 71 (1938): 2:294–95, 295n35; Duke de la
Rouchefoucault Liancourt, *Travels through the United States of North America* [. . .], 2nd

ed. (London, 1800), 4:228–29; Edwin G. Burrows, *Forgotten Patriots: The Untold Story of American Prisoners during the Revolutionary War* (New York: Basic Books, 2008), 241–48, 325n1.

20. Stephen Berry, *Weirding the Civil War: Stories from the Civil War's Ragged Edges* (Athens: University of Georgia Press, 2012); Megan Kate Nelson, *Ruin Nation: Destruction and the American Civil War* (Athens: University of Georgia Press, 2012), 229, 234–35, 238.

21. Max Page, *The City's End: Two Centuries of Fantasies, Fears, and Premonitions of New York's Destruction* (New Haven, Conn.: Yale University Press, 2008).

Acknowledgments

Thanks, first, to Robert Barry, Howard Caretto, Peter Onuf, Robert Rothblatt, William P. Tatum III, David Waldstreicher, and the reader for Yale University Press, who read an early draft (many pages longer than this) and made crucial suggestions. I am intensely grateful to all of them in very different ways and for many other reasons. A second Yale Press reader gave useful suggestions on a subsequent draft. Gregory E. Gorbett, professional fire investigator, shared his expertise, and Mark Boonshoft, Abigail Chandler, Cassandra Good, Paul Grant-Costa, Nancy Isenberg, Cynthia Kierner, Jason Mancini, Holly Mayer, David Naumec, and Mariam Touba also offered insights on particular sections. For their recurring generosity, special thanks to Richard D. Brown and Wayne E. Lee.

Christopher Minty and Vaughn Scribner have been delightful correspondents; I am grateful to them for continually sharing their findings and insights. Thanks to the dozens of scholars and historians who answered questions by sharing their kindness and knowledge and brilliance, their access, their referrals, and their time; I can't thank everyone I want to in this space, but thanks to Don N. Hagist and John Houlding for help with identifications, to Joshua Kavaloski and Brett Martz for translation assistance, and to Todd Braisted, Peter N. Moore, Jessica Sheets, and Peter William Walker for sharing some great sources. I previously thanked Patricia Bonomi, George Boudreau, Jessica Carp, the late Robert Carp, Francis Cogliano, Gary Gallagher, Frank Grizzard Jr., the late Richard E. Mooney, and Peter Onuf for "The Night the Yankees Burned Broadway: The New York City Fire of 1776," *Early American Studies: An Interdisciplinary Journal* 4, no. 2 (2006): 471–511, copyright © 2006 the McNeil Center for Early American Studies. I have used scattered elements of this earlier work with permission. I also drew some elements from Benjamin L. Carp, "'The First Incendiary': A Female Firebrand and the New York City Fire of 1776," in *Women Waging War in the American Revolution*, ed.

Holly A. Mayer, © 2022 by the Rector and Visitors of the University of Virginia. Any such elements are reprinted by permission of the University of Virginia Press.

The William L. Clements Library granted two Jacob M. Price Fellowships, the Massachusetts Society of the Cincinnati sponsored a research fellowship at the Society of the Cincinnati Library, and I received a fellowship from the David Library of the American Revolution. I also received support from two PSC-CUNY Awards, jointly funded by the Professional Staff Congress and the City University of New York. The Ethyle R. Wolfe Institute for the Humanities at Brooklyn College provided teaching release. The Daniel M. Lyons fund at Brooklyn College has provided crucial support.

Because I have studied this subject for many years, I am grateful for previous funding from the American Antiquarian Society, American Philosophical Society Library, John Carter Brown Library, Carnegie Trust for the Universities of Scotland, Gilder Lehrman Institute for American History, Huntington Library, Leverhulme Trust, Massachusetts Historical Society, North Caroliniana Society, Tufts University, University of Edinburgh, University of Virginia, and Virginia Historical Society.

Thanks to the librarians, archivists, and museum professionals at institutions listed earlier and at the British Library, Brooklyn Historical Society, Chester County History Center, Columbia University Libraries, Connecticut Historical Society, Connecticut State Library, Hampton National Historic Site, Historical Society of Pennsylvania, Library of Congress, Maryland Center for History and Culture, Morris-Jumel Mansion, Morristown National Historical Park, Museum of the City of New York, National Archives of the United Kingdom, National Library of Scotland, National Maritime Museum, New York City Fire Museum, New-York Historical Society, New York Public Library, New York Society Library, New York State Library, Northumberland Estates, Princeton University Library, Rhode Island Historical Society, Rutgers University Libraries, Trinity Wall Street, and especially the staffs of the Brooklyn College Library and Graduate Center Mina Rees Library at CUNY. Thanks also to databases maintained by Adam Matthew Digital, Ancestry, Chester County Archives, fold3, Gale Primary Sources, Harvard University Libraries, HathiTrust, the Internet Archive, JSTOR, the Norman B. Leventhal Map and Education Center at Boston Public Library, Project MUSE, Readex, and Yale University Libraries.

I am also grateful to participants in the New York City Seminar at the Gotham Center for New York City History; the Late Antiquity, Medieval, and Early Modern Colloquium at Brooklyn College run by Lauren Mancia; the CUNY Early American Republic Seminar, especially Miriam Liebman and Helena Yoo Roth; the Washington Early American Seminar at the University of Maryland; and the Yale Early American History Seminar, especially Jay Gitlin and Teanu Reid.

I received valuable feedback at conferences offered by the Society for Military Historians, Institute for Thomas Paine Studies, Consortium on the Revolutionary Era, Seton Hall University, National Society for the Sons of the American Revolution, Thomas Jefferson Foundation and University of Hong Kong, Agora Institute, Urban History Association, and Conference on New York State History, and at presentations for Brooklyn Lifelong Learning and Historic Huguenot District.

Saleema Josey helped secure the book's images, Edward Charnley assisted with Audit Office records, and Matthew Grace looked up materials I couldn't reach. Thanks to Sydelle Kramer for contributions to the book's proposal and to William Keegan for his enthusiastic and brilliant work on New York's geography. Thanks to Adina Popescu Berk, Ash Lago, Joyce Ippolito, Mary Valencia, and everyone else at Yale University Press, and to William G. Henry, Judy Loeven, and Enid Zafran. Thanks to Lorraine Greenfield and Anne Ciarlo of the Brooklyn College History Department, and thanks to my colleagues and students at Brooklyn College and the CUNY Graduate Center, who brought me home. I have learned a lot from them, and I am excited to keep learning.

While I deeply appreciate the collective kindness that made this work possible, I also take full responsibility for any errors I have made.

There are many who have passed since 2010 who will always be with me, particularly Herbert Carp, Anne Geiger, Carlos Mena, Kenneth Negin, and Leonard Sadosky. I also wish to acknowledge the kindness and inspiration of Edwin Burrows, Jesse Lemisch, Pauline Maier, John Murrin, William Pencak, and Alfred Young.

Thanks to colleagues, friends, and family who have been there for me. Love to my mother, my in-laws, my brothers, my aunts, my cousins, all my nieces and nephews, and the Octetters.

I will never stop being grateful to my wife, Jessica; I am still in awe of her many talents, and I deeply appreciate her love and support. This book is dedicated with love to our son, Jedidiah, a truly amazing person.

Index

References to illustrations and maps are indicated by italicized page numbers.

soldiers; punishments; rebels; Washington, George; Washington, George, options for New York City; *specific state and regional militia and troops*
Continental Association, 20
Continental Congress: articles of war and punishments of soldiers, 57–58, 76, 97, 209; on Boston under siege, 32, 37; British towns, seeking destruction of, 211–12; Bunker Hill and, 25; censorship and control of information in newspapers, 178; Committee of Secret Correspondence, 184; destruction of towns making reconciliation impossible for, 33–34; disavowing incendiarism, 77, 188; Great Fire reports sent to, 175–76; Loyalists punished for opposing, 21; moderates from New York attending, 19; New York City's defense and, 40, 75–76, 83; "no damage" resolution on New York City, 78–79, 85, 95, 171, 184–85, 189, 241, 244, 247, 274nn16–17, 274n20; soldiers of color in American Revolution and, 133; veterans and, 237; wartime damage claims and, 235; Washington's relationship with, 172–73, 184–85, 244; Washington's retreat from New York City and, 77, 79, 246. *See also* Treaty of Paris
Continental Journal (Boston), 183
Cooper, Myles, 206
Cooper, Samuel, 37
Cornwallis, Lord, 194
Coromantee rituals, 133
corporal punishment. *See* punishments
Cortlandt, John, property surviving Great Fire, 148
courts-martial. *See* punishments
Coventry, Connecticut, 132, 196
Cresswell, Nicholas, 134, 217
Cruger's Wharf, 136, 230–31
Cruikshank, Isaac, *139*
Cummins, Mr. (landlord), 65

Cunningham, William, 20, 107, 112, *158*, 159–60, 162
Curwen, Samuel, 128
customs house, 10, 20, 145, 281n8

Dalrymple, John, 33
Danbury, Connecticut, 210
Darby, William John, 227–33
Dash, John Baltus, 1, 44, 69, 101, 108, 112, 126–27, 143, 236
Dawkins, Henry, *17*
Deane, Silas, 34, 63, 184–85
Declaration of Independence, 47, 50, 76, 133, 177
DeLancey, Ann Heathcote, 111
DeLancey, Oliver, burning of estate of, 207
DeLancey faction, 13–14, 20
Devereux, James, 127–28
Dickinson, John, 32, 34
Dissenters, 13–14, 18, 101, 151, 192, 246. *See also* Congregationalists; Presbyterians
Donop, Carl von, 149, 156–57
Dorchester, Baron. *See* Carleton, Guy
Dorothy, 107, 117
Douglas, William, 63, 69, 82, 89–90
Douw, Volkert P., 188
DuBois, Peter, 100, 128
Duchess of Gordon, 42, 44, 46
Duer, William Alexander, 236
Dumas, Charles, 63
Duncan, Henry, 92, 136–37, 144
Dunmore, Lord, 32–33, 75, 112, 139
Durkee, John, 94, 116, 132–35, 246, 290n36
Dutch Reformed North Church, 86, 101

Eagle, 47, 49, 86, 92, 107, 114–16, 144, 180
Earl of Suffolk, 105, 111
Elliot, Andrew, 106, 228
Elsworth, William, 233
English Neighborhood (now Englewood Cliffs), New Jersey, 167